COLONIZING KASHMIR

SOUTH ASIA IN MOTION

COLONIZING KASHMIR

State-building under Indian Occupation

HAFSA KANJWAL

STANFORD UNIVERSITY PRESS
Stanford, California

Stanford University Press
Stanford, California

Printed in the United States of America on acid-free, archival-quality paper

Library of Congress Cataloging-in-Publication Information

Names: Kanjwal, Hafsa, author.
Title: Colonizing Kashmir : state-building under Indian occupation / Hafsa Kanjwal.
Other titles: South Asia in motion.
Description: Stanford, California : Stanford University Press, [2023] | Series: South Asia in motion | Includes bibliographical references and index.
Identifiers: LCCN 2022044637 (print) | LCCN 2022044638 (ebook) | ISBN 9781503635388 (cloth) | ISBN 9781503636033 (paperback) | ISBN 9781503636040 (ebook)
Subjects: LCSH: Bakhshi, Ghulam Mohammad, 1907–1972. | Muslims—India—Jammu and Kashmir—History—20th century. | Jammu and Kashmir (India)—Politics and government—20th century. | India—Colonies—Administration—History—20th century. | India—History—1947–
Classification: LCC DS485.K27 K355 2023 (print) | LCC DS485.K27 (ebook) | DDC 954/.6—dc23/eng/20220923
LC record available at https://lccn.loc.gov/2022044637
LC ebook record available at https://lccn.loc.gov/2022044638

Cover photograph: Market day on the lake in Kashmir. Bridgeman Images.
Cover designer: Lindy Kasler

For my parents, Yousuf and Rubina
And my grandfather, Nanu

CONTENTS

Contents

ACKNOWLEDGMENTS

To work on Kashmir, especially today, is not easy. As I write, Kashmiri academics, journalists, artists, activists, and human rights defenders are being intimidated, harassed, suspended, and detained by the Indian government for documenting and representing India's long-standing colonial occupation. Many Kashmiris are not able to leave Kashmir for higher education or other professional opportunities, and others have been unable to return. I want to first and foremost acknowledge those in Kashmir and elsewhere who have spoken and continue to speak truth to power throughout history and today: their courage, resilience, integrity, and commitment to justice, hope, and love will endure. Nonetheless, as India continues to find different ways to silence and criminalize the truth tellers, the future of knowledge production on Kashmir remains endangered.

Being in the US academy, I have had the privilege of being able to research, write, and publish this work. Although the experience has not been easy, I am incredibly grateful for the mentors, colleagues, and friends along the way who sustained this journey.

I remember wanting to write a book on Kashmir when I was in high school and coming across the many works on Islam, history, and politics written by Professor John Esposito at my local Barnes & Noble. I was lucky to be his student as an undergrad at Georgetown. He has mentored generations of us, and his concern and interest in our lives well after we graduated are a testament to his care. At Georgetown, courses with John Voll, Osama Abi-Mershed, Judith Tucker, and Ashwini Tambe ignited my love and interest in history, research, and teaching.

This book began as a joint doctoral dissertation in history and women's studies at the University of Michigan with support from the Rackham International Research Award, Center for the Education of Women, and the

Department of Women's and Gender Studies. At Michigan, my advisors, Farina Mir and Mrinalini Sinha, introduced and guided me—as a very fresh graduate student—through the foundational debates in South Asian history, encouraged me to be intellectually rigorous, and inspired some of the questions of this work. With their perceptive comments, Kathryn Babayan and Fatma Müge Göçek helped me think of my project in new ways. I am so grateful to Nadine Naber for being a model feminist scholar-activist and allowing me to feel that there was a path for me in academia.

At Michigan, I had a wonderful group of fellow travelers. Tapsi Mathur has been my "ride or die" since day one; everyone should be as lucky as I am to have a friend like her. Faiza Moatasim is the one I am always in awe of: she is wise and perceptive and gives the advice you need, not want. Nama Khalil, Nida Abbasi, Gurveen Khurana, Saima Akhtar, and Laura Miller are the loveliest of friends and confidantes. I loved learning from and spending time with Diwas Kc, Leslie Hempson, Hoda Bandeh-Ahmadi, Sean Chauhan, Danial Asmat, Sara Grewal, Purvi Mehta, Anneeth Kaur Hundle, Zain Khan, Ahmad Huzair, Farida Begum, Zehra Hashmi, and Sana Ahmed.

I have been fortunate to work at the supportive History Department at Lafayette College. I thank all of my colleagues in the department, especially Paul Barclay, Rebekah Pite, and Christopher Lee for their time and constructive feedback during my book workshop. The Academic Research Committee provided additional funds for follow-up visits to the archives. Neha Vora, Rachel Goshgarian, Youshaa Patel, and Lindsay Ceballos have been amazing allies and friends during the tenure track. Randi Gill-Sadler is like none other: her beautiful friendship, brilliant mind and spirit, and commitment to liberation have kept me going.

A number of friends and colleagues provided incredibly useful comments or suggestions at different stages of the book. Mona Bhan and Haley Duschinski have not only been extraordinarily generous and supportive mentors throughout, but they also helped me think through some of the more difficult aspects of this project as well as the types of interventions it can make. Cabeiri Robinson's valuable comments during my book workshop strengthened the book significantly. Teren Sevea, Saadia Toor, SherAli Tareen, Randi Gill-Sadler, Fatima Rajina, Siraj Ahmed, Darryl Li, Andrew Amstutz, and Neha Vora also provided feedback at critical moments. Alden Young, Shenila Khoja-Moolji, and Stan Thangaraj gave helpful book publishing advice. Atiya Husain, one of my dearest and oldest friends, my "dear diary" since high school, came in at a pivotal time to provide incisive feedback on the broader aims, arguments, and stakes of this project. I am beyond thankful we have each other for all the ups and downs.

A number of people sustained me intellectually, emotionally, and spiritually, especially these past few years: Marina and Rabail Sofi, Ifrah Magan, Nouf Bazaz, Abdullah al Arian, Farah el Sharif, Zara Ahmad, Nadia Khan, Nimrah Karim, Haniya Masud, Haben Fecadu, Fatima Asvat, Aastha Mehta, Vina Lervisit, Yousra and Sameera Fazili, Sarah Waheed, Linah Alsaafin, Gulshan Khan, Shereena Qazi, Sabahat Adil, Laila al Arian, Nate Mathews, Shalini Kishan, Nafeesa Syeed, Shajei Haider, Sabra Bhat, and Sarwat Malik.

I am grateful for colleagues who invited me to speak or write on my research or on Kashmir in recent years. Special thanks to SherAli Tareen, Amber Abbas, Navyug Gill, Ayesha Jalal, Dina Siddiqi, David Ludden, Zia Mian, Manan Ahmed, Suchitra Vijayan, Bilal Nasir, Rob Rozehnal, Audrey Trushchke, Ali Asani, Saliha Shah, Ovamir Anjum, Ali Riaz, Rohit Singh, Jamal Elias, Mohammad Khalil, Homayra Ziad, Chandni Desai, Khadijah Abdurahman, Nayanika Mathur, Sami al Arian, Layan Fuleihan, and Hatem Bazian.

A number of libraries and archives made this work possible. In particular, I am very thankful for the helpful staff at the Srinagar State Archives for their assistance and patience, as well as good cheer, especially Mohd. Shafi Zahid, Mudasir, Shagufta, Shaheena, and Azra.

In Srinagar, I also thank the resourceful staff people at the Iqbal Library at Kashmir University, SPS Library, Cultural Academy, Nawa Kadal College, Press Information Bureau Library, Department of Information and Government Press (especially Zahoor), Research and Oriental Library, Legislative Assembly Library, Sri Pratap College, Amar Singh College, and the Government College for Women. In Delhi, thanks to the staff at the National Archives of India, Nehru Memorial Museum and Library, and India Council of World Affairs.

So many people in and beyond Kashmir guided and shaped the direction of this research or also provided assistance in sharing archival material. They include Ghulam Nabi Khayal, Hasrat Ghadda, Shabir Mujahid, Anwar Ashai, Altaf Hussain, Hilal Azhar, M. Ashraf Wani, Nighat Shafi, Abdul Majid Baba,

S. B., Abdul Haseeb Mir, Neerja Mattoo, Jeelani Qadri, Zahid G. Muhammad, Sheikh Showkat, Toru Tak, Zahir Uddin, P. G. Rasool, Sanjay Kak, Qurrat ul Ain, Javeed ul Aziz, Ehsan Fazili, and Shafi Shauq. Saleem Malik, Rafi Butt, and Urwa Sahar helped with translations and research assistance. Audra Wolfe came in at a critical stage and gave this book direction and Regina Higgins was instrumental in helping this book take its final form.

My editors and staff at Stanford, including Thomas Blom Hansen and Dylan Kyung-lim White, have been wonderful to work with. I am thankful to them for believing in this project.

I am incredibly grateful to be researching and writing on Kashmir at a time when it is not a lonely endeavor, among those for whom knowledge production is a political, personal, and intellectual commitment. In particular, I would like to acknowledge those who have fundamentally shaped and transformed my work and also provided a much-needed sense of community. Mona Bhan, Haley Duschinski, Deepti Misri, and Ather Zia provide a model for engaged scholarship and an immense amount of guidance and support. Mohamad Junaid and Suvaid Yaseen give me clarity, honesty, perspective, and some much-needed lighter moments. My sincerest thanks also to S. M., Fatimah Kanth, Goldie Osuri, M. A., Haris Zargar, Uzma Falak, Abir Bazaz, Idrees, Cabeiri Robinson, Mohammad Tahir, Ahmed bin Qasim, Zunaira Komal, Nishita Trisal, Dean Accardi, Iffat Rashid, Iymon Majid, Huma Dar, Nosheen Ali, Samina Raja, Mehroosh Tak, Idrisa Pandit, Imraan Mir, Sarbani Sharma, Bhavneet, Dilnaz Boga, and Shirmoyee Ghosh. There are a number of others, especially in Kashmir, whose work has influenced me and who have been working to change the narrative for decades. I am indebted to them, as well as the new generation of Kashmiri scholars who I know will continue to transform the field.

There are so many friends in Kashmir who have helped me, kept me company, taken me around, and shared their stories, especially during my fieldwork. A special thanks to R. F., A., Raashid Maqbool, Amjad Majid, M. S., Saima Iqbal, M. Yaseen, P., I. N., Aaniya and Seerat Farooqi, M. S., Faizaan Bhat, and many more. Archival work in Delhi would not have been possible without the hospitality of the Khurana, Mathur, and Shah families, as well as Uzma Khan.

My family in Kashmir—including my Mamu, Mami, Chacha, and

Chachi—are an endless source of love and prayers. They took such incredible care of me, and the times I've spent with them have been some of the best in my life. Zainab and Imaan went along with my shenanigans and made everything exciting. My younger Chacha passed away during my fieldwork; I know he would be supremely proud to see this book. My loving family in South Africa, Rooksana and Ebrahim Essa and Shenaaz Essa, as well as the extended family, have warmly taken me in as a daughter. Asma Khaliq, Danny, and Noura are my joy in NYC.

My younger sister and brother, Shifa and Omar, are my sources of tough love and encourage me to be the best version of myself. I am so thankful for Faroukh, Samra, and now, baby Rayaan and Minna, who arrived at the final stages of writing.

My maternal grandfather is the reason why I wrote this book. This book is the story of his generation. He, along with my beloved grandmother both passed away in 2019—not a day goes by without me missing them. Nanu was so eager to share bits of his life story, and out of everyone in my family, he was the most excited and proud that I had chosen this academic path. I am lucky to be his granddaughter and to have witnessed his immense faith, humility, kindness, and keen desire for adventure and exploration.

I've known my husband, Azad, for almost as long as I've been working on this project. He is my greatest blessing and a reminder that *naseeb* takes a life form of its own.

My parents, Yousuf Kanjwal and Rubina Hassan, left Kashmir in the early 1990s, in an attempt, like so many other families, to build a better life for their children. They left the only home they had ever known and their families. My father instilled the love of Kashmir in me at a very young age and made sure we never forgot our roots. My mother urged us to always be principled, considerate, and honest in what we do. Their children's education and future was the most important thing to them, and for that they worked. And worked. Despite not fully understanding the strange path I have taken and at times being nervous and scared of its implications, they paved the way selflessly in order for me to have the opportunities I do today. To them and my Nanu, this book is dedicated.

COLONIZING KASHMIR

INTRODUCTION

In 1952, Jawaharlal Nehru, the first prime minister of independent India and the Indian nationalist stalwart known for his role in the decades-long anti-colonial struggle against the British, wrote a letter to Sheikh Abdullah, the first prime minister of the state of Jammu and Kashmir, who played a towering role in the state's politics for a larger part of the twentieth century.[1] In the letter, Nehru demands that the state's new Constituent Assembly affirm its contested accession to India, so that the Kashmir issue—which had embroiled the new Indian state in a dispute with neighboring Pakistan since 1947—could be laid to rest in the international arena. Nehru, speaking of the character of Kashmiris, writes: "It must be remembered that the people of the Kashmir Valley and round about, though highly gifted in many ways—in intelligence, in artisanship, etc.—are not what are called a virile people." He adds, "They are soft and addicted to easy living. . . . The common people are primarily interested in a few things—an honest administration and cheap and adequate food. If they get this, then they are more or less content."[2] That Kashmiris had been brought to starvation and famine a number of times in the nineteenth and early twentieth centuries did not seem to factor into Nehru's patronizing understanding of them as being "soft" and "addicted to easy living." The parallels between British colonial attitudes toward Indians as unmanly and lacking virility and Nehru's understandings of Kashmiris should not be surprising, the latter's ironic reputation as an anti-colonial nationalist (and being of Kashmiri descent himself) notwithstanding.[3] These attitudes are fundamental to the process of colonial domination.

A year later, the Indian state, with the cooperation of several Kashmiri leaders, turned against Sheikh Abdullah, who, despite playing a supporting role in Kashmir's accession to India, was now perceived as working against Indian interests. After successfully arresting Abdullah and leading a coup against him, the Indian government placed Bakshi Ghulam Mohammad, who had previously served as deputy prime minister in Abdullah's cabinet, in power on August 9, 1953. Bakshi, a Muslim, became the second prime minister of the Jammu and Kashmir state. A tall, imposing figure, with a mustache, who often wore a long, buttoned overcoat or jacket with a salvar (pants) and Kashmiri karakul (hat), Bakshi was commanding and authoritative. During his decade as prime minister, the Kashmir assembly confirmed Kashmir's accession to India and sought greater financial and administrative integration with the Indian Union.

The 1953 coup that brought Bakshi to power was one of the most significant events in Kashmir's modern history. Its aftermath entrenched India's colonial occupation over Kashmir. It denied the people of the state their right to self-determination. But it also led to what has been described by some as Kashmir's "golden period," marked by increased development and modernization, as well as a rise in economic and educational opportunities—modalities of rule that were reliant upon the very assumption that Kashmiris were "addicted to easy living" as Nehru suggested. This book is fundamentally interested in two seeming paradoxes: the first, how India's period of decolonization simultaneously marked its emergence as a colonial power in Kashmir, in what is otherwise seen as the early "postcolonial" period or the heady "Nehruvian era" after Indian independence. The second paradox is that of development and progress in Kashmir under India's colonial occupation. I contend that one of the key mechanisms of effective control by which India's colonial occupation took place was through the installation of local client regimes, such as Bakshi's, as well as the particular forms of state-building and governance that took place under these regimes. I examine the role that Bakshi's government played in securing Kashmir for India, as well as the excesses, contradictions, and consequences of its state-building practices. Challenging the binaries of colonial and postcolonial, I historicize India's colonial occupation through processes of integration, normalization, and empowerment to highlight the new hierarchies of power and domination that emerged in the aftermath of India's "decolonization" from British colonial rule.

State-building refers to "the establishment, reestablishment, and strengthening of public structures in a given territory capable of delivering public goods" as well as the "processes through which states enhance their ability to function."[4] As states build their capacity, they come into greater contact with different groups in society, which in turn creates further expectations of state capacity. State-building necessarily requires a political arrangement—some form of sovereignty—as well as control over basic functions such as security, law, finances, education, and development. My reference to state-building relates to those processes that were part of the responsibility of the Kashmir government. The Kashmir government was a client regime of the Indian state, meaning it was politically, economically, and militarily dependent on and subordinate to India. For my analysis, however, it is important to distinguish between the Kashmir government and the Indian government, especially given the legally autonomous status of the Kashmir state within the Indian Union at the time, even as that autonomy was deeply contested in practice. It is also important to distinguish state-building from nation-building, the latter of which has been defined as the "most common form of a process of collective identity formation with a view to legitimizing public power within a given territory."[5] While the two are distinct, there are some overlaps; for example, building educational institutions is a form of state-building, while the educational curriculum developed in those institutions—especially if geared toward narrating a particular history and cultural identity—can be a form of nation-building.

This is not a book about how Kashmiris became alienated or estranged from India. It is also not a book about India's mistakes in attempting to "accommodate" Kashmir within its union after accession, which led to an armed rebellion in the late 1980s. Such approaches are built on two fallacies: first, that Kashmiris were emotionally integrated into the Indian nation-state from which they would somehow become "alienated," and second, that "conflict" was a result of misguided center-state relations and not India's denial of self-determination and an imposition of a colonial occupation. And yet, these fallacies dominate much of the historical and political scholarship on Kashmir, as well as the understandings of most Indian scholars—including in the US academy—on Kashmir.[6]

Rather, this book poses the inverse question and a number of related questions: How did India acquire Kashmir without the popular consent of its people? How did India—through its client regimes—exercise state-building in a manner that entrenched its colonial occupation of Kashmir in the early post-Partition period? How did India and its client regimes normalize its occupation both within Kashmir and also for Indian and international audiences? What were the different modalities of rule that were in operation during this time? What can the case of Kashmir tell us about how state-building occurs in other politically liminal sites, tied to the emergence of the (post-) colonial nation-state?[7] In these contexts, how do nation-states manage these restive populations, and how do they establish their legitimacy? And finally, what insight can Kashmir provide us in ongoing theorizations of colonialism, settler-colonialism, and occupation?

A Brief History

Historically, Kashmir was an independent kingdom, led by a series of Kashmiri Buddhist, Hindu, and Muslim rulers. Starting in the sixteenth century, the region was ruled by the Mughals, the Afghans, and finally, the Sikhs. The events of the mid-nineteenth century were to shape the course of Kashmir's modern history. On March 16, 1846, the English East India Company sold a cobbled-together territory of Jammu and Kashmir to Gulab Singh, a warlord from the Hindu Dogra family in Jammu, in return for his assistance in helping the British defeat the Sikhs in the Anglo-Sikh wars of the mid-nineteenth century. The Treaty of Amritsar is recalled as a "sale deed" in Kashmir as Singh agreed to pay the British government a sum of Rs. 75 lakh and an annual token for recognition of supremacy of "one horse, twelve shawl goals of approved breed, and three pairs of Cashmere shawls." When Kashmiris resisted this treaty, the British threatened an invasion and the Dogras were able to secure the region, consolidating their newly acquired princely state. This was to be the first in a series of treaties in Kashmir's modern history where the people were completely left out of a momentous decision that would come to shape their lives.

Kashmir became one of over 565 princely states under the Dogras, within the broader ambit of British colonial rule. As Mridu Rai states, the monarchical Dogras were vested with a new form of "personalized sovereignty, erasing earlier traditions of layered authority shared simultaneously by various levels in Kashmiri society."[8] They inherited a diverse territory, which included the regions of Jammu, Ladakh, the Kashmir Valley, Gilgit and Baltistan, and later, Poonch.

By the last British census before Partition, in 1941, Muslims constituted the majority of the entire princely state and were nearly 77 percent of the total population. Hindus comprised just over 20 percent of the total population. The Dogras' native region of Jammu had a population that was over 60 percent Muslim, and the remainder, Hindu. The Muslims of Jammu would later be ethnically cleansed in 1947, making Hindus the majority. The Kashmir Valley was majority Muslim (over 90 percent) and also had a small but significant Pandit, or Kashmiri Hindu, community (around 5 percent), as well as a smaller percentage of Sikhs. Finally, the sparsely populated region of Ladakh was both Buddhist and Muslim, in almost equal measure. Muslims in the princely state were also diverse; while Kashmiri-speaking Muslims dominated in the Valley, other regions included Punjabis, Rajputs, and Baltis, as well as nomadic tribes such as the Gujjars and Bakerwals. There were also Shia Muslims, particularly in the region of Kargil in Ladakh as well as in the Valley.

Decolonization led to the creation of two new nation-states—India and Pakistan. After a controversial accession by the last Dogra ruler, Maharaja Hari Singh to India in October 1947, the two countries would immediately go to war over Kashmir. As a result of the first of four wars between India and Pakistan in 1948, two-thirds of the former princely state—known as the state of Jammu and Kashmir and including the regions of Jammu, the Kashmir Valley, and Ladakh—was controlled by India. One-third of the princely state was controlled by Pakistan, which included Azad Jammu and Kashmir and the Northern Areas, today's Gilgit-Baltistan. A UN ceasefire line, later renamed the Line of Control, divided the two parts. Given the challenges of conducting sustained research on both sides of the Line of Control, I focus in this book on the part of the former princely state that is controlled by India. Scholarship on the part of the former princely state controlled by Pakistan describes its own diverging political trajectory within the Pakistani nation-state.[9]

In Indian-controlled Kashmir, the Indian government, led by Prime Minister Nehru placed Sheikh Abdullah, a Kashmiri Muslim who was one of the leaders of the anti-Dogra struggle in Kashmir, in power. Abdullah supported the accession, thinking Kashmir would have a greater autonomous status under India. Under Sheikh Abdullah's rule (1947–1953), the state of Jammu and Kashmir acquired a status of legal provisionality as an administered, but autonomous, territory of the Government of India, pending a United Nations–mandated plebiscite to determine the future of the entire region. Its autonomy was enshrined in Article 370, which gave Jammu and Kashmir a special status within the Indian constitution, allowing the state to make its own laws and have its own prime minister, flag, and constitution as well as the ability to restrict residency rights of land ownership and employment to Kashmir state subjects (the latter under Article 35A). It was the only state that would have this status and indeed, the only state that negotiated its status in this manner with the Indian Union.[10] As early as 1949, Sheikh Abdullah began to backtrack. He was increasingly concerned with rising Hindu nationalism in India as well as the Indian government's attempts to erode the agreed-upon autonomy of the Kashmir state by moving beyond the restricted mandate of communications, defense, and foreign affairs and interfering in the state's internal matters, including finances and judicial authority. Amid rising tensions and realignments in the region with the emerging Cold War, his retreat resulted in India gaining a more significant stronghold in Kashmir.

The Compulsions of State-Building

After the 1953 coup, Bakshi's government faced a number of important challenges that would come to define its state-building policies. Primarily, the Indian government tasked Bakshi with promoting Kashmir's fiercely contested accession to India domestically and internationally while repressing popular political aspirations for merger with Pakistan or independence. Thus, from the onset, Bakshi had to emotionally integrate Kashmiris to India and deny the possibility of a plebiscite for Kashmir, even as Kashmir was still being debated at the United Nations. After violently quashing protests that arose in the aftermath of Sheikh Abdullah's arrest, Bakshi turned his attention to implement a number of educational and economic policies meant to empower the population—including the rural masses—and help Kashmiris see the practical benefits of acceding to India.

The notion of "emotional integration" here is important. Bakshi's period oversaw crucial shifts in India's political and economic relationship with Kashmir toward concrete, material integration. Yet, Bakshi knew that in order for this relationship—and his rule—to be legitimized, Kashmiris had to be convinced that this relationship was in their best interests, and they had to develop an *emotional* bond in favor of India, based on their political and sociocultural identification with the Indian state.

In many ways, then, Bakshi's state-building project was an earlier iteration of what Mona Bhan has termed "heart warfare" when speaking of relations between the Indian army and border communities in Ladakh, also part of the Jammu and Kashmir state, in the aftermath of the 1999 Kargil war. Through a large-scale counterinsurgency development intervention, called Operation Sadhbhavna, the army deployed "heart warfare, healing, and compassion . . . [as an] emerging yet pervasive strategy of governance in war-torn regions where states are heavily invested in rebuilding their authority and legitimacy."[11] As a "sentimental undertaking," heart warfare transformed "subversive (or potentially subversive) subjects into law-abiding citizens, who would pose no future threat to India's territoriality and political integrity."[12]

Other occupying powers have referred to such strategies as "winning hearts and minds." In Bakshi's Kashmir, the concept was resonant, although the context was different. Here, it was the Kashmir government, not the Indian army, that was engaged in "certain modes of consent and subjectification."[13] Furthermore, there was no active armed resistance that the Kashmir government was engaged with, as would happen decades later. Thus, the role of a civilian government relying on such strategies is striking, but also points to the longue durée of India's colonial occupation and its recurring modalities of control. With the concept of emotional integration, this book builds upon recent anthropological research that showcases how colonial occupations can function as both the assimilation of *territory* and the intentional assimilation of *people*.[14]

Bakshi's policies were driven not only by a desire to secure Kashmir's accession to India and contain political dissent. As I detail in the first chapter, Bakshi was compelled to respond to the economic and social aspirations of the people. Enacting the aims of the anti-monarchical struggle against the Dogras that he had played a part in, Bakshi had to build a modernizing state that was committed to rectifying the ills of the past and empower society through a *Naya,* or New, *Kashmir.*[15] He had to ensure a better quality of life for those he now ruled over, especially Kashmir's majority-Muslim populations who had long suffered under unjust economic and social policies. Meanwhile, given the frictions that existed between Kashmir's diverse regional and religious groups under the Dogras and under Abdullah, he had to ensure his state-building policies were inclusive so that there were no communal or regional tensions that would undermine the Kashmir government.

Bakshi also had to enable a process of normalization. Targeted toward local, domestic, and international audiences, the Indian government and its varying client regimes often deploy the trope of normalization to disguise its colonial occupation, project Kashmiris as being content and thriving under Indian rule, and dismiss dissent as not being indigenous to the region but sponsored by foreign actors, namely Pakistan. Normalization in the context of Kashmir meant that the people of the state had accepted the accession to India (or whatever the latest colonial maneuver may be), seeing it as politically and economically beneficial for Kashmir, while also creating an ideological acceptance of the natural, indeed time-immemorial, relationship between Kashmir and the Indian nation-state.

Normalization is integral to processes of colonization, settler-colonialism, and occupation. India and its client regimes' oft-repeated "Kashmir is normal" trope belies the immense amount of violence inherent to the production of normalcy in the aftermath of the 1953 coup. As Michel-Rolph Trouillot argues in the context of European colonization in the Caribbean, "Built into any system of domination is the tendency to proclaim its own normalcy."[16] To even admit that people are discontent or that there is resistance means to "acknowledge the possibility that something is wrong with the system."[17] Although the Kashmir government claimed that Kashmiris were content, a series of measures, as I detail in chapter 7, were set in place to curb any form of dissent or resistance. As this book shows, the careful manufacturing of normalization through both punitive measures and propaganda has an inherently intricate relationship to state-building. Furthermore, structures of colonial occupation necessitate the banality—and thus, the normalcy—of the everyday that obscures its multipronged violence.

Bakshi's state-building policies were designed to reconstruct Kashmir's local culture, politics, and economy altogether and alter people's day-to-day lives, revealing the reach of the state in society. What is astounding about this state-building project is how thorough it was; Bakshi left no stone unturned in transforming the state and utilized a range of actors, including Kashmiri bureaucrats, educators, intelligentsia, workers, peasants, tourism operators, and Indian filmmakers, for this purpose. With financial assistance from the Government of India, the Kashmir government established a number of public institutions and developmental projects, including schools, colleges, and universities; hospitals, roads, tunnels, irrigation and power projects; as well as cultural centers, stadiums, and social welfare associations. In the 1950s and early 1960s, Bakshi's government used state-building to empower the population of Muslim-majority Kashmir and emotionally integrate it into India and to normalize India's colonial occupation for international, Indian, and local audiences.

The Politics of Life

Colonizing Kashmir centers the varying modes of control in the aftermath of Partition and Kashmir's disputed accession to India, and especially during Bakshi's rule. It argues that the early decades of India's colonial occupation were marked by what Neve Gordon calls a "politics of life," in which the Indian government and Kashmir's client regimes propagated development, empowerment, and progress to secure the well-being of Kashmir's population and to normalize the occupation for multiple audiences.[18] Relying on a biopolitical mode of governmentality, the politics of life entailed foregrounding the day-to-day concerns of employment, food, education, and provision of basic services.[19] At the same time, questions of self-determination and Kashmir's political future were being suppressed. Nehru is purported to have told Sheikh Abdullah, "India would bind Kashmir in golden chains."[20] The government intended to ensure that with an improved standard of living and greater prosperity, Kashmiri—especially Kashmiri Muslim—sentiments would shift in favor of India, toward a form of emotional integration. The politics of life played out in multiple spheres—both in the discursive realms of cinema and international diplomacy and in the realm of planning, policy, and bureaucratic strategies.[21]

A reliance on the politics of life did not entail forgoing more coercive and lethal measures—as chapter 7 of this book highlights, they were indeed used. Yet, it denotes an emphasis in the modes of control that were being deployed. In the early years of India's colonial occupation, the Indian and Kashmir governments perceived Kashmiris as malleable—while they may have had varying political aspirations, Kashmiris were viewed as having the potential to be integrated subjects as long as they could experience the benefits of Indian rule. In his memoirs, Sheikh Abdullah stated that this approach to state-building, including policies like subsidized rations, was the brainchild of D. P. Dhar, a Kashmiri Pandit leader who served as a cabinet minister under Bakshi and was close to the Indian leadership.[22] According to Abdullah, Dhar and others "propounded the theory that Kashmiris knew little of politics, what they cared about was a hearty meal, and they could be won over gastronomically," comparing this approach to the use of opium during British imperialism in China.[23] This gastronomic approach—not unlike Nehru's contention that Kashmiris were "addicted to easy living"—was foundational to the politics of life.

Bakshi's efforts to treat his government as a site of advancing the politics of life emerged in two key ways. First, his state-building project drew upon the history of Kashmir under Dogra rule as well as British colonial tropes of Kashmiris that had been internalized by India's post-independence leadership as well as the Kashmir client regimes. British narratives of Kashmir depicted the people as always in want, despicable, greedy, cunning, and weak. Given how central economic and educational empowerment had been to Muslim demands under the Dogras, the Indian and Kashmir governments, led by individuals such as Nehru and Dhar, acted upon the assumptions that Kashmiris were not able to think beyond their immediate material comforts and that dissent could be contained as long as basic needs were met.

Fundamentally, for both the Indian and Kashmiri leaders, the Kashmir issue in the years following 1947 was not political but economic—linked to a better standard of living—and thus could be managed through state planning. This biopolitical approach is endemic to the politics of life and informed Bakshi's policies of abundance, creating conditions for making Kashmir a space for a different kind of politics. Abundance—and primarily abundance under India—referred to the many benefits that Kashmiris could incur under Indian rule, well beyond what could have been possible under any other political setup and well beyond what was provided to Indian states.[24]

Second, state-building policies were primarily geared toward Kashmir's Muslim-majority population, most of whom were located in the Kashmir Valley. The Kashmir Valley posed a particular challenge of legitimacy for the Kashmir government, as it was there that demands for a plebiscite were raised, especially amongst Kashmiri Muslims in the aftermath of the UN resolution of 1949.[25] The regions of Jammu and Ladakh also had significant Muslim populations. However, in the case of Jammu, the Muslim demographic decreased significantly. As sections of the region became a part of Pakistan-controlled Kashmir, or Azad Kashmir, many Jammu Muslims migrated to Pakistan or, as I discuss in chapter 1, were killed by the Dogra state and its affiliates in 1947. Given that the demographics had now shifted in favor of Hindus, the Muslims who remained in Jammu were not viewed with much concern by the Kashmir government. In Ladakh, the Muslim population was sparse and did not necessitate the attention of the Kashmir government either. Indeed, political mobilizations in both Jammu and Ladakh—led by Hindus and Buddhists—called for greater integration with the Indian Union and did not pose the same challenges as the Kashmir Valley.[26]

In addition, the Kashmir Valley faced a different political trajectory than Jammu and Ladakh in subsequent decades, as the region erupted into a mass uprising and armed rebellion against the Indian state in the late 1980s. Although my primary focus is on the impact of state-building in the Kashmir Valley, I consider how the other regions of the state influenced the shape of economic, linguistic, and cultural policies.

Most importantly, Bakshi's government took a keen interest in the empowerment of Kashmiri Muslims—notwithstanding the ethnic and sectarian divisions in this group—and they became the principal beneficiaries of several economic and educational policies. The reasons are many and go beyond charges made in some Kashmiri Pandit or Indian circles that the Muslim-led bureaucracy was communally minded and, therefore, preferred to patronize Kashmiri Muslims only. The first reason is that Kashmiri Muslims constituted the majority of the population of Kashmir. The second is that most of them had remained illiterate and financially disadvantaged under Dogra rule. They were demanding that they also benefit from the social and economic progress that other communities in the state, including Kashmiri Pandits, had made. The third, and crucial, reason is that the focus on Kashmiri Muslims reflected a strategic desire on the part of the new government to maintain political stability in the aftermath of the accession and arrest of Sheikh Abdullah. In the eyes of the Indian and Kashmir governments, the Kashmiri Muslim political identity was suspect; indeed, as some have argued, it was increasingly pro-Pakistan as a result of the oppressive nature of Abdullah's rule.[27] The new government could ill afford strong political sentiments in favor of Pakistan and a deeply held anxiety about the Indian state.[28] Muslims were also seen as being sentimental and easily influenced by discourses that relied on emotional calls for religious solidarity and unity with Pakistan. As Bakshi came to power at this moment, the development of a secular, modern Kashmiri Muslim identity—one that was neatly aligned with the alleged secularity of the Government of India—was critical to his government's policies.

As much as this book is about state-building, it is also about state dissolution. Bakshi's state-building efforts were frustrated and tempered by his need to secure popular and affective sources of legitimacy for the new political order as well as keep up with the demands of the Indian state. This book reveals the tensions within the state-building project: while the Kashmir government attempted to empower different groups in society, these policies were marked by religious and regional tensions between them and within them, as well as corruption, political suppression, and coercion.

Even as the project intended to emotionally integrate Kashmiris into India, it ended up continuing a sense of distinctiveness and resentment. While the Kashmir government attempted to cultivate particular subjectivities that would lead to consent for its—and by extension, the Indian state's—rule, it simultaneously created opportunities for resistance, as evidenced by the rise of various groups within Kashmir that were contesting the accession. Furthermore, Bakshi's usefulness for the Indian government eventually reached an apex. Increased corruption and repression in the state made the Indian government wary, as did Bakshi's resistance to eroding the state's autonomy even further by changing the nomenclature of the head of state from prime minister to chief minister, as in Indian states.

In September 1963, under the guise of the Kamraj Plan, the Indian government requested that Bakshi step down from power. The plan called for the voluntary resignations of high-level officials in order to devote their efforts to rebuilding the Congress Party in the aftermath of a disastrous war with China. Months later, in December 1963, the *moi-e-muqaddas*, a relic revered by Kashmiri Muslims, said to be the Prophet Muhammad's hair, was stolen from the Hazratbal Shrine in Srinagar. The event came to be known as the Holy Relic Incident. There were mass protests throughout the state, and hundreds of thousands of people were on the streets. The Holy Relic Committee, composed of Muslim leaders throughout Kashmir, was formed to recover the relic. Bakshi—and by default the Indian state—was blamed for the disappearance. The relic was recovered a few weeks later under mysterious circumstances. However, mobilizations continued and paved the way for a mass movement for self-determination against the Indian state, underscoring the tenuous nature of Bakshi's state-building project during the prior decade. At the end of Bakshi's decade of rule, the state was brought into the political and economic fold of the Indian Union. However, the people of the state—particularly Muslims in the Kashmir Valley, were not. Rather than empowering them, Bakshi had further entrenched India's colonial occupation over them. Ultimately, the government provoked opposition from the very class it sought to emotionally integrate into the Indian Union, sowing the seeds of its own disintegration. This resistance became heightened in the late 1980s, manifesting in an armed uprising and a popular rebellion that erupted against Indian rule, and continues until today.

A Colonial Occupation

Building on recent Kashmir scholarship, this book is anchored in an understanding of Kashmir and its relationship to India as a colonial occupation and in particular foregrounds the role of a client regime in Kashmir in entrenching the colonial occupation. Even though India is a *postcolonial* nation that emerged from British colonial rule, it has itself become a colonizing force. Its colonialism, as we will see below, is disavowed or ignored, especially among postcolonial scholars of India. There remains an attachment in scholarship to seeing colonialism as emerging only from the West to the Global South, in addition to situating our present moment as a decolonial one.[29]

Both tendencies fail to account for power dynamics in the Global South and the ways in which (post)colonial nation-states are also enablers of imperialism or colonialism.[30] Even in more rigorous analyses where the colonial analytic persists, terms such as *neo-colonialism* and *neo-imperialism* continue to depict ongoing forms of economic exploitation and political subordination by the West of its former colonies in the Global South, obscuring colonialism within the Global South.

Colonizing Kashmir pushes back against such reductive understandings of colonialism and coloniality that see colonial powers and nation-states as being entirely different constructs, arguing that it is precisely in spaces like Kashmir where postcolonial studies, in its "ambiguous spatio-temporality," confronts its limitations, especially given ongoing forms of colonialism.[31] Scholars have advanced the terms *postcolonial colony*, *postcolonial informal empire*, *postcolonial occupation*, and *third world imperialism* to reflect how "formerly colonized nations assert their sovereign status through vociferous proclamations of territoriality and violent enactments of military might" that have implications for both indigenous communities and stateless peoples within their borders who are denied self-determination.[32] One reason that these forms of colonialism remain obscure is that "geographic contiguity and internal cultural cohesion" disguise imperial or colonial dynamics.[33] Thus, the fact that Kashmir is geographically contiguous to India creates the possibility for a less visible kind of colonialism than is possible overseas. Such contiguity results in what Goldie Osuri calls a "broader concealment of the relationship between postcolonial nation-states and their [own colonies]," as well as the concealment of "the manner in which postcolonial nationalism is also an expansionist project."[34] My book, then, attempts to understand the forms colonialism takes today within (post)colonial nation-states.

Recent Kashmir scholarship has contested triumphalist narratives of the postcolonial Indian nation by examining how colonialism, imperialism, occupation, and settler-colonialism are all important analytics to understand India's relationship with Kashmir (and elsewhere).[35] Building upon this body of work, my use of the term *colonial occupation* highlights these varying, often overlapping, and sometimes contradictory strategies and practices.[36] This book further develops our understanding of the modes of control used by the Indian government and its client regimes, which have varied over time, underscoring the multiple trajectories and manifestations of colonialism, occupation, and settler-colonialism in Kashmir.[37]

A number of the signature features of late colonialism, as recognized and theorized by leading scholars in the field, constitute Kashmir as a colony. First, the denial of sovereignty and the absence of popular consent are integral to colonial formations. In Kashmir, the colonial nature of India's rule stems primarily from the fact that the "state subjects of Jammu and Kashmir cannot be said to have ceded sovereignty to the Indian state through popular collective will."[38] The accession treaty signed by the maharaja, the formation of the Kashmir constituent assembly, and elections in Kashmir are all identified as evidence of India's sovereignty in Kashmir. However, these events occurred in the absence of popular collective will with no consideration given (despite multiple UN resolutions calling for self-determination and a plebiscite) to the political aspirations of the people.

The sovereignty claims of colonial states are also derived from "the authority of [their] own particular narrative of history and identity."[39] Indian narratives hold Kashmir as being integral to India since time immemorial (especially given the construction of Kashmir as essentially Hindu), thus legitimating both secular and Hindutva claims over Kashmir. Colonial rule is driven by territorial conquest, largely for the purposes of resource extraction for the metropole, and it relies on labor and explicit racial logics. Resource extraction, especially of Kashmir's water resources, is an important part of India's colonization, as is the racialization and exotification of Kashmiris in Indian imaginaries. Colonial rule is also borne of strategic geopolitical interests. Kashmir's pivotal location fortifies India's geopolitical interests with regard to Central and East Asia and also "secures its geo-political hegemony in South Asia."[40] Nation-states like India also derive a more symbolic benefit from colonization. Kashmir consolidates India's identity as a nation-state: it produces "nationalist consensus in its mainland," which has served to maintain and reproduce India both territorially and symbolically as a secular nation (especially during the Nehruvian period) and a Hindu homeland. In binding the nation together, Kashmir can "be used to paper over the unfulfilled needs and demands of postcolonial India's own disempowered people."[41]

Another distinguishing feature of colonial rule is the presence of compradors, or native political elites that colonial powers utilize to facilitate effective forms of governance, especially in instances of indirect rule. Indirect rule is often developed in response to demands for self-rule or self-determination by the colonized.[42] This comprador class in turn attempts to negotiate and gain from colonial structures. Examples include Kashmir's client regimes, such as Bakshi's government, which helped reinforce Indian rule in Kashmir by demanding increased financial integration, economic rights, and educational access. Far from denying the colonial logics inherent in the relationship, these examples are evidence of colonial rule. The demand for jobs, education, and greater representation (by the Congress and others) occurred under British colonial rule in India, too, and is widely understood as part of the colonial framework rather than a negation of it.

Defining India's relationship with Kashmir as an occupation has been deployed by a number of Kashmir scholars, who have examined the ways in which occupation has been critical to the foundation of what is often touted as the world's largest democracy. The term *occupation* has its roots in international humanitarian law and refers to military control by a power over a territory that is outside its sovereign jurisdiction. This control is meant to be temporary, until a permanent settlement is reached, and international law seeks to regulate the relationship between the occupier and the occupied. Recent scholarship on occupation has problematized "the very nature of occupation," arguing that many occupations, like Kashmir, remain outside the bounds of international law and are prolonged, not temporary, often resulting in processes that overlap with settler-colonialism (through land grabs and demographic engineering) as well as colonialism (through resource appropriation).[43]

Mohamad Junaid has argued that occupation is a process that involves "concomitant strategies and practices," many of which operate in Kashmir.[44] Developing occupation frameworks in relation to Kashmir allows us to see how India's occupation operates through illegitimate elections portrayed by the Indian government and its client regimes in Kashmir as exercises in democratic action and popular will (what Ather Zia calls the "politics of democracy") and preemptive detention of political opponents, as well as more spectacular forms of military violence and dispossession.[45] In addition, particular forms of law and constitutionalism—such as states of emergency—are constitutive of occupations.[46] Haley Duschinski and Shrimoyee Ghosh argue that India's occupation should be seen as "occupational constitutionalism," whereby legal mechanisms and processes produce foreign dominance through annexation of Kashmir's territory and sovereignty after Indian independence. These constitute "a state of emergency and permanent crisis in Kashmir," a point I develop in my seventh chapter.[47] This occupational constitutionalism originates in Article 370 of the Indian constitution, which, the authors argue, was initially intended to form a constitutional framework of sovereignty and self-determination for the Jammu and Kashmir state but became "a constitutional mechanism of incorporation in the Indian Union."[48] Given my focus on emotional integration, I also draw from an understanding of occupation as an affective category, "at once a regime of power and a structure of feeling that shapes the logics of rule while transforming space, place, nations, and communities."[49]

On August 5, 2019, the Indian government "dismantled" Kashmir's special status under Article 370, setting into motion policies intended to "carry out far-reaching changes to demographic and land-holding patterns."[50] Kashmir scholars have increasingly turned to the framework of settler-colonialism—which focuses on the acquisition more of land than of labor and resources—to understand "India's escalating assaults on Kashmiri sovereignty."[51] These assaults include laws that enable Indian citizen-settlers to buy land and achieve "domicile" status in Kashmir (which in turn gives them voting and employment rights) and the Indian army to make land grabs, as well as providing Indian corporations opportunities for investment and resource extraction. While some scholars have argued that settler-colonialism and colonialism are antithetical, I situate settler-colonialism as a variant of colonialism and thus constitutive of colonial occupations.[52] Furthermore, Samreen Mushtaq and Mudasir Amin argue that settler-colonialism should also be placed within the framework of military occupation. They describe the long history of settler-colonialism in Kashmir, starting from 1947, as "a shrewd combination of eliminationist and assimilationist tactics undertaken by India to erase the distinct historical and political context of Kashmir."[53]

These tactics include what Mushtaq and Amin call "practices of memoricide": "the erasure of history of one people overwritten by that of another" in order to "create a narrative over time that has appropriated local histories and people's notions of belongingness."[54] Settler logic removes such notions of belongingness in an attempt to construct a new identity, an identity that is inextricably tied to the settler state. In particular, both the Indian and Kashmir governments have attempted to erase from historical consciousness the involvement of the Indian state and Hindu nationalist militias in changing the demographics of the Jammu province from a Muslim to a Hindu majority.[55] For Kashmir's identity to be mapped neatly onto India's "secular politics of inclusion," violence against Muslims in Jammu had to be elided, and ideas of a new, secular Kashmir had to be propagated.[56] The Indian army's usurpation of territory, especially of ecologically critical forestland, since 1947 also demonstrates the settler-colonial logic that has governed Kashmir.[57]

Patrick Wolfe argues that settler-colonialism "is inherently eliminatory but not invariably genocidal" and that elimination can also take place via assimilation.[58] This means that elimination logics are more than the liquidation of indigenous or colonized communities; rather, in their positive aspect, they mark "a return whereby the native repressed continues to structure settler-colonial society."[59] Calling for a broader understanding of the term *genocide*, Wael Hallaq pushes back against Wolfe by arguing that colonialism is always "inherently genocidal," even though it is normalized in modern history, "whereby the totalizing act of decimating 'traditional' cultures comes to be regarded as 'natural' development."[60] For Hallaq, colonialism, including settler-colonialism, is a "structure of thought," a "modern project of total transformation, one that perpetually aims at reengineering the subject as nature."[61] Colonialism's genocidal intent lies in its relationship to modernity and the total transformation that engenders.

Nonetheless, Wolfe's other main argument that we should see settler-colonialism not as an event but rather as a structure—that is, "elimination is an organizing principle of settler-colonial society rather than a one-off occurrence"—is an important one for Kashmir.[62] It helps us understand how the Indian government has used assimilationist tactics as a form of elimination since 1947, especially in the context of a global decolonial moment where conventional killing would provoke condemnation from the international community, including the United Nations, as well as threaten India's position vis-à-vis its leadership in the Non-Aligned Movement. Drawing from J. Kehaulani Kauanui and other indigenous studies scholars, however, it is important to situate settler-colonialism as a "structure that endures indigeneity, as it holds out against it."[63] Kashmiris, like all other colonized and indigenous communities, have resisted Indian sovereignty, as well as Indian declarations of normalcy, through practices of "refusal, or everyday practices of rejecting externally imposed institutions of settler state sovereignty and asserting . . . political orders that challenge settler logics of inclusion."[64]

Four decades after accession, and especially during the Bakshi period, India's (settler) colonial occupation primarily utilized assimilationist strategies. Assimilationist policies—what I refer to in this book as integration—seek to erase the historical specificity and sovereignty of a given community and forcibly bring it into the fold of the settler state. Assimilation as integration is "one of a range of strategies of elimination that has become favoured in particular historical circumstances."[65] It is inherently destructive—perhaps what Hallaq would refer to as genocidal. This book incorporates an understanding of assimilationist settler-colonial logics and how they intersect with state-building practices.

Decades of assimilationist policies still failed to bring Kashmiris into the Indian national fold, leading instead to anti-colonial resistance in the form of the armed rebellion and the popular mass uprisings in the late 1980s. Junaid situates this period of a "military occupation" as an "ensemble of spatial strategies and violent strategies that the occupier state employs to dominate physical space in a region where its rule lacks, or has lost popular legitimacy and thus faces an imminent challenge of being popularly supplanted."[66] Seeking to quash the resistance, the Indian government turned to more necropolitical forms of control, whereby different modes of killing and containment are used in order to subject the population at large to death.[67] With over 750,000 Indian troops deputed to Kashmir, the decades after the armed rebellion have been marked by the deaths of over 100,000 Kashmiris and thousands more raped, disappeared, arbitrarily detained, and tortured. This period largely relied on an immense amount of militarization and control through violence, as well as a heightened state of emergency through draconian laws such as the Armed Forces Special Powers Act in 1990. However, as Kashmir scholars like

Mona Bhan have highlighted, assimilationist strategies of development and humanitarianism still continued throughout the military occupation, once again underscoring the overlapping modes of control in Kashmir.[68]

Interventions

Kashmir is not a unique political entity and nor is it an exception. A number of other nations and communities have been brought into the fold of nation-states without their consent or remain under colonial occupation, dispossession, war, and apartheid. These include, but are not limited to Hawaii, Puerto Rico, Palestine, Hong Kong, Tibet, East Turkestan, Chechnya, and Western Sahara. They include indigenous and First Nation communities in Canada, the United States, and Australia, as well as the Kurds, Papuans, and Oromo and Tigray people.

This book calls for the creation of a historiography of states that do not exist, have not been allowed to exist, and peoples who have been denied self-determination and the right to exercise their sovereignty. These are states-in-waiting, not-yet-in-formation, in varying stages of political liminality. Sometimes the disastrous results of former colonial machinations and divisions, places like Kashmir are now meshed with the colonial, expansionist policies of the nation-state. They unsettle and threaten hegemonic forms of nationalism. Their histories are deeper than those constructed by modern day borders; they exist at the confluence of multiple routes and civilizations. Like Kashmir, some of them have been on the agenda of the United Nations, at the receiving end of resolutions that have collected dust over the years. Most have become pawns in the international liberal order, subject to the whims and political agendas of regional and global superpowers. The ways in which nation-states manage these places and peoples differ. Some are subject to intense forms of violence and dispossession on a daily basis, while others have been forcibly integrated—or assimilated—in an uneasy "peace." The people in these places attempt to make their voice heard through anti-colonial resistance, as well as everyday acts of "refusal" that resist ongoing forms of colonialism, occupation, and settler colonization.[69]

Many movements or struggles in these places are often depicted in both scholarship and popular narratives as "ethnic conflicts," "secessionist movements," "territorial disputes," "insurgencies," or "terrorism." These depictions are as ahistorical as they are dehumanizing. They are inherently colonial in their upholding of a hegemonic idea of the territorial nation-state to the detriment of those who refuse inclusion. While territory defines the space of the nation-state, the territorial boundaries of the nation-state are not primordial, and nor should we treat them as such. It is critical to consider the colonial processes through which these boundaries are consolidated. More crucially, the way we think about the territorial sovereignty of the nation-state does not always align with how people inhabit these spaces. These are spaces where people have their own histories, identities, spatial imaginaries, and political aspirations. Their lived experiences under occupation, colonialism, and settler colonization must be accounted for. This book urges us to think beyond the foregrounding of nation-states and their territorial sovereignty or integrity in understanding these "disputes" or "conflicts." It asks what kinds of histories are possible when we do not take the narratives nation-states tell about themselves for granted. In doing so, it "allows us to rethink the nature of India's sovereignty claims, as well as sovereign power more generally in the modern world order."[70]

Given the area studies frameworks that dominate the discipline of history, these places are not often conceptualized together. Building from recent studies of governance, development, and state-building in other contemporary colonies, this book situates what the Kashmir context can advance in this body of work and how it can help us think through comparative regions.[71] In his recent work on comparative settler-colonialisms, Mahmood Mamdani argues that nationalism and colonialism were co-constituted and that the birth of the nation-state entailed homogenous nation-building through large-scale ethnic cleansing, civil wars, and genocide.[72] His insight certainly applies to the context of India, Pakistan, and the Partition, as well as the Jammu Massacre. However, it may function to dismiss the violence in Kashmir in the four decades after accession, which happened through parallel processes such as the politics of life, development, integration, and normalization. By leaving these assimilationist processes invisible in the analysis of the making of the colonial nation-state, existing power structures and the state form are reified. This book provides insights into the role of state-building under colonial occupations;

rather than being an exception, I argue that these spaces are integral to the formation of nation-states.

In challenging the sovereignty claims of the (post)colonial nation-state, this book also contributes to global histories of decolonization as well as histories of the third world. It is part of a constellation of counter-narratives about how global decolonization has played out after World War II, challenging ideas that it was liberatory.[73] In particular, I critique narratives about the third world as an emancipatory, anti-colonial project. In his discussion of the "built-in flaw" of the third world project, Vijay Prashad discusses how newly independent governments reinforced social hierarchy and were unable to meet the economic demands of their people.[74] Yet, his discussion does not include a major built-in flaw: the ways in which the third world project replicated European claims to sovereignty and territoriality. While the third world project countered European colonization and sought to build a different type of world, triumphalist and romanticized narratives of the third world ignore the presence of South-South colonization, as well as the political condition of those who were excluded from the decolonial movements that gained traction during that time. Instead, I situate the postwar "decolonial" third world moment as one in which the sovereignty of the (post)colonial, third world nation-state was affirmed, a new moment of the assertion of state boundaries and territorial claims, or as Bhan and Duschinski formulate, third world imperialism. These were advanced through moments like the Bandung Conference in 1955 as well as the Pancheel Agreement in 1954 between India and China, which normalized notions of territorial integrity through principles of noninterference, leading to the undermining of Tibetan claims of sovereignty.

In these triumphalist narratives, India figures as a prominent example of third world anti-colonial struggle as well as the beacon of the Non-Aligned Movement. However, this book complicates this narrative by "suggesting that India's adoption of an anti-colonial positionality in the international arena in effect strengthened its capacity for colonial domination in Kashmir."[75] Positioning India's first prime minister, Jawaharlal Nehru, and the Nehruvian moment, as anti-colonial erases the histories and legacies of India's colonial state-formation, including in Kashmir. That Nehru identified "the United Nations as the principle institution for planetary justice" and key to the third world project, while undermining multiple UN resolutions calling for a plebiscite in Kashmir, reveals the inherent contradictions of this "emancipatory" third world project.[76]

Aside from contributing to the discussion of decolonization in India, my primary intervention in South Asian historiography is to challenge scholarship on India's foundational moment, including India's state-formation and nation making and the transition from the colonial to the (post)colonial nation-state. This book builds on recent scholarship that focuses on the legacies of British India's indefinite colonial borders, as well as the contingencies that marked India's nation-state formation. In particular, this scholarship seeks to understand how the "territorially circumscribed nation-form and the sovereignty of the nation-state [have] played out since decolonization."[77] Scholars have examined how princely states and frontier regions like the Northeast, the Himalayan border with China, and Hyderabad were incorporated into India, arguing that "a relation of hierarchy," "democratic deficit," and "violence and coercive force" were constitutive of India's relationship with these troubled regions or borderlands.[78]

However, even in these important works, India's expansionist strategies and its sovereignty claims are rarely depicted as colonial maneuvers, despite the violence used to overthrow the Nizam's sovereignty and annex Hyderabad, the indirect rule used in the Northeast to suppress demands for self-determination among the Nagas or the people of Manipur, or the exploitative resource extraction in the Northeast.[79] Even as there is an understanding that India's policies were not "a radical departure from colonial practice" or were "reminders of the horrors of colonial violence," there is little articulation that India is fundamentally colonial.[80] What does it mean to act like a colonial power instead of being a colonial power—where is the line drawn? Does the fact that a nation was previously colonized mean that it cannot colonize? This book argues that the quest to consolidate the Indian nation-state was a colonial quest; India's foundational years need to be reexamined through this framework. Arguing that there were simply continuities with colonial rule discredits the ways in which Indian sovereignty manifested on its own terms and had its own logics and intent.

There has been scant scholarly attention on the role of Kashmir in India's nation-state formation, an irony, given how crucial Kashmir was to India's self-definition as a secular nation in the early years of independence. For example, in the 2007 volume *From the Colonial to the Postcolonial: India and Pakistan in Transition*, not one of the sixteen essays is about Kashmir, admittedly an issue that has been fundamental to understanding the "transition." The editors refer to the "spiritual and political price to be paid for this postcolonial concern with the territorial integrity of India" and suggest that there is "no denying that some social groups—admittedly not a majority of the population were coerced into being Indians. The historical incongruity of a nation emerging from colonial rule imposing with an iron fist its own rule on a reluctant minority cannot go unnoticed."[81] While Kashmir goes unnoticed, the example that the authors give of this "minority" is the Nagas—who were forced into being Indians through "strategies of which sheer and awesome military force was a very powerful component." The Nagas' case, the editors argue, "only highlights the colonizing tendencies that an anti-colonial nationalism may also display as it mutates into official nationalism with the assumption of power by the nationalists."[82] In addition, the editors note that the case of the Nagas was somewhat different from "the many ethnic and secessionist movements that grew in India and Pakistan after Independence," of which we are to assume Kashmir is one.

This example reveals a number of classic tendencies in the scholarship on Indian nation-state formation and decolonization. First, it shows how many scholars of India remain committed to a methodological nationalism or statism, which naturalizes the (Indian) nation-state form and denies its coloniality.[83] Once again, nation-states can act like colonizers, have "colonizing tendencies" (as India did with the Nagas) and take on structures of or continuities from colonial rule, but somehow, they can never be actual colonizers. Second, the authors refer to "concern with the territorial integrity of India" as a postcolonial, not a colonial concern. The use of the term "spiritual and political price" here is also for India—we must lament what India's colonizing tendencies did for an otherwise abstract ideal of India. What, then, is the physical, material, and existential price for those who were "coerced into being Indians"? Finally, the erasure of Kashmir and possible assumption of Kashmir (and many other places) as "ethnic and secessionist movements" are rife in postcolonial and subaltern studies of India. I have referred to this as epistemological violence on Kashmir, given the reflection of a colonial commitment to the integrity of the Indian nation-state form, as well as the nation-state's historical narrative.[84]

Colonizing Kashmir builds upon a body of Kashmir scholarship that poses a much-needed corrective to studies of "postcolonial" South Asia, or subaltern studies. This "postcolonial" scholarship, as Huma Dar has argued, remains unable—or unwilling—to move beyond its "unacknowledged, un-interrogated nationalism amongst those otherwise apprehensive of nationalism."[85] It is part of a broader "sanctioned ignorance" in which, Ather Zia maintains, "the Kashmir issue and the demands of Kashmiris have been overwritten, invalidated, and criminalized by India."[86] The Subaltern Studies Collective, in particular, has played a role in this "sanctioned ignorance" (despite one of its founders coining the term). As Mohamad Junaid discusses, the collective examined the "heterogeneity of colonial subjects, [but] omitted using its own conceptual tools to analyze the constitutive hierarchies in postcolonial India," especially in relation to those for whom India's rule was colonial.[87] He continues, "Of the 83 articles published . . . [in] their flagship publication . . . there was not a single article on Kashmir—even during the 1990s when the collective had gained global recognition and Kashmir was under intense military repression."[88] Instead, Kashmir was "subsumed under the overarching master-sign 'India.'"[89]

Many postcolonial scholars of India have continued to solidify the fiction of a unified India in which Kashmir's incorporation is a natural teleology—seen as a given historically, geographically, and politically. In this understanding, the "division" of a time-immemorial "India" into India and Pakistan or the quest for freedom or self-determination of various communities is an aberration to the ideal of a unified nation. However, what we know today as "India" is a nation-state borne out of a particular decolonizing/recolonizing moment; its form as a nation-state could have come about in a number of different iterations.

There is also a body of work that, while acknowledging "regional" political aspirations, seeks to figure out ways to better incorporate them into the broader "nation." For example, in the introduction to the edited volume *Kashmir: History, Politics, Representation*, Chitralekha Zutshi asks how "borderland" regions such as Kashmir, Kurdistan, or Palestine and their "national movements and their people's interests [can] be accommodated within states rather than being seen as threats to the national interest."[90] The relationship between the "region" and the "nation" becomes one of an ideal, if sometimes contested, affiliation. This methodological nationalist framing once more privileges the Indian nation-state as needing to improve its efforts to accommodate the Kashmir region (perhaps through even more Indian-styled democracy and elections). In this perspective, the region remains a subservient category, but the category of "India" especially in its territorial form remains the norm to which the region must be accommodated under. I ask why we are compelled to examine Kashmir as a "region" and India as a "nation." More importantly, why does Kashmir have to be accommodated within India?

My work emphatically pushes back against these territorial and historical conceptions of India, whereby all other political visions and aspirations become mere aberrations. By idealizing and valorizing the territorial boundaries of the nation-state, Indian nationalist, postcolonial, and subaltern scholarship naturalizes the relationship between India and Kashmir, without critically analyzing how this relationship was constructed in the first place. A result of such impoverished analysis is that the "the Kashmir issue" is simply reduced to a "crisis of federalism," a "crisis of democracy," or "internal colonialism."[91] This verbal gymnastic foregrounds India's inability or challenges in managing "difference," a fault that can be rectified through more inclusive practices. As mentioned earlier, one of the ways in which this is iterated is through the use of security and statist language such as "separatism" and "ethno-nationalist" insurgencies.[92] For example, Rekha Chowdhary argues, "The present phase of separatism in Kashmir can be explained with reference to the failure of Indian nationalism to accommodate the ethno-nationalist identity politics of Kashmir."[93] This failure, she argues, has resulted in a "deep-rooted sense of alienation in Kashmir but also in the shaping of this identity in a direction that is incongruous with Indian nationalism." Anti-colonial resistance and a struggle for sovereignty is simplified to Kashmir's "ethno-nationalist identity politics" that must be accommodated (one wonders whether the British could have better accommodated Indian nationalists and their "identity politics"). From a settler-colonial framework, the liberal desire for accommodation or inclusion is not so divergent from the desire to eliminate through assimilation. These flawed understandings not only obscure India's colonial occupation, but they also valorize Indian nationalism as the universal normative that a Kashmiri "ethno-nationalism" must be subsumed under. As Junaid has pointed out, Indian scholars' evocation of Kashmir in these terms of accommodation echoes the statist rhetoric of "Kashmir is an integral matter [or part] of India."[94] Fundamentally, it reveals epistemic complicity on the part of these scholars in India's colonial occupation.

Rejecting accounts that rely on pre-constituted, naturalized geographies of the "territorial integrity" of the Indian nation-state, as well as the ad nauseum Indian statist and scholarly narrative that Kashmir is "integral" to India, I historicize how Kashmir was made integral to India through state-building policies, both discursively but also through the planning and assimilationist processes of emotional integration and normalization. Rather than taking territory as a given or naturalizing Kashmir's association with the Indian state, I show how Kashmir was territorialized through state-building practices that attempted to also transform people's subjectivities, while simultaneously producing tension and resistance.

Finally, this book also contributes to scholarship on secularism in India. Given the expansion of right-wing Hindu nationalism in the past few decades, discussions of the death or crisis of "Indian secularism" have come to the fore in both scholarly and popular discourses.[95] In this narrative, India had a "distinctive" brand of secularism, one in which there was not an opposition to religion but rather a "principled distance" between religion and state that attempted to balance the claims of individuals and religious communities and oppose "institutionalized religious domination."[96] The idea of India as a "secular republic" was evidenced by its constitution. Some scholars have challenged how India's secular credentials played out in its post-independence history by examining how Muslims, in particular, were erased or marginalized in Indian nation-state making. They have also examined how "the Indian state is directly involved in the Hinduisation of the country."[97] Yet, in debates over whether India is truly secular or secular enough, the secular still remains a normative ideal that the Indian republic should aspire to.[98] I draw from interventions in critical secularism studies that show how secular power exacerbates religious tensions and is involved in—not distant from—the "regulation and management of religious life."[99]

In particular, I am interested in the relationship between secularism and (settler) colonial occupation. Nehru promoted the use of Kashmir to serve as a litmus test for India's alleged secularism and a bulwark against Hindu communalism. In a public rally in Calcutta in 1952, he argued, "There can be no greater vindication . . . of our secular policies, our Constitution, than that we have drawn the people of Kashmir towards us. But just imagine what would have happened in Kashmir if the Jan Sangh or any other communal party had been at the helm of affairs. The people of Kashmir say that they are fed up with this communalism. . . . They will go elsewhere and they will not stay with us."[100]

Given the primacy of Muslim-majority Kashmir in "exemplifying India's exceptional status as a tolerant, secular state,"[101] what exactly does that secularism entail if India's secular credentials are grounded in the context of a colonial occupation? The "secular," I argue, was deployed as a mechanism to entrench India's colonial occupation and criminalize Muslim political aspirations or "alternative visions of nationhood and belonging."[102] For Kashmiris to want to "go elsewhere," according to Nehru, was a rejection of Hindu—not secular—nationalism. Yet, Kashmiri Muslims viewed "Indian secularism as an alibi to forcibly integrate Kashmir into the predominantly Hindu Indian nation-state."[103] Ultimately, Kashmiri Muslims were politically useful for India's "secular politics of inclusion"; this forcible inclusion aligned with assimilationist settler-colonial narratives about Kashmir's history and recent past.[104] As a number of my chapters reveal, the secular was used to both erase Muslim histories of Kashmir, while taming "Islam's assumed fanaticism under Hinduism's influence."[105] In addition, I show how Hindu geographies, imaginaries, and histories were central to these secular discourses, revealing the close relationship between secularism, settler-colonialism, and Hindu majoritarianism.

In the field of Kashmir studies, my research foregrounds the role of the Kashmir governments, or client regimes, as well as the perspectives of diverse Kashmiri political elite, bureaucratic, and educated classes as they sought to resolve the socioeconomic problems of the people. In doing so, I draw from a recent strand in South Asian historiography that examines governance, citizenship, and development in the immediate post-Partition moment, as well as the role of the everyday state and state/society relations.[106] This historiography challenges simplistic divisions of the state-versus-society paradigm and examines how the new citizens of India and Pakistan were involved in nation- and state-building, showing how the state is often a site of competition or dispute among different groups. In addition, it underscores that the state is not as monolithic or coherent as accounts of its reach make it out to be and that it is responding to both local concerns as well as broader postwar international development schemes. While these insights are relevant to the Kashmir context, my contribution to this literature is to examine how state-building practices, governance, and development operate differently in the context of a colonial occupation and where the transition from subject to citizen remains opaque.

Studies of the various post-accession Kashmir governments have largely focused on political leaders' actions as they attempted to navigate relations with the Indian state.[107] In shifting away from seeing the Kashmir governments as only "puppet regimes" of the Indian state, I attend to the ways in which state-building policies shaped and were shaped by people in Kashmir, highlighting how local aspirations intersected and conflicted with broader political realities.

One of the Bakshi government's most important features was its greater reach toward the masses in the state, including workers, peasants, and artisans. On some level, ordinary people became a part of the project of reform, either by pushing for better schools and colleges in their areas or seeking employment in government service. In this way, state-building constituted a local logic, borne out of local concerns and needs and binding the government and people in new ways. The Kashmir government played a crucial role in responding to the demands of the local population, providing services, acquiring new obligations, and expanding its capacity and bureaucratic apparatus. At the same time, it is important not to conflate participation by people in the state-building project with giving the Kashmir government legitimacy. Instead, building on Ilana Feldman's work on Gaza, I distinguish between "bureaucratic authority" and "state legitimacy." The Kashmir government was able to exert authority, where "both practitioners and the public recognize its demands as being authoritative," and thus took part in it, but that did not entail that the government was seen as legitimate, even though it aspired for that.[108] Rather, people realized that their continued participation could procure them particular benefits—at least for the short term. In this way, I argue that Article 370—the clause in the Indian constitution that provided some autonomy for the Kashmir state—was significant. However, instead of creating a state-form that was truly autonomous or negotiated its own form of sovereignty, the Kashmir state, through its state-building measures, reinforced India's colonial occupation.

My research also brings the Bakshi period to the forefront of understanding Kashmir's contemporary history. A vast majority of scholarly work has focused on Sheikh Abdullah and his role in Kashmiri politics. Indeed, because of Abdullah's towering role in politics before and during Partition, in some works, Abdullah is credited for developments that actually happened under Bakshi's government, including providing free education in Kashmir.[109] There has been no scholarly work that has discussed Bakshi Ghulam Mohammad and his tenure as prime minister in its entirety. Those that have covered some aspects of his rule or looked at the early post-accession period in Kashmir have primarily examined it through the lens of federal-state relations. Bakshi's government is usually characterized as the first in a series of governments through which the Indian state attempted to erode Kashmir's autonomy, a process that Sheikh Abdullah withstood, leading to the eventual "disenchantment" of Kashmiris from the Indian Union.[110] Alternatively, other scholars have argued that Bakshi's government provided the state with one of the longest periods of stability due to financial assistance from the Government of India to ensure economic prosperity.[111] Yet, this stability did not last long. Most scholars conclude that the increasingly undemocratic, authoritarian, corrupt, and highly coercive nature of Bakshi's government led once more to increasing anti-Indian sentiments in Kashmir.[112]

This book intervenes in the study of the Bakshi period in a number of ways. Most importantly, it seeks to disrupt the exclusive prism of India-Kashmir and/or federal-state interactions through which much of the existing scholarship on the Bakshi period has been viewed. To be sure, the overarching context of Bakshi's need to gain legitimacy for Kashmir's accession to India is crucial to understanding this period. Still, an exclusive focus on the "contractual relationship" keeps us from seeing the ways in which Bakshi was also attempting to implement a project of sociocultural reform that had its roots in the pre-Partition period.[113] Foregrounding India's role as a hegemonic, paternal state and Bakshi as an obedient, willing collaborator who was simply implementing the demands of the Government of India overlooks the intricacies of local politics and negotiations that traced their roots well before 1947, as well as Bakshi's agency. In particular, I examine how Bakshi exercised and developed his own theory of the political, relying on the politics of life to procure whatever benefit he could for Kashmir and its people. Yet, these local dynamics clashed with the imperatives of the colonial occupation, ensuring that his political praxis remained insufficient and would eventually become counterproductive. His rule elucidates how a client regime was able to utilize India's ambition for colonial expansion to assert a socioeconomic quest for modernization.

Sources and Organization of the Book

This book draws upon a wide array of bureaucratic documents, propaganda materials, memoirs, literary sources, and oral interviews in English, Urdu, and Kashmiri. I conducted my archival fieldwork between 2013 and 2014, with shorter stints in the summers of 2011, 2012, and 2016–2018. I was based primarily in Srinagar, the capital of Indian-occupied Kashmir, with short interludes at the National Archives of India and the Nehru Memorial Library in New Delhi. At the Jammu and Kashmir State Archives in Srinagar, I examined bureaucratic correspondence from the Departments of Education, Information, and Home as well as administrative reports and government propaganda materials. To bring forth diverse Kashmiri voices, I collected several published memoirs and literary works through various local libraries, bookstores, and private archives. In addition, I conducted twenty-five oral interviews with former students in local colleges and members of the state bureaucracy on their memories of the Bakshi period. In New Delhi, I examined published materials on Kashmir in the early Indian state and newspaper clippings. My initial visit to the National Archives of India in 2014 proved unproductive, as most files relating to my period were "non-transferrable," indicative of the multiple ways in which the Indian state seeks to restrict access to information and knowledge-production on Kashmir. My second trip, in 2018, resulted in acquiring limited correspondence between the Indian government and the Kashmir state on financial integration and agricultural subsidies. However, much of the additional material remained inaccessible, a limitation I hope will be rectified for future historians.

Colonizing Kashmir is divided into seven chapters and an introduction and a conclusion, highlighting how Bakshi's state-building sought to establish normalcy, territorialize Kashmir in the Indian imagination, create economic dependency, shape Kashmiri subjectivities and culture, and manage dissent. Chapter 1 provides a genealogy of Bakshi's state-building project, rooted in the late Dogra period and Kashmir's anti-monarchical mobilizations. I discuss Bakshi's early life and political philosophy, linking it to socioeconomic conditions under the Dogras. I foreground the Naya Kashmir manifesto as the basis of Bakshi's state-building policies. The chapter discusses the momentous events surrounding the contested accession to India and the contestations surrounding Abdullah's government, as well as Bakshi's rise to power.

The second and third chapters lay out the Bakshi government's use of the "politics of life" in the realm of discourse. Chapter 2 draws upon bureaucratic directives and communication with the press, political speeches, news articles, photographs, and state propaganda materials to understand how Bakshi's client regime established legitimacy in the eyes of non-client powers. It brings attention to the unique set of political compulsions Bakshi's government faced on three primary fronts: within a conflict of narratives and aspirations in Kashmir, with skeptical Indian policy makers and the broader public, and in the international arena in the context of shifting political realignments during the Cold War. I argue that Bakshi's government utilized the power of media as propaganda and maintained strict controls over the flow of information into and out of the state to project normalization, as well as progress, in Kashmir for these multiple audiences. These critical policy interventions came at a time when Kashmir was still being contested in the United Nations. Bakshi's efforts to target Muslim-majority countries and the Soviet Union, in particular, were crucial to unraveling the "disputed" status of the region, securing India's claims over Kashmir, and eroding the calls for a plebiscite on the international front.

Kashmir was the place to be in the 1950s and 1960s as film crews across India descended upon the state, and a record number of tourists—mostly from India—visited the Himalayan hotspot. In chapter 3, I examine tourist guides and videos, advertisements, film, and bureaucratic correspondence with Indian film companies to show how they contributed to an affective desire for both the land and its people. This colonial gaze depicted the region as fertile for adventure and at the cusp of modernization as a result of its relationship with

India. At the same time, Kashmir's sacred territoriality for Indian Hindus was mobilized through the Amarnath Yatra, which was also extensively promoted by the Kashmir government, paradoxically propagating a land that was both modern and timeless, secular and Hindu. Tourism and cinema served to territorialize India's colonial occupation in both its secular modernizing and religious avatars and enabled an unquenchable desire of Indians toward Kashmir (and some Kashmiris) that would continue to undergird India's rule in Kashmir.

The next three chapters situate the "politics of life" through government planning in economic development, education, and cultural reform. While they highlight how these policies attempted to entrench India's colonial rule, they also discuss the unintended consequences and effects of these policies, both for undermining their original intent and for producing contradictions and creating empowered subjects who began to articulate their own demands. Chapter 4, which incorporates five-year plans, administrative and budget reports, political speeches, Indian and international media reports, and state propaganda materials, focuses primarily on the economic policies of the Bakshi government and draws attention to how these developmentalist policies reflected the particular political context in Kashmir. It looks at financial integration with the Indian state, the subsidization of rice, and the creation of the Banihal Tunnel. I argue that Kashmir's political status engendered a form of developmentalism that focused more on short-term strategic interests than on long-term economic growth. As a result, the state's economic goals of self-sufficiency were undermined as the state became increasingly dependent on the Government of India. Also, I highlight how corruption became an intrinsic component to the functioning of developmentalism in Kashmir, leading to the Ayyangar Commission of Enquiry of corruption after Bakshi stepped down from power. This chapter showcases how Bakshi's client regime incorporated Kashmir's economy into the larger economic body of India.

Chapter 5 uses education plans and reports, as well as college journals, memoirs, and oral interviews, to examine how the state's education policies sought to incorporate its citizenry into the Indian social and political body. I argue that educational policy was the cornerstone of constructing a modern, secular Kashmiri subject. However, because the government targeted Kashmiri Muslims as its principal beneficiaries, the educational policies of the state, which included specific quotas for various religious communities and language policies, created tensions between and among Kashmiri Muslims and Kashmiri Pandits, leading the latter to bring the government's secular credentials into question. Debates over education reflected the conflicting aims and complex interests of the Kashmir government as well as the fraught nature of intercommunal relations under both secular rule as well as a colonial occupation.

Chapter 6 looks at poems, shorts stories, novels, cultural journals, and bureaucratic correspondence to explore the government's attempts to revitalize Kashmiri culture. It reveals the role of the cultural intelligentsia in Kashmir in buttressing the state-building project and constructing a Kashmiri cultural identity. At the same time, I argue that the bureaucratization of culture produced its own contradictions in eliciting conformity and resistance, highlighting the extent to which dissent is always integral to cultural projects.

Chapter 7 examines sovereign modes of control and the unraveling of the state-building project as it generated dissent among various groups within Kashmir. By focusing on the workings of dissent and repression, I argue that the local state was at the forefront of repression against those individuals and groups that challenged the government's stance on Kashmir's political status. The state's repressive practices led to an enduring state of emergency, well before the armed uprising. It was also under Bakshi that a popular and organized post-Partition indigenous resistance emerged. Groups like the Political Conference and the Plebiscite Front demanded the implementation of the plebiscite. This chapter explores how the state managed to eventually fold the leadership of both organizations into the political mainstream, highlighting once more the strategies of repression and co-option that undergird a colonial occupation. I conclude with reflections on what the case of Kashmir tells us about the present, one in which processes of settler-colonization and military occupation have brought to the fore the contestations inherent in the liberal, secular, democratic nation-state.

Chapter 1

GENEALOGIES OF COLONIAL OCCUPATION AND STATE-BUILDING

Becoming Khalid-i-Kashmir

Bakshi Ghulam Mohammad was born on July 20, 1907, in downtown Srinagar, in a neighborhood called Safakadal.[1] His family came from a working class Muslim background, and he had four brothers and two sisters. With his uncle's financial assistance, Bakshi attended one of the local Christian missionary schools, founded by Tyndale Biscoe, a British missionary. Because of his family's dire economic conditions, Bakshi dropped out of school after completing the eighth grade, which at the time was considered "middle pass" and an appropriate qualification for certain forms of employment, including teaching.[2]

For someone who had barely completed the eighth grade to become the prime minister was no ordinary feat. Yet, the personal is never far from the political. Bakshi's personal life and experience enabled an embodied relationship with the politics of life, and his background—reflective of the socioeconomic conditions of many Kashmiri Muslims—informed his political praxis. Furthermore, Bakshi's project of state-building was grounded both in the context of Kashmir's experience under Dogra rule as well as the contentious relations between Sheikh Abdullah and the Government of India in the aftermath of the accession.

Dogra Rule

Bakshi was born during a time of immense repression and economic hardship, especially for the region's Muslims. The Dogras, Kashmir's princely rulers, oversaw an extremely despotic rule, which, as Mohamad Junaid argues, was "singularly devoted to extracting maximum tax and free labor from its (primarily Muslim) subjects."[3] As upper-caste Hindus, the Dogras also established what Mridu Rai has termed a "territorially bound Hindu sovereignty," or a Hindu state. As a result, by the first two decades of the twentieth century, the majority of the Muslim population were suffering economically, politically, and socially. Most were illiterate and had no land ownership rights. Peasants and artisans were forced to pay crippling taxes to the Dogra state and high prices for foodstuffs.[4] As Iffat Malik details, everything was taxed: "crops, fruit, grazing for animals, handicrafts (shawls, carpets, etc.), marriage ceremonies, labour services—including grave-digging and even prostitution."[5] Grain was controlled and trade prohibited between the towns and the countryside, leaving peasants at the brink of starvation and resulting in multiple famines. Epidemics and outbreaks of cholera were frequent. Kashmiri Muslims were legally not allowed to leave the state, but their dire conditions led to large-scale migrations to neighboring Punjab. Muslims in the Valley were also not allowed to bear arms or serve in the Dogra army.[6] Others were made to take part in *begar*, or forced labor without compensation.[7] While a small but growing number of middle-class Muslim families were involved in business, trade, and religious leadership, very few were educated in modern educational institutions, a reality that was in stark contrast to Muslims in other parts of the subcontinent. Similarly, there were very few Muslims in the government bureaucracy. Some of the religious elite (*pirs*) received "land grants, tax exemptions, and sustenance" and were complicit with the actions of the Dogra state by forcing peasants to hand over their remaining grain to ensure their class dominance.[8]

The Dogras banned the consumption of beef and generously constructed and maintained Hindu temples, while ignoring Muslim sites of worship. They gave Hindus exclusive privileges to government employment as well as massive land grants and institutionalized the Dharmath Trust, which was meant to establish control over all aspects of Hindu worship. Celebrating Hindu rituals and ceremonies with much fanfare, they also utilized colonial textual and architectural claims to "decree Hindu precedence over shrines disputed between Kashmiri Pandits and Kashmiri Muslims."[9]

The small minority of Kashmiri Pandits had significant political and administrative presence and fared better than their Muslim counterparts in terms of education and employment. Many of them were the face of the Dogra state because they served as revenue collectors. They received favorable treatment to the extent that they were identified with the ruling class in the eyes of many Kashmiri Muslims.[10] This was to have important implications for relations between the two communities, as "religious identity gradually came to overlap with class identity."[11]

Yet, Kashmiri Pandits had their issues with the Dogra state. As increasing numbers of Punjabi Hindus were employed by the Dogras, Kashmiri Pandits mobilized, first in 1912 and then in 1927, to ensure that only Kashmir state-subjects would be able to secure employment in the bureaucracy. Through the "Kashmir for Kashmiris movement," the hereditary state-subject, as Cabeiri Robinson illustrates, "emerged as the primary category to identify the state's people and the legal provisions for state-subject recognition were codified and elaborated by the Maharaja's government between 1912 and 1932."[12] Later, the state-subject category would be important in determining who qualified as "Kashmiri" in both post-Partition India and Pakistan—and the category was integrally linked to education and employment, two aspects of state-building.[13]

The British were partly to blame for the plight of the Muslims—while some individuals, including Robert Thorp, wrote about the conditions of Kashmiri Muslims, most British government officials turned a blind eye and some profited from the use of *begar* labor and tourism.[14] In addition, as Rai argues, the British underwrote the "sovereignty of the Dogra rulers while encouraging them to derive their legitimacy from arenas that bypassed" their Muslim subjects.[15] In effect, the British buttressed the Hindu state. It was only when the devastating famine of 1877 occurred, decimating over half the population of the Valley, that the British finally demanded the presence of a British resident and a transformation in agrarian policy. However, Altaf Hussain Para notes, "The British intervention was more motivated by its own colonial compulsions than by any 'good' of the people of the state."[16]

The conditions that most Muslims were subject to did not escape Bakshi's early childhood in Srinagar. While he was in school, Bakshi had impressed local Christian missionaries with his leadership qualities and involvement in extracurricular activities. The missionaries encouraged Bakshi to serve in one of the mission's schools in Ladakh. For two years Bakshi lived in Skardu and Leh as a teacher and headmaster. He also travelled with the missionaries to Shigar in Gilgit.[17] Back in Srinagar, there were rumors that, as a result of working with Christian missionaries, Bakshi had converted to Christianity.[18] Upon hearing this, his family encouraged him to return to Srinagar. Soon after, he was married and started working at a local branch of the All-India Spinners Association. During his stay in Ladakh, Bakshi came across the ideologies of Gandhi and the Congress. He was an avid follower of Gandhi and became one of the first links between the Congress and Kashmir.[19] He then worked as a salesman in a *khadi* (cotton cloth) store on Hari Singh High Street and was known as the "Kashmiri Gandhi" for his calls to boycott British goods.

Upon Bakshi's return to Srinagar, the atmosphere was politically charged, the result of the glaring inequalities of Dogra rule. In the 1920s and 1930s, inspired by anti-imperialist and nationalist movements across the subcontinent, Kashmir's Muslims, too, demanded political and social rights from the Dogras. Their efforts led to major contestations over defining Kashmiri Muslim identity on questions of nationalism, secularism, and sovereignty.

Starting in 1907, the Muslim leadership, consisting primarily of "clergy, landowners, and wealthy traders," issued a series of memorandums indicating their demands.[20] In 1924, prominent Muslim leaders wrote a memorandum to the British viceroy, Lord Reading, during his visit to the state. The list of grievances included better wages for the workers who were striking at the government silk factory, improvements in education for the Muslim community, greater representation of Muslims in the government administration, land reform, abolition of *begar*, and a representative legislative assembly.[21] Muslim mobilization increased once a small number of them began to receive higher education in cities like Aligarh and Lahore. There, they were influenced by the modernist or left-leaning progressive politics of the Muslim intelligentsia. Upon their return, they created the Reading Room Party in 1930 to seek ways to empower the beleaguered Muslim community in the Valley.[22] In Jammu, a similar organization, the Young Men's Muslim Association, was formed in 1922.[23]

One of the prominent leaders that emerged at this time was Sheikh Abdullah. Abdullah was born in Soura in 1905 in a small business family. He received his master's degree in Aligarh and returned to the Kashmir Valley, hoping to secure a position in government administration. After failing to do so, he became active with a number of groups, including the Reading Room Party, in order to mobilize Kashmiri Muslims to agitate for greater rights.[24] A turning point in Muslim mobilization occurred in July 1931, when the state police opened fire on a procession that had gathered to protest the arrest of Abdul Qadir, a Pathan Muslim who had raised his voice against state tyranny.[25] The Dogra state killed twenty-one people—the day is commemorated in Kashmir as Martyr's Day and the day the freedom struggle commenced. As a result of the violence, riots broke out in other areas, and businesses owned by Hindus were attacked.[26] Although issues of religious concern prompted the events, Shahla Hussain argues that the riots were a result not of religious bigotry but of underlying socioeconomic issues.[27]

After the events of July 1931, the Dogra government responded to public pressure by setting up the Glancy Commission to examine the concerns of the state's Muslims. Following from the grievances expressed in the 1924 memorandum, the commission once again focused on issues of exorbitant taxes, *begar*, education, restoration of Muslim shrines, and employment in government services. An important development of the commission was the establishment of a legislative assembly, the Praja Sabha. Initially, the body just had advisory power, but by 1939 it had power to make laws and included a majority of elected members. Political parties became legal for the first time, and newspapers and political meetings were also permitted.

Abdullah and the emerging Muslim leadership established the All Jammu and Kashmir Muslim Conference in 1932 in order to politically unite the Muslims of the state. Rai argues that the exclusion of Muslims from the economic and political resources of the Hindu-led state led to a religious sensibility that informed political mobilization, so religious discourses became inseparable from the discourse of rights.[28] The Muslim Conference initially received support from various Muslim groups in the state, including Muslims in Jammu as well as the Kashmir Valley. However, regional as well as "sectarian and class divisions within the Kashmiri Muslim community prevented the forging of a unified movement for rights" against Dogra rule.[29] Furthermore, while the leadership of the party sought Hindu-Muslim unity and the empowerment of all communities in the state, non-Muslims, especially in Jammu and Ladakh primarily saw their efforts as supporting *Muslim* empowerment.[30]

As Abdullah grew in popularity, he became involved in political developments outside the state. The divisions within the Muslim Conference and his desire to separate from the influence of Punjabi Muslims, as well as his closer ties to the Congress, caused Abdullah to shift his approach.[31] Kashmiri Pandit writer and reformer Prem Nath Bazaz, as well as Indian national leaders such as Jawaharlal Nehru, convinced Abdullah to extend the framework of the party to include Hindus, Sikhs, and Buddhists in a broader non-religious, class-based struggle against the Dogras.[32] The Muslim Conference was subsequently renamed the National Conference in 1938 and became more left-leaning in orientation.[33]

A majority of the Muslim leaders from Jammu, as well as some from the Kashmir Valley, were opposed to the new orientation of the National Conference and withdrew from the party, leaving it primarily Valley-centric. As Mohammad Yusuf Ganai details, these leaders, including Chaudhri Ghulam Abbas from Jammu, who would later revive the Muslim Conference in 1941, "had an apprehension that the conversion would weaken the movement because the non-Muslims would not participate in the National Conference sincerely but for the sake of the safeguard of their vested interests."[34] Yet, religious differences were not the only factor in breaking away from the National Conference. There were regional ones too. Abbas and other Muslim leaders from Jammu did not see the National Conference as representing Jammu Muslims.[35]

Bakshi played an instrumental role in the anti-Dogra agitation. When the Muslim agitation against Dogra rule began in 1931, Bakshi, at twenty-four years old, aligned himself with Sheikh Abdullah and the Muslim Conference. He was tasked with bringing traders, unions, and laborers into the fold of the Muslim Conference. After the organization was split into the National Conference, Bakshi—who initially voted against the conversion—went along with the shift and, as district president, organized branches of the party throughout the Valley.[36] He was also involved in establishing a number of youth federations. His anti-government activities led to a number of arrests, and many times he was forced to go underground. For his activism, he was referred to as "Khalid-i-Kashmir" after the iconic Khalid ibn Walid, the Arab Muslim general who was credited with expanding the Islamic empire in the seventh century.

Naya Kashmir

To understand the genealogies of Bakshi's state-building plan, it is important to consider the influence of the Naya Kashmir manifesto, a document that would serve as a model for the post-Partition period, although it would never be fully implemented.[37] The forty-four-page manifesto outlined an ambitious program for a future secular and democratic state, borrowing heavily from Soviet-style models of governance and planned economy. As Robinson argues, the manifesto is the first adoption of the concept of popular sovereignty for Kashmir state subjects, "based in the region's previous land rights movements and protests."[38]

On September 29, 1944, leaders of the National Conference convened their annual meeting in Sopore, a town in the Baramulla district of the Kashmir Valley. One of the important challenges Abdullah faced was to bring together the various regions of the state and position the party as offering socioeconomic transformation for all communities. And so, with the help of prominent leftists in the subcontinent, especially B. P. L. Bedi, his wife Freda Bedi, and K. M. Ashraf, the Naya Kashmir manifesto was released at the annual meeting. The manifesto was published in a small red booklet. It bore an image of a Kashmiri peasant woman holding the flag of the National Conference, with a white plow above her head. The manifesto was intended to counter decades of oppression and poverty under the Dogras. National Conference leaders declared that they were building a Naya Kashmir in order to "raise ourselves and our children forever from the abyss of oppression and poverty, degradation and superstition, from medieval darkness and ignorance into the sunlit valleys of plenty ruled by freedom, science and honest toil."[39] Instead of seeing the struggle in religious terms—a Hindu state versus the Muslim masses—the manifesto declared that the struggle was along class lines: "it is for the poor, against those who exploit them; for the toiling people of our beautiful homeland against the heartless pranks of the socially privileged."[40] The writers of the manifesto were conscious of the changes happening around the world, in the Soviet Union and elsewhere, and positioned the document as specifically formulating "more concretely [the National Conference's] own conception of the New Kashmir it strives to build."[41] The National Conference went beyond the Muslim Conference's earlier demands for better educational and economic rights, and also called for a responsible government and democracy in a socialist welfare state that would reduce the monarch to a titular figurehead.

In this document, the Jammu and Kashmir state was a distinct country with a Muslim majority, but with significant provisions for its Hindu, Sikh, Christian, and Buddhist minorities. Geographically, the manifesto covered the regions of Jammu, Kashmir, Ladakh, and the frontier regions, adopting the areas that constituted the Dogra princely state of Jammu and Kashmir. Politically, the document called for a representative legislature called the National Assembly. It also called for universal suffrage and decentralized governance "based on devolution of decision making and administrative responsibilities to districts, *tehsils* [subdivisions of districts], towns, and villages."[42] One of the more interesting aspects of the manifesto was its weightage toward the state's minorities, which included "Pandits, Sikhs, and Harijans," who were given two—instead of one—votes in the assembly during a transitional period.[43] A reason for this weightage could have been to deflect concerns of Muslim majoritarianism that the minorities in the state held toward the National Conference.

On the economic front, the manifesto drew a revolutionary new economic plan that abolished feudalism and gave land to the tiller, established cooperative associations, and placed emphasis on state-led industrialization. Under the plan, the state would control the means of production so as to ensure the fairest distribution of goods and services to its citizens. A crucial aim of the economic goals of the state was to achieve "national self-sufficiency as far as is consonant with the economic welfare of the general mass of the people of the State" and raise the "standard of living according to a definite specified programme of nation-building."[44] Culturally, the manifesto designated Urdu as the official language of the diverse state and called for the development of the region's cultural heritage, with an emphasis on its religious pluralism. It articulated basic human and political rights, including the right to education; freedom of speech, press, and worship; and equality of all citizens, regardless of race, religion, nationality, or birth. It also had a charter on women's and workers' rights, which included the right to divorce, equal wages, and paid maternity leave. One of the important themes that emerged in the manifesto was the need to integrate the diverse ethnic and religious groups in the state and secure their role in building a New Kashmir; Kashmir was to be a polity based on progressive politics, not one that was divided because of its religious and ethnic difference.

As Chitrelekha Zutshi details, the manifesto came at a time when it appeared that the National Conference's popularity was waning with the reemergence of the Muslim Conference, increasing divisions amongst the various groups in the state in the lead up to Partition, its close relationship with the Indian National Congress, as well as its perceived concessions to the Dogra state.[45] Furthermore, during a massive shortage of fuel and grain during the winter of 1942–43, there were allegations of corruption against the National Conference, especially against Bakshi, who had been appointed by the Dogra government's prime minister as the Muslim member of a "committee that supplied fuel and grain to inhabitants of the provinces" that were the hardest hit. Many "alleged that the committees had refused to them grain and fuel because of their affiliation with the Muslim Conference."[46] This incident would serve as an antecedent to the immense allegations of corruption during Bakshi's actual rule, but it also suggests the close familiarity Bakshi had with the desperation of the people of the state, which would come to play an important role in shaping his economic development policies—and indeed, the politics of life.

While Naya Kashmir appeared to revitalize political life in the state, especially in rural areas, and provided a blueprint for the activities of the National Conference, Abdullah's detractors, including Mirwaiz Yusuf, declared that it held Kashmiri interests above Muslim interests. In a meeting of the recently revived Muslim Conference, in November 1945, the manifesto was denounced.[47] A number of Hindu groups in the state, conscious that they would lose their socioeconomic privileges were the manifesto to be implemented, also opposed the manifesto for pandering primarily to Muslim concerns and felt that siding with the maharaja, not the National Conference, was a better course for them.[48] Moreover, the manifesto was vague on the future of Kashmir after the British left the subcontinent.

Naya Kashmir was a progressive project of state *and* sociocultural reform located in the particular context of the late Dogra period; however, as I will show in this book, parts of it were still utilized by Bakshi in his project of state-building and reform nearly a decade later.[49] In moving the manifesto out of the context of its own production and into the period of Bakshi's government, I will highlight how we are able to see the duration and continuity of the ideas of state-building that undergird the project, the ways in which the local leadership attempted to fulfill (many times unsuccessfully) its aims of economic, educational, and cultural transformation, as well as the tensions inherent in many of the demands of the manifesto.

Ethnic Cleansing, Accession, and War

Political developments in Kashmir in the 1940s allow for a more nuanced perspective into what is otherwise simply seen as the anti-colonial nationalist movement against the British in the subcontinent. There was a wide range of emergent political visions, subjectivities, demands, and formations—including those that were anti-monarchical, anti-colonial, anti-feudal, Hindu nationalist, socialist, communist, and Muslim nationalist (pro-Pakistan). Some of these overlapped, offering visions of political possibilities or formations that challenged or moved away from the "nation" or the emergent Indian state: for example, the All India State Peoples' Conference brought together representatives from the princely states but was also linked to Sheikh Abdullah and the Naya Kashmir manifesto. Others, like the socialists and the communists, were drawing from and linked to more global contexts. The emergence of these contesting visions underscores how concepts of participation and engagement on questions of governance and sovereignty were a part of the formation of the political domain in Kashmir.

Throughout the 1940s, it appeared that the National Conference was increasingly becoming allied with the Indian National Congress, while the Muslim Conference was more sympathetic to the Muslim League and calling for merger with Pakistan. Yet, there were no easy overlaps between the Muslim League and the Muslim Conference and the Indian National Congress and the National Conference, and other groups had formed too, such as the Kisan Mazdoor Party, founded by Prem Nath Bazaz to represent the aims of the rural classes. While Abdullah had a popular base in the Valley, the Muslim Conference was the more dominant of the two parties in Jammu and Poonch. Matters became increasingly fractious between the various groups in the days leading up to Partition. In 1946, Sheikh Abdullah launched the Quit Kashmir movement against the Dogra Maharaja Hari Singh, calling for an end to his monarchical order. This move was in direct contrast to the party's earlier stance of allowing the maharaja to serve as titular head. Most scholars have seen Quit Kashmir as an attempt by Abdullah to "revive his party's flagging popularity," which had resulted from his growing closer to the Congress, a position that was unpopular in the Valley, especially among members of the newly formed Kisan Mazdoor Party and the Muslim Conference.[50] At a meeting sponsored by the Kisan Mazdoor Party in May 1946, a number of political groups in the state called for an Azad (Free) Kashmir, demanding "the liberation of the princely state of Jammu and Kashmir and the creation of a free state in which the people of the state would be sovereign."[51]

During the Quit Kashmir movement, Bakshi escaped to Delhi and Lahore to gain outside support for the agitation in Kashmir, writing pamphlets about the conditions of Kashmiri prisoners in Dogra jails.[52] Meanwhile, Abdullah and other leaders were arrested—including those of the Muslim Conference, who were also attempting to organize separately against the Dogras—keeping them out of the negotiations over the future of the state.

In mid-August 1947, the two new nation-states of India and Pakistan were formed. The leaders of the princely states, including Jammu and Kashmir, were given the option of joining either, depending on the geography and demographics of the people of the state. Because of the geographic and demographic diversity of Jammu and Kashmir, it remains unclear what the people would have demanded; some scholars have argued that while most non-Muslims were not in favor of accession to Pakistan, Muslims in the Jammu and Poonch region were in favor of Pakistan. In the Valley, there was support for the Muslim Conference and the National Conference. Yet, even those who were loyal to Abdullah as a local leader maintained an inclination toward Pakistan. Others have suggested that Kashmiri political and public opinion was not overwhelmingly in favor of India *or* Pakistan and that most would have preferred independence.[53] In sum, there were a variety of political opinions in Kashmir at the time of Partition: pro-Pakistan Muslim parties (many members of the Muslim Conference, who on July 19, 1947, declared their support for accession to Pakistan), pro-Pakistan socialists (some members of the Kisan Mazdoor Party and the Kashmir Socialist Party), pro-India or continued rule by the maharaja (most Hindu or Pandit parties, such as the Praja Parishad), pro-India with a strong desire for autonomy (a number of National Conference leaders), and pro-Independence, a sentiment initially supported by some members of the Muslim Conference, National Conference, and Kisan Mazdoor Party and shared by a number of individuals across the spectrum, including within the Dogra state bureaucracy.[54] There were diverse political visions for the future of the princely state. To claim that one party or leader had more authority or popularity than others, as both Indian nationalist and National Conference histories have done with Sheikh Abdullah, is misleading. However, once India and Pakistan formed, the range of political possibilities narrowed and other political visions were eclipsed by the two new nation-states.

How state-formation and state-building would occur in Kashmir was an important component in shaping political inclinations. One of the main reasons Sheikh Abdullah and some of his followers—although not all members of the National Conference—were averse to the Muslim League and joining Pakistan was that they envisioned it as a party of landed elites with feudal interests that would not allow them to implement the Naya Kashmir manifesto, which included land reform. In addition, the Congress and Jawaharlal Nehru presented to Abdullah a democratic and multiethnic framework that would supposedly secure Kashmir's autonomy in order to protect its identity as a Muslim-majority state. It was the "progressive agenda of social transformation which prompted Abdullah to opt for India," and he gave Nehru assurances of the same while he was imprisoned.[55] The point about the provision of autonomy in the context of state-formation is crucial for understanding why Abdullah later turned away from the Government of India.

At the time the decision was to be made, however, leaders of both the Muslim Conference and National Conference were in jail. The maharaja vacillated in his decision, perhaps also wanting an independent state that was separate from both India and Pakistan.[56] Nehru, realizing Abdullah's support was crucial for any agreement with the Government of India, urged the maharaja to release Abdullah from jail, which he did in September 1947. Nehru had made his claims on Kashmir clear even before Partition, declaring at different moments that Kashmir would be an integral part of a future India. He bolstered the leadership of Abdullah and the National Conference in order to facilitate that process—although, as we have seen, neither Abdullah nor the National

Conference was the sole representative of the people of the state.[57] Nehru wanted to control Kashmir to "vindicate Congress's secular ideology and to address India's security concerns," while other members of his party, such as Sardar Patel, wanted "Kashmir's accession to India based on its Hindu past."[58] Gandhi also visited Kashmir in the first week of August, which many argue was another attempt by the Indian leadership to convince the maharaja to accede to India. Both secular and Hindu nationalist elements of India's nationalist leadership converged on one demand: to incorporate Kashmir into the Indian nation-state—eventually, at whatever cost.

Two other important events would reveal India's intentions in Kashmir. First, the Boundary Commission, established to set the boundary between the nation-states of India and Pakistan, gave India three townships in a Muslim-majority district in Gurdaspur in Punjab, which adjoined Jammu and should have technically gone to Pakistan under the terms of the Boundary Commission's reference.[59] This allocation provided India with crucial road access to Jammu; without it, India's only link to Jammu and Kashmir would have been a difficult mountainous terrain, which would have made accession impossible. Second, as the maharaja vacillated, he signed a standstill agreement with Pakistan, which gave him time to make his decision. The agreement "ensured the continuation of essential relations, in communications, posts, and trade."[60] The Indian government did not sign the agreement, suggesting "India had decided to take Kashmir with or without the state ruler's consent."[61]

Meanwhile, between August and October, a local rebellion in the area of Poonch against Dogra high-handedness, repression, and heavy taxation spread to Mirpur and Jammu and was crushed by the maharaja's soldiers. The Dogra army had begun "to disarm Muslim peasants (as well as Muslim soldiers) and redistribute weapons to Hindu and Sikh landlords."[62] Hindu and Sikh refugees fleeing Pakistan also made their way to Jammu, sharing stories of the atrocities committed against them and retaliating against Muslims in Jammu. Aided by Indian Rashtriya Swayamsevak Sangh (RSS) jathas as well as troops from the Indian state of Patiala (another princely state), the Dogra forces took part in a violent campaign from October to November 1947, resulting in an estimated 200,000–250,000 Muslims from Jammu province being killed and an equal number or more fleeing to Pakistan, where they settled in government-run camps in

West Punjab.[63] Here, the intersection of the two princely states as well as right-wing Hindu nationalist movements in cleansing Muslims from parts of the state provides a different lens into political visions and aspirations as well as ideas of sovereignty, that shaped events in Kashmir at the time of partition. There were also reports of thousands of women being abducted, as well as violent incidents between Hindus/Sikhs and Muslims. While histories of what is referred to as the Jammu Massacre have been silenced by the Indian and Kashmir government historiographies, recent scholarship has uncovered the Dogra state's actions as an explicit attempt at demographic change, resulting in an ethnic cleansing whereby the population of Jammu turned from a Muslim majority to a Hindu majority.[64] The reason to "cleanse" Jammu of its Muslims was most likely "in case retaining the Kashmir Valley and other Muslim majority provinces of the state became tough."[65] By October 24, the Poonch rebels, many of whom who had served for the British during World War II, formed a provisional revolutionary government of Azad (Free) Kashmir in western Jammu, where they declared the overthrow of the maharaja's government and included leaders from "the Kashmir and Jammu provinces" of the princely state.[66]

In late October, Pathan Muslim *lashkars*, or militias, from northwest Pakistan, supported by officials in the Pakistan state, made their way to Kashmir in order to support the local rebellion and "liberate their co-religionists from the Hindu yoke."[67] The speed with which the Pathan Muslims moved toward Srinagar "created panic in the state administration and among the local population, particularly in the rank and file of the National Conference."[68] Accounts of what became known as the "tribal invasion" are sparse. They state that on their way, the Pathan Muslims attacked Hindus and Sikhs in retaliation. There were reports of looting, arson, and destruction, including a violent attack on a Catholic convent and mission hospital in the town of Baramulla in North Kashmir.[69] Many people fled their homes. Andrew Whitehead argues that "the attackers were indiscriminate in their violence and so lost much of the goodwill they might have enjoyed as self-proclaimed liberators from Hindu princely rule."[70]

The maharaja escaped Srinagar "along with the vast treasure from the state exchequer" and sought military help from the newly formed Indian government under Prime Minister Jawaharlal Nehru.[71] Under advice from

Mountbatten, the Government of India made the Dogra ruler sign an instrument of accession on October 26, 1947, before it would lend its assistance; its army officially arrived in Srinagar, the summer capital of Kashmir, on October 27. However, some scholars have argued that Indian military units from the state of Patiala were already secretly operating in Kashmir, making the Indian army's arrival an invasion.[72] Others dispute the date the accession was signed, arguing that the Indian army was already making its way to Kashmir before the maharaja could have signed the treaty. Whatever the case, the accession gave India control over Kashmir's defense, communications, and foreign affairs but also promised that the state's future would be determined "by a reference to the people." Having been recently released, Sheikh Abdullah gave his consent for the accession, and the National Conference raised militias and home guards against the raids. Abdullah was tasked with leading the interim government.[73]

The government of Pakistan rejected the accession and also sent its troops, leading to the first India-Pakistan war, in November 1947, "and two different internal governments claimed to be the government of the entirety of the former Princely State and its state subjects."[74] Meanwhile, violence continued in the "lower mountains of the Jammu Province, often displacing the residents of entire villages. Minorities in each of the controlled territories were also collected at refugee transit camps, similar to those organized in the Punjab, and sent to territories held by the opposing armies."[75] The worst violence against Jammu Muslims by Dogra state forces occurred during the week of November 5, over a week after the contested accession. Abdullah's interim government, then, alongside the Indian government, was complicit in ethnically cleansing Muslims from the Jammu region both by failing to protect them and in forcibly transporting them across the border. Displacement over the course of the massacre and the war caused a massive refugee crisis; most refugees were unable to go back to their homes as a result of the imposition of a UN ceasefire line (known today as the Line of Control that divides the princely state).[76] However, they remain Kashmir "state-subjects" and have political claims on the future of Kashmir.

Indian nationalist narratives surrounding these events have largely revolved around the tropes of Pakistan as the "aggressor," the "invading tribals" from Pakistan causing India to come to the state's defense, and the accession being a valid treaty that legally binds Kashmir to India. This colonial narrative, depicting the Indian nation-state as the savior of a hapless Kashmiri population, obfuscates a number of important points and has been increasingly met with resistance in recent scholarship.

First, it completely denies Kashmiri agency and the role that an indigenous uprising of Poonchis and Mirpuris played during this time.[77] Second, it grossly excises the historical records as well as memories of the Jammu Massacre, while perpetuating the "Kashmir Valley's resistance against the invading Pakistani 'tribals'. . . as a triumph of an Indian secular nationalist project over Pakistani Muslim nationalism."[78] For the Indian nation-state, the truth of the violence and brutality against the Muslims of the state, as well as the role of Indian RSS jathas and Patiala state forces, would undermine Kashmir's belonging to India on the grounds of secularism. Furthermore, it would complicate India's desire to depict Maharaja Hari Singh as 'legitimate,' and hence his accession to India as "a valid sovereign act."[79] So, the Indian leadership—relying on settler logics of erasure of histories—buried the Jammu Massacre altogether.

Nehru, in a letter to Sardar Patel in November 1947, was cognizant of the "RSS volunteers that had been organized in East Punjab to be sent to Jammu for a campaign against the Muslims there." Yet, instead of being angered by the actual violence against Muslims, Nehru was more concerned with its optics—"the potential to crack open the whole Kashmir position if an anti-Muslim drive took place in Jammu."[80] Furthermore, instead of holding those who were responsible for violence in Jammu accountable, Nehru "employed the discourse of 'otherness,' blaming the 'tribal invaders' for the extreme violence," despite the fact that "the violence inflicted by the Muslim tribesmen . . . was minor compared to the scale of horror inflicted by the Dogra forces."[81] From the beginning, Nehru's and India's reliance on the colonial optics of normalization in Kashmir, only to be interrupted by "Pakistani aggression," was set into motion.

Beyond statist discourse, rarely does one hear Indian postcolonial or subaltern scholars speaking of the Jammu Massacre, even though they are all too eager to overemphasize the Pakistan-sponsored "tribals." Here, too, lies another bias. The "tribals" constructed as violent Pakistani-Muslims are seen as inherently foreign and thus having no justification to make any claims on Kashmir. Meanwhile, India's claims are naturalized, and its "foreignness" masked. This is especially ironic considering the economic, cultural, and religious ties that Kashmiris had with the areas of the subcontinent that would become Pakistan. Meanwhile, scholars have argued that around 65 percent of the "tribals" were actually native Kashmiris who had risen in revolt against the Dogra state.[82] This point is important to highlight because India's colonial occupation rests on these characterizations of the events surrounding 1947 in Jammu and Kashmir. India evidently "saved" Kashmir from Pakistani aggression, even as we have seen that it overtly and covertly made its own aggressive claims on Kashmir well before Partition and well before the "tribal invasion." As Iffat Malik explains, the Indian government had already "premeditated the outcome and already decided to send troops to the State in order to prevent it from falling into Pakistani control, irrespective of Hari Singh's signature."[83] This level of premeditation was not as fully reflected within the Pakistani leadership, which was relatively ambivalent about its active involvement in securing Kashmir's accession to Pakistan (especially given its limited resources) until the rebellion against the maharaja began and the Pathan Muslims were becoming mobilized.[84]

Furthermore, whether or not the maharaja signed the treaty under duress or before or after the Indian army landed in Kashmir, even if it occurred with the approval of Sheikh Abdullah, is immaterial. The maharaja, representing a state buttressed by the marginalization of the majority of its population and facing an internal revolt—one that had just committed an ethnic cleansing against the Muslims of Jammu—had fundamentally lost his moral and legal authority to represent the will of the people of Jammu and Kashmir. It appears the Indian government knew this too. As Mohamad Junaid argues:

> But it is a fact that Indian leaders made signing of the accession treaty a legal condition for their military help in securing the Dogra state, which, if they considered Hari Singh the sovereign, should not have been necessary at all. After all, Hari Singh could have asked for help as a sovereign ruler, and India would not have broken international law by providing it. And if they did not think Hari Singh had sovereign rights, as Congress leaders had repeatedly asserted previously, why was there the need to have him sign the document at all? Quite plausibly, M. K. Gandhi, and especially Nehru,

> knew about Hari Singh's involvement in abetting the genocide in Jammu, and yet they supported his decision.[85]

Therefore, the Treaty of Accession should not be treated as a legally binding treaty, but rather one in which two parties—neither of which had any right to decide any arrangement for the people of Kashmir—were attempting to maintain control and hold possession over the territory. This was, simply put, a colonial treaty, not unlike those the British had negotiated with princely rulers.

Finally, India's circuitous intentions in Kashmir are evidenced by its actions toward the princely states of Junagadh and Hyderabad.[86] Unlike Kashmir, both states had a Muslim ruler but a Hindu majority. In both these states, India overruled the aspirations of the ruler in favor of the will of the majority of the people (which it did not do in the case of the Hindu maharaja in Kashmir). In Junagadh, the nawab had signed an accession treaty with Pakistan. Economic and military pressure on the state led the nawab to flee to Pakistan, and "Indian troops marched into Junagadh on November 9. . . . A referendum was held on February 20, 1948, the result of which was overwhelmingly in India's favor."[87] In Hyderabad, the nizam wanted to remain independent. In September 1948, Indian troops took the state through violent military action in which many Muslims were killed.[88]

After the first India-Pakistan war, India took the dispute to the United Nations in mid-1948. The UN called for a plebiscite in the region under UN Security Council Resolution 47 in 1948 and negotiated a ceasefire line (later, the Line of Control) in 1949. Both the Indian and Pakistani leadership agreed to the resolution. There were a number of similar resolutions in subsequent years. India claims that the resolutions called for the withdrawal of Pakistan's troops from the territory, and because Pakistan did not remove troops, it was Pakistan's fault that the plebiscite never took place. Yet, Pakistan argues that the resolutions had also called for a removal of Indian troops and that the two countries had been unable to come to an agreement about the manner of troop removal and the authority that would oversee the plebiscite. Furthermore, Pakistan was hesitant to remove troops first given that the Indian government had already buttressed the National Conference government and was using elections to the Kashmir Constituent Assembly as a substitute for the plebiscite. Despite the UN resolutions not being implemented, they continue to bear significant moral weight as they firmly situate Kashmir as an international dispute and shape Kashmiri political demands for self-determination from the latter half of the twentieth century up until the present.

After the war, one-third of the region, known as Azad Kashmir and the Northern Areas (now Gilgit-Baltistan), came under Pakistani control, while the remaining two-thirds, which included the Kashmir Valley, Jammu, and Ladakh, was controlled by India. The Azad Kashmir government and Sheikh Abdullah's interim government were both seen as local authorities by "international authorities and relief workers," who were in the region for the purposes of "refugee relief, protection of minorities, and prisoner exchanges."[89] Neither recognized the other, however, and debates arose over the nature of leadership that would oversee the plebiscite. Sheikh Abdullah's government abolished the Dogra monarchy but retained the son of the maharaja, Karan Singh, as a titular sadar-i-riyasat (head of state).[90] The National Conference now dominated the political scene in the state, as most of the leaders of the revived Muslim Conference went to Pakistan and were instrumental in the formation of the new Azad Kashmir government.[91]

Sheikh Abdullah's Rule (1947–1953)

With Sheikh Abdullah and the National Conference in power, it appeared that the Naya Kashmir manifesto could be implemented. Internationally, especially among Western powers, the possibility of Kashmir being a site of advancing socialist transformation and land reform became a cause for concern. Within Kashmir, Sheikh Abdullah's rule was one of severe economic hardship, political suppression, and nepotism.[92] The fear of Pathan Muslims reaching Srinagar had buttressed some support for the National Conference. The party responded to the attack by organizing militias, including a women's self-defense corps.[93] It also utilized propaganda elements, such as plays, theater, and poetry, through a cultural front. However, the National Conference arrested or exiled any individual that contested its vision, including Kashmiris that supported merger with Pakistan. Newspapers and periodicals that disagreed with Kashmir's accession to India were banned—a policy more illiberal than that of late Dogra rule. Meanwhile, Abdullah was sent by Nehru to the United Nations Security Council in February 1948 to defend India's position on Kashmir.

One of the primary reasons Sheikh Abdullah agreed to the Treaty of Accession was Nehru's promise that the state would have substantial autonomy. The 1947 Treaty of Accession made Kashmir "a part of the Indian Union"; however, "India had only accepted this on condition that it be ratified by a popular referendum."[94] In October 1949, the terms of the accession were adopted into the Indian constitution via Article 370, which granted the state and its subjects a special autonomous status within the Indian Union and stipulated that all the other articles of the Indian constitution that gave power to the Indian government would be applied to Kashmir only with the concurrence of the state's newly formed Constituent Assembly. Thus, the Indian constitution was not to be directly applicable to the state of Jammu and Kashmir. Article 370 is what enabled the state to have its own flag, constitution, and assembly, and it also allowed the head of state to retain the title of Prime Minister, instead of Chief Minister as in Indian states. An offshoot of Article 370, Article 35A, protected "proto-citizenship rights to property by ensuring that only state subjects with proof of permanent residency status [could] own land in the state."[95] Article 35A, in particular, was a legal continuity from Pandit-led agitations decades earlier that had sought to define and give certain privileges and rights to Kashmir state-subjects.

In the eyes of Abdullah and members of the National Conference, Article 370 allowed for a distinction between Kashmir state-subjects and Indian citizens, while maintaining a formal—but restricted—link with the Government of India. Most scholars have viewed Article 370 as a means to protect Kashmir's interests from being subsumed under the larger Indian Union. However, Indian government officials, including Gopalaswami Ayyangar, who served as minister for Kashmir affairs, depicted Article 370 as "designed to *temporarily* manage the constitutional relationship between J&K and India until the political will of the people could be established and a final settlement reached through the state's own constitutional drafting process."[96] Iffat Malik reports, "The high degree of autonomy granted to the state by Article 370 was intended to be temporary. It was generally assumed that once accession had been ratified, greater integration would follow."[97] Furthermore, Article 1 of the constitution "describes Jammu and Kashmir as an integral part of the Indian Union"—a contradiction to Article 370.[98] Thus, as Haley Duschinski and Shrimoyee Ghosh argue, Article 370 has emerged as "asymmetric in the opposite sense to that intended," since "it has given the Indian Union greater powers over J&K than it has over Indian states."[99] The reason is that Indian presidents have used it to pass "one Presidential Order after another," which A. G. Noorani maintains was "unconstitutional" after the dispersal of the State's Constituent Assembly in 1956 and meant that the orders could not achieve the ratification that was needed.[100] Through these presidential orders—with no oversight—a number of "central" acts were applied to Jammu and Kashmir. Thus, I situate Article 370 as yet another colonial arrangement legally differentiating the colony (Kashmir) from the colonial power (India). The temporary state of autonomy that was to be established through Article 370 should be seen as a mode of India's colonial occupation, not as a remediation of it. This becomes especially evident since the Indian government did not uphold the alleged promises of autonomy.

India allowed for the formation of a constituent assembly as well as a state constitution in Kashmir, based on its "understanding that the constituent assembly would ratify Kashmir's accession to India, thus avoiding the necessity of complying with the United Nations–mandated plebiscite."[101] India claimed that local elections for the Constituent Assembly in 1951 served as a referendum, implying that the people accepted Indian rule. Despite the United Nations arguing that local elections were not a substitute for the plebiscite, the Indian state has consistently maintained its "democratic" character in Kashmir through local elections. Yet, the formation of the Constituent Assembly was not a democratic exercise. The 1951 election "that decided the composition of the Assembly is believed to have been rigged," especially given that the National Conference won all seventy-five seats and that seventy-three of its candidates ran unopposed.[102] This is true of all elections throughout Kashmir's post-Partition history, with the possible exception of those held in 1977, during which Sheikh Abdullah was elected and the Janata Party in India condemned any form of election rigging.[103] Furthermore, opposition parties that did not agree with the state's accession to India were not able to participate; the election was entirely dominated by the National Conference. The farce of elections, or the "politics of democracy" as with Article 370, has also served as an extension of the colonial occupation and a normalization technique of the Indian government.[104]

While "autonomy" appeared attractive on paper, it was harder to execute politically. During his time in power, aside from suppressing voices of dissent, Abdullah was determined to maintain Kashmir's autonomy and keep Kashmir financially independent from the Government of India. Thus, it was difficult for a number of reforms based on the manifesto to take place, because a substantial amount of funding was required that the fledgling government did not have access to. Indeed, food prices rose because no imports were allowed in—Abdullah wanted Kashmir to be self-sufficient—and peasants were forced to part with a quarter of their paddies under a system of procurement called *mujawaza*. The paddies' produce was intended for use by government-owned rationing centers, but corruption among government officials led much of the food to be sold in the black market. Customs duties and taxes were high, and Syed Mir Qasim, a leader in the National Conference who later became chief minister, describes how during political tours, the Kashmir leadership saw "hungry people scramble for leftover food dumped in garbage cans."[105]

Despite the widespread political and economic instability, Abdullah's government was determined to implement one aspect of the Naya Kashmir manifesto. In 1950, the government passed landmark land reforms that transferred land to the tiller without any compensation for the landlord. While Abdullah's intentions were to improve the socioeconomic conditions of Kashmiri peasants, the land reforms had a dual purpose. Mir Qasim explains that the "tillers who had got land through our land reforms would vote for India if a referendum was held as they were apprehensive that this land might be taken away from them to be returned to the original owners if Kashmir became part of Pakistan."[106] Abdullah's land reforms were a precursor to Bakshi's politics of life.

Although the move had support in the Muslim-majority areas, given that they were the prime beneficiaries of the reforms, many other groups within the Jammu and Kashmir state were not supportive of the step. Protests erupted in Jammu, where a number of Hindu landlords were forced to give up their land and felt that the new government was catering exclusively to Kashmiri Muslims, claiming that the National Conference had proved itself as a "Muslim communal party," not a secular nationalist one.[107] Already angered by the abolition of the Dogra monarchy as well as the increase in employment and educational opportunities meted out to Muslims, Jammu Hindus also protested the Valley being given more favorable treatment than the other regions in the state. Many Buddhists in Ladakh also wanted full integration with the Indian Union and were not in favor of autonomy. Members of the Indian government, including most Congress officials, also opposed the land reforms, arguing that it would create ill feelings among minorities in Kashmir. While Nehru was sympathetic to this concern, he also knew that Abdullah's support of the accession was based on a promise of being able to execute the Naya Kashmir manifesto under India, and thus he did not strongly register his protest.

To address some of the lingering concerns with regard to the nature of the state's relationship with the Government of India, the Indian leaders invited Kashmiri leaders for talks in Delhi from June to July 1952. On July 24, the Delhi Agreement was signed, which considered Jammu and Kashmir as a part of India (rendering the plebiscite obsolete) but also affirmed autonomy for the state. Matters like fundamental rights, financial integration, and the jurisdiction of the Supreme Court remained unsettled.[108] The agreement confirmed that Kashmiris would be treated as citizens of the Indian government. Yet, even after having signed the agreement, Malik argues that both "Abdullah and the Indian government proceeded to abuse it, the former by persisting with calls for independence, the latter by asserting its authority beyond the spheres allocated to it."[109]

The Praja Parishad, founded by Balraj Madhok, emerged as a leading political party in Jammu. It shared the Rashtriya Swayamsevak Sangh (RSS) ideology of Hindu nationalism and accused Abdullah of trying to "Islamize the administration."[110] After the Delhi Agreement, the organization launched a popular agitation in 1952, primarily calling for full integration into the Indian Union, which was supported by Hindu nationalist groups like the Jana Sangh, led by Shyama Prasad Mukherjee, in India.[111] Abdullah dismissed the agitation as reactionary and arrested many of its leaders. Meanwhile, leading members of Nehru's cabinet as well as Karan Singh, the maharaja's son, gave their support to the agitation. Singh repeatedly told Nehru that he was against autonomy for Kashmir and preferred greater integration.[112] Once more, Nehru was less concerned with the rise of Hindu nationalism than with what it would mean for Kashmir's relationship with India: "In the name of close association with India," he complained to Singh, "they are acting in a manner which might well imperil that very association."[113] He also bemoaned the coverage the agitation received in Pakistan.[114]

The combination of economic and political instability, the authoritarian policies of the National Conference, the Praja Parishad agitation, and the attitude of the Government of India, which did not seem interested in holding the plebiscite to determine the wishes of the people of the state, drove, as Zutshi argues, "Kashmiri Muslims toward extolling the virtues of Pakistan and condemning India's high-handedness in occupying the territory."[115] Indian intelligence reports based on intercepted letters reveal how various pro-Pakistan Muslims in Kashmir were touring villages and conducting "pro-Pakistan propaganda," arguing that the Praja Parishad movement should be an eye-opener for those who wanted to "link their destinies with Hindu India."[116] Others expressed concern that India would eventually allow non-state subjects to acquire property in the state, which would convert the "Muslim majority of the Valley into a minority."[117] One letter from "Tayab," based in Delhi, to Ghulam Mohi-din Hamdani, the deputy development minister in the National Conference government, urged the minister to take the Praja Parishad movement and its popularity in India seriously, as it showed that most Indians were against Muslims. He called for all the ministers of the Kashmir government to take a decisive and united stand in regard to how they wanted to move forward. He also claimed that the non-Muslim members of the National Conference, including Pandit leaders like Pandit Shiv Narain Fotedar, were spreading "poison" in India against the Kashmiri Muslim leadership.[118]

Another intercepted letter—from Ghulam Hassan based in Aligarh University to Mohammad Sharif in Nawa Kadal—argued that, in light of the developments in Jammu, the Kashmiri Muslims should start a movement "launched on the issue of civil liberties" and not an alliance with Pakistan "because the slogan for accession to Pakistan will give a handle to the government to suppress us easily." However, "indirectly, it will be a movement for alliance with Pakistan. A movement started for freedom of speech and press will prove to the world that the present government has deprived the people of Jammu as well as Kashmir of their rightful freedom and this will bring the Kashmir issue nearer to solution."[119] Ghulam Hassan urged the recipient of the letter to discuss this matter with Ghulam Mohiuddin Karra, who would eventually start the oppositional Political Conference. Almost all the letters from this time detail the poor living conditions and the negative attitude toward Muslims in India, as well as the rising anti-India and pro-Pakistan sentiment among Kashmir's Muslims. With this intelligence, it appears that the Indian government knew that it would have to take decisive action soon were it to hold on to Kashmir.

The immediate impact of the Hindu nationalist mobilizations cannot be understated. The specter of Hindu communalism not only impacted Kashmiri Muslims but also influenced Abdullah's thinking, and he began to doubt the safety of Kashmir's Muslims in a Hindu-majority India.[120] Aside from the state's economic woes, Abdullah resisted increasing Indian influence in Kashmir's affairs, including attempts to further integrate the state into the Indian Union.[121] Indian officials were interested in maintaining the pretense of autonomy for the international community, while using the Constituent Assembly to finalize Kashmir's accession to India, after which they would push further integration. Nehru's duplicitous stance applied to the plebiscite as well: as early as the end of 1947, it had become evident that he was not serious about the plebiscite, notwithstanding what he said in public.[122] After 1954, once Bakshi was in power, Nehru was able to able to publicly transform India's disapproval of the US-Pakistan military pact into a complete rejection of the plebiscite option. Nehru was also well aware of the complete lack of democratic principles when it came to his government's policies in Kashmir. The journalist Balraj Puri states that Nehru told him that India had "gambled" at the international stage on Kashmir, and it couldn't "afford to lose." He admitted, "At the moment, we are there at the point of a bayonet. Till things improve, democracy and morality can wait."[123] Nehru, who continues to be painted as a beacon of anti-colonialism and a stalwart of the Non-Aligned Movement, unapologetically advanced and justified India's colonial occupation.

Realizing that Kashmir could well get out of India's clutches, Nehru recognized that it was time to let Abdullah go. The reasons for Abdullah's political transitioning away from India and subsequent dismissal have been discussed at length elsewhere; the primary point to note here is that the Government of India was concerned with his ties to Western leaders and diplomats, his many speeches suggesting that independence was a better course for Kashmir, and his insistence that the accession was *not* final and that a plebiscite must still take place.[124] His treatment of the Praja Parishad movement, including the arrest and subsequent death of Shyama Prasad Mookerjee, the leader of the Hindu nationalist Jana Sangh, also raised the ire of officials in the Indian government and the broader Indian public. Members of Abdullah's cabinet who were in favor of increased integration with India, including Bakshi, who served as deputy prime minister, G. M. Sadiq, and D. P. Dhar, were alarmed by the increased political and economic instability. They regularly kept the Government of India updated about the political developments in the state.

The Government of India, along with the sadar-i-riyasat Karan Singh, orchestrated Sheikh Abdullah's removal with the assistance of Bakshi and his associates. B. N. Mullik, the director of the Indian Intelligence Bureau, planned the operation, and Nehru was directly involved.[125] Bakshi agreed to take on the role of prime minister, as long as Abdullah was arrested so that he would not be able to organize demonstrations.

Having been told that he was meeting an emissary of Pakistan, on August 8, 1953, Sheikh Abdullah was arrested in Gulmarg, and the state police, now under the command of Bakshi, conducted a series of raids and arrests of his closest associates. There was spontaneous uproar in Kashmir over Sheikh Abdullah's arrest and removal from power, and for weeks the political situation remained extremely volatile with strikes, processions, and political gatherings. Despite the authoritarianism of Abdullah and the National Conference, Kashmiris took to the streets, protesting the high-handedness of the Government of India in meddling in Kashmir's affairs by removing Abdullah from power. Bakshi's opponents labeled him a *ghaddar,* or traitor, for going against his former political partner. In the ensuing riots and protests, Bakshi's government, aided by Indian troops, clamped down heavily against the protestors, and while estimates vary, anywhere from sixty to as many as fifteen hundred people were killed.[126] Many more were arrested and tortured in jail, and shopkeepers were forced to open their shops. There were nearly three weeks of strikes, primarily in the Valley.

Mir Qasim records in his memoirs that, sitting in his law chambers in Anantnag in South Kashmir, he witnessed "waves after waves of protest marches surging past" for days.[127] Because of Mir Qasim's political affiliations with the

National Conference and Bakshi, the people's anger turned against him and crowds threatened to burn down his house. G. M. Sadiq called him to Srinagar to join the new cabinet. Along the way, he encountered crowds of people demanding the release of the bodies of people shot by police. Qasim reported that a crowd twenty-thousand strong had proceeded toward the Dak Bungalow in Shopian where he and his fellow travellers were staying. "Nobody was willing to risk their life to rescue us. . . . We slipped out in burqa. Srinagar was in chaos. Bakshi's house, despite the police, was also under attack."[128]

The 1953 coup was a pivotal moment. That India and Nehru would go against the very man who had enabled Kashmir's accession to India once he began to resist Indian diktats was revealing. The stark coloniality of India's rule became more evident for Kashmir's Muslims. Furthermore, historian Mohammad Ishaq Khan argues that the dismissal of Sheikh Abdullah began to cause rifts between communities in Kashmir, as many Hindus and Pandits felt vindicated by his arrest. He recalls that his father "swore to take revenge against his Hindu neighbors . . . because they clapped with glee at Sheikh's arrest." For his father, to see Pandits celebrating the dismissal of their "savior," who had protected them during the Pathan Muslim raids, was incomprehensible.[129]

Khalid-i-Kashmir

Bakshi was not known as an ideologue within the ranks of the National Conference. Indeed, his strengths were his ability to administer and mobilize. Thus, we don't have a complete picture of Bakshi's political position on the future of Kashmir. Although Bakshi's letters to fellow National Conference members expressed excitement at growing ties with the Congress during his time in Lahore for the Quit Kashmir movement, a number of oral interviews conducted with those who were part of the political milieu at the time or related to Bakshi confirmed that in 1947, at a working committee meeting of the National Conference, when asked whether Kashmir should accede to India or Pakistan, Bakshi replied "Pakistan."[130] His reasons for favoring Pakistan were less ideological—he did not necessarily believe in the two-nation theory—and more pragmatic. He knew that up until then, Kashmir's economic, educational, and political ties had been closer to the territories that would become Pakistan than to India—Lahore was far more familiar to the average Kashmiri than was Delhi.[131] Knowing Sheikh Abdullah's indecisive personality, however, he added that the party should commit to what was decided at the meeting, as the cost of vacillating would be too high and average Kashmiris would suffer.[132] Abdullah opted for India, and from that point onward, Bakshi appeared committed to safeguarding Kashmir's accession to India. However, Abdullah narrates that in 1950, Bakshi expressed his support for the Dixon Plan, which divided the state and suggested independence for the Kashmir Valley, leaving us once more unable to fully comprehend his actual political ideology.[133]

In the aftermath of accession, Bakshi remained a bulwark for the National Conference. He was active in Jammu, where the political situation had deteriorated as a result of the violence against Muslims by the Dogra army. Bakshi organized border defenses against the Pathan Muslims alongside the Indian army and assisted in restoring essential services and providing shelter, clothing, and food for refugees. He enjoyed a close relationship with the Indian army and various generals at this time. He established a fleet of buses for public transport, which had not existed under the Dogras. Because of his ability to mobilize and maintain internal security, Sheikh Abdullah named him deputy prime minister.

B. N. Mullik, the former director of the Indian Intelligence Bureau, writes in his memoirs that Bakshi's allegiance to India was "not based on such strong ideological grounds."[134] It is, of course, difficult to ascertain Bakshi's intentions. Nonetheless, those who were close to him describe him as being "practical" and "pragmatic." An interview I conducted with his nephew, Nazir Bakshi, provides some context for Bakshi's decision-making at the time of Sheikh Abdullah's arrest. Nazir Bakshi said, "Once Kashmir had already acceded, [Bakshi] decided that India was too powerful for Kashmiris to fight. So he decided to get the best out of India."[135] This is why when Sheikh Abdullah was becoming increasingly vocal against India, "Bakshi believed that he was leading Kashmiris down the wrong path."[136] Perhaps Bakshi came to believe that an independent Kashmir seemed implausible, as it would be unable to defend itself against the various regional and Western powers that had a stake in the future of the state. He may have also believed that without the support of either of the neighboring countries, Kashmir would be unable to survive politically. Acceding to Pakistan now was out of the question as it was increasingly coming under the influence of foreign powers and would be unwilling to provide Kashmir with an autonomous status. Furthermore, as his nephew suggested, Bakshi was also concerned with the violence that the Indian state would unleash upon Kashmiris were they to change their political course. As for taking on the role of prime minister, Bakshi believed it was better "to have a Kashmiri Muslim as the prime minister, instead of someone from outside of the state."[137] Nazir Bakshi's sentiments about Bakshi's political thinking appear to be confirmed by the statement made by B. N. Mullik—that Bakshi's allegiance was based not on "strong ideological grounds," but practical ones.

While it may be difficult to ascertain what Bakshi would have preferred for Kashmir's future, we can be sure that he was committed to the politics of life. Having worked in grassroots politics for the National Conference—and given his own personal background—he was well aware of the poverty in the state. In an oral interview, Hassan Shah, a former bureaucrat, narrates, "Bakshi's close assistant, Ram Lal, who was from Jammu would tell me how Bakshi kept his old, ragged, torn shirt and pant [*kameez shalvar*] in a box. Ram Lal would tell me how Bakshi would look at it daily to remind himself of his mission to the poor and his own humble background."[138] Keeping these considerations in mind, after taking power, Bakshi made it his priority to get the "best out of India." This entailed securing as many material and financial benefits for Kashmir as possible.

Bakshi embodied the politics of life in a number of ways. His leadership style was unique in that he sought an affective, intimate relationship with the people of the state. He received common people in his office weekly and heard their complaints, taking decisive administrative action on the spot. Countless people would visit him to receive "admission, appointments, and loans."[139] Often, they didn't even have to come to him. In my oral interviews, I heard many stories of how Bakshi would dole out jobs to people he saw on the street. Hassan Shah stated, "Bakshi would stop young boys and ask them if they went to school. If they had passed the eighth grade, he would employ them in the government, often writing their appointment on matchboxes and slips of paper."[140] He was seen as being generous even to opponents, including members of the various pro-plebiscite or pro-Pakistan groups, whom he had detained, by taking care of the economic and social needs of their families.[141]

A government official describes a particularly compelling incident:

> I was visiting with him in district Pulwama. We reached a village where he addressed the crowd, as was his routine. People told him their complaints, and many came to him. An old man, too, came towards him. His son was suffering from an eye disease, and he was fearful that his son would lose his eyesight. Those days, there was no eye specialist in this town. Bakshi got the boy admitted in a hospital in Srinagar for his complete medical treatment. After many years, I went again with Bakshi to that district. Coincidentally, we were in the same area and a crowd assembled around him. When he saw the same old man, Bakshi made a gesture and called him with his name and asked if his son had recovered completely. The old man, smiling, answered that his had recovered and even goes to school, and he brought the boy in front of him. I was surprised that here was a Prime Minister, who had many preoccupations in different works and who met thousands of people in a week, who remembered the name of an old man, and also his problem.[142]

This account suggests a number of things. First, people expected that Bakshi and, by extension, the Kashmir government, would address their problems and did not hesitate to make their demands known. Two, Bakshi may not have been able to secure legitimacy, but he was certainly imbued with authority, through which the public recognized his actions as being authoritative and enacted through practice.[143] It was his authority, not his legitimacy, that enabled people to partake in the activities of the Kashmir state, as they were "averted from the challenges of consent and coercion and focused on the mundane, the day to day, the getting by."[144] With his towering build and commanding voice, Bakshi offered a paternalistic mode of leadership. Hagiographic accounts repeatedly made reference to how he bore the weight of Kashmiris on his "Atlantean shoulders."[145] His sheer physicality, level of activity, and ability to get things done embodied the politics of life for those around him. Bakshi personally engaged people he would meet in various towns and villages throughout Kashmir on government policies. He "told them that he expected them to play their role in the fields of state affairs and its economy, agriculture, industries, and in social development. . . . People asked different questions, and Bakshi resolutely answered their questions."[146] Through this, people saw themselves as playing an agentive role in their own progress.

Observers labeled him as the Bud Shah Thani (Second Bud Shah, after the revered medieval ruler of Kashmir, Zain-ul-abidin of the Shahmiri dynasty, who was known for his contribution to Kashmiri arts and culture). He was portrayed as a great rational modernizer of Kashmir, but one who was also firmly in touch with his spiritual side. Like many Kashmiris, he was a firm believer in the power of shrines, especially Char-i-Sharief, the historic shrine of the Kashmiri mystic Nund Rishi, and would often seek advice from a number of holy men. He revered Kashmir's multireligious spiritual traditions and folk literature and music. Bakshi's influence was not limited to Kashmir; he also appeared to give hope to the Muslims of India and would even receive letters from Indian Muslims asking to be employed in the state. Other Indian Muslim leaders urged him to "take out some time for Indian Muslim's problems . . . which he may be able to solve, otherwise country and nation will face tragedy because of sectarianism."[147]

Bakshi's plans for Kashmir could not take place while Kashmir's political status was still undetermined. Political sentiment in Kashmir notwithstanding and despite Kashmir's status remaining unresolved in the international arena, Bakshi adopted a series of measures intended to settle the political question of Kashmir once and for all and pave the way for his state-building project. Decisions were made on key issues of governance quickly, defying democratic procedure.

On October 5, 1953, members of the state's constituent assembly gave Bakshi a "unanimous vote of confidence." Under Sheikh Abdullah, Kashmir had greater financial autonomy and rarely accepted funds from the Government of India. In order to go forward with his modernizing agenda and to propel the aims of the Naya Kashmir manifesto, Bakshi sought Indian financial aid. The Government of India insisted that the state ratify the accession before it would agree to provide significant financial assistance. To ward off any possibility of a plebiscite, in February of 1954, Bakshi called upon the Constituent Assembly to ratify the state's accession to India. Subsequently, Kashmir became financially integrated into India, and the latter provided the Kashmir state with grants to implement its development policies.[148] Through the removal of customs duties in April 1954, which Abdullah had been adamant in maintaining, Bakshi further integrated Kashmir's economy into India's.[149] He also raised the salaries of all government servants and workers.

Additional attempts at greater political integration occurred in the first few years of Bakshi's rule. Through the Constitution (Application to J&K) Order 1954, many provisions of the Indian constitution were extended to the state with the approval of the Constituent Assembly. They included "the right to legislate in the State on the majority of items on the Union List, gave the Supreme Court full jurisdiction in Jammu and Kashmir, put the State's financial and fiscal relations with the Union government on a par with other States, and extended fundamental rights to Jammu and Kashmir with the caveat that they could be suspended in the interests of 'security' and without judicial review."[150] In addition, several central departments, such as Audit, Customs, Finance, and the Election Commission extended their jurisdiction to Kashmir.[151] In 1956, the state's Constituent Assembly also approved a draft of the constitution of the state that declared Jammu and Kashmir an integral part of the Indian Union, effectively putting the plebiscite to rest.[152] The Kashmir constitution went into effect on January 26, 1957. The Indian Parliament was also allowed to legislate upon a wider range of subjects. In 1958, further bureaucratic integration was achieved when the Indian Administrative Services and the Indian Police Services were authorized to function in the state.[153]

These integration-as-assimilation policies were implemented in the absence of a democratic order in Kashmir, as the National Conference was the only party that was allowed to contest elections in the state—political parties or candidates that contested Kashmir's accession to India were not permitted to run. The 1957 and 1962 elections for the Legislative Assembly (formerly, the Constituent Assembly) were also rigged, even as Nehru kept using the elections to sell normalcy to the international community.

Bakshi's Government

Bakshi's cabinet ministers who oversaw various portfolios were primarily those Kashmiris—both Muslims and Pandits—who sought greater integration with the Indian government for ideological or practical reasons. Many bureaucrats who sympathized with Abdullah had been arrested or sidelined;

others remained in the new administration but were discreet about their political proclivities. Bakshi hired a number of Kashmiri Muslims for different posts in his administration, and they would come to play an important role in his state-building policies. Many came from upper-caste Muslim families or *pirs* (those affiliated with religious shrines), as well as from families that were involved in business and trade. Some had family members who had served under the Dogras. They were educated in government-run schools or schools run by the *anjuman* (association) Nusrat ul Islam. Many had gone for further studies to places like Aligarh or Lahore and had taken part in the anti-Dogra movement. A wide range of ideological currents in British India, including Muslim nationalism and secular nationalism, as well as more left-leaning or radical socialist ideas, influenced them—what a Kashmiri doctor described as "being caught up in the middle. . . . This is what happened to most Kashmiris who were educated."[154]

After Partition, most bureaucrats were not ideologically pro-India but wanted to secure economic and social security for themselves and their families, a desire that was shaped by their memories of and anxieties about abject marginalization and discrimination under the Dogras. Mostly, they were eager to be modernized, and their interests were defined by a desire to "consolidate class interests, [obtain] political and economic empowerment and upward mobility, and end monarchical rule."[155] As I've written elsewhere, many of them thought that the political situation would eventually be resolved—that there would be a plebiscite—and preferred to be a part of Pakistan, despite being complicit in the everyday work of the state and bureaucracy.[156] Many of them were also fearful of expressing any dissent, especially as government repression against those who spoke out grew. Over time, their political subjectivities continued to be shaped and reshaped by the restrictive conditions under Indian rule.[157]

Chapter 2

NARRATING NORMALIZATION

Media, Propaganda, and Foreign Policy amid Cold War Politics

By mid-1950s, just a few years into Bakshi's tenure as prime minister, a number of Indian and international journalists visited Kashmir to observe social and political developments in the disputed state. Hosted by the state's Department of Information, they visited newly built schools, large-scale development projects, and tourist areas, accompanying Bakshi on his tours.[1] Their accounts of Kashmir under Bakshi were largely positive, and in some cases, nearly euphoric, as they noted shifts in land reform, education, tourism, transportation, employment, irrigation, agriculture, industry, and food availability.

A. M. Rosenthal, the *New York Times* special correspondent who travelled to Kashmir in 1955, wrote, "The road over the Banihal Pass, Indian Kashmir's only land link with the outside world, has been widened and improved. Indian civil planes fly in and out of Srinagar's airport every day. In the Sindh Valley a hydro-electric plant, the first to be built in almost half a century, will open this summer."[2] Speaking of his trip to parts of rural Kashmir, Rosenthal emphasized, "The people of the poor and once forgotten villages have begun to have demands. Not long ago, they not only did not demand but did not know that better things were theirs by human right. The people are getting many of their demands fulfilled and the pace is faster than ever before in Kashmir history."[3] A few articles also noted the increase in tourist traffic in the state. For example, the *Economist London* reported: "Kashmir is booming. There have never been so many tourists and they have never brought so much [money to spend]. This year, 70,000 tourists are expected."[4]

In addition to praising development activities, journalists' accounts were centered on the figure of Bakshi, described as a capable administrator and uniquely positioned, because of his background and personality, to address the plight of the Kashmiri masses. Taya Zinkin, a correspondent of the *Manchester Guardian*, accompanied Bakshi on a tour in 1956. About her time in Kashmir, she wrote, "The relations between Bakshi . . . and his people are unique in India."[5] Positing Bakshi as a well-liked populist leader, she added that touring with him "requires a sturdy constitution and all round athletics from knowing how to ride, swim, and climb to the art of elbowing one's way out from an over-enthusiastic concourse of friendly and overpoweringly persistent welcomers."[6]

Bakshi's ability to interact freely with the crowds took journalists by surprise: "The Prime Minister moved unescorted among crowds who garlanded him, and peasants showered lumps of sugar, signifying a sweet welcome, on his car. While everywhere there were shouts of 'long live' and women sang, 'our bread-winner has come.'"[7] Paul Grimes, a correspondent for the *New York Times*, described how Bakshi would meet with common Kashmiris every Friday from 9:00 a.m. to 1:00 p.m.: "An hour before he arrived today, nearly 200 Kashmiris were squatting on the broad lawn in front of his office. They included Moslems, Hindus and Sikhs, shy teen-age boys and elderly women, Western-dressed business leaders and bazaar peddlers in bell bottomed pajamas and karakul caps."[8] That Bakshi was able to appeal to a broad cross-section of Kashmiri society was a common theme in many of these accounts.

The international press had not always written such glowing reports on Bakshi and developments within Kashmir. A few years earlier, Bakshi's government faced a crisis of legitimacy after coming to power in the wake of Sheikh Abdullah's arrest. Given the persona Abdullah had managed to cultivate as the sole representative of Kashmiris, the crisis of legitimacy was not limited to Kashmir; it reverberated within India and in the international arena. Prominent international newspapers criticized the Government of India for forcibly removing Sheikh Abdullah. Newspapers in the US and Europe questioned the sincerity of "Nehru's devotion to peace and justice," and one Swedish paper declared, "Home-made imperialism has replaced European imperialism."[9] International reports asserted that the new government was not popular and that Kashmiris were becoming more inclined toward Pakistan.

An editorial in the *New York Times* reported that "Moslems in Srinagar . . . have undertaken to parade in demonstration against this coup and have been fired on by Indian police and troops. . . . One thing is obvious: the present government of Kashmir is not an instrument of popular will."[10] It argued, "There can be no equitable solution of the problem unless and until there is a genuinely free plebiscite, so that Kashmiris can live under a Government of their own choosing."[11]

A series of photographs James Burke took for *Life* magazine in 1953 included images of "pro-Abdullah protesters" who had been repressed by Indian police in Kashmir. In one black-and-white photograph, over two dozen Indian troops were surrounding three demonstrators and making them "rub out statements they had written on the street."[12] In another photograph, hundreds of Kashmiri men are seen running away from Indian police, some of whom appear to be charging at the protestors with batons.[13] Even as late as 1957, an editorial in *Life* magazine, clearly concerned with the US bolstering the legitimacy of the UN as a foreign policy goal, claimed that India is "both defying the Security Council's order and repudiating its own pledged word to hold a plebiscite in that divided and hate-ridden land." The editorial even referred to the state government as a "puppet Constituent assembly."[14]

After the 1953 coup, the circulation of these photographs, combined with various adverse reports in the international press, once again brought the Kashmir issue to the forefront of international attention, raising questions over the nature of India's claims on Kashmir as well as the aspirations of the Kashmiris themselves. Then, there was the question of the pending UN resolutions. All these developments created a heightened sense of political instability. As a result, Bakshi had to not only obtain legitimacy for his government within Kashmir but also counter adverse narratives against the coup in India as well as in the international community.

How do we understand the dramatically diverging narratives that emerged in the immediate aftermath of Sheikh Abdullah's arrest and those that appeared just a few years into Bakshi's rule? How was Bakshi able to placate local, Indian, and international concerns about India's high-handedness in Kashmir and about the woefully undemocratic coup that brought him to power? This question can be examined through a geopolitical lens, as a result of shifting political alliances in the emerging Cold War context. However, it becomes imperative to also foreground the role of the Jammu and Kashmir state's Department of Information and its aggressive propaganda efforts in deploying the politics of life to position Kashmir as a haven of progress and development and to project normalization. Bakshi's efforts to target Muslim-majority countries and the Soviet Union, in particular, were crucial to unraveling the "disputed" status of the region, securing India's claims over Kashmir, and eroding the calls for a plebiscite on the international front. Shrimoyee Ghosh has referred to this as the "domestication" of Jammu and Kashmir into Indian jurisdiction, whereby the colonial occupation was "largely viewed by the international community as constitutional questions integral to India" unrelated to issues of sovereignty or self-determination.[15] I argue that state-led propaganda played a fundamental role in pivoting the question of Kashmir from a political one of sovereignty to one of governance, where progress and development became the primary frame through which the question of Kashmir was mediated and subsequently domesticated. In doing so, Bakshi attempted to position Kashmir as an experiment in secular, modernizing, anti-colonial, democratizing, socialist state-building and himself at the forefront of this experiment.

Media as "Publicity"

Publicity for the state was split between the Indian government's Ministry of Information and Broadcasting (MIB) and the state government's Department of Information. Although the two were in close contact, they were managed and run separately, even while targeting similar audiences, such as foreign embassies. This suggests an attempt to foreground Kashmir's autonomous status for international audiences. The MIB, which led the Indian state's propaganda efforts on Kashmir, published a magazine called *Kashmir*, for which it solicited articles from the Department of Information on arts, culture, industry, trade, and development.[16] The MIB also separately published a series of books, pamphlets, and brochures including such titles as *Muslim Press on Kashmir*, *Kashmir's Accession to India*, and *Inside Pak-Held Kashmir* for distribution to various Indian embassies around the world, making the case for India's position on Kashmir. While the MIB was primarily targeted toward international audiences, the Department of Information also targeted Indian and local audiences by creating its own content, managing the flow of information into and out of Kashmir, and having complete, draconian control over the media to the extent of deploying the local, Indian, and even international media to do publicity for the state. Simply put, the government heavily managed press freedom and actively discouraged independent media outlets challenging the state.

Propaganda efforts began under Sheikh Abdullah, and soared under Bakshi. During Sheikh Abdullah's tenure, the department initiated plans to publish three magazines—*Kashmir Today* (English), *Tameer* (Urdu), and *Yojna* (Hindi)—designed to make the case for Kashmir's accession to India on political, cultural, and economic grounds to multiple audiences. Journalists who visited the state were to be "shown such things as will enable them to appreciate . . . that things are perfectly *normal*, that the National Conference has a tremendous hold on the people and that the government is a thoroughly popular one."[17] Facts that might challenge this narrative were erased. In one incident, the director of the department, a Kashmiri Pandit official, J. N. Zutshi, requested that a contributor delete a section that included the massacre of Muslims in Jammu, arguing that there was no use introducing "controversy" into the publication—a practice of memoricide that replicated the Indian and Kashmir government's erasure of the Jammu Massacre.[18] Zutshi also kept a close eye on reports in the international press and complained to the MIB about a letter to the *Commonwealth* paper by Josef Korbel, a member of the UN Commission for India and Pakistan, claiming people were deeply unhappy with Indian rule and had come up to him saying they wanted to join Pakistan.[19] Given that Korbel was a member of the UN commission, the department was particularly concerned about the state government's loss of credibility as a result. Zutshi would take a similar approach when leading the propaganda efforts during Bakshi's tenure.

Government-sponsored magazines began to be regularly published after Bakshi came to power and had a circulation in 1966 of 4,820 (*Kashmir Today*), 6,222 (*Tameer*), and 3,456 (*Yojna*).[20] Their primary aim was to publicize the plans of the state government, but they also served as literary and cultural spaces by publishing poems, short stories, and reflections, as well as in-depth reports on various development initiatives, education, archeology, and Kashmiri culture and history.[21] This literature was distributed, in accordance with Bakshi's orders, to the president of India, all the ministers of the Government of India and the various states (especially the information ministers), judges, trade agencies, the secretary of the Congress party, governors, members of the parliament, universities, and local libraries, as well as all the newspapers of India.[22]

Within Kashmir, the Department of Information utilized Radio Kashmir to host a series of programs publicizing new policies and reiterating the state's defense for arresting Abdullah. A similar counter-propaganda department had been set up under Abdullah to counter Pakistan and Azad Kashmir Radio, which, the government was concerned, had major "emotional appeal" for the public. Under Bakshi, however, in addition to highlighting Kashmir's accession to India, the department issued a series of programs in which cabinet members and leading administrators discussed development schemes that the new government was seeking to implement. The Government of India subsidized community radios—in one year alone, two hundred were distributed.[23] In November 1961, Zutshi let the finance minister, G. L. Dogra, know that seven district information centers had been built to publicize the plans and activities of the various government departments through poetry sessions, dramas, film shows, skits, and debates, in addition to government publications and important newspapers and magazines from outside the state. Zutshi stated that these had proved "very effective . . . and have consequently become very popular among the public."[24] By focusing the content of the materials on issues pertaining to development and progress and creating means for people to hear of the successes of the administration—sometimes directly from officials—the state government created a perception of accountability and active state-building, while shifting away from the larger concerns of Kashmir's political status.

In addition to publishing its own content, the Department of Information also fostered close ties with local, Indian, and international media in an effort to bring them into line with the state's narrative on sociopolitical developments. On the local level, the minister for information, G. M. Sadiq, wrote a letter to the editors of all the major newspapers in the state requesting ideas for better "publicity" in the state. Almost all the editors—most of whom belonged to the Kashmir Journalists Association—assured Sadiq of their cooperation. They recommended that the department set up a press advisory board and help journalists visit different parts of the state with government officials on tours. They also recommended issuing government gazettes that would keep them abreast of the latest developments and spreading government advertisements more equally among the different papers. One editor complained that journalists from Delhi were given more access to official tours and recommended that local journalists be provided with the same benefits. However, all agreed that they would provide their full "cooperation" to the government, one going so far as to say that "nationalism" was his creed.[25]

The overwhelming support that Sadiq received from the news editors cannot be seen in a vacuum. It is possible that many of the editors of the various papers did genuinely believe in "full cooperation" with the government. At the same time, however, the Kashmir government made it next to impossible for independent newspapers to operate without government approval. Since Sheikh Abdullah's time, but especially during Bakshi's rule, editors were obliged to apply to the Department of Information for permission to start newspapers.[26] The department sent all requests to the Central Information Department (CID; police intelligence) to get a background check on whether the individual had been involved in any "politics." The superintendent of police had an acute sense of each applicant's political or religious ideology. For example, one applicant Ghulam Nabi Durrani, had his application to start *Parwana* rejected because the CID mentioned that he was a "zealous Muslim Leaguer, and an anti-national, not fit to be publishing a paper."[27]

If a paper was approved, it would receive advertisements from the government, amounting to between 250 and 5,000 rupees, a significant source of revenue because private advertisements were not as regular or common.[28] These advertisements were also given to papers in India that spoke favorably of the Bakshi government. Press correspondents of both Indian and local papers had to be accredited to be invited to various government functions and press conferences.[29] Correspondents could easily lose their press accreditation for being critical of the government.

The Department of Information kept a daily register of all the papers published and distributed in the state and also kept a list of "approved" papers. Memos circulated around the department of the list of active papers, background information about their editors and publishers, how often and the language in which they were published, and whether they were affiliated with any organizations, as well as their circulation. Notes on the ideological aspect of each paper were also included. For example, in one memo, the *Khidmat*, an official paper of the National Conference, was said to condemn "all mischievous efforts which are against Kashmir's accession to India."[30] The *Martand*, a paper for the Kashmiri Pandit community, was seen as "aligning its politics of the government generally in respect to political issues." The *Hamdard* was said to be "critical of the government policies and is not certain of its attitude towards accession…it gives publicity to pro-Pakistan organization activities also." The department was also concerned with papers published in other parts of the state. For example, there were concerns over the paper *Jai Sundesh Sansar*, described as a "mouthpiece of P. N. Dogra, of Praja Parishad," whose writings were "intended to rouse public opinion in Jammu against the present government."[31] Thus, concerns were not restricted to parties not in favor of accession, but also included those seeking full integration with India. The department closely monitored papers daily and sent any questionable articles to the legal department to decide on a course of action.

At times, the Department of Information would take legal action against certain papers. For example, in July 1958, J. M. Zutshi sent a letter to Shri J. K. Nair, the legal advisor to the government, saying that the editor and publisher of the paper *Sach* was in detention and that a paper could not be printed when its editor was in jail. The editor's offense was supporting "Abdullah's stand for [a] plebiscite to determine the future of the state" and "toeing the line of those elements which aim at creating chaos and confusion in the state."[32] Zutshi requested an amendment in the Press and Publication Act allowing government action against writings opposing the "state's accession to India." Another Kashmiri Pandit department official, J. N. Bhan, tried to bypass the Press and Publication Act and booked the paper *Khalid* under Section 32 of Defense Rules, saying that the paper described the policies and actions of the Pakistan government in a favorable light and also highlighted the persecution of minorities in India, which "disturbed peace" in the state.[33]

It was not just the local editors and journalists who were monitored. Any adverse, anti-Bakshi comments made in the Indian or international press were dealt with directly. The government also monitored Srinagar-based correspondents for international media, including the Srinagar correspondent for the *London Times*, S. P. Sahni, who was contacted for writing a story on the increasing influence of the Political Conference (a pro-plebiscite group). While not revealing what was said to Sahni, the Department of Information official noted, "Mr. Sahni agreed in the future he would avoid giving publicity to [the Political Conference] and serve as their propaganda."[34]

Because of these clear restrictions on the press, editors of papers often attempted to toe the government line to ensure that their publication could continue to be published and that they would not lose government ads or face legal action. As a result, newspapers in circulation at the time did little more than provide "publicity" for the government. Although papers like the *Khidmat* or the *Martand* published articles criticizing issues of governance or complaining of corruption, there was no space to critique or discuss the political future of Kashmir. Restricting dissent to matters of governance created the illusion of transparency as well as a tolerance for dissent. In reality, the government had full control over the contours of dissent in Kashmir.

Appealing to Indian Audiences

After Abdullah's arrest, there was much confusion over the political desires of Kashmiris and the mysteries surrounding the fall of Abdullah, who had played such a critical role in bringing Kashmir to India. An article in the *New York Times* suggested that "some leading Indians are becoming reconciled to losing at least the predominantly Moslem part of the state," while holding on to hope of obtaining Ladakh and Jammu.[35] Others raised concerns over the amount of funds New Delhi spent on the state.[36] Furthermore, there was an active anti-Bakshi lobby in India. A campaign against the Bakshi government led by Mridula Sarabhai, a Congress leader, was accused of weakening and undermining the links between Kashmir and India and promoting nullification of the accession of Kashmir with India.[37] Sarabhai actively campaigned within the Indian parliament and civil society to revive and consolidate Sheikh Abdullah's leadership, and Bakshi's government was concerned about her influence.[38] Perceptions of political instability also led tourism—both international and Indian—to drop after the 1953 coup.

Commentary after August 8, 1953, in the Indian media further highlighted the precarious nature of the Kashmir issue, raising questions of "development" and the "economy" as potentially overcoming political concerns. One correspondent declared that "in order to retain his hold over them, Bakshi is calling their attention to their economic interests. . . . Change of emphasis is significant and should be welcomed."[39] Another correspondent wrote that the task before the new government was that "living standards must be improved. . . . A study of local conditions in Kashmir gave me the impression that economic considerations may exercise a reasonable amount of influence on the masses in their final choice of association between India and Pakistan."[40] These examples suggest that within India there was an acknowledgment of the instability of the political question of Kashmir's future. There was also an expectation that material progress in the state would work in India's favor, especially as it had a better economic standing than Pakistan. In other words, even within India, it was not a given that Kashmiris saw themselves as an "integral" part of India—they had to be made to do so.

And so, in addition to censorship and monitoring of the local press, the Kashmir government also actively attempted to control press coverage in India and beyond. It invited Indian and international correspondents to visit Kashmir and approved hundreds of requests from Indian and international media personnel who wanted to report on the state. All were required to obtain permission to enter. Most requested to meet with Bakshi and his cabinet and observe schools, small industrial enterprises, agriculture, and tourism and community projects.[41] The Department of Information provided them with housing and additional amenities, including transportation. For this purpose, the government set aside a special fund called the Entertainment of Press Correspondents.[42] The funds were so in demand that in 1957, as early as June, the funds for the year under this portfolio were "almost exhausted."[43]

It was clear from the start that the government would use the funds to secure positive press coverage. In 1957, when a reporter named Rangaswami of the *Hindu Madras* visited Kashmir, J. N. Zutshi suggested he was a "friendly correspondent," so the government should provide him with free transport and cover part of his expenses.[44] Although reporter Michael Davidson of the *Sunday Observer* in London represented a conservative newspaper, it was noted that if "given adequate facilities he is likely to present our point of view in a favorable light."[45] Attempting to influence the narrative of journalists visiting Kashmir with access and amenities was a regular practice at this time.

The Indian government also facilitated these visits and sent press from India to attend different events, such as the opening of various development projects, a university's convocation, and the Festival of Kashmir, a cultural program.[46] In September 1956, a delegation of Indian journalists visited during the Festival of Kashmir, attending musical events and athletic meets and touring development projects and the silk factory and woolen mills, as well as meeting with various ministers and Bakshi. These visits would result in entire issues of a given newspaper or magazine featuring Bakshi's Kashmir, especially the educational and economic uplift of the people, development projects, five-year plans, and tourism.[47] This level of access was intentional. While it appears the reporters were centering "soft" topics like development and tourism, for both the Indian papers as well as the Kashmir government, this was done with a political end in mind: to refocus the narrative on Kashmir toward one of economic progress, development, and "normalcy"—and not a political dispute in the international arena.

Just before the UN Security Council debate on Kashmir, directives came from the Ministry of Information and Broadcasting that the Department of Information should encourage press to cover "economic and social progress achieved by Kashmir after accession."[48] And so the department sent state-prepared supplements and detailed information about five-year plans and various development schemes to Indian newspapers that were published, oftentimes, verbatim.[49] Indian papers also regularly requested publicity information on Kashmir, utilizing state propaganda for their reports. The Department of Information provided advertising to papers throughout India—in one report, over seventy-five Indian papers including *Blitz, Indian Express, Souvenir, Times of India,* and the *Hindustan Times* received advertisements publicizing development in the state.[50] Editors requested that the government provide them with material so that they could issue special Kashmir supplements. In October 1957, Motiur Rahman Shamim, the editor of *Roshni*, sent a message to the department stating that he and a group of people had formed the Bihar State Muslim Youth-Kashmir Front, with a "view to educating the public on the stand of the Government of India vis-à-vis Kashmir."[51] He requested that the Kashmir government provide him with advertisements and articles so that the paper could "expound the policies of the Kashmir government."

Indian papers began to speak positively of Bakshi's government, its allegiance to India, its avowed secularism, and its emphasis on economic and social progress that had brought together Kashmiris to develop a modernizing, socialist order. In a series of articles for the *Indian Express* in October 1956, G. N. S. Raghavan, a special correspondent, stated that "Kashmir today is assuredly not a troubled state. On the contrary, it is achieving economic and social progress at a rate and under conditions of political stability and mass enthusiasm which the rest of India might envy."[52] A political correspondent for the Calcutta-based *Amrita Bazar Patrika* wrote, "Conscious of the fact that mass support for them could depend on how expeditiously and effectively relief was provided for the people, the [Kashmiri] leaders took speedy decisions and introduced a number of economic reforms."[53] The emphasis on economic reforms led a journalist from the *Hindustan Times* to claim, "Going around the countryside either in Jammu or in Kashmir province, one no longer finds people obsessed with politics. Instead of people's grievances, one hears demands for opportunities to develop their towns and villages and to improve their living conditions."[54] Moreover, "the cultivator, businessman and administrator are all busy with tasks connected with greater production of food, expanded trade and planned constructive activity. . . . Jammu and Kashmir is witnessing a social and economic revolution."[55]

Implicit in these observations was an understanding that this new emphasis on economic development was intended to set aside local concerns for Kashmir's political future and instead, as the *Amrita Bazar Patrika* correspondent suggested, obtain political loyalty for the new government and, by extension, India. Raghavan noted that apart from the detention of Sheikh Abdullah and his associates "on grounds of security of the state," Kashmir was "being administered in the normal democratic manner, with a vigorous though small opposition in the Constituent Assembly," and the press enjoyed "the same measure of freedom as in the rest of India."[56]

These reports also provide a glimpse into some of the deeper anxieties that arose within Indian discourses about the importance of holding on to

Kashmir. *Amrita Bazar Patrika* hailed the "decision of a Muslim-majority area to remain with India" because that "proves and at the same time strengthens the secular character of Indian polity so necessary if India has to become a strong stable democracy."[57] In other words, Muslim-majority Kashmir being a part of India would provide a check on the "communal," or Hindu nationalist, elements within India. This perspective—often repeated in other accounts—"shackled Kashmir to the project of improving Indian democracy and made the Muslim-majority region serve as a litmus test of India's alleged promise of secular equality."[58] Kashmir's incorporation, then, was more about how India wanted to define itself amid a range of contested visions and less about what the people of Kashmir actually wanted. Here, the relationship between secularism and colonial occupation becomes evident.

The Kashmir government wanted to ensure that press coverage in India remained positive and that Indians were also brought into the narrative of progress and development happening in the state, perhaps to enable continued economic and political support from the Government of India for the Bakshi regime. As a result, most mainstream Indian publications did not critically examine the political developments in the state, nor did they seem to venture beyond the contours set by the Department of Information.

The Cold War Context

In a letter to Prime Minister Nehru, Karan Singh, the sadar-i-riyasat, who played a crucial role in ousting Sheikh Abdullah from power and replacing him with Bakshi, stated that Bakshi and his government were "shocked" to learn of Nehru's talks with Mohammed Ali Bogra, the Pakistani prime minister, regarding the plebiscite administration in 1953.[59] According to Singh, Bakshi and his cabinet were upset that Nehru, for such a vital decision, had not taken the viewpoint of those in government in Kashmir. Singh said that "this came as a personal blow to Bakshi because he has taken considerable personal risk and sacrifice for these ideals...he cannot carry on government if his position amongst people will be untenable."[60] Singh reiterated that pro-Pakistan elements were still active and the government had to resort to "severe" measures to bring forth law and order after Sheikh Abdullah's arrest. He encouraged the Government of India to support the Kashmir government by passing a resolution affirming the accession of the state to India and condemning the plebiscite; otherwise, "internal dissentions will develop, pro-Pakistan intrigues will start, and whole internal position might once again deteriorate. . . . Only a bold stand can save the situation."[61]

Singh's sentiment in the letter to Nehru suggests that the Kashmir government, perhaps for purposes of its own survival, was driving the political question of Kashmir toward the finality of the accession to India. Although Nehru had expressed his lack of sincerity toward the plebiscite as early as 1948, he had to balance India's interests in maintaining Kashmir with assuring the international community that his government was serious about coming to a settlement, which included a plebiscite, with Pakistan.[62] Given Nehru's anti-imperial foreign policy and positioning as a voice of the marginalized, it would become increasingly difficult for him to preach decolonization elsewhere—as he had in Korea--and not resolve the Kashmir issue closer to home.[63] Thus, while Nehru was tied down internationally, Bakshi had free rein to render a situation in which the plebiscite was made obsolete.

Kashmir, alongside Korea and Palestine, was one of the top issues discussed at the UN immediately following Partition. After the initial two resolutions of the newly formed United Nations Commission for India and Pakistan (August 13, 1948, and January 5, 1949) calling for a ceasefire, demilitarization, and an eventual plebiscite, progress at the UN was slow because of disagreements over the nature of demilitarization as well as the Indian demand that Pakistan be treated as the aggressor and unilaterally withdraw its troops. Most delegates at the UN and practically all the resolutions of the Security Council treated Pakistan as an equal party to the Kashmir dispute.[64] India maintained that holding a plebiscite was the exclusive concern of the Kashmir government (and later used elections to the Constituent Assembly as a replacement for the plebiscite), whereas Pakistan insisted an outside agency direct the plebiscite to guarantee its impartiality. Subsequent missions and interventions, including those of McNaughton (1949), Nimitz (March 1949), Owen Dixon (April–August 1950), and Graham (July–September 1951 and February–May 1952), failed to result in agreement between the two countries but represented a strong desire by the international community for mediation and resolution of the issue, with the demand for a plebiscite still looming large. After the failed Graham mission, direct negotiations commenced between the Pakistani prime minister Mohammad Ali Bogra and Nehru—to which, according to Karan Singh, Bakshi had raised objections.

The primary players in the early years of Bakshi's rule were the United States, the United Kingdom, and the Soviet Union. For both the US and the UK, Kashmir's geostrategic importance was evident even before 1947, as a buffer against the Soviet Union. One Indian author, in a scathing critique of American and British imperialism in the region, argued that the US planned to use Kashmir not only "as a military base against the Soviet Union and China" but also "as an issue for sowing animosity between India and Pakistan."[65] He contended that Kashmir was to be a "stronghold from where its rulers can exercise a direct whip-hand over India and Pakistan." From his perspective, a situation whereby US military forces were present in Kashmir during any interim period would be used against Indian interests.

Others have argued that after 1947, the two world powers wanted this issue to be resolved as it would help clear the way for the "settlement of other disputes" between the free and the communist world.[66] Yet, there were differences as well. Rakesh Ankit argues that Kashmir "impinged upon Britain's continued post-imperial presence in India and Pakistan" to secure a "smooth transition from empire to commonwealth," while for the US, "Kashmir was a spanner in the American wheels of collective security against the Soviet Union and Communist China."[67] American and British concerns also revolved around the popularity of communists in Kashmir, which had been made possible by the number of left-leaning officials in the Kashmir government such as G. M. Sadiq, (education minister), Mir Qasim (revenue), D. P. Dhar (home affairs), and G. L. Dogra (finance).[68] The US was increasingly wary of India's foreign policy and non-aligned stance and closer relations with the Soviet Union, as well as its mediation in Korea in 1952. Neither the US nor the UK wanted an independent Kashmir because of the possibility of it becoming communist and closely aligned with the Soviet Union. Finally, both the US and the UK, facing significant backlash over their role in the Partition of Palestine, were looking to placate the Muslim world using Kashmir.

Following Partition, the US sought to keep Pakistan as a close ally in the anti-communist block and in its delicate relations with the Muslim world.

Pakistan, in turn, was also willing to accommodate the US against the Soviet Union in hopes of having American support against India on Kashmir. This perhaps explains the critical coverage in the US press of India's position on Kashmir, as well as the "puppeteer" Kashmir government, in the years following Partition, especially immediately after the coup. Indeed, there was a strong interest in the US press regarding Kashmir in the early 1950s, much of it in favor of a UN-backed resolution.

Nehru, in particular, was seen as intransigent and as gravely contributing to the Kashmir impasse by rejecting all proposals at the UN, to which Pakistan had been more amenable. The *Life* magazine article also highlights how the US wanted to bolster the legitimacy of the UN.[69] Both the Indian state and the Bakshi government expressed concerns that Kashmir was becoming a part of power bloc politics and that the US and its allies had a vested interest in ensuring Kashmir merge with Pakistan.[70] After Sheikh Abdullah's arrest, without mentioning—but referring to—the US, Bakshi told the press that Abdullah was attempting to create an independent Kashmir with the connivance and support of foreign powers.[71] Yet, this fear seems far-fetched given that it was not in the interests of the US or the UK to have an independent Kashmir.

Initially, the Soviet Union was cold toward independent India because India was seen as being a part of the British Commonwealth and because of Nehru's repressive treatment of the Communist Party in India.[72] The Soviets also saw Pakistan as being feudalistic and anti-worker. Thus, Soviet perspectives on the Kashmir issue were noncommittal. Debidatta Aurobinda Mahapatra details in his dissertation on the India-Russia partnership that the Soviet representative was either absent or abstained during voting when the Kashmir question came up at the UN in 1948 and in 1949, believing both India and Pakistan to be part of the Anglo-American bloc.[73] However, the Soviets became increasingly concerned that the US and the UK were using Kashmir to set up military bases against them, a worry that was not completely unfounded.[74] In 1949, India voted with the Soviet Union at the UN, affirming concerns about growing Indo-Soviet relations. Matters turned in India's favor at the UN in 1952, when on January 17, the Soviet representative, Jacob Malik, declared that a plebiscite under the UN would be a plebiscite under the US and accused America and Britain of "crude, imperial intervention" in Kashmir.[75] India saw this as "a warning to

Pakistan" and an "acknowledgment of India's independent approach to world problems and a bid for [the] country's friendship."[76] Kashmir was officially a pawn in Cold War politics.

The UK attempted to pivot toward greater neutrality between the two countries, as it wanted to ensure that India would remain in the Commonwealth and to protect its own economic interests.[77] On the other hand, the US and Pakistan solidified their growing ties by signing a defense agreement in May 1954; furthermore, in September 1954, Pakistan joined the Southeast Asia Treaty Organization (SEATO) and in September 1955, the Baghdad Pact (later, the Central Treaty Organization or CENTO), both of which were US-backed.[78] These developments significantly impacted the resolution of the Kashmir issue, as both India and the Kashmir government took serious offense to the military deal and decried Pakistan's increased armament and America's involvement as endangering India's security.[79] While the Pakistani leadership justified the alliance as strengthening Pakistan against India and scholarship has described it as addressing Pakistan's concern about India, the US placed certain safeguards to assure India there were no threats against it and that those armaments were not to be used against India. Instead, according to Hamza Alavi, the US initiated the alliance to secure its own anti-communist interests in West Asia, and Pakistan was "drawn to West Asia following on the role that it was assigned by the US in Western military strategy."[80] Nevertheless, the response against the military deal was strong. Pakistan was isolated from the non-aligned Afro-Asian countries (besides Turkey, Iraq, and later Iran) for being fully in the imperial camp. On March 5, 1954, Nehru "reiterated that the US decision on military aid had changed the context of the Kashmir dispute, thus rendering the [talks of 1953] irrelevant."[81] He denounced the appointment of the plebiscite administrator, and India also sent back the visas of the US observers who were to join the UN Commission.[82] Given that Nehru had long ago decided that he was not truly committed to the plebiscite, this outrage was opportunistic—it finally gave India the exit strategy it needed from resolving Kashmir according to the aspirations of its people. The most consequential impact of the US-Pakistan military alliance was the betterment of India-Soviet relations.[83]

Amid this early Cold War context and the intrigues between the new world powers, Bakshi strategically used propaganda and media, targeted generally toward international audiences but specifically toward Muslim-majority countries and the Soviet Union, to portray Kashmir as benefiting from the accession to India and rejecting the need for a plebiscite. Starting in 1955, international press reports by journalists invited to witness progress in the state reflected a different tone on developments in Kashmir. In a crucial three-part series from Kashmir in July 1955, A. M. Rosenthal of the *New York Times*, pleasantly surprised by the cordial treatment given to reporters, declared that even though a majority of people in Kashmir would vote for either Pakistan or independence, "time, money, hard work, and power" were the main factors in New Delhi's favor. He argued that India was patiently biding its time, providing benefits to Kashmiris, and expecting that those who would prefer Pakistan or independence would be in the minority, eventually.[84] To talk of a plebiscite, he argued, would "make people uncertain of tomorrow, and would stop work and progress to create instability."

Pursuing the Muslim World

Kashmir played a crucial role in shaping India's foreign policy toward Muslim-majority countries. The Department of Information prioritized visits from journalists from prominent Muslim-majority countries, such as Afghanistan, Iraq, Turkey, Egypt, and Indonesia.[85] Kashmir was also leveraged to portray India as a country that respected religious diversity. As Taylor Sherman has highlighted in the case of Hyderabad, the Indian state was keen to secure India's reputation as a secular state both home and abroad, and one strategy was with its positive treatment of Muslims, including in Kashmir.[86]

Among Muslim-majority countries, the issue of Kashmir was also complicated by a desire to maintain relations with both India and Pakistan, officially taking a position of neutrality. Turkey, a partner in the Baghdad Pact, made it clear that new Turkish-Pakistan ties would not draw the country into Pakistan's dispute with India over Kashmir.[87] However, prominent leaders and religious figures within these countries favored Pakistan's position and demands for international Muslim solidarity. In October 1954, for example, the *New York Times* reported that leaders from fourteen Muslim-majority countries "have begun a propaganda campaign in support of Pakistan in her seven-year-old dispute with India over Kashmir . . . [with] editorials from Egyptian and Iranian newspapers that were sharply critical of India for failure to proceed with the appointment of a plebiscite administrator in Kashmir."[88]

Egypt was one such case. Egypt had close ties with India, especially given their common struggle against British imperialism and Egypt's recognition of the need for Indian support in Arab causes such as Palestine. But Egypt wanted to be seen as the leader of the Muslim world and thus could not denounce Pakistan's position.[89] On February 17, 1950, the Egyptian government offered to mediate informally between India and Pakistan.[90] In addition, influential groups within Egypt, including religious figures at al-Azhar and leading newspapers were sympathetic to the cause of Kashmiri self-determination. The issue became a diplomatic crisis in 1950–1951, when Egyptian diplomats and religious leaders ostensibly departed from the official state line and began to speak out against the Government of India. A group calling itself the Friends of Kashmir also began to issue statements, leading the Indian embassy in Egypt to reprimand the Egyptian authorities.[91] While the diplomatic row was eventually resolved, there were concerns the Kashmir issue would be positioned as an "Islamic" one, and the Government of India would lose its standing in the international arena if that were the case.

And so, it is no surprise Bakshi viewed developing ties with the broader Muslim world as strategically important and that as "prime minister," he attempted to craft his own brand of foreign policy. He invited political and diplomatic leaders and media delegations from Muslim-majority countries to visit Kashmir, and the Government of India facilitated these visits with accommodations and transportation. Here, the narrative of economic development and progress in a modernizing Muslim society served as the cornerstone. Press delegations from Egypt and Syria visited Kashmir in 1955.[92] Upon Bakshi's invitation, the king of Saudi Arabia, on his visit to India, also visited Kashmir that year.[93] All these delegations were invited to meet with Bakshi, members of his cabinet, and other leaders and observe the progress in the state. Their itineraries were filled with these meetings as well as tours to major tourist attractions, including the Mughal Gardens, the Dal Lake, and schools and major development schemes. Upon their return to their respective countries, the media accounts were resoundingly pro-Bakshi and thus, pro-India.

In April 1954, the foreign minister of Indonesia offered to mediate between India and Pakistan.[94] Later that year, the Government of India invited an Indonesian press delegation—comprising five journalists—to tour India for four weeks. Upon Bakshi's invitation, they also visited Kashmir during this time. A report from Asa Bafagih, editor of Djakarta's Islamic daily *Duta Masiaraket*, compared Bakshi to the second caliph in Islam:

> Our thoughts naturally go several centuries back to the days of Islamic democracy practiced so well by Caliph II, Umar ibn Chattab. . . . What impressed us was not merely the direct manner in which Bakshi government dealt with people's problems but even the more great measure of freedom which they enjoyed in this regard. . . . Here we saw real democracy at work without show or pretense. There was nothing but simplicity, modesty, love and genuine concern for people's welfare.[95]

The editor of Djakarta's Socialist daily *Padoman*, Mr. Rosihan Anwar, placed blame on the great powers for causing further instability in Kashmir. "On the international chessboard, it has become no more than a pawn in the great power rivalry of the United States, Britain, and Russia." The writer blamed the "tribal invasion" on Great Britain, with the assistance of Pakistan troops that "invaded the Kashmir valley." He further charged the US with creating additional problems by providing Pakistan with military aid and said that as a result, the plebiscite would not likely occur and the status quo should be held. Mrs. Herawati Diah of the *Madjalah Merdeka* stated that Bakshi had a "magnetic personality" and "answered all our questions on the Kashmir problem with perfect candor and sincerity." According to Diah, Bakshi told the delegation that Sheikh Abdullah had "made a blunder," which had been roused by "interested foreign powers."[96]

The press reports by the Indonesian journalists are revealing. First, they seem to be taken in by the figure of Bakshi himself—signaling once more that his "magnetic" presence alone was propaganda for the Kashmir government. Second, the Indonesian journalists simply reiterate the talking points of the Kashmir and Indian governments, focusing specifically on how imperialist forces were seeking to cause problems in Kashmir. This suggests how the appropriation of an anti-colonial and anti-imperial positionality allowed Bakshi (and the Indian government) to strengthen India's claims over Kashmir, especially toward an emerging non-aligned bloc, including a number of Muslim-majority countries. Socialists and leftists, as well as those espousing a politics of anti-colonial Muslim solidarity, were incorporated into this messaging. Of note here is that the Indian government's publication *Muslim Press on Kashmir*, featuring the writings of various Indian Muslim press outlets in favor of the government's position on Kashmir, was also distributed to Muslim-majority countries. The following year, in November 1955, the Indonesian vice-president, Dr. Mohammad Hatta, visited Kashmir, hailing the economic ties between India and Indonesia and praising Bakshi for his warmth and hospitality.[97]

Iran was also actively recruited in Bakshi's propaganda efforts, despite being a part of the US-backed military Baghdad Pact alongside Pakistan. In 1955, Bakshi invited the Iranian ambassador to India, A. A. Hekmat, to give the keynote address at the sixth convocation of the University of Jammu and Kashmir. In his speech, Hekmat praised the government's policy of free education as indicative of its interest in the promotion of knowledge. He urged the Kashmir government to continue on its path and develop the study of agriculture, sericulture, horticulture, industries, and crafts. He also praised the non-communal and nonsectarian outlook of the government.[98] In 1958, a press delegation, including the editor of the *Bamshad*, based in Tehran, stated that the accession of Kashmir to India was an established fact and Pakistani forces must vacate the region to create a "suitable atmosphere for negotiations and good will between India and Pakistan." The press report highlighted the support Bakshi received from Kashmiris, arguing that just because Kashmiris were Muslim didn't mean they could not be a part of India, because "religious difference can't separate Indian people from each other."[99] Here again, India's alleged secularity was used as a justification to deny self-determination.

And finally, in 1960, the press counselor of the Iranian embassy in New Delhi, Mahmood Tafazzoli, spoke with Kashmiri Persian scholars and writers on a tour to Kashmir. He mentioned that the Indo-Iranian Society would be setting up branches across India and that the one in Kashmir would have the most potential "in view of the traditional affinity of culture between Kashmiris and Iranians."[100] He was pleased that Persian was still read and understood by a large number of people and said that Iranians would be excited to hear that Kashmir "contained a treasure of Persian literature which was being preserved."[101] With Iran, the Kashmir government was able to appropriate Kashmir's rich Persianate history in an attempt to bring Kashmir into the fold of greater Indian-Iranian relations.

In the case of Egypt, the shifts in discourse surrounding Kashmir in the media also had an impact. A 1956 edition of *Kashmir Today*, distributed to all embassies around the world, featured an article on the Suez Canal, which was extraordinary given the usual focus on Kashmir. The article highlighted how India had always supported the anti-colonial movement and had spoken out in favor of the rights of Egyptians regarding the canal.[102] The article positioned the Indian state—and subsequently, the Kashmir government—in an anti-colonial vein and connected Kashmir and the Suez Canal in a broader matrix of anti-colonialism. The Egyptian government increasingly saw India as an ally against Western imperialist designs in Kashmir and began to restrict Pakistan from using Arab and Islamic forums against India.[103] Consequently, Egypt would abstain from voting on a UN resolution on Kashmir calling again for a plebiscite in 1957.

In addition to these diplomatic initiatives, during Bakshi's tenure, anti-Pakistan propaganda reached new levels, targeting both local and international observers. The Department of Information kept a close eye on Pakistan-based newspapers, often reprinting and distributing editorials or opinion pieces critical of conditions in Pakistan. The department especially highlighted the poor development conditions on the other side of the ceasefire line. Here is an information officer's description from one such publication:

> A veritable iron curtain has been thrown round the area and no outsiders—not even Pakistanis—save those permitted by the Pakistan government are allowed to enter the territory. . . . Local population kept down with a firm hand and even elementary civic rights are denied to it. . . . There is no legislature and people have no say in the administration. . . . Governments have been changed ten times during the last nine years or so. . . . The Azad Kashmir government cannot even appoint a peon. . . . [There is an] imposition on martial law, ban on public meeting and banishment and detention of political workers. . . . [The] number of people jailed [is] 4,632.[104]

Indeed, the difference in development between the two regions was a point often repeated by the Indian state. Krishna Menon, India's representative to the UN, remarked, "Why is it that the five-year plan is making vast strides in the state which the Jammu and Kashmir government administers, yet there is no such thing at all or even a semblance of it anywhere in those [Pakistan-administered] areas?"[105] The report described the poor development situation in Pakistan-administered Kashmir, declaring that rice sold for 100 rupees per standard unit of measure (as opposed to 8 on the Indian side).[106] Geared toward international observers, comparisons between economic developments in both regions highlighted the economic benefits of merging with India, once more deflecting from questions of self-determination.

By inviting leaders, representatives, and journalists from Muslim-majority countries to observe Kashmir's progress, Bakshi isolated Pakistan's calls for international Muslim solidarity on the issue of Kashmir. On their return to their respective countries, the leaders and journalists made statements about the status of Kashmir, highlighting how, under Bakshi, it benefitted economically from its relationship to India.[107] Bakshi's efforts and broader geopolitical developments had an impact in various international forums as well. In 1957, when Iraq asked the Arab League to support Pakistan's claims on Kashmir, most countries were opposed.[108] The government relied upon narratives of progress to project its legitimacy to a broader international audience, and Bakshi positioned himself amongst an international coterie of Muslim leaders as a secularizing but faithful, modernizing, anti-colonial Muslim leader—one who had, in the perspective of one Indonesian journalist, even espoused the characteristics of an ideal Islamic democracy.

Encounters with the Soviet Union

As the Soviet Union and India came closer together after the US-Pakistan military alliance, the highest-profile visit to Kashmir occurred in 1955, when a Soviet delegation consisting of Nikolai Bulganin, the Soviet premier, and Nikita Khrushchev, who at the time was the first secretary of the Communist Party of the Soviet Union, arrived in Srinagar on a two-day visit in December.[109] This transformative visit was to fundamentally change Kashmir's status in the international arena.

In Srinagar, the Soviet delegation received a grand state welcome by Karan Singh and Bakshi, addressing large crowds. The date of their arrival, December 9, was declared a public holiday. The *New York Times* reported that nearly sixty thousand men, women, and children gathered from distant towns and villages and stood in the cold for the welcome.[110] A contingent of the national militia conducted a guard of honor and salute, while the Soviet and Indian anthems played in the background.[111] The whole city was decorated with "arches, buntings, and festoons." In an oral interview, Abdul Khaliq, a retired engineer who had been in secondary school on that day, said the government had arranged for busses from various towns and villages and told people that they would "get a free ride and lunch to Srinagar."[112] Thousands thronged the busses that let people off on the banks of the Jhelum River to watch the river procession of the Soviet and Kashmiri leaders. Khaliq recalls that people cheered and shouted, especially as they learned that important foreign dignitaries had arrived in Kashmir. "We had no idea what they were there for, but Bakshi manipulated the situation so that the cheering crowds were interpreted by the Soviets as our happiness being under India. When it was all over, we weren't even given the promised ride back to our town or village. . . . We had to make our own way home."[113]

Khaliq's description reveals the breadth of the government machinery to enlist Kashmiris for propaganda efforts during the Soviet visit and manipulate the "public spectacle" that enabled not only the narrative of normalization but also, more importantly, produced Bakshi's political power.[114] The cheering crowds, despite the "absence of belief or emotional commitment," were interpreted as accepting Indian rule—and simultaneously induced "complicity by creating practices in which [Kashmiris were] themselves accomplices" in their loss of self-determination.[115]

Bakshi and the other members of his administration took the Soviet delegation around Kashmir, highlighting the steps toward economic development the Kashmir government had taken in recent years with the help of the Indian government. At each stop, large crowds were gathered. The Soviets also visited the state emporium and saw *Bambur Yamberzal*, a Kashmiri opera.

The Soviet delegation was keen to discuss the historic ties between Kashmir and Central Asia and expressed an interest in renewing "ancient" contacts—including trade and cultural connections. The delegation included artists from Muslim regions of the Soviet Union, who performed in a cultural show, and the dances presented by the Kazakh artists were said to have resembled Kashmiri dances. Bakshi, in his speech to the delegation, highlighted the historic ties between many parts of Central Asia and Kashmir. Both governments deployed Kashmir's links to Central Asia in an attempt to secure India's rule.

Bakshi's hospitality succeeded. At a reception in Srinagar, Khrushchev did the unexpected: he declared that Kashmir was India's internal affair. He spoke of the different nationalities and faiths living as friends in Kashmir, wanting to work for the well-being of their state. He asserted that its people had already decided Kashmir's status and that his country did not want to intervene in India's internal affairs.[116] He criticized Pakistani politics, stating that the Pakistani ruling circle was interested not in its people or state but in the politics of the US.[117] Later on, Nehru would insist that the Soviet leader made these comments about Kashmir on his own accord and the Indian leadership had not asked him to make any statements.[118] In a letter to Nehru, Karan Singh calls the visit a "resounding success," adding that the Soviet reference to Kashmir as the northern part of India was of "great political value. . . . The Russians are the first great power to have accepted the accession of Kashmir to India as final."[119]

Press commentary in the US, predictably, did not praise the Soviet visit. An editorial in the *New York Times* referred to it as a "traveling salesmen trip" and said that the Soviet statement that "Kashmir is already a part of India by virtue of the will of the Kashmiris" was not merely "telling a big lie" but "also trying to pay a cheap bribe for Indian sympathy, even if that means a vicious slap to the United Nations."[120] The editorial declared that the "ultimate sovereignty over Kashmir has not been decided by anyone, much less the Kashmiri people."

The Soviet delegation's visit to Kashmir served as a critical turning point in support of India's case on Kashmir. The US and the UK felt that India and the Soviet Union were openly aligned against their policies at the UN. After being shown Bakshi's Kashmir, the Soviet Union squarely situated itself with India. At the UN, India became emboldened as a result of Soviet support and would not even entertain the idea of the plebiscite. Pakistan once again brought Kashmir—after a hiatus of three years—to the Security Council in 1957, after the Kashmir government's Constituent Assembly had ratified a new constitution. Pakistan called for deployment of a UN force. A draft resolution circulated by the US, the UK, Cuba, Colombia, and Australia affirmed earlier resolutions and called for Gunnar Jarring, the president of the Security Council, to lead a mission to examine proposals that would lead to demilitarization. It was vetoed by the Soviets.[121] Subsequently, the Soviet veto or threat of a veto led the other world powers to cease any further resolutions against India. Indeed, Soviet support of India's case was critical in maintaining the status quo, eroding calls for a plebiscite on the international front and ultimately, creating an "intractable" barrier in resolving the Kashmir dispute.

Closer to the end of Bakshi's rule, major shifts in geopolitics once again repositioned world powers on Kashmir. US strategy toward the region shifted after 1958 until the 1962 India-China War. For US policy makers, India's importance as a balance against China grew, and the resolution of Kashmir's status was placed on the backburner. About China, the Soviet Union and the US converged geopolitically. Subsequent US presidents, including Dwight Eisenhower and John F. Kennedy, would warm toward India, and relations with Pakistan would take a downward trajectory.[122] As Pakistan and China became more closely aligned, Soviet-Pakistan relations also changed in the second half of the 1960s, and new Soviet leaders envisioned that good relations with both India and Pakistan would deter American and Chinese influence in the region. The Treaty of Tashkent that ended the 1965 India-Pakistan war would solidify the USSR's new stature as peacemaker.

However, the developments that had occurred in the previous decade had effectively crushed all proposals for an eventual resolution and plebiscite for Kashmir, further exhibiting how state-building solidified India's colonial occupation. Amid a shifting geopolitical context during the Cold War, Bakshi's government successfully used propaganda and media to portray normalcy and progress in a time of political uncertainty to multiple audiences. What is most crucial about this deployment is the agentive role of Bakshi and the Kashmir government in developing and propagating these policies, whether it was by inviting international delegations to Kashmir or closely monitoring the flow of information into and out of Kashmir. The Kashmir government attended to its own internal and external compulsions in putting forth this vision of Kashmir. The government had multiple audiences for its propaganda—Kashmiri, Indian, and the international community—and catered to these spheres in different ways. For the Indian public, emphasis was on how effectively the government used Indian financial resources for progress and development in the state. For the Muslim world, the focus was on Bakshi as a modernizing Muslim leader and his unique brand of leadership. In all respects, the Kashmir government was consolidating its own authority on its own terms.

What this chapter also underscores is that the support of Western imperial powers for a resolution actually undermined Pakistan's claims as well as the quest for a plebiscite. Bakshi and the Indian government were able to leverage an anti-colonial, socialist, third-world positionality in the face of a growing US-Pakistan nexus. This example reveals the limitations of the third-world project, and how India's status as a leader in the Non-Aligned Movement allowed it to suppress the demand for a plebiscite in Kashmir. Furthermore, the transformative visit of the Soviet leaders to Kashmir placed them squarely on India's side during a critical period at the UN. Eventually, even the world powers had to come into line. Starting in 1955, the American and international press was far more complimentary to Bakshi's Kashmir, even if critical of India. Many of the media narratives began to focus on development in the state. Bakshi had effectively tied the question of "progress" in the state to Kashmir's political future. Indeed, in 1956, the former prime minister of the UK, Clement Attlee declared, "Judging by the results, the present regime is successful. It is also thoroughly democratic with local self-government. . . . I think that Kashmir has definitely opted for union with India."[123]

Chapter 3

PRODUCING AND PROMOTING PARADISE

Tourism, Cinema, and the Desire for Kashmir

In March 1963, Shakti Samanta, the proprietor for the Bombay-based Shakti Films, wrote a letter to the inspector general of police of the Kashmir government, seeking permission to film the motion picture *Kashmir ki Kali* in the Kashmir Valley. He affirmed that the film, which featured Sharmila Tagore and Shammi Kapoor, two of the top Indian film stars at the time, was a "simple social romance and it has nothing to do with politics or any sort of propaganda. Neither it is against any religion or community."[1] He further assured that his crew "will not picturise or take any photograph of the prohibited areas on account of the present emergencies."

In the 1950s and 1960s, dozens of Indian filmmakers wrote similar letters to the Kashmir government, seeking permission to shoot their films in Kashmir.[2] They all followed a similar script: they sent a synopsis and assured the Kashmir authorities that the films would have no religious or political propaganda. The authorities required that prohibited areas relating to national defense be excluded from the shoots and that the film would be "submitted to the defense authorities for scrutiny from the security point of view before it [was] exhibited."[3] If a film was approved, a government order would be issued in its favor. Bakshi also invited prominent Indian filmmakers to come to Kashmir and shoot their films in the region's mountainous landscape, legendary gardens, and fresh lakes.

Pretty soon, Indian actors and actresses and entire film teams were descending upon Kashmir, making blockbuster technicolor "holiday films" like *Junglee* (1961), *Arzoo* (1965), *Jab Jab Phool Khile* (1965), *Phir Wohi Dil Laya Hoon* (1963), *Janwar* (1965), and of course, the abovementioned *Kashmir ki Kali*, which would become one of the highest grossing films of 1964.[4] Amid "growing modernity and increasing consumer culture," Kashmir became the go-to destination for Indian cinema, and millions of Indians—many who would never be able to physically travel to Kashmir—were able to "visit" the famed "paradise" in movie houses across the country.[5] Once the films were released, the filmmakers would thank the Government of Jammu and Kashmir for its assistance and full cooperation.

In their letters to the Kashmir government, Indian filmmakers attempted to suggest that the holiday films set in Kashmir would generate more tourist traffic for the state. The filmmaker Nassir Husain, who was the director of the hit *Phir Wohi Dil Laya Hoon*, featuring Joy Mukherjee and Asha Parekh, wrote a letter to the Kashmir government stating that the film would "help with the tourist trade" and that it would be shown abroad.[6] The linking of the visual medium and tourism promotion to Kashmir became extremely lucrative. Aside from the feature-length holiday films, directors were also requesting permission to make films or documentaries about Kashmir's scenic beauty, lakes, mountains, seasons, arts, culture, and development projects. The Films Division of the Government of India made two short films entitled *Spring Comes to Kashmir* (1956) and *Magic of the Mountains* (1955).[7] These films, created by Indian directors, were made to promote tourism to Kashmir, particularly by middle-class Indian tourists, and they contributed to a visual aesthetic about Kashmir that was commensurate with the Bakshi government's own efforts to bolster tourism to the state.

Given perceptions of instability, tourism in the state dropped immediately after the 1953 coup. Visitors to Kashmir also complained of the difficulties in travel as well as poor amenities once they arrived. Amid growing insecurity over the future of Indian rule in Kashmir, Bakshi's government, in conjunction with the Indian government and tourism promoters across India, paid special attention to the development of Kashmir's tourist industry. While Bakshi himself certainly did not plan for what has been described as Indian cinema's "Kashmir obsession," his government's propaganda objectives converged all too well with the fervor for Kashmir in Indian cinema. What, if not "excitement, modernity, youthfulness, and escape," could have better described the image Bakshi wanted to project of Kashmir?[8]

The feature films and documentaries, as well as the Indian and Kashmir government tourist propaganda materials, which included guide books, itineraries, advertisements, posters, and images, represent a "body of related and contextualized visual documents" that were "participating in a larger network of circulated ideas" about the place of Kashmir.[9] Defining place was a key tool for "sustaining imperialism" in a time when empires or nation-states were disavowing their territorial conquests.[10] Using the example of the Japanese empire in Taiwan, Manchuria, and Korea, Kate McDonald argues that for imperial formations, "the project of territorial acquisition to one of territorial maintenance necessitated the production of new social and spatial imaginaries of the nation that could coexist with the imperial territory of the state."[11] Since India had occupied the territory of Kashmir, it became imperative to determine how Kashmir coexisted within the imaginaries of the Indian nation. Furthermore, McDonald contends that "place served both as an axis along which colonial difference could be defined and exploited" as well as "a symbol of national identity that could encompass the entirety of the imperial territory without distinction."[12] Below, we will see how Kashmir was represented as a state of exception from metropolitan Indian norms but was also integral to the imaginary of the Indian nation. Importantly, tourism enabled this process to take shape as it produced "firsthand experiences and representations of the space of the nation and of the colonies as places within it."[13]

Unlike Shakti Samanta's claim that his film had "nothing to do with politics," cinematic and touristic representations of Kashmir played a role in the production and reproduction of Indian colonial desires, anxieties, and claims over the occupied territory. Not only did the Indian and Kashmir government enable tourism by providing the transportation and infrastructure necessary for tourist travel, but Indian tourism to Kashmir also served to build and maintain India's colonial occupation through the territorialization of its landscape and people. In some ways, then, India's sovereignty was exercised through and with tourism and cinema.

Tourism, especially in the context of Kashmir and other contested regions, is often understood as a form of peace building, a way of bringing together different communities to promote understanding and harmony.[14] However, tourism is a highly political phenomenon that has shaped state- and nation-building and understandings of what constitutes cultural identity and history.

In Kashmir, where occupation and the forcible integration of the region into India have prevailed, travel, tourism, and cinema emerge as sites where the "pleasures of imperialism" meet the "politics of empire" and where one entity has the power to promote certain ideas about the other.[15] It is no surprise that in 1960, an article in *India Weekly* called Kashmir a "tourist's paradise. . . . It occupies the leading most position on the tourist map of India."[16] For an occupied territory to occupy such a position brings into sharp relief the relationship between tourism, desire, and colonial control. Marketing Kashmir as a premier destination was inherently an ideological act as it relied on representations of the place, its history, and its people and factored in what got included or excluded in that representation. Most importantly, this designation was not a given; the centrality of Kashmir in the Indian imagination was manufactured through tourism's and cinema's maintenance of India's colonial occupation.

Tourism promoters and filmmakers produced and promoted Kashmir as a "paradise." I incorporate cinema in my analysis of tourism not only because it was a medium that was used to bring more tourists to Kashmir but also because it is a technology that serves a similar role to tourism and shaped meanings of Kashmir as a "territory of desire" for the Indian masses.[17] The Bakshi government's development of the tourist industry was practical. Tourism was deployed as a major source of revenue for the state (numerous accounts referred to tourism as the "backbone" of the state's economy), created new forms of wealth and employment for ordinary Kashmiris, and expanded the state's control over the local economy.[18] It was, as were Bakshi's efforts to reach out to Indian and foreign journalists, part of his plan to legitimize his rule by trumpeting the progress that was being made, to project normalization to Indian and international observers, and to promote integration with the Indian mainland. In a 1959 special issue of *Kashmir Today* dedicated to tourism, the minister for health and tourism, G. M. Rajpori provides insight into this position by stating, "The promotion of inter-state tourist traffic in the country provides great opportunities for a closer understanding among the people of different states and thereby welds these diverse types of people together emotionally, socially and culturally."[19] Combined with the Indian films shot in Kashmir, tourism was a critical component in consolidating the desire for Kashmir in the Indian colonial imagination and reordering a religious, spatial, and gendered imaginary of Kashmir that was both linked to and in need of India. Kashmir was a place to be seen and experienced and, in turn, to claim.

The production and dissemination of colonial tropes to propagate a particular view of life in Kashmir was meant to appeal to the sensibilities of middle-class Indian Hindu citizens. Cinematic and tourist representations promoted a Kashmir that was inherently Hindu, revealing the centrality of Hindu sacred geographies in the "secular" Nehruvian period and a people that were at the cusp of modernity, waiting for the benevolent largesse and protection of the Indian state.[20] Gendered representations also sexualized the land and its people, putting forth ideas of a feminized paradise that must be penetrated experientially. Tourism and cinema served to territorialize India's colonial occupation in both its secular modernizing and Hindu nationalist avatars and in some ways highlighted the co-constitutive relationship between the two. It also enabled an unquenchable desire of Indians toward Kashmir (and some Kashmiris) that would continue to undergird India's strategic rule in Kashmir.

"A Special Place"

Historical accounts in Persian and Sanskrit and colonial texts have always posited Kashmir as "a special place."[21] Rafiq Ahmad argues that "tourism imaginaries of Kashmir from the colonial past to the 'neo-colonial' present have remained essentially frozen in time even as Kashmir has actually moved from a romanticized space of the colonial past to a 'strange confined space' of the 'neo-colonial present.'"[22] Similarly, the idea of Kashmir as a paradise was certainly not a post-1947 construction. The Mughal emperor Jehangir reportedly used that term as the Mughals sought their summer escape from the plains of Hindustan into the Kashmir Valley, building an array of gardens and providing patronage to miniature artists who captured the beauty of the Valley.[23] In the seventeenth to nineteenth centuries, European travelers to Kashmir perceived it not just as a respite from the oppressive summers in the plains but also "as a place of romance, and for displaced Europeans, the 'Eastern' equivalent of 'Western' places of leisure," such as the "Switzerland of the East."[24] While the beauty of Kashmir acquired much fame, Ahmad argues that European accounts "resorted to an ethno-centric tradition of comparison between Kashmir and Europe," one in which Kashmir was never to be

Europe—it was a "degraded, primitive society lying frozen in time, incapable of change; incapable not because they do not want to, they cannot. A sense of paradise lost and bestowed on the wrong people became prevalent in European discourse about Kashmir."[25]

In the realm of the visual lens, Ananya Jahanara Kabir describes the "immense symbolic capital of the Valley's topography that . . . accrued since its indirect incorporation within the British empire in 1846" as British "photographers, surveyors, and archeologists . . . were transformed into the tourist as domesticated imperial adventurers."[26] The camera's gaze toward the landscape helped construct the Valley as a desired space, as the rumors of Kashmir that had previously existed in the European imaginary through poems such as Thomas Moore's "Lalla Rukh" were verified.[27] Kashmir was a pivotal location in the rivalry between Britain and Russia, and thus, British interest in the region was also due to the geopolitical context of the Great Game.[28] British photographs were published, sold, and circulated in albums, frames, and postcards across Europe. With the proliferation of photographs of Kashmir to those who had never even visited, the "value" of Kashmir increased.

The legacy of "desire" was transferred from colonial European orientalism to colonial Indian nationalism, which, Ahmad argues, "using the same methodology of tourism imaginaries and the power (political, cultural and technological) of discourse . . . turn the . . . space into a space of 'epistemic violence.'"[29] Ahmad suggests that tourism in the contemporary moment serves to integrate Kashmiris into the Indian national identity, project normalization and peace, and serves "as an anti-secessionism strategy in the garb of economic development and the preservation of cultural heritage."[30] I extend Ahmad's argument to Bakshi's tenure and specify how Kashmir was (re)produced in the Indian colonial imaginary and how Indian tropes both sustained and departed from European orientalist accounts.

Beyond the Permit System

Under Sheikh Abdullah's government, any non-Kashmiris who travelled to Kashmir had to obtain a special permit. Even Kashmiris who travelled to Jammu or India had to obtain a permit from the inspector general of police. Abdullah had insisted on the permit not only for security reasons but also to consolidate Kashmir's autonomous status. Yet, visitors complained of the lack of amenities at the checkpoints and the long waiting lines. The procedure for issuing special permits was also time-consuming—Indian nationals had to be recommended by a gazetted officer, a municipal commissioner, or a member of Parliament. For unattested applications, police reports were required. Kashmiri nationals in India who wanted to return home had to approach the trade commissioner in Calcutta, Bombay, Amritsar, or Pathankote.[31] Tourists from abroad, who held tourist visas, could only approach regional tourist officers in Calcutta, Bombay, Madras, or New Delhi for the special permit. For Pakistani nationals, permits were not issued except in special circumstances and only with the permission of multiple Indian state bureaucracies. Flights in and out of Kashmir were also controlled. These bureaucratic controls led many to reconsider visiting Kashmir.

Additionally, advance notice was given to local intelligence agencies if "undesirable characters" were proceeding to Kashmir. All of this was done "very informally and in secret" and officials were concerned about the "legal validity of searching passengers proceeding to Kashmir, a state which has acceded to the Indian union."[32] In the days surrounding Abdullah's arrest, the Ministry of Defence ordered that all "permits issued up to date" should be cancelled and that applicants should apply again so that "applications [can be] scrutinized with view to preventing undesirable persons crossing into [the] state."[33] While the report did not specify who these "undesirable persons" were, it is possible it referred to people who were pro-Pakistan or wanted complete integration, such as Hindu nationalist groups.

As early as 1948, however, Bakshi expressed his discomfort with the permit system, arguing that it hampered the movement of traders between India and Kashmir. He also felt that any "genuine Indian national going on a visit to Kashmir should not be stopped."[34] In an interdepartmental meeting in January 1954, various officials recommended eliminating Kashmir entry permits altogether, and Bakshi insisted on abolishing the checkpoints as well in order to make entry for tourists easier. This required coordination with the Government of Punjab, and in March 1954, an official in the Indian defense department sent a letter to Punjab's chief secretary requesting abolishment of the checkpoints stating, "It is our endeavor to help tourist traffic to Kashmir in all possible ways. . . . It would save annoyance to the visitors and would indeed help considerably in the promotion of tourist traffic to Kashmir."[35] While it remains unclear when the checkpoint system was ultimately abolished, amendments to the permit system were made until it was permanently abolished in April 1959.[36] The decision was transformative. Removing the permit system made it significantly easier for Indian tourists to go to Kashmir.

Concerns within the Indian and Kashmir government over the standards of tourism arose when an article by an American tourist, Julie Smith, the chief public relations officer of Pan American Airways, appeared in five hundred American newspapers complaining about her terrible visit to Kashmir. Her complaints included the lack of reception arrangements at the airport for tourists, lack of guides, lack of fixed prices, a poorly run visitors bureau, and no reliable travel agents, as well as exploitation by local vendors, including boatmen.[37] In 1954, the Armed Forces Information Office also stated that many of the tourists that had come to Kashmir recently were from Bombay and belonged to the "monied classes."[38] As a result, there were not enough appropriate accommodations to meet their needs. The report warned that many of the tourists were "dissatisfied with the arrangements and facilities. . . . Some of them are so disgusted that they say that they have made a mistake in coming to Kashmir."[39] Others similarly complained of irregular bus schedules, high food prices, and poor accommodations for women and vegetarians.

Visiting India's "Best Holiday Resort"

Given the concerns surrounding the quality of tourism, one of the primary objectives of Bakshi's government was to consolidate the tourism industry and in doing so, to facilitate Indian colonial travels to Kashmir and the meaning-making that it enabled. Promoting "paradise" went from being a mainstay of European imperial travels to a full-blown state-building project under Bakshi. This involved a thorough restructuring of transportation, infrastructure, accommodation and other needs, while also decreasing the costs and troubles associated with travel to Kashmir, establishing the rise of organized mass tourism. While the Department of Tourism was in charge of improving the tourist infrastructure inside and outside the state, the Department of Information extensively publicized Kashmir's tourism opportunities, encouraging outsiders to travel and see for themselves the progress that was being made in the state. The tourists' journeys actually began with these promotional materials, which included radio announcements and features, as well as filmed announcements in theaters in India that "Kashmir is once again open to visitors as before."[40]

The government sought to make traveling to Kashmir enticing for Indian tourists, in pursuit of building affective connections between the nation and the occupied territory. This was a stark departure from the majority of American and European tourists who had frequented Kashmir prior to 1947. In deciding what types of tourists to focus on, J. N. Zutshi of the Department of Information lamented that the Government of India was more focused on foreign tourists and suggested the publicity efforts target Indian tourists primarily, saying that "it would be no use reverting to the vicious circle created by the dependence of our tourist industry on the British or Americans" and that "domestic" tourists "formed the pivot of the tourist industry of Kashmir."[41] Consequently, travel agencies were opened in a number of major Indian cities, such as Bombay, Calcutta, New Delhi, Madras, and Agra, in order to entice middle-class and urban Indians to come to Kashmir. These publicity efforts had their intended results. The percentage of tourists who were domestic was 86.6 in 1951, which increased to 94.13 in 1955; the percentage of foreign tourists was 13.35 in 1951, which decreased to 5.87 in 1955.[42] While Zutshi does not provide additional reasons for why tourism from India should form the "pivot" of the tourist industry, a closer look at the promotional materials involved underscores the intentions behind such a push.

The Kashmir government, in collaboration with the Government of India, prioritized addressing the concerns about tourism circulating in the public sphere during Abdullah's rule. The tourism department became a vast organization with branches both inside and outside the state. An interdepartmental meeting in January 1954 strategized the ways in which tourist traffic could be brought to Kashmir, suggesting concessions, improving facilities and accommodations, making arrangements, fixing itineraries, providing ration cards for tourists (for rice, firewood, flour, sugar, and kerosene), building better hotels and huts, and improving air and bus transportation. Subsequently, other steps were taken to improve the experience of tourists, and the Kashmir government was involved not only in luring tourists to visit Kashmir but also in playing a role in all aspects of their stay. Accordingly, an article in *The Mirror* in September 1962 remarked, "Nowhere else in the world does a Government-sponsored department look after the visiting tourist without any charges, as is done in this state."[43]

Getting to Kashmir was made much easier with various options for tourists based on their time or money, involving "webs of infrastructure, enjoyment, and mobility" that linked India to Kashmir.[44] Better-off tourists could reach Kashmir by air from Delhi, a journey that took "only three hours and a half to reach Srinagar" and cost Rs. 110.[45] Indian Airlines operated daily services between Delhi and Srinagar, with stops in Amritsar, Pathankot, and Jammu. Those who had their own vehicles could drive: starting from Delhi, "one would do best to follow the Grand Trunk Road through Karnal, Ambala, and Ludhiana, as far as Jullundur, then turn north and take the new road to Pathankot via Mukerian, and proceed to Srinagar via Jammu."[46] This journey often took two days, with a stopover at Kud or Batote. Since parts of the Gurdaspur district were given to India at the time of Partition, there was now a direct road connecting the state to the Indian mainland. Otherwise, taxis or busses were usually hired at Delhi or at Pathankot, to which there was a twelve-hour overnight train service from Delhi. Access to Kashmir was also made easier by deluxe busses that would bring in tourists from Pathankot to Srinagar with a round-trip fare of Rs. 45 per passenger in 1951.[47] Regular bus service ranged between 3 and 16 Rs.[48] Jammu and Kashmir tourist information officers were posted at centers where the journey to Kashmir by air, bus, or car began.

The varying modes of transportation, as well as the relative ease and adventure in traveling to Kashmir, are depicted in a number of the holiday films, which feature young Indian men or women, tired of their lives in metropolitan centers in India "escaping" to Kashmir, often as a getaway from parental authority, or for relaxation or leisure and sporting activities. In *Arzoo*, the hero, Gopal, takes a flight to Srinagar, where he sits next to and meets the heroine Usha, played by the actress Sadhana. In *Kashmir ki Kali,* Shammi Kapoor's character drives a stylish Studebaker convertible from Delhi to Kashmir, passing through memorable landscape, singing "I will have to fall in love with someone, sometime, somewhere." In *Janwar*, Shammi Kapoor's character and his friend, played by the comedic Rajendra Nath, take a train to Kashmir, which Kapoor almost misses at a stop while he is refilling his water. He ends up stepping into a girls' compartment, resulting in the ire of his later love interest, played by the actress Rajshree. In *Phir Wohi Dil Laya Hoon* a taxi full of young women—all friends of the heroine, Mona, played by Asha Parekh—go to Kashmir on holiday while the hero, played by Joy Mukherjee, hitches a ride and sits on top of the car. The group stops to snack at various points, complete with a song sequence and some playful scenes. No matter the mode of transport, the holiday films suggest that it is the journey to Kashmir, not just Kashmir, which is memorable, as it is filled with humor, adventure, and play. En route to Kashmir, the characters are able to express their deepest desires or initiate a love story that will later be fulfilled in Kashmir itself. Kabir argues that the "car embodies the changes in this cinematic formation of the youthful modern urban Indian subject," suggesting a link between Kashmir, modernity, and youthful urbanity.[49]

Upon their arrival, visitors were led to the massive Tourist Reception Center, the largest in Asia at the time and open twenty-four hours a day, which Bakshi built in Srinagar for those who needed assistance in finding a place to stay, guidance on their itinerary, or making complaints. Additional tourist agencies housed in the center arranged for houseboats, camping, fishing, shooting, and transportation. A hostel was also attached to the center, where tourists could stay at a nominal cost until they made their arrangements. The center hosted regular cultural programs (no doubt, in response to tourists complaining of the "lack of entertainment in the city"), which featured "light Indian and Kashmiri music followed by typical Kashmiri tea and *bakerkhani* [pastry]."[50]

Government funds went toward improving the condition of houseboats, and the number of hotels, youth hostels, and restaurants increased. Tourists were given a variety of options for their accommodations. They could stay in European-style hotels like the Nedous or the Boulevard, which cost between 26 and 40 Rs. per night for a double room. The tourist department ran the 167-room hotel, Lalla Rookh, which was deemed Srinagar's most modern structure.[51] There were also "Indian-style hotels" like the Kashmir Guest House and the River View, which ranged from 8 to 16 Rs. per day for a double room. Houseboats, popularized through films such as *Jab Jab Phool Khile*, were a common choice for those who wished to stay a while (a houseboat for one month ranged between 250 to 800 Rs., or 12 to 30 Rs. per day). Houseboat owners like Raja in *Jab Jab Phool Khile* or Mamdu in *Arzoo* were depicted as loyal servants, who catered to every whim of the visitor and provided a "native" perspective to the tourists' stay. The government also built a number of bungalows, huts, and camps in major tourist areas. People involved in the tourist industry were trained in best practices. It was not just individuals or families who would make the trip to Kashmir; oftentimes, arrangements were made for large parties of the National Cadet Corps, scouts, or college students.[52]

Once in Kashmir, tourists had a variety of options to choose from, including visiting various Mughal gardens like Nishat and Shalimar, health resorts like Gulmarg or Pahalgam for day-long trips, the Dal Lake, or other points of historical interest. The government constructed roads that linked important tourist resorts of the Valley with Srinagar and created access for areas that had been previously inaccessible, such as Yusmarg and the Lolab Valley. In each new tourist attraction, a rest house was constructed. For those tourists who were more active, the government also introduced activities such as skiing, horseback riding, boating, swimming, trekking and mountaineering, golf, tennis, shooting, and fishing. These new modes of leisure and pleasure were also depicted in the holiday films. In *Janwar,* the young Indians, including the hero and the heroine, go to Kashmir to play in a tennis tournament (which they win), and in *Arzoo,* Gopal goes to Kashmir for a skiing competition in Gulmarg (which he also ends up winning). Even in *Phir Wohi Dil Laya Hoon,* Mona and her friends visit Kashmir for a youth festival. Almost all the movies show the characters horseback riding in the vast meadows of Kashmir, surrounded by mountains, jet-skiing in the Dal Lake, or trekking in the snow-covered mountains. Kabir points out that the "announcement of the Valley as the locus for novel modes of leisure and pleasure was thus intimately tied to the novelty of cinema in color."[53]

Advertisements in Indian newspapers promoted the number of leisure activities. One advertisement issued by the director of tourism stated, "No matter what sort of holiday you want, Kashmir will be able to provide it. The excitement of mountain climbing, the thrills of hiking along scenic trails, angling in the swift, clear streams, and everything that you need to make your holiday most enjoyable is available in Kashmir—the beautiful Kashmir, with more facilities and holiday attractions this year!"[54] The advertisement listed the seasons affiliated with each activity. For example, golf and tennis were popular from April to October, while skiing was popular from the last week of December to February. In the film *Arzoo*, the different developments in the characters' romance also revolved around the seasons—love and romance in the spring and summer, heartbreak in the fall, and a reconciliation on the snowy mountainside in the winter. No matter the time of the year, Kashmir abounded with extravagant adventure and fun, and each season had its own charm—a representation that further cemented the yearlong fascination with Kashmir.[55]

In addition to adventure, the tourist's experience was also replete with consumerism. The proliferation of tourist discourses incorporated the desire for Kashmiri art and handicrafts, commodities that were increasingly sought across India. The focus on traditional handicrafts was part of broader Indian development strategies to "support Indian culture, encourage diverse Indian production, and build rural employment"; in Kashmir, however, it took on an additional significance when linked to tourist and cinematic imaginaries of desire and colonial fantasy.[56] The government ran the Kashmir Government Arts Emporium and the Central Market, as well as the Government Silk Factory, where many goods were available at fixed prices. The Government Arts Emporium also had branches in Jammu, Amritsar, Jullundur, New Delhi, Lucknow, Bombay, Madras, Bangalore, and Calcutta. Tourist guidebooks showed images of Kashmiri artisans, painstakingly huddled over their craft, as well as images of different arts and handicrafts. One guidebook linked the beauty of the landscape to the artisan's inherent talent: "The glorious surroundings of Kashmir have bred in the Kashmiri an instinctive feeling for beauty, and his deft fingers can turn any raw material into articles of exquisite delicacy."[57]

Handicrafts included wood carving, an "ancient craft" that produced tables, screens, dressers, or cigarette boxes; papier-mâché decorations that were still in the hands of the descendants of the original craftsmen; and needlework, which could be used for rugs or wall hangings. Handmade products also included "silver of exquisite craftsmanship, tastefully embroidered shawls, magnificent hand-made carpets, furs, homespun tweeds and blankets, semiprecious stones, and a hundred other things."[58] Kashmiri embroidery, including *tilla*, *sozni*, and *ari,* was especially valued, on shawls, fabrics, cushion covers, and saris, and it required "exquisite needlework and Mughal patterns."[59] Shawls especially had been of great value since "antiquity. . . . Kashmir shawls are said to have been admired in the days of Mahabharata."[60] Holiday films featured Kashmiri commodities—from the *tilla pherans* (long, loose embroidered Kashmiri dress) and silver headdresses on the leading actresses to the carpets and the wood carving found in homes and houseboats. Documentaries on tourism in Kashmir depicted Kashmiri boatmen bringing various handicrafts to Indian tourists in houseboats.

Commodity promotion showcased a Kashmir that was defined not just by its natural beauty but also beauty through its art and handicrafts. Kabir argues that this fetishization of Kashmiri commodities contributed to a "postcolonial discourse on and consumption of Kashmiri handicraft" that was "itself implicated within the construction of Kashmir as pastoral fantasy." For Indian tourists, acquiring a souvenir from Kashmir allowed them, as consumers, to remind themselves of their journey and continue a relationship with an "absent Kashmir."[61] For future travelers, the handicrafts were "food for imagination" and secured their "desirability to the desirability of the place of its making."[62] For what is the consumption of souvenirs if not attempting to capture that which "remains out of one's reach?"[63] It was precisely because the artisans were deemed to be seeped in history, culture, tradition, and antiquity that the modern Indian desire for the non-modern other became more pronounced. This naturalization "firmly linked Kashmir's landscape . . . antiquity, and . . . indigenous crafts traditions in the collective Indian imaginary."[64] Furthermore, I suggest that the circulation of Indian capital in Kashmir tied Kashmiri artisans and Indians in a political economy that was based on desire and dependence. The greater the demand for Kashmiri handicrafts, the more the Kashmiri artisan was forced to perform "antiquity," participating in a network of production, circulation, and exchange of paradise that was to further contribute to the Indian colonial gaze.

"A Fine Race"

Tourism relied on a continuation of and a departure from European orientalist imaginaries of Kashmir and Kashmiris. Not only did the various stakeholders bolster the transportation and infrastructure necessary for a modern tourist experience, but they also crafted particular imaginaries that tourists were supposed to take back with them. These imaginaries transformed as the Indian and Kashmir government needed to articulate shifting meanings of the place of Kashmir, its people, and its position within the Indian state over time. Yet, what remained consistent is that Kashmir was positioned as both the inferior, unmodern "other" but paradoxically also a version of what the Indian nation had the inherent potential of being. It was this context that was intended to foster affective and dependent ties between Indian citizens and Kashmiri natives.

If Kashmiris had been depicted as being backward during the British colonial period, they were racialized, fetishized, or erased completely in tourism propaganda materials during Bakshi's rule. Most of the guidebooks included a brief section on "the people," which spoke of the diversity of the local population, as well as their cultural habits, including customs, language, holidays, food, and dress. References were made to the people inhabiting the various regions—Ladakh and Jammu—as well as the various ethnicities, including the Dogras, Paharis, and Gujjars, although most of the attention was given to Kashmiri-speaking people from the Valley. A tourism guidebook from the Indian Ministry of Information and Broadcasting described the people of the Kashmir Valley as "physically a fine race, the men being tall and well built and the women and children possessing charming features. Lively and intelligent, they are full of fun and fond of amusement."[65] The only other facts the guidebook found pertinent were that "their staple food was rice" and "they drink large quantities of tea."[66]

Interestingly, these descriptions of Kashmiris travelled beyond India, showing how widespread they were. Mrs. Herawati Diah of the *Madjalah Merdeka*, an Indonesian newspaper, visited Kashmir with a state-sponsored delegation. Upon her return, she wrote that an average Kashmiri had "light skin" as compared with "an average Indian in other parts of India," and "his features resemble that of an European, rather than an Asian. He has a large pointed nose, hazel eyes and a physical constitution which is the envy of the members of this delegation."[67] Diah's description of the physical appearance of Kashmiris is striking—especially as it mirrors the tropes found in colonial-era narratives, as well as contemporaneous Indian depictions that sought to enable a "desire" for not only the land but also its people.

Another guidebook described Kashmiris as "fair of complexion and regular of feature, its people are mostly of the Aryan type. . . . They have a keen sense of form and color and make excellent craftsmen."[68] The racialization of Kashmiris as "Aryans," repeated elsewhere, was linked to a broader project of religious nationalism that was constitutive of the secularity of the Nehruvian period.[69] In the context of the Brogpa community in contemporary Ladakh, Mona Bhan notes that the racialization of Kashmiris as "Aryans" must be read within "the context of India's historic attachment to Aryanism and its intersections with India's religious and territorial politics in Kashmir."[70] As evidenced by the tourist guides, this racialization is not a contemporary development resulting from the rise of Hindu nationalist politics—it was integral to how Kashmiris were imagined in the early post-independence period. The "fetish for the Aryan seed" should not only be seen "within colonial and global circuits of myth and fantasy" but also within India's "occupational regime in Kashmir that operates in and through registers of race, religion and sexuality."[71] Ascribing Aryanism to Kashmiris was to epitomize the Kashmiri Pandits, who were Brahmans, as the aborigines of the land and situate Kashmir and Kashmiris through a "primordial Hindu subjectivity," a topic I return to at the end of this chapter.[72]

The maintenance of colonial difference between Indians and Kashmiris also relied on the portrayal of Kashmiris as a formerly provincial people who were at the cusp—thanks to their links with India—of entering a more cosmopolitan, modern era. In a letter to the Department of Information on November 22, 1954, M. N. Malhotra, the general manager of Movie Makers, a Bombay-based company that made educational short films, drafted a proposal to the Kashmir government for "making short color subjects with the object of obtaining as wide a coverage as possible for Kashmir, the pleasure resort, the home of ancient and traditional arts, crafts, and cultures."[73] In the proposal, which was meant to "renew an invitation to even the habitual visitors to this colorful valley," he argued that "physical attributes of Kashmir Valley are not the only assets that can be exploited. . . . Many aspects of the unending variety of life of the humble peasant folks and craftsmen of Kashmir and its primitive tribes who live in the interior of this colorful valley" should also be showcased.[74]

Here, as with other colonial narratives, Kashmir and Kashmiris were denied coevalness; rather, they were seen with reference to a (primitive) time other than that of the present India and Indians.[75] One of the ways in which this came across was through dress. Kashmiris were always depicted in "traditional" clothing; for the women, this included a loose *pheran*, *shalwar* (loose pant), silver headdress, and a *dupatta* (scarf), while for the men this entailed a *pathan* suit (long tunic with pant), a vest, and some sort of hat. Alongside the traditional forms of dress were also pastoral occupations, highlighting how Kashmiris were still stuck in "premodern paracapitalist purity."[76] In the films *Magic of the Mountains* and *Spring Comes to Kashmir*, Kashmiris mostly are depicted working as agriculturalists or laborers—women picking saffron from the fields; men, women and children packing fruit to be exported; a young girl selling flowers to Indian tourists from her *shikara*; and artisans engaged in their "ancient" crafts. In the holiday films, this difference is more stark because the Indian characters are usually professionals—doctors or businessmen—and dress in more Westernized, modern clothing. The way Kashmiris were depicted reflects how Indian colonial imaginaries constructed them as occupying a different time and space.

While there were brief references to the people of Kashmir in the guidebooks and the documentaries, in the holiday films, Kashmiris were remarkably all but erased, even while the Indian characters repeatedly appropriated Kashmiri culture and dress. Across all the films, an Indian character inevitably "goes native" by donning Kashmiri clothes. Kabir argues, "Kashmiris were never in the picture in their own right. . . . The postcolonial playground itself a space disjunct from the nation is sustained through their neocolonial erasure from the landscape of love."[77] Across the six holiday films viewed for this chapter, there were only two Kashmiri characters, both of whom are assumed to be Muslim. One was Raja, played by Shashi Kapoor, an innocent, rustic, uneducated houseboat owner who falls in love with an Indian tourist, Rita, in *Jab Jab Phool Phile*. His innocence is underscored in one of the songs from the film, "Pardesiya," where he sings "Don't look into the eyes of foreigners. . . . The foreigners have to leave one day." The use of the term *foreigner* to describe the Indian tourist is telling and signifies the difference between the metropole and the colony from the perspective of the lone Kashmiri character. In another scene, Raja asks Rita to teach him to read and write. Initially, he says he would like to learn Arabic but then acknowledges that Hindi would be best. Here, the recognition that Kashmiris are "not yet complete or fully formed national subjects" is evident and positions the Indian tourist as the one who has the capacity to nationalize, or integrate, the colonized subject.[78] Raja's dismissal of Arabic for Hindi also suggests the rejection of more Muslim expressions of cultural belonging in order to integrate.

Yet, the film is mired in contradiction, highlighting the paradox in representations of Kashmiris. When Raja goes to the metropole to visit Rita, he is appalled at a party by the easy way she carries herself with other men. In another song, "Yahaan Mein Ajnabi Hoon," Raja laments how he feels like a stranger in her world and declares, "But I am a man of a very old civilization. . . . How can I forget that I am an Indian." In contrast to Rita, who is seen as being too Westernized, Raja, the uneducated Kashmiri houseboat owner is depicted as the authentic Indian, highlighting how "the Kashmiri indigenes must of necessity remain not only the corrective measures against this modernity, but in fact, quintessentially Indian."[79] The theme of "reconciling concerns of modernization with the compulsions of tradition" was certainly not new to Indian cinema; here, however, it was the Kashmiri native that served as the upholder of Indian tradition and civilization.[80] The second Kashmiri character, in the film *Arzoo*, is Mamdu, an even more simpler houseboat owner who provides comedic relief with his rustic personality, his poorly constructed Urdu and mock Kashmiri, and his lack of education. His role, as a loyal servant to Gopal, the hero, is primarily to enable the blossoming love between Gopal and Usha, as well as their subsequent reunion. Here, not only Kashmir but the lone Kashmiri character's only purpose is to provide the impetus for the love story.

Aside from racialization, exotification, or erasure, Kashmir was also feminized in tourist discourses. European orientalist accounts posited Kashmiri women as possessing "all the beauty, the physique, and the charm that position her in harmony with the natural beauty of the surrounding landscape."[81] Furthermore, they "express 'unlimited sexuality,' are 'more or less stupid,' and above all they are often 'willing.'"[82] The tropes continued well into the post-independence period. Nehru spoke of Kashmir in explicitly gendered terms:

Like some supremely beautiful woman, whose beauty is almost imper-

> sonal and above human desire, such was Kashmir in all its feminine beauty of river and valley and lake and graceful trees. And then another aspect of this magic beauty would come to view, a masculine one, of hard mountains and precipices, and snow-capped peaks and glaciers, and cruel and fierce torrents rushing down to the valley below. I watched this ever-changing spectacle and sometimes the sheer liveliness of it was overpowering and I felt almost faint. As I gazed at it, it seemed to me dreamlike and unreal like the hopes and desires that fill us and so seldom find fulfillment. It was like the face of the beloved that one sees in a dream and that faces away on awakening. But Kashmir calls back, its pull is stronger than ever, it whispers its fairy magic to the ears and its memory disturbs the mind. How can they who had fallen under its spell release themselves from this enchantment?[83]

Nehru's depiction of Kashmir as an "enchantress" replicates European colonial orientalist discourses and objectifies the land. For Nehru, Kashmir is a "supremely beautiful woman," who ignites "hopes and desires" that rarely find fulfillment. This sexualized imagery of Kashmir, whose "pull is stronger than ever," rekindles fantasies of Kashmir as a feminized paradise that must be explored and penetrated experientially, a trope that has only continued as the "Indian military has long asserted its masculine presence, the use of sexualized language feminized Kashmiri mountains and landscapes [by] . . . comparing them with women's bodies," as Mona Bhan argues.[84] Moreover, in this gendered representation, Kashmir was denied any agency—or any ability to provide consent for the actions of those who have "fallen under its spell." Kashmir, in fact, cannot actually call back; it is simply "her" beauty alone that does so by disturbing "the mind."

Tourist propaganda materials replicated Nehru's colonial and gendered gaze toward Kashmir through the bodies of Kashmiri women. The continued fascination with the "Kashmiri belle" is displayed in a number of guidebooks, which feature orientalized images of rustic beauty. The films produced by the Film Division of India also focus primarily on fair-skinned Kashmiri women—working in the fields surrounded by mountains, picking fruit from trees, looking shyly toward the camera, smiling, and wearing the quintessential *pheran* with the silver headdress and scarf. The *Guide to Kashmir*, published in 1954, states, "There is an Arabic proverb which says three things ease the heart from sorrow—water, green grass and the beauty of women. If this be true, there is no place for sorrow in the valley of Kashmir for there you will find all the three things in ample measure, and a lot else besides, to charm away the gloom and monotony of everyday life."[85] It was through the bodies of women—meant to be at one with and not separate from the landscape—that Kashmir was depicted as a "welcoming," inviting, playful place to the Indian tourist. That the beauty of women was intended to "charm away the gloom and monotony of everyday life" depicts the level of sexualized objectification that was naturalized in tourist discourses and was part in parcel of Indian colonial desires for not just the place, but also its people.[86]

The participation of Kashmiri women in these documentaries was not without controversy. J. N. Zutshi, from the Department of Information, requested Miss Mehmooda Ahmed, the principal of the Government Girls College for Women in Srinagar to assist Mr. Baskar Rao of the Films Division in securing a Kashmiri folk dance to be included in his film. The participation of students from the women's college in the documentary elicited some discontent from the public and within the bureaucracy. Miss Mehmooda, in a letter to Mr. Mohi-ud-din, presumably a bureaucrat who had passed on a community complaint alongside his own, stated that "it was done in a purely private and voluntary capacity . . . obviously after taking full permission from their parents."[87] She continued, "A documentary is a purely cultural affair, its purpose is to develop and enhance our cultural heritage of which we should feel justly proud."[88] This incident reveals some of the Kashmir bureaucracy's anxieties—particularly around gender and representations of Kashmiri women—surrounding the development of these tourism propaganda materials, highlighting how these representations were contested even among local officials.

While the guidebooks in the early years of Bakshi's rule depicted Kashmiris as rustic and awaiting modernity or simply erased them all together, later guidebooks reflected the transformations that occurred as a result of Kashmir being under Indian rule. The images in these guidebooks shifted to depict how Kashmiris had already benefited from India. As early as 1954, the draft proposal from Movie Makers suggested the importance of showing how:

> The People's Government headed by worthy statesmen is providing an in-

> spiration to the rest of the world in high endeavors and national integrity. . . . All this could be pictorially treated by montaging how the leaders of today's Kashmir function; how they maintain intimate contact with the people they serve and in the atmosphere of such mutual trust and enthusiasm, how the whole country is putting its shoulder to make a success of the Kashmir Five Year plan—which is already under way.[89]

The Kashmir leadership was invoked in order to show the development of the five-year plan. In 1962, closer to the end of Bakshi's rule, tourist materials no longer erased Kashmiris from the prescriptive lists of sights. Rather, the modernizing Kashmiri subject was integral to the tourist's gaze. Unlike previous guides, which had focused on landscapes and were interspersed with images of the poor Kashmiri peasant or artisan or women dressed in *pheran*, in these new guides there were images of children attending classes, men working at construction sites, women in crisp white *kameez shalvar* (tunic and pant) attending colleges, men in pants and blazers, and doctors and patients interacting at hospitals.[90] For middle-class Indian tourists, Kashmir was now a place they could identify with and lay claim to, as the guides affirmed the benefits of Kashmir's accession to India; it was a place that was now bustling with economic activity as a result of Indian benevolence. Tourist materials also began to show tourist women in their swimsuits amid the scenic landscape in an attempt to highlight the modernity and openness in the region. These changing depictions over time underline the importance of framing tourism discourses as reflecting shifting colonial demands and strategies.

Claiming the Land

In addition to discourses about the people of Kashmir, there were also discourses about the place of Kashmir—and in particular, the land. These discourses primarily sought to naturalize the boundaries of the territorial nation-state. Here, it becomes important to assert the "centrality of land to the ideological project of observational travel and imperial tourism" and, of course, to processes of settler-colonialism.[91] For Indians to imagine the land and the territory of Kashmir as part of the spatial imaginary of the nation was not a natural process; it had to be constructed, and it was primarily through tourism discourses and travel that this construction took place. In these representations, Kashmir was depicted as a fertile land, ripe for exploitation, as well as a place of potent healing potential. It was also depicted as a natural playground for fun and leisure, particularly for a young Indian urban class. Central technologies like guidebooks, itineraries, documentaries, and holiday films allowed travelers to see patterns in how they were to make sense of the place of Kashmir and lay claim to the land and how it was envisioned within the space of the territorial nation-state.

Combined with the gendered, sexualized representations of the people were the gendered discourses surrounding the land, in particular the fertility of the Kashmir Valley. A documentary boasted of the "luscious fruits of Europe and Asia that grow in profusion" in the summer.[92] One tourist guidebook reported that "rice and wheat are staple crops; among vegetables, cucumbers, turnips, radish, cabbages, tomatoes, peas, carrots, beans, asparagus, and spinach grow in plenty. Fruits which are abundant and are exported in large quantities include apples, peaches, plums, apricots, walnuts, and green almonds."[93] Another guidebook declared, "Perhaps no state in India has better facilities for fruit growing than Kashmir—the apple, vine [*sic*], mulberry, gooseberry, currant and strawberry—Kashmir has truly become the Orchard of India. At Banihal . . . the motor trucks are full of Kashmiri fruit, connecting Valley to Jammu and the plains of the Punjab. . . . The road has been considerably improved and traveling over it is a thrilling experience."[94] Words like *abundance* and *plenty* heightened the notion of the fertility of the land and its ability, as the "orchard of India," to make India bountiful.

The reference to the "motor trucks" in the newly constructed Banihal Tunnel was intended to convince travelers of the successes of Indian rule in enabling sites of economic production, distribution, and circulation. These later guides intended to project a "modern" Kashmir and highlight Kashmir's rapid modernization. Kashmir was no longer an underdeveloped, backward society; it was on par with Indian states and, thus, a critical constituent of the broader Nehruvian modernizing political order. Advertisements emphasized the "modern" hotels, with their nightclubs, cocktail bars, continental cuisines, ballrooms, salons, cinemas, and telephones.[95] By bringing attention to infrastructure that had been recently developed, these tourist guidebooks were able to trumpet the successes that had resulted from Kashmir's accession to India as well as the continued need for the link between India and Kashmir for the latter to develop. In addition, they also meant to underscore the ways in which India stood to benefit commercially (for example, through the export of Kashmiri fruits) from this relationship. Visual imagery in films and documentaries depicted gushing water from the rivers, perhaps to signal Kashmir's hydropower potential for India.

In addition to depicting Kashmir as "a pastoral space where the idea of a new Indian could materialize, and a new kind of youthful identity," tourism guidebooks also portrayed Kashmir's landscape as a place of healing and rest.[96] The springs of Kashmir, such as those in Chesmashahi Garden, were said to have medicinal value.[97] Another guidebook stated that "the waters of Kokernag are considered highly digestive and many patients suffering from chronic dyspepsia have benefited from its continued use."[98] A newspaper advertisement in Calcutta stated, "The climate, its pure breeze, its variety of temperatures, and its gorgeous hills and lakes have a tonic effect on health. You will be infused with new vigor, new blood, and new life. Visit Kashmir."[99] Another called Kashmir the "land of health" that allowed the visitor "real rest in the deep shade of mighty oaks and spreading chinars. . . . Only in a setting such as this can nature the healer do her work." The holiday films suggest that Kashmir was an escape from urban life in India—filled as it was with newfound anxieties around middle-class aspirations, consumerism, and modernity. Kashmir as a place separate from but connected to urban India as a result of its healing properties exemplifies the role it played in constructing the social imaginary of modern India. In other words, ideas of modern India were being fashioned concurrent with the construction of its colony in Kashmir.

The technology of guidebooks, filled with itineraries of day- or week-long trips in Kashmir, became instrumental in laying claim to the actual land. Over time, tourist propaganda materials became repetitive: tourists were encouraged to visit the same gardens, lakes, resorts, and ancient monuments and were also given detailed accounts for expeditions or routes for important treks. This "affective use of the Valley's topography" formed impressions of particular sites.[100] These detailed routes—not unlike those embarked upon by colonial travelers—covered much of the breadth of the land, from Baramulla in the north to Udhampur in the south, and relied on the guides' intimate knowledge. The listing of the various sites of interest was also a method of claim-making on the differential Kashmir landscape, whether it was the lakes, the springs, or the mountains. Holiday films participated in this realm of "intertextuality," with familiar locations: Dal Lake, Gulmarg, Pahalgam, and the poplar-filled road from Srinagar to Baramulla in North Kashmir. All this was meant to be explored and experienced and, in turn, to be claimed. In this way, the territory of Kashmir and its place in the Indian spatial imaginary was naturalized.

Depiction of Sacred Geographies

Tourism propaganda materials depicted a history of Kashmir that was not only linked to India but was the heart of Indian civilization from the ancient to present times. This was done, primarily, by foregrounding Kashmir as a "sacred site of Hinduism, home of India's spiritual and syncretistic traditions, and pivotal to the idea of an eternal Indian civilization," while ignoring or overlooking others—including its Muslim histories.[101] Settler-colonial representations of Kashmiri history were selective, partial, and distorting, ignoring complex historical processes and providing a simplified narrative of Kashmir's "natural" incorporation into the Indian nation. In their travels, Indian tourists saw and experienced Kashmir in ways that legitimated India's symbolic claims over Kashmir and promoted the naturalization of Indian empire on colonized land.

Tourism promoters signified the territory of Kashmir by propagating "place myths" of its history. Kashmir was reinvented as an exceptional space—one that could simultaneously appeal to Hindu nationalists by being an ancient, authentic Hindu space as well as to secular nationalists as a result of its contemporary hybrid identity and harmony. As Meena Gaur argues, "Contrasting political projects were vying for space in the years following the independence of India, and any formulaic reading of the films and cultural politics from this [Nehruvian] period would be a gloss over what were far more complex articulations of region, religion and secularism in India."[102] Nonetheless, even as the political leadership of India and Kashmir propagated the idea of Kashmir as the only Muslim-majority region in India to dismiss the two-nation theory of Pakistan and promote its own secular ideals, the tourist propaganda materials foregrounded Hindu sacred geographies and histories.

Guidebooks propagated the notion that "in classical India, Kashmir had an honored place," as a result of its various Hindu kings and history.[103] This was primarily done through the oft-repeated "origin myth" of Kashmir: "according to tradition, Kashmir was once a vast mountain lake called 'satis.' . . . It is said that the drainer of this lake was an ascetic, Kashyapa," and that is how the Valley was formed. Invoking Aryan heritage, the guidebook continues: "Like other parts of northern India, Kashmir was also inhabited by Aryans when their hoards came from Central Asia. . . . Originally Hinduism was prevalent in the whole of the country."[104]

Following from debates in contemporary South Asian historiography about the construction of Hinduism in the British colonial period, one could challenge the use of the term *Hinduism* to describe the traditions operating in Kashmir in the ancient and medieval period. However, here, I am interested in the use of particular texts to construct the historical narratives found in these guidebooks. This mythologized version of history—which was repeated in nearly all guidebooks of this time—was based on the Sanskrit text *Rajatarangini,* written by Kalhana in the twelfth century.[105] Khalid Bashir describes the text as largely "fictional . . . characters in flesh and blood and supernatural beings with their paranormal actions. . . . Kings take the forms of gods, and gods come down from the heavens to deliver justice. . . . It elevates mixing of fiction and history to an art form."[106] Kabir highlights the role of the British state, as well as the Dogras, in characterizing the *Rajatarangini* as "legitimate historiography," and others texts as "myth and fable."[107] Both Kabir and Bashir push back against "the epistemological equivalence of myth and history," as evidenced by the use of the *Rajatarangini.*[108] But why was this text highlighted above all others? The repeated references to *Rajatarangini* as *the* authoritative text on Kashmir's history—both by the Indian and Kashmir governments—signified "Kashmir as a glorious Hindu kingdom of the past" and placed Kashmir "at the historical origins of India," which itself was being constructed as Hindu.[109]

Some guidebooks situated the Hindu origins of Kashmir as far back as 3000 BC, and its Buddhist origins going as far back as 250 BC. Kashmir's Buddhist history shone during the time of Ashoka, when a Buddhist council was held there and "Buddhism and Hinduism existed side by side for several centuries. . . . In this Hindu-Buddhist period, many fine temples and monasteries were erected."[110] As Kabir argues, the Valley's hospitality to "Indic religions" like Buddhism and Hinduism highlighted the vertical connection between the histories of Kashmir and India, again propagated by colonial officials as well as the Dogra state.[111] Other guidebooks depicted Kashmir as the place of Shiva philosophy and Sanskrit learning. In *Srinagar and Its Environs,* Samsar Chand Koul writes:

> There is still a custom in vogue in the plains of Hindustan, which requires a boy who is to be invested with the sacred thread, to walk seven steps towards Kashmir. The underlying idea is that the boy is sent to Kashmir to receive his education and returns after completing it. No person in India was in those days recognized as a scholar unless he had a certificate to that effect from the Kashmir University.[112]

In this depiction of Kashmir, the "sacred thread" is a reference to Kashmir being a site of Brahman, and hence upper-caste, learning and edification, once more primarily situating Kashmir as central to Hindu sacred geographies.

Moreover, guidebooks—while making passing references to important Muslim sites such as the Jamia Masjid and the Hazratbal Masjid—demonstrated Kashmir's antiquity through Hindu architecture, which included the Shankarcharya temple in Srinagar as well as the ruins of the temple of Martand on the way to Pahalgam.[113] Nestled atop a hill, the Shankarcharya temple, "built by king Gopaditya who ruled Kashmir towards the earlier half of the fourth century BC," served as the central point for the tourist's experience; tourists were encouraged to begin their journeys there so as to have a "panoramic view of the entire city and its environs."[114] Almost all the guidebooks encouraged visitors to start their visit by climbing up Shankarcharya Hill to the temple of Shiva.[115] In the film *Arzoo,* upon arriving in Kashmir, the first site Gopal visits with the houseboat owner, Mamdu, is Shankarcharya. On the way up, Mamdu praises Nehru saying, "Mr. Nehru used to stay here. . . . Whenever I think of Nehru, it moves me." Gopal, the Indian tourist responds, "Yes Mamdu. . . . Even God feels the need for good men." Here, the secular Nehru is deployed in a scene about Shankarcharya, revealing the extent to which the centering of Hindu geographies was integral to secularist discourses.

One of the guidebooks dismissively acknowledges that "[Shankarcharya's]

Hindu origins not withstanding, the Musulmans call it the Takht-i-Sulaiman."[116] For the tourist then, the beginning of one's journey to Kashmir should be blessed with a visit to a Hindu temple—its relevance for Muslim sacred geographies was immaterial; indeed, the view from Shankarcharya was meant to situate the centrality of Hindu sacred geographies to the tourist's experience. Other sites, including springs, temples, villages, and natural landscapes were also situated amid "Hinduism's primordial relationship with Kashmiri topography and political economy."[117] Koul, in *Srinagar and Its Environs,* discusses the importance of various springs scattered across the city for Hindus, while disparagingly referring to springs near Muslim shrines as not being kept clean.[118] In the guidebooks, most of the "ancient" monuments mentioned are from Kashmir's pre-Islamic past.

The Indian and Kashmir government invoked Kashmir's Muslim-majority status in order to buttress India's *secular* credentials. Yet, in myriad ways, Kashmir's "Muslim" history was underplayed, demonized, or erased completely in tourist discourses. There are brief references to Kashmir coming "under the influence of Islam" by the end of the thirteenth century and "remaining under the suzerainty of Muslim conquerors" for a considerable time.[119] That the Muslims are referred to as "conquerors," whereas earlier Hindu or Buddhist rulers—despite their varied origins—are seen as indigenous to Kashmir completely erases Muslim belonging to the territory. The only deserving Muslim historical figure was Sultan Zainul-ab-din, who was often compared to the Mughal emperor Akbar for his "tolerance" and ruled Kashmir in the early part of the fifteenth century as part of the Shahmiri dynasty.[120] Zainul-ab-din was positioned against Sultan Sikander, who—like Mughal emperor Aurangzeb—was depicted as an iconoclast and a Muslim fanatic, a charge that Khalid Bashir contests in his study.[121]

Tourist discourses also privileged Kashmiri Pandit belonging to the Valley. The draft script for a Movie Makers documentary on Kashmir positions the Kashmiri Pandit community as the "very first Arians to have settled in the Valley but the many invasions have reduced them into a minority. . . . The conversion of these Arians has had many aspects, from peaceful preached Islamism to the forcible ways of invaders who also destroyed their ancient temples."[122] These narratives replicated colonial and Dogra discourses that, as Kabir argues, "privileged Kashmir not merely as a Hindu enclave within a Muslim population but in retrospect rather shamefully as a pure Brahmin Hindu enclave," dismissing its Muslim masses "as latter-day interlopers."[123] This led to a "fervent linking of Kashmir's Pandit culture to Kashmir's pre-Islamic heritage."[124]

As mentioned earlier, the holiday films featured only two simple Kashmiri Muslim characters, contributing to an erasure of Muslims overall and propagating ideas of eternal Hindu belonging in Kashmir and racist narratives of Hindu superiority over Muslims in terms of intelligence. Other characters donned a "Muslim" identity for comedic relief, including wearing the *burkha* or dressing up as an elderly *hakeem* to get close to the heroine. Aside from perfunctory Arabic idioms and references to Urdu poetry, according to Gaur, "the traces of Muslim religiosity and culture are obliterated from the representations of Kashmir, while portraying it as a place which is fundamental to the imagination of Hindu pasts, and central to the question of origins and belonging in India."[125]

After situating the ancient and medieval history of Kashmir, the guidebooks also addressed Kashmir's contemporary history: the people's demand for a more democratic administration before 1947, Kashmir's accession to India, and developments that had occurred in the state since 1947. One guidebook simplistically stated, "In October 1947, Kashmir acceded to India and since then has registered an all-around improvement in education, health and economic well-being of people," while others focused on the "tribal raid" from Pakistan and India's role in "saving Kashmir."[126] There was no reference to the contested nature of Kashmir's sovereignty, as well as the demand for a plebiscite to determine the future of the region (not to mention the events in Jammu). The history of Kashmir—from antiquity to the present—was depicted as being teleologically in favor of India, and the transition from the Dogras to the Indian nation-state was naturalized as seamless.

Tourism discourses also relied on the pilgrimage to Amarnath as central to promoting Kashmir's sacred Hindu geographies. One guidebook declared, "Kashmir is a holy land, the ultimate pilgrimage for the Hindu pilgrims in the north of Hindustan. . . . Compared to this homeland, Banaras [regarded as the spiritual capital for Hindus because it is on the Ganges river] stands as a molehill before a mountain."[127] Many of the guidebooks had a special section dedicated to the Amarnath Pilgrimage, while Karan Singh, the sadar-i-riyasat of the state, wrote an entire guidebook entitled *Pilgrimage to Shree Amarnath Kashmir*, where he describes his own pilgrimage in detail, including the relevance of various mountains, lakes, and glaciers for Hindu sacred geography and his feeling of awe about the thousands of great intellects of India who had traversed the same journey.[128]

Although the origins of the cave and the pilgrimage remain contested, the Dogras provided state patronage for the pilgrimage. It took on renewed significance when Indian tourism to Kashmir increased after 1953 and the pilgrimage became popularized.[129] Every year, thousands of devotees made the fourteen-thousand-foot trek to the cave of Amarnath, where they worshipped at the self-formed icy lingam (that waxed and waned), believed to be an embodiment of the Hindu deity Shiva, as well as at three blocks of ice representing the Hindu deities of Shiva, Parvati, and Genesha. Most pilgrims reached the cave during Raksha Bandhan every year, an auspicious day when the lingam was supposed to be at its largest. Amarnath was believed to be the place where Shiva told Parvati the secret of life and eternity and the Himalayas were constructed as the "dwelling place of Hindu gods," according to mythology.[130]

The Kashmir government provided accommodations, supplies, and transport for the pilgrims' journey, including for those who started by foot from Srinagar. Most pilgrims would start from Pahalgam, where hotels, tents, and huts were available, and then travel by foot or horseback.[131] British newsreels in this period regularly covered the annual Amarnath pilgrimage and showed video footage of how difficult the journey was for those who came from the hot plains of India to a "bitter cold they have never known."[132] Kashmiri porters carried Indian pilgrims for part or most of the difficult journey, which included a portion where they had to walk on ice. There were a number of Hindu holy men, or sadhus, along the route who would encourage the pilgrims to continue their journey, and doctors were present as well for those who fell ill. The icy waters along the route were considered sacred, having been sent from Shiva for their physical and spiritual cleansing powers, once more furthering the connections between Kashmir's rivers and Hindu sacred geography. Karan Singh describes how he felt his body and mind were "made pure and free from the tentacles of desire, and fear, ego and attachment [to] concentrate upon the unalloyed purity of nature and thereby perhaps achieve spiritual illumination."[133] At the cave, pilgrims could cleanse themselves of their mortal sins and begin their life anew. The pilgrimage was depicted as being too difficult for the average European, but for Hindus, it seemed to "draw upon sources of spiritual strength."[134] That the Amarnath pilgrimage was so physically challenging only heightened its appeal and importance for the Hindu faithful across India.

The journey to Amarnath was also featured in a number of Indian films. The 1954 film *Amar*, directed by Mehboob Khan depicts the main character's journey to the cave in search of redemption after committing a heinous crime.[135] In *Jab Jab Phool Khile,* the Indian tourists are told that "a visit to Kashmir without Amarnath is like going to the Ganges and not taking the holy dip." And so Rita and Raja, as well as the remainder of the party, go to Amarnath. Raja (the Kashmiri Muslim character) tells Rita that he prayed in Amarnath last year and that if two drops of water land on one's face, one's prayer will come true. Kishore, Rita's friend and potential fiancé, declares that he doesn't believe in these superstitions. Here, again, the Kashmiri Muslim character is meant to represent the true, authentic Indian civilization, one who remains committed to Kashmir's Hindu sacred geographies, as the modern Indian tourist from the metropole remains aloof.

Although studies have looked into the intensification of the Hindu nationalist rhetoric around the Amarnath pilgrimage after 1990, I suggest here that the larger infrastructure of religious tourism that served India's Hindu-nationalist state-building agenda in Kashmir had already commenced under Bakshi. The Kashmir government utilized vibrant images and religious symbolism to encourage Hindu pilgrims to visit Kashmir. With a growing stream of religious pilgrims visiting Amarnath every year, Kashmir was constructed not simply as a site of desire for middle-class Indian tourists but also as a site of religious attachment for Indian Hindus and integral to Hindu sacred geographies. This in turn strengthened nationalist claims and desires over Kashmir. Other articles recommending the Kashmir government explore the full possibilities of breaking new ground for tourism by examining other important archeological sites also reveal the importance of deploying archeological and religious sites as a tool of legitimation for Indian settler-colonial claims to Kashmir.

Perhaps no scene in the holiday films can best represent the ultimate purpose of Indian tourism to Kashmir than a scene in the beginning of the film

Janwar. The character Chintu, Shammi Kapoor's comedic friend played by Rajendra Nath, is depicted as being keenly interested in *rashtriya sadhbhavna*, or national integration. He declares that he wishes to marry a woman from another state as part of his attempt to promote this ideal. Later, on the train ride to Kashmir for a tennis tournament, he gleefully tells Shammi, "Now we are going to Kashmir! And in the little heaven my desire for *rashtriya sadhbhavna* will be complete." His exclamation underscores the gendered, commoditized, and orientalized construction of the place and its people.

The Kashmir and Indian governments' emphasis on developing the tourist industry began to have its desired effect. A 1963 report published by the Indian government declared that one crore (ten million rupees) had been spent on the promotion of tourism in Kashmir.[136] In 1951, 9,330 tourists from India and 1,250 foreign tourists visited Kashmir. By 1960, the numbers jumped to 63,370 and 11,190 respectively.[137] Most of the foreign tourists were from the United States, the United Kingdom, Germany, and Australia, but Kashmir certainly became *the* tourist destination for Indians.[138] For Bakshi, the returns were manifold. Both the tourist industry as well as Indian cinema were meant to create affective ties that would shape the sentiment of the Indian public toward Kashmir and encourage greater Indian state investment in Kashmir. By projecting Kashmir as a "modern playground," Indians would be able to see that their country's financial and other investments in Kashmir were materializing.

Yet, for the Indian state too, tourism to Kashmir contributed to the building and maintenance of Indian colonial rule. Tourism to Kashmir was not simply for enjoyment and leisure; it determined the fate of individuals and communities and had the power to interpret or invent cultural meanings of the self and the "other." In this sense, tourism was a form of governmentality. The development of tourism was directly linked to Indian nationalist desires for Kashmir as a place that was, in its pure essence, what India could be. Yet, paradoxically, Kashmir was also a place that needed India for it to prosper. What is most compelling of the promotion of tourism is that it revealed the one space where there was commensurability between the Kashmir government and the Indian state. The Kashmir government played a role in re-territorializing Kashmir as a resort for the Indian tourist, in turn promoting and acquiescing to India's colonial gaze, while also profiting from the tourist industry.

Much of the tourist industry revolved around the Muslim-majority Kashmir Valley; Ladakh and Jammu were not "exploited" to the extent the Valley was, although both had their own tourist potential. The Valley, in particular, was "not merely the symbolic space for the articulation of Indianness but a space wherein the slippages between Indian and Hindu are all the more emphatic and out of place."[139] Thus, through tourism and the film industry, the convergence of both secular and Hindu nationalism is evident, and the centrality of Hindu sacred geographies to Indian secularism becomes more apparent. This chapter has showcased the importance of spatial politics to the survival of colonial rule. If accession and Article 370 allowed India to justify its political rule over Kashmir, then tourism and cinema allowed India and Indians to maintain Kashmir as a place of their own.

Chapter 4

DEVELOPING DEPENDENCY

Economic Planning, Financial Integration, and Corruption

On August 9, 1953, a day after Sheikh Abdullah's arrest, Bakshi Ghulam Mohammad broadcast a policy speech on Radio Kashmir.[1] He accused Abdullah of threatening to disintegrate Kashmir and make it a pawn in international power politics, foregrounding the economic reasons that led to Abdullah's arrest. He detailed the economic crisis the state faced, especially the pitiable state of the peasants taxed for their goods. He declared that the "key to the present crisis lies in the deep-rooted economic discontent of the masses of the state. This crisis cannot be overcome by the termination of the state's association with India or by merger . . . with Pakistan," and he argued against depending on "foreign charity."[2] He affirmed his government's pledge to "build anew the economic and social life of the people of the state in accordance with [our] genius traditions and resources, with the help of and in partnership with the people of India and those other states who are friendly towards us."[3]

The largest problem confronting his administration was not political nor military but was "the economic distress which has been on the increase since 1947 and is today at its worst."[4] He emphasized that Kashmir would benefit from its economic ties with India because of an "urgent need to pay attention to the economic reconstruction of the state."[5] Making reference to the progressive economic policies of the Indian state in comparison to the feudal landlordism that had overtaken Pakistan, Bakshi reasoned, "Can there be a better position of security or more honorable status for a small state with its poor resources, backward economy and complex geographical situation?"[6]

Bakshi praised the Government of India for providing income and employment to a larger number of people and also taking over key offices such as communications and national highways, while allowing the Kashmir government to "secure an autonomy in our economic policy which is unknown in any federal state."[7] India, he argued, didn't impose financial integration; it was for the Kashmir state "to decide in our own interests whether, how and when the customs duties would be abolished." He thanked the Government of India for providing the state with loans, especially during the Emergency Administration from 1947 to 1948, financial aid to balance the budget, and grants from the national five-year plan in community development projects.

Bakshi reiterated that Abdullah's economic policies had caused violent dislocations, unemployment, economic maladjustments, and a heavy fall in living standards, shaking confidence in the competence of the government to solve economic problems. In his speech, he listed a series of economic policies relating to rural development, agriculture, infrastructure, and industry, reassuring people that his government was committed to the ideals of the Naya Kashmir manifesto.[8] Blaming the previous government, members of the new state legislature also made reference to the manifesto, declaring that under Abdullah's government, "the New Kashmir programme [had] remained confined to paper plans only."[9] It was now the task of Bakshi's government to implement its vision, to finally produce the new Kashmir and "uplift the lot of our unfortunately backward countrymen and enable them to realize their ideas and aspirations."[10]

In addition to establishing legitimacy, the new government had an even greater task at hand: determining the contours of the state's financial relationship with the Government of India and collecting funds to promote economic development. Bakshi's government had to set itself as more economically progressive than the governments of its predecessors—those of Sheikh Abdullah and the Dogras—and fulfill the promises of economic transformation made during his radio address after Abdullah's arrest. As this chapter demonstrates, even Abdullah's government had certain political compulsions when pursuing particular development policies; his were to gain greater support for the National Conference and societal approval of Kashmir's accession to India. However, Abdullah was not interested in increased financial, legal, and economic integration with the Government of India, preferring Kashmir to have greater autonomy.

Bakshi was also concerned about the finality of the accession as well as securing the position of his government. Yet, Bakshi departed from his predecessor most explicitly in creating greater economic ties between the Government of India and the Kashmir government. Bakshi saw financial integration with the Government of India as imperative to addressing Kashmir's economic concerns, which, if increased, would cause greater political upheaval than what had existed at the time of Abdullah's arrest and would further undermine the accession. As a result, to create economic betterment for Kashmir's peasants, workers, and artisans, Bakshi reframed the discussion surrounding economic development. The radio address was an important discursive shift; the problem of Kashmir became one of economic miseries instead of its future political status between India and Pakistan. Bakshi centered economic development as a panacea to overcome the state's political problems and also deployed the politics of life as a reason for the state to merge with India. In this chapter, I use the term *developmentalism* to describe this strategy of combining economic development with the establishment of political legitimacy.

Development discourse enhances state power and capacity. While states may have varying intended outcomes, the economic logic of developmentalism lies in its ability to demand state intervention and international assistance. Drawing from James Ferguson's theorization of development as "anti-politics," whereby political realities are whisked out of sight "all the while performing, almost unnoticed . . . [the] pre-eminently political operation of expanding bureaucratic state power," I detail the economic policies of the new government, as it navigated Kashmir's fraught political context while addressing people's economic concerns and demands for a better standard of living.[11] Economic planning was not just a means to usher in an era of modernization but a modality of control used to manage a restive population—to bring forth a new Kashmir incorporated into the larger economic body of the Indian nation. Bakshi became the "architect of modern Kashmir"; indeed, as we will see in this chapter, Kashmir entered a "golden age" of large-scale modernization, including agricultural reform, infrastructural growth, and increased employment opportunities. These developments resulted from a complete renegotiation of Kashmir's financial relationship with the Government of India. The Kashmir government placed certain fiscal demands on the Indian state; yet, this renegotiation came at a cost. Kashmir's political status engendered a form of developmentalism focusing more on meeting short-term strategic interests than on long-term economic growth and diametrically opposite to the strategy of the Government of India elsewhere. This strategy was ultimately detrimental to the Naya Kashmir manifesto's economic goal of self-sufficiency, further entrenching India's colonial occupation.

The Political Compulsions of Development

Modern governments have grounded their legitimacy on their ability to enact and implement development schemes. A limited number of studies on the history of economic development in Kashmir have located economic causes for the militancy of the 1980s, particularly economic development measures taken by the post-1947 governments.[12] Siddhartha Prakash argues that state interventions in agriculture and industry were constantly subjected to the pressures and pulls of various interest groups, so that policies conceived to benefit the broader society were often implemented by a small group of the population for their own benefit.[13] As this group began to get richer at the expense of the poor, "militancy and the dream of an independent state began to have its own appeal."[14] Sumit Ganguly contends that modernization in the context of Kashmir was uneven; while economic development certainly occurred and introduced Kashmir to possibilities of alternative futures, the political process choked off such possibilities because economic development and political mobilization didn't go hand in hand.[15] Ganguly's account shows how the *lack* of political freedom undermined economic development. Prakash's account argues that a particular type of economic development occurred in Kashmir, one in which the bureaucratic and elite classes benefitted, while others did not. Ganguly's analysis does not take into account that economic development in Kashmir *was* political—it was not just that the lack of political mobilization undermined economic development, but rather, developmentalist policies were already constrained as a result of India's colonial occupation, as the Kashmir government promoted short-term economic interests over long-term economic growth. While Prakash accounts for the shortsightedness of the Kashmir government, his analysis simply portrays the government as a set of corrupt bureaucratic and elite actors attempting to benefit themselves and various interest groups at the expense of the poor.

He does not attempt to explain the political context as to why the Kashmir government resorted to these policies. Indeed, what he labels as "economic mismanagement and political nepotism," was intentional.[16] What is missing from both accounts is any understanding of or engagement with the nature of the economic relationship between India and Kashmir, what it sought to achieve, and how economic planning became a mode of control. Furthermore, both accounts fail to consider how economic state-building policies consolidated India's colonial occupation of Kashmir.

More recent work by anthropologist Mona Bhan examines the construction of dams in the border town of Gurez, positioning it as a "corporate arm of India's occupation" that seeks to "bring Kashmiris into the fold of capitalist modernity while assimilating them into India's productive work culture."[17] Building from Bhan's work, this chapter provides a longer history of how "Kashmiri political aspirations for freedom" were deflected through economic development, financial integration, and corruption.

Economic Challenges under Sheikh Abdullah

Developmentalism in post-1947 Kashmir occurred in the broader context of decolonization and Cold War politics. Because of the perceived successes of Soviet-style planning, the ideology of state-led modernization captured the imagination of political elites throughout the Third World, including South Asia.[18] Kashmiri political elites, including both Sheikh Abdullah and Bakshi, influenced by leftists and communists in the subcontinent, were undoubtedly swept up in this fervor, and as participants in the drafting of the National Conference's Naya Kashmir manifesto in 1944, relied heavily on Soviet-style economic policy planning. Having witnessed the economic marginalization of Kashmiris under the Dogras, the National Conference leadership viewed the state as imbued with the political will and power to transform the lives of its citizens. Political discourses also depicted the idea that economic development could bring various communities closer to each other.[19]

The manifesto envisioned a National Economic Plan seeking first, to achieve national self-sufficiency and second, to raise the standard of living for men and women in society. The planned economy of the state was to provide work for all adult able-bodied citizens.[20] The manifesto gave a detailed account of what a higher standard of living would entail, including better nutrition and more clothing, housing, water, lighting, education, provision of food stores, insurance, banking, medical aid, recreation, and affordable transportation.[21] Because the people of the state primarily relied upon agriculture, economic reform revolved around the abolition of landlordism, distribution of land to the tiller, and establishment of cooperative associations, where the sale of crops and produce would be regulated. The plan also mentioned that exports of food would be prohibited until "the needs of the state have been provided for, both immediate needs and the needs of a healthy reserve."[22] The state was to achieve self-sufficiency in foodstuffs and crops. The plan called for the people's control of forests, to ensure that the people of a locality derived the "fullest benefit from forest land."[23] Technological advancements were to help in improving the quality and quantity of crops produced, in addition to introducing modern methods of animal husbandry, dairy farming, fruit cultivation, and beekeeping. The plan also included a peasants charter abolishing forced labor, debt, and levies and promising the benefit of modern scientific research.

Another economic aim of the Naya Kashmir manifesto was the development of industry. The plan abolished big private capitalism and private monopolies and declared that all industries would be owned by the state except for those small-scale enterprises in conformity with the National Plan.[24] Industries to develop in the state included hydroelectric power, mining, transportation, textiles, furniture, medicines, and paper, as well as handicrafts and cottage industries, including wool, silk, wood, papier-mâché, rugs, embroidery, metalwork, and honey and saffron cultivation.[25] A workers charter protected the right to participate in trade unions, eight-hour workdays, weekly wages, leave, pensions, and the right to recreation.[26] Although the manifesto was written in the waning years of Dogra rule, it called for a strong planned economy in a sovereign state that the National Conference would lead, one that would aim to protect the rights and standard of living of workers and peasants, protect and promote the state's resources for its own benefit, and most importantly, achieve national self-sufficiency.

Following the partition of the subcontinent and the contested accession of Kashmir to India, Kashmir's economy faced serious challenges, and the Naya Kashmir manifesto had to adjust to new political and economic circumstances. Prior to 1947, Kashmir's economy was intrinsically linked to the area in Punjab that became a part of Pakistan. The rivers connecting the two regions provided transportation for timber, while the roads carried fruit, vegetables, carpets, and handicrafts.[27] Partition disrupted trade in 1947, and new avenues for Kashmiri exports had to be created. Peasants, nearly 90 percent of Kashmir's population, also suffered from a feudal system of agriculture with levies and heavy taxation, which was the primary source of revenue for the Dogras.[28] Sheikh Abdullah's government took a few steps toward reconstructing the economy, made difficult by the division of the territory, local resistance to the accession, refugee rehabilitation, and political problems in Jammu, where the right-wing Praja Parishad was contesting the state's autonomy and seeking greater integration with India. Given that political stability in the region depended on the sentiments of the restive peasantry and because it wanted to execute one of the major components of the Naya Kashmir manifesto, the government implemented land reform. In 1948, the Kashmir government abolished jagirs, *muafis*, and *mukarari* lands, except those granted to some religious institutions.[29] The Big Landed Estates Abolition Act followed in 1950, intended to end landlordism and give the land to the tiller.[30] The amount of land that each proprietor could hold was limited to 22 ¾ acres (equivalent to 182 *canals*). As a result of this act, "4.5 lakh acres of land held in excess of 22.75 acres . . . excluding orchards were expropriated from as many as 9,000 and odd land owners, and out of this ownership rights of over 2.31 lakh acres of land were transferred to cultivating peasants."[31] Kashmir became the only state in the subcontinent where such sweeping land reforms occurred without any compensation to the landlord.

Nevertheless, a number of scholars have noted that the reforms were not as far-reaching as is understood.[32] For one thing, the same bureaucracy that existed under the Dogra period was in charge of its implementation, leading to allegations of corruption and favoritism. Landowners also exploited loopholes in the law.[33] Well-off families with a significant amount of land split up their joint families so that the land was divided among multiple family members. Moreover, because orchards and fuel and fodder resources were exempt from the reform, a number of landowners converted their land into these exemptions. Some peasants also received land that was not productive.[34] As Daniel Thorner observed in 1953, the reforms benefitted those at the village level who were already important; they did very little for petty tenants and landless laborers. As a result, new forms of rural hierarchies, or neolandlordism, came into being.[35] Furthermore, Javeed ul Aziz and others have noted that the land reforms antagonized a number of Hindus both in the Kashmir Valley and in Jammu who were among the primary beneficiaries of the feudal system under the Dogras. In some quarters, the land reforms were seen as "communal" because they benefitted a largely Muslim peasantry. This sentiment led to the popularity of groups such as the Praja Parishad.

Nonetheless, the political benefits of land reform were more far-reaching than the logistics of its actual implementation. Beginning in the last few years of Dogra rule when the National Conference faced opposition from the Muslim Conference and up until the years of Sheikh Abdullah's government, the party needed support to fight against the Dogras and later, accede to India. Land reforms resulted in strengthening the political and social base of the National Conference and Sheikh Abdullah, especially in rural areas.

In 1950, the state had one of the lowest per capita incomes and consumption levels in the subcontinent.[36] Despite this, keeping with the manifesto's call for self-sufficiency, Abdullah determined to keep Kashmir financially independent from the Government of India by broadening the tax base of the state instead of depending on external assistance. With no imports allowed, food prices rose and the cost of living became high. A system called *mujawaza*, begun under the Dogras, also forced peasants to give a large percentage of their paddy to the state.

In 1950, members of Abdullah's cabinet who were more open to greater financial integration with India, including the finance minister, G. L. Dogra, began a series of conversations with Indian officials to mitigate the economic crisis in the state. Dogra was concerned that "circles in the Government of India did not appear very much keen for the integration. . . . I found that they were rather hesitating and this was perhaps due to the fact that the center will be a losing party if the integration takes place."[37] Dogra argued that greater financial integration would significantly lower the costs of the Kashmir government's expenses—as those areas would be taken over by the Indian government. This included the expenses for the local militia, which he argued was engaged in national defense and not local policing, so these costs should be borne by the Indian government. Dogra knew that financial integration would not be in the Indian government's best interests but suggested that there were political angles to consider.

Customs duties, the primary source of revenue for the government and a burden for the average consumer, became a primary point of contention in these discussions. Integration would abolish customs duties, yet Kashmir officials were concerned they would lose their primary source of revenue. While the Government of India argued that this revenue could be met by a sales tax, as with Indian states, Kashmir officials—including Bakshi—argued that the sales tax would not yield even a quarter of the income derived from customs and that the Indian government "must agree to subsidize on a permanent basis and for all times to come the revenues of the state at least to the extent of the customs duty regardless of what new taxes may or may not be introduced in the state later on."[38] Responses from various Indian finance officials suggested that this step would alienate other part B states like Hyderabad and Rajasthan, which were similarly deprived of the revenues from custom duties but were told to raise their revenue through other taxes.[39] Indian officials feared that it would lead to "demands being made by other part B states for a modification of their respective financial integration agreements in a manner more advantageous to them" and would result in discontent. They also complained that while the Government of India incurred large amounts of expenditure in relation to the state, "the state does not make any contribution at all to the central exchequer."[40] From the perspective of Indian finance officials, there was "not much advantage to Government of India entering into a complete federal financial integration arrangement with Jammu and Kashmir—but if it happens—worthwhile for us on wider grounds and as a term of a comprehensive settlement of all outstanding issues to accept a financial arrangement which is on lines uniform with that entered into with the other part B states even if taken by itself it may appear to be financially disadvantageous."[41]

From these discussions, it appears that while key members of Abdullah's cabinet, including Dogra, Sadiq, and Bakshi, pushed for greater financial integration, Indian officials were less than enthused. Meanwhile, Sheikh Abdullah and Mirza Afzal Beg resisted the attempt because it entailed a loss of autonomy, and a final settlement between the state and the Government of India had not yet occurred. Other disagreements arose over the different expenditures the Government of India would be responsible for in a future financial integration; the Indian government resisted paying for the militia, arguing it was a "police" force and not defense force and thus was under the purview of the Kashmir government. The Kashmir government also wanted all the loans provided for development under the category "Aid to Kashmir" forgiven and future loans to be given as grants-in-aid. Kashmir officials also wanted the Indian Finance Commission to be excluded from dealing with the Kashmir government and wanted to deal only with the Ministry of Home. The Ministry of Finance responded that there would be no compensation for the loss of revenue from the customs tax, no support to the Kashmir militia, no writing off of loans, and no exclusion of the Indian Financial Commission as it pertained to Kashmir. All requests were denied.

As a result of these outstanding issues, there would be no agreement on financial integration during Abdullah's rule. Yet, what is clear from these conversations is that various officials of the Kashmir government—those who would come to power once Bakshi became prime minister—were the primary party seeking greater financial integration for practical purposes. Indian officials were either ambivalent or opposed to greater integration since it was seen as having very little financial benefit for India.

Toward Financial Integration

There are continuities in the development policies between Bakshi's and Abdullah's governments, particularly in conceptualizing post-Dogra Kashmir as being in need of economic development and desiring empowerment for the rural masses. However, Bakshi saw the 1953 arrest as a critical turning point in determining the future political and economic stability of Kashmir. His economic vision for the state differed from Abdullah's in that he viewed economic and financial integration with India as the only means to promote the overall aims of the Naya Kashmir manifesto, a position that would later emerge as contradictory. In other words, he was willing to compromise on the primary aim of "national self-sufficiency" to achieve the secondary aim of a higher standard of living for the people of the state. As a result, he pursued a number of policies distinct from his predecessor, and this became central to his government's self-fashioning.

The intrigues surrounding Abdullah's arrest and the subsequent protests were covered in previous chapters, but one of the important points to foreground here is that members of the new government saw progressive economic development as a means to secure support from people in the state to remain with India. Indian intelligence reports described a staggering economic situation in both the Kashmir Valley and Jammu in the waning years of Sheikh Abdullah's government. These reports described the "worst possible life, a life of affliction and suffering; a life of poverty and want; a life of utter helplessness and oppression. . . . Everywhere you will hear people talk of hunger and starvation." And they carried accounts of the rampant corruption of government bureaucrats. One intelligence report declared that "not even 1 percent people are happy or contented."[42] While customs duties on luxury items decreased, they remained high for essential items such as salt and medicines.

Iffat Malik argues, "Both Bakshi and the Indian government realized that . . . the only way the people of Kashmir could be kept under control and convinced of the merits of closer ties with India was to provide the region with economic prosperity."[43] This underlying compulsion informed both governments' economic policies and resulted in a shift in the minds of Indian officials from Abdullah's tenure. They now understood the importance of economic aid to ensure the permanence of Kashmir's accession to India. Given the local outcry after Abdullah's arrest, members of the new government understood that its legitimacy was in question, especially after the contested accession. The government soon realized that earning the loyalty of the population required immediate measures ameliorating the economic conditions, especially among the rural masses. If it failed, the situation was sure to deteriorate out of the Indian and Kashmir governments' control. Shifting the discourse from political grievances to exclusively economic ones and articulating an ambitious economic plan would enable the new government to not only implement the Naya Kashmir manifesto but also assert its authority.

Yet, it was clear that large-scale modernization and development required substantial funding. Abdullah attempted to maintain a degree of financial autonomy for the Kashmir state, which meant that the government had to establish a variety of taxes and duties in order to broaden its revenue base to meet expenditures. His government's first year of the five-year plan was barely implemented because of a lack of financial resources and the technical infeasibility of the projects. Bakshi was well aware that increased taxation was one of the primary reasons for public discontent under Abdullah. In contrast, he aggressively sought financial aid from the Government of India for the state to proceed with its development initiatives.

First, Bakshi informed the Government of India that "he would like Kashmir to integrate with India without the name of financial integration being used too much," perhaps knowing the local and international political consequences that would have.[44] He continued that the center should assume direct responsibility for income tax and central excise taxes on items such as tobacco, as well as administrative departments such as the postal service, telephones, telegraphs, radio, broadcasting, and national highways. He argued that the state was surrendering its sovereign right in abolishing customs duties and stated that Kashmir could not be compared to other financially integrated states, as it had a "unique position constitutionally but also industrially." He declared that the center must meet the deficit in the budget caused by the abolishment of customs duties, arguing that the alternative, to impose a sales tax, would cause further political instability. He also argued that because the central government was taking over the national highways, the levy tolls would have to be abolished—and the center should cover this loss, too. To cover the gap, he negotiated a deal in which the Government of India would allocate an additional 250 lakh rupees to the state annually, a proposal the Government of India had previously rejected.[45] Once they agreed, on April 13, 1954, Bakshi abolished the customs duties.

Calling Kashmir a "border state," Bakshi argued that the 60 lakhs currently spent on the militia also be taken over by the Indian government. The loans previously given to the state under the Aid to Kashmir account, which was related to matters that the central government had jurisdiction over, should be forgiven. He suggested all discussions regarding future grants-in-aid should be discussed between the two governments and not by the Indian Finance

Commission because political factors should be considered. Because of the "special circumstance" in which the state was placed, he requested that the Government of India provide grants-in-aid, not loans, for various development projects, as the interests on the loans caused great strain on the state's budget.

Despite the Indian government previously declaring a uniformity of treatment among all states in the matter of grants-in-aid and other forms of financial assistance, it approved all Bakshi's terms. In turn, the Indian government insisted that the state accept the extension of the auditor general of India as well as the authority of the Indian Supreme Court over Kashmir, a bargain Bakshi was all too eager to make but one that would significantly constrain Kashmir's autonomy. Once financial integration officially began under Articles 278 and 295 of the Indian constitution on May 14, 1954, other related laws began to apply to Kashmir, since having separate laws for items like capital taxes, foreign exchange, and insurance would cause "unnecessary confusion and hardship." The net recurring burden on central revenue as a result of financial integration was 2.5–3 crore rupees per year. The Kashmir government had access to financial assistance on varying central schemes pertaining to commerce and industry, food and agriculture, and education and health as a result of the new financial arrangement.

The Kashmir government estimated that between 1951 and 1956, it received a total of Rs. 1274.15 lakhs in financial assistance from the Government of India; in 1956–1961, it received Rs. 3392.07 lakhs; and in 1961–1965, it received Rs. 7514.00 lakhs.[46] This amount did not include funds spent on centrally operated and sponsored schemes like the national highway, telegraphs and telephones, broadcasting, regional engineering and medical colleges, tunnels, and regional research laboratories.

In its first iteration, the Indian Planning Commission advanced a loan of $14.9 million to the state in December 1953.[47] As Siddharth Prakash details, starting in the 1950s, the center funded nearly 90 percent of the state's five-year plans, while "backward" states such as Bihar received 70 percent.[48] In addition, during the five-year period between 1957 and 1962, Kashmir received the highest per capital grant-in-aid—Rs. 41.7— almost seven times the average (Rs. 6) of Indian states.[49] At the start of the third five-year plan, the proposed per capita outlay was also the highest among all the states, averaging Rs. 91 against

Rs. 141 in Kashmir.[50] The government also received special grants in the form of food subsidies as well as additional central assistance for the development of border areas, state police, additional battalions, and border check posts. Furthermore, "central aid has formed an important part of the revenues of the state . . . indicated by the fact that grants-in-aid contributed 30.7 percent of the State's revenues against 10 percent for all states."[51] Even as the total cash loans from the central government increased during Bakshi's rule, "neither the principal nor the regular interest was typically paid," effectively making them grants-in-aid.[52] In sum, the Kashmir government received far more grants-in-aid than Indian states, giving it less liability than those receiving more loans.[53] Furthermore, "Kashmir's share in the divisible pool of central taxes also increased, even though it was the least-taxed state in India."[54] Clearly, Kashmir was treated as a unique case in the broader context of economic planning in India.

When the overreliance on Indian government funding caused tension within the Kashmir legislative assembly, Bakshi defended his government's position unambiguously and unapologetically: "We have been receiving aid from India from the very beginning and are receiving it today and shall continue to receive it as long as the conditions make it necessary."[55] He argued that accepting Indian aid meant the Kashmiri government did not have to increase taxes, which would be sure to cause strong resistance and create further political instability.[56] He defended the acceptance of Indian aid by stating that Sheikh Abdullah's government had also taken aid from the Government of India to make up for the deficit, while his administration was using it exclusively for development. Reframing the patron-client relationship, he argued that his government was not taking loans from a foreign government and that "India is our own country. . . . Opponents don't see it as that," likening India to a more prosperous older brother from whom a younger brother (Kashmir) was seeking help.[57] On another occasion, he noted that because the state had limited resources at its disposal, "it would have been impossible for [us] to undertake huge projects if the central government had not allocated generous funds to the state for its various schemes and programs."[58] In other words, if Kashmir had not acceded to India and accepted Indian government money for its economic projects, Bakshi argued, its economic and political situation would have remained volatile. Nonetheless, Bakshi managed to use the threat of political instability shrewdly (and successfully) to make a set of demands on the Indian state. By abolishing taxes, removing customs duties, and accepting Indian funding for development projects, Bakshi departed from the policies of his predecessor and not only further integrated Kashmir economically to India but also created greater economic dependence on the Indian state, thus entrenching the colonial occupation.

While we know that the Government of India increased its spending in Kashmir under Bakshi, it is difficult to ascertain the extent to which the Government of India was implicated in directing the actual course of development planning because of the restrictions on access to files on Kashmir in the National Archives of India. As with Indian states, the Government of India would provide a series of economic schemes that state governments were expected to implement. From the Srinagar State Archives, however, it is clear that a number of schemes were drawn up locally, in light of local concerns, while others were implemented upon the request of various ministries in the Government of India. Nonetheless, discourses of the Nehruvian state's socialist planning clearly influenced local officials, who were often sent on trainings to India and elsewhere on particular economic concerns. What were the new government's economic plans? Who were they targeted toward, and why? How were they similar to or different from states in India or even from Pakistan? And how do we understand their impact? It is to these questions we now turn.

The Developmental State: Agriculture, Industry, and Infrastructure

Overall, the Bakshi government oversaw either the creation or implementation of three five-year plans intended to address the economic crisis within the state and improve the well-being of the population. Bakshi revitalized the entire bureaucracy to implement the development goals in the first five-year plan, which began in the last year of Sheikh Abdullah's administration (1952) but had made little progress due to limited funding. Accusing Abdullah of not consulting with the broader public, Bakshi went on to appoint a series of committees to analyze the inefficiencies in policies surrounding food, industry, land reform, employment, and cooperatives, among other issues, and determine a new course of action.[59] Intimate knowledge about the economic needs of the population made specific policies possible.

Agriculture was the mainstay of the Kashmir economy. Nearly 90 percent of the population depended on it.[60] The government prioritized agricultural reform over industrial development for two reasons: first, because of the political need to appeal to the large peasantry, and second, because of the economic conditions in the state that prevailed under the Dogras. The state's constitution gave special attention to "organize and develop agriculture and animal husbandry by bringing to the aid of the cultivator the benefits of modern and scientific research and techniques so as to ensure a speedy improvement in the standard of living as also the prosperity of the rural masses."[61]

Informed by the findings of the Wazir Committee, a damning account of Sheikh Abdullah's economic policies, the new government went beyond the previous administration in executing agricultural reform. Within just a few days of taking power, Bakshi's government gave the Wazir report new life. Because it detailed the economic grievances of the peasantry, the new government was able to use it to develop policies that would ameliorate these grievances. Two crucial new policies were implemented: the abolishment of *mujawaza,* a compulsory procurement of nearly a quarter of food grains from peasants by (often corrupt) officials, and the subsidization of rice and wheat.

Since the state was being subsidized with rice and wheat from the Government of India, *mujawaza* was no longer necessary. A peasant now had the option of selling his paddy to the government in the various centers around the state but was not required to do so. Restrictions on purchase of paddy or transporting it to other parts of the Kashmir Valley were also removed. Ration holders also increased by 25,000.[62] The abolishment of *mujawaza* lessened tensions between rural and urban dwellers.[63] In addition, land reform continued under Bakshi. By 1961, nearly 8 lakh acres of land had been transferred to tillers, as opposed to 4.5 lakhs under Abdullah. This meant that around 70,900 Muslim peasants in the Kashmir Valley and 25,000 lower-caste Hindus in Jammu became peasant proprietors.[64]

While the abolishment of *mujawaza* was aligned with the aims of the Naya Kashmir manifesto, the Kashmir government's reliance on agricultural subsidies from the Government of India was a more complicated affair, highlighting the ways the government prioritized short-term political gains over long-term development. Abdullah had encouraged Kashmiris to survive on a diet of potatoes (for which he earned the nickname "Aalobab," or father of potatoes) rather than relying on rice subsidies from India. Immediately after his arrest, the government received agricultural subsidies from the Government of India, drastically decreasing the price of rice and grains. It was estimated that rice subsidies under Abdullah were 19 lakh rupees; under Bakshi, the cost, met almost entirely by assistance from the Government of India, reached 150 lakh rupees per year.[65] As a result, in some areas, the price of rice went from 60–70 rupees per standard unit of measure (khirwar) to 8.[66] Immediately after Bakshi took power, the Government of India made an emergency allotment of seven lakh maunds of rice. Nearly nine hundred vehicles brought the rice from Pathankot to Srinagar.[67] This was, indeed, a critical step taken by the new government. For a peasantry that had suffered a severe shortage of grains in the 1920s, as well as increased prices under the black market during Abdullah's government, these subsidies were a welcome and immediate relief.[68] The price of rice and paddy was finally within the reach of the consumer's purchasing power. In contrast to Abdullah, Bakshi came to be known as "Battbab," or father of rice. Moreover, given the shortage of salt during Abdullah's time, the government also began to import salt, available for purchase without any restrictions.[69]

As with the funds for development, Bakshi managed to leverage the threat of political instability in the state to secure an ongoing and high amount of food aid.[70] For example, in 1956–1957, officials in the Ministry of Food were aghast that the Kashmir government would continue to request such high amounts, even as the production of rice was increasing within the state. They were willing to give 20,000 tons, not the 36,700 tons the Kashmir government requested. Indian government officials repeatedly requested that the Kashmir government increase the price for local procurement, so that there would be a decrease in the demand. At times, they suggested an increase in the price of the subsidized rice or a reduction in the amount of rice meant for one adult per day (from sixteen ounces to twelve). Bakshi protested, stating that the food supply remained perilous, especially after crops had been damaged by floods and hail storms. He also repeatedly stated that "the position of Jammu and Kashmir was materially different from other states. . . . There were other political factors. . . . The Government of India should not risk with the state as numerous political implications were involved in the distribution of rice at reduced prices."[71] He also refused to raise the price of rice because of upcoming elections. Bakshi would specify not only the amount, but the type of rice that Kashmiris preferred (an indigenous variety from Punjab), which the Government of India should try to obtain, arguing that opponents of the present government would start a whisper campaign that "India is selling inferior rice to Kashmiris." Eventually, the Ministry of Home wrote to the Ministry of Food and Agriculture, requesting it to take into consideration the "special circumstance" of the state. Additional tons of rice and paddy would subsequently be deployed.

In April 1957, Kashmir officials panicked that there were only a few weeks' worth of food grains. Bakshi insisted that the Indian government must expedite food supplies—requesting over 50,000 tons for the years 1957–1958—citing the negative impact of news reports in Pakistan about the food crisis in the state. Minister of Food and Agriculture Ajit Prasad Jain insisted that the Kashmir government cut down on its rice requirements, while Bakshi once more argued that "the food problem of our state should be viewed as part and parcel of the overall situation."[72] Despite food shortages, dependence on American food aid, and food riots in many parts of India, Nehru intervened, requesting the minister for food and agriculture to "do our best" to send something to Kashmir. He also recommended that instead of the rice being transported from the ports at Bombay or Calcutta, it should be bought by the Punjab government and then sent to Kashmir to reduce the long transportation time.

These examples highlight how integral the rice subsidization policy in Kashmir was to India's colonial occupation. Subsidization of rice and paddy in Kashmir was in sharp contrast to the Government of India's overall food policy, which suggests the need for the Government of India to maintain a different development strategy in Kashmir and also shows how Bakshi was able to leverage political instability in Kashmir to get the best deal for food aid for Kashmir—oftentimes to the sheer dismay of some Indian officials. The Government of India did not make emergency allotments of rice to any other state, although rice was partially subsidized in some other politically challenging states, including in the northeast state of Assam. In the years following independence, the Indian political leadership sought to transform India's eating habits, encouraging citizens to rely less on foreign food imports. Instead of the usual staples, Benjamin Siegel notes, "India's new citizens were asked to adopt 'substitute' and 'subsidiary' foods—including bananas, groundnuts, tapioca, yams, beets, and carrots—and give up a meal or more each week to conserve India's scant grain reserves."[73]

Furthermore, the Indian National Congress struggled to formulate a postcolonial nationalism with limited resources "because it was torn between using the state for development and urging the people to shape their own destiny outside of the state."[74] Unlike the discourse of "scarcity" in India, Bakshi's government utilized a narrative of "abundance" in Kashmir—integral to the politics of life. Consumption of rice and wheat was encouraged through the provision of subsidies, and as we have seen, Bakshi defended the fact that Kashmir was heavily dependent on external aid. In a reply to local critics, he asserted, "I consider it my foremost duty to feed the people well. It is no crime."[75] Since the new boundaries of postcolonial Indian citizenship relied upon values of "adversity, austerity, and sacrifice," it appeared that Kashmir under Bakshi was not to fit so easily into the model of postcolonial citizenship the Government of India had envisioned.[76] In direct contrast to Abdullah, Bakshi envisioned a political economy in which Kashmir would receive ongoing aid from the Government of India—as a result, his was a time of plenty. The provision of food subsidies and the narrative of "abundance" suggest the political compulsions of both the Government of India's and the Kashmir government's development policies. To get the most from the Indian government, all Bakshi had to do was to refer to the "political sensitivities" or compulsions he was subject to. The provision of aid and abundance *under India* was intended to remake sentiments *toward India* and provide legitimacy to Bakshi's government. If Kashmiris could see for themselves the real, tangible benefits of joining with India, they would be likely to consent to Indian rule. This is fundamentally how the politics of life operated. In subsequent years, the diets of Kashmiris, especially in the rural areas, began to change and rely heavily on rice. Rice became associated with a mark of social status, and the flood of rice into Kashmir during Bakshi's time remains one of his lasting legacies.

At the same time, the importation of food and grains contradicted the Naya Kashmir manifesto stipulating that the state should be able to feed its citizens. It appears that the Kashmir government did make some effort to achieve self-sufficiency in food, suggesting that the importation of agricultural subsidies was initially seen as a short-term political strategy to manage the unrest in the state after Sheikh Abdullah's arrest.[77] Bakshi was aware of the eventual need of the state to be able to feed its own people after the unrest died down—especially given its importance in the Naya Kashmir manifesto. The government urged Kashmir's farmers to increase production by investing in lift irrigation, application of fertilizers, and popularization of china paddy that was said to yield at least seventeen maunds more per acre than the local variety.[78] Irrigation was given nearly 17 percent of the total plan allocation, and fifty-two irrigation schemes were established.[79] In one year, four thousand acres of land were brought under cultivation.[80] Introducing irrigation to previously uncultivated lands created an increase in food production: "between 1951–52 and 1964–65, the food production in the state increased from 82.56 lakh to 166.10 lakh maunds and the annual growth rate of 8.8 percent registered . . . first three Five Year Plans was more than the all Indian average of 5.13 percent per annum for the same period."[81] Javeed ul Aziz attributes this increase in productivity not to improved seeds and fertilizers, which were used marginally, but to the intensification of irrigation. The construction of irrigation canals in particular regions, including Sonawari to the northwest of Srinagar, also proved politically rewarding.[82] As Aziz suggests, "The vast economic benefits which the people obtained provided sound basis for transforming the affected areas into political constituencies for the leaders who were thought to be responsible for the work."[83]

Yet, throughout Bakshi's rule, the government continued to rely on food subsidies. Even in terms of irrigation, the Kashmir government lagged behind Indian states. In 1961, "the number of tractors and irrigation pumps used in the state was 132 and 85 respectively, whereas the corresponding number for Punjab was 7,866 and 8,524 respectively."[84] Because of the growing population, large amounts of otherwise fertile lands were converted into residential areas, leading to a "horizontal expansion of construction work, consuming the fertile tracts of land, thereby shrinking the already meager agricultural space of the Valley."[85] Even the National Conference, meeting in Baramulla for its twenty-second plenary session, expressed disappointment with the food situation and called for more scientific processes as well as releasing pressure on land, which would mean opening up avenues for alternative occupations for the rural populations.[86]

Why did the government's attempts to produce more food falter? It is possible that continued food aid from the Government of India reduced any incentive for the Kashmir government to make serious, long-term investment in agriculture. In addition, many landowners switched their land to orchards since those were exempt from land reforms and not under the control of the state. Because of their favorable cost-benefit ratio, some peasants began to cultivate cash crops like fruit and saffron, instead of subsistence ones like rice and wheat.[87] These cash crops were able to reach local markets as well as markets in the northern Indian states because of improvements in roads and transportation, including the Banihal Tunnel. The transition to cash crops meant that these goods were exported, and there was less subsistence farming in the state, leaving the population once more dependent on Indian food imports.

In addition to the lack of significant government support for long-term agricultural development, the government also provided limited support to promote industrial development, in contrast to the plans of the Naya Kashmir manifesto. Government propaganda materials routinely publicized the establishment or development of existing industries, including fisheries, animal husbandry, horticulture, sericulture, sheep breeding, forestry, and mineral development. New factories were established for watch assembly and manufacturing steel, barbed wires, radios, cycles, cement, brick and tile, ceramics and concrete. A joinery and tanner was created.[88] In a speech to the Kashmir legislature, Karan Singh stated that given the "natural features" of the state, large-scale industrialization could not be undertaken for some time to come.[89] Indeed, Shahla Hussain details how "India refused to set up industry in Kashmir due to a lack of raw materials and high transportation costs."[90] The market was flooded with finished goods from India, further restricting the growth of indigenous industries. Between 1962 and 1963, the value of imports into Kashmir was over 5,500 quintals. The value of exports was just under half of that.[91]

Much of the industrial development was in small-scale cottage industry for handicrafts, shawl-making, embroidery, carpet weaving, woodcarving, papier-mâché, and silverware to complement the development of tourism in the state. The government reorganized the emporium to facilitate a market for goods to be sold. It also modernized the silk and woolen factories. When the government held its first industrial exhibition in 1955, trade outside Kashmir for these goods increased considerably. In the first year of his rule alone, Bakshi approved Rs. 1,500,000 in loans for craftsmen, artisans, and traders.[92] These developments created a larger market for Kashmiri goods, yet they also led Kashmiri traders to depend on the consumption practices of the Indian market, and as we examined in chapter 2, the desire for Kashmir's handicrafts was linked to Indian colonial imaginaries of Kashmir. Thus, the primary developments in industry were linked to these colonial imaginaries.

Based on the recommendations from the various committees formed in the government's initial months as well as the manifesto, the government also embarked on a series of large-scale transportation projects. Along with irrigation canals and dams, the government initiated a number of bridges, roads, and power development schemes. As deputy prime minister, Bakshi played an important role in improving the government transport department; as prime minister, he continued to improve city bus services, connecting cities with various towns and remote villages.[93] Under the plan, the government developed 1,852 miles of new roads, making trade and commerce more profitable.[94] Indeed, private sector transport went from 1,872 vehicles in 1947 to 6,325 under Bakshi. Developments in transportation created employment for nearly ten thousand people.[95]

One of the massive and most consequential infrastructure projects in Kashmir's history was the Banihal Tunnel in 1956, which would dramatically alter the economic life of the state. Prior to the completion of the tunnel, the isolated Kashmir Valley was accessible from India only by a two-hundred-mile road that "twists and turns, runs along the sides of great mountains, and winds its way gradually to the nine thousand feet high Banihal Pass, where snow lingers in the shade even on the hottest days."[96] The road was blocked by heavy snowfall during the long winter months, leaving the Valley completely isolated during that time. The only year-round road connection from the Kashmir Valley to the rest of the subcontinent was in Pakistan—and thus, inaccessible.

Every winter, the Kashmir government anxiously hoped that grain supplies would arrive before the roads would close on account of the weather; in the past, the state had suffered famines because of delays, leaving the population with great food insecurity.

Abdullah's government had begun discussing a tunnel soon after accession, but it remained in the planning stage until 1954, when Bakshi's government began construction. Considered "the greatest single achievement of our times," the Banihal Tunnel, designed by two German engineers, was nearly 8,120 feet long, in the form of a single tube accommodating two-way traffic as well as two footpaths.[97]

Upon completion, the tunnel linked the Kashmir Valley with Jammu, thus creating an all-weather physical, social, and commercial link between the Valley and the Indian mainland, allowing trade to flow between Kashmir and India and increasing tourist traffic in the winter months. The tunnel also reduced the journey to Kashmir by one and a half hours, which was critical to the commercialization of the fruit industry in the state, as perishable goods could now reach new markets in India.[98] Aside from improving trade and transportation, the tunnel also symbolized the goal of connecting Kashmir to India. Both the Kashmir government and the Government of India aspired to year-round communication, trade, and transport, in the hope that they would cultivate a sense of emotional and physical integration.

The cost of financing the tunnel elicited debate once more between the two governments. An official in the Indian Ministry of Finance wanted initially to provide the funding as a loan, declaring that the tunnel should not be seen as a national highway, the responsibility of India. Bakshi, arguing that his government could not undertake the project as a loan, insisted that it should be considered a national highway. Pressure came from Nehru that the tunnel be pushed through "as fast as we can" and that the Ministry of Finance and Ministry of Transport should decide on the financing. Eventually, the tunnel was treated as a national highway, and funds were provided to the Aid to Kashmir grant, costing the Indian government nearly three crore rupees.[99]

On December 22, 1956, the tunnel was inaugurated with much fanfare. The vice president of India, Sarvepalli Radhakrishnan, declared at the ceremony that Banihal was a "permanent and lasting physical link between the Kashmir

Valley and the rest of the country." Arguing that construction would not have been possible without the unstinting and generous assistance of the Government of India, Radhakrishnan also commended the inclusion of expertise from a foreign country—Germany—allowing the Kashmir state to be showcased on the international stage. Bakshi also spoke at the ceremony. He argued that while the accession had been complete, the lack of a year-round transport link had remained a barrier blocking the relationship between India and Kashmir; with the advent of the tunnel, people's hardships would be minimized. There would be new "avenues of prosperity for the people of the state," and it would "also considerably bring Kashmir nearer [to] India." By creating a physical link between India and Kashmir, the tunnel enabled the accession to be territorialized and made into a concrete reality.[100] Similarly, as Bhan argues in the case of another development project, dams, the Banihal inaugural ceremony was intended to "generate narratives of 'national' unity and pride . . . [and] cement the nation through gravel and concrete."[101]

Large-scale construction projects such as the Banihal Tunnel also increased the Kashmir government's technical expertise, an essential resource for further developing the state's infrastructure. Between 1952 and 1963, the number of technically qualified individuals in the state increased by nearly a hundredfold, from 57 to 4,770.[102] The government invested significant funds in electric power schemes, including the Sindh Valley Hydro Electric Scheme, a ten-mile-long canal and powerhouse. Power generation increased tenfold, from 4,000 kilowatts to 31,000 kilowatts, between 1947 and the end of the second five-year plan. Many villages became electrified as a result. The power project was noted internationally as well. A report in the *New York Times* commended "Indian money and Kashmiri engineers" for this feat that took six years and cost $5 million, stating, "For Kashmir, the plant is a symbol of some of the benefits of association with India."[103] Bakshi's government also constructed dams throughout the region, and implemented anti-flood measures.[104]

How are we to understand the impact of these modernization schemes? Some scholars have focused on the "spectacle" of developmentalism and how certain projects of the state, including housing, irrigation, and infrastructural schemes, can be seen as spectacular displays of state power meant to awe or inspire the local population and in turn underscore legitimacy for the government. Large-scale development projects were used to 'signal' modernization to the population at large. Much like the opening of irrigation dams in rural Sindh in Pakistan, which Daniel Haines examines, the large-scale modernization projects of Bakshi's government "underscored the ideas of development, modernity and progress" and signaled modernization to locals, demonstrating state power.[105] With their use of modern technology and machines, they ushered in a new era of "progress." As some newspapers reported, people came to see and marvel at the work that was being done. One correspondent noted, "If nothing else, the tractors and the bulldozers have convinced the people that development work is really in progress."[106]

Bakshi's projects, however, were not simply "spectacle." This becomes clear when we compare projects like the Banihal Tunnel with other iconic development projects. Consider, for example, Korangi Township in Pakistan, a satellite town constructed during the military rule of Ayub Khan for several hundred thousand residents southeast of Karachi. Built with funds from USAID and the Ford Foundation, the project was heralded in international media as the largest slum clearance and urban rehabilitation program in Asia. And yet, from the very beginning, Korangi Township was flawed, and residents quickly deemed it a failure for lacking basic amenities. From the Pakistani government's perspective, however, Korangi succeeded at its more important objective: enacting sovereignty. In a study of the project, historian Markus Daechsel has written that Ayub Khan's government was "only interested in demonstrating its ability to make decisions and to deploy executive power over its territory."[107] The "spectacle" of Korangi was geared toward international observers in an effort to justify Pakistan's close alliance with the United States during the Cold War, as well as its ability to enact development schemes. The government was not actually interested in practical implementation or success on the ground; in the end, Daechsel argues, the postcolonial Pakistan state deliberately enacted development failure.

Bakshi was up to something different with the Banihal Tunnel. An infrastructural project like the Banihal Tunnel had to succeed, and it did, as a "concrete expression of Kashmir's integration with India."[108] Bakshi and the Indian government needed the tunnel to construct the physical, emotional, and psychological ties between India and Kashmir. And so, while Bakshi's government was certainly interested in the propaganda value of the tunnel for international spectators, the tunnel was primarily a modality of control for the broader populace. The Banihal Tunnel enabled the Kashmiri government to relinquish notions of sovereignty by physically linking the state directly to India; it remade the public in relation to its integration schemes.

Furthermore, unlike later infrastructural projects that resulted in "regimes of immobility" and "structures of chaos," the success of Banihal depended on its ability to make Kashmiris mobile, and it wasn't reliant on "separations and enclosures."[109] Much of the infrastructure of the post-1990s moment has relied on providing mobility for the Indian army, while restricting it for Kashmiris. This was not the case during Bakshi's time, as the presence of the army in civilian areas was limited. Movement and mobility to and from India via the Banihal Tunnel were thus constitutive of India's infrastructural ambitions in this time as well as the politics of life, in order to create better emotional and economic integration between Kashmiris and Indians. This example highlights the different aims and meanings of infrastructure over time, even under conditions of a colonial occupation.

In the decade of Bakshi's government, development euphoria took over the administration and made inroads into Kashmiri society. Roads, transport, small-scale industries, power plants, and improved agriculture and irrigation techniques all signaled modernization to the Kashmir masses. Most importantly, a growing Kashmiri Muslim middle class emerged, buttressed by shifts in land reform, public service employment, and economic opportunities. Bakshi's patronage also extended to a nouveau riche of "bureaucrats, businessmen, and politicians,"[110] which effectively served as a collaborator or comprador class. As Hussain argues, "the new class of collaborators accepted liberal financial aid as the price of integration."[111]

A number of development indices increased. Per capita income rose from Rs. 188.41 to Rs. 236.86. In the first two five-year plans, the government created 33,569 jobs. Policies of agricultural reform, including food subsidies and the abolishment of *mujawaza*, played an important role in improving the lives of Kashmiris, especially in rural areas. With increased incomes, consumption also increased, especially of motorcars, radios, fans, and refrigerators.[112] Nonetheless, the overall rate of growth remained low, as the government failed to generate higher revenue. The revenues of the government rose from Rs. 523 lakhs in 1953–1954 to Rs. 2,453.46 lakhs at the end of Bakshi's government, an increase of only 7–8 percent each year.[113] Financial assistance from the Government of India was the main factor in prohibiting economic growth.

In the early 1960s, *Kashmir Affairs*, a Delhi journal edited by Balraj Puri, a journalist from Jammu, published an issue dedicated entirely to Kashmir's economic affairs. The issue made "startling revelations" about Kashmir's economy, which "despite highest per capita revenue, highest per capita central aid, highest per capita plan, and lowest per capita taxes among the states of India, is lagging behind the rest of the country in its economic growth and productivity."[114] Several observers noted how the government was not solely concerned with speedy economic growth, because a number of its economic policies were "politically motivated." Kashmir's tax revenue was only 31 percent of the state's entire revenue, while the average for Indian states was nearly 66 percent. Thus, a vast majority of the state's revenue came from Indian aid, causing "an overdependence on union grants."[115] Because of the abundance of Indian aid, the authors noted that per capita revenue was far ahead of all other states.[116] Yet, the state had the lowest per capita productivity and one of the lowest rates of growth. Although incomes were increasing, money was not being spent on income-generating projects. In regard to the state's budget, the journal noted that a far greater percentage was spent on the Departments of Information, Police, and Intelligence in comparison to other states in the Indian Union. This suggests that because of the government's "political motivations," greater effort had to be placed on building and policing its narrative of development than on policies resulting in greater long-term economic benefits.

As mentioned earlier, the government proclaimed that it had made significant improvements in agriculture and industry. The journal challenged this notion, stating that agriculture had not improved; while there were new fertilizers and land reforms, the state still had the lowest per capita agricultural output and no food self-sufficiency.[117] Industries fared no better; the journal reported that their working expenses exceeded their income and thus, were a drain on the system.[118] As a result of limited industrialization, the state also imported far more goods than it exported, causing a trade deficit. While the government invested less in industrialization, it increased investment in the public service and civil administration structure, creating one of the largest bureaucracies among Indian states. This was complemented by All-India Services (including Indian Administrative Service, Indian Forest Service, etc.) which became applicable to Kashmir in 1956. Ensuring the largest employer in the state was the government bureaucracy was another attempt to contain political aspirations.

Puri was not alone in his unease with the government's narrative on development and economic progress. Members of the Plebiscite Front, an opposition group I discuss in chapter 7, argued that India should focus on "creating jobs that would generate income and tax revenue alike" instead of "pouring money into the state."[119] Furthermore, others complained that Kashmiris were now completely dependent on the Banihal Tunnel for trade. They argued that "reopening old routes and rivers that connected the state to the rest of the world would revive Kashmiri self-sufficiency."[120] These old routes went through Pakistan, and their closure had devastated the local economy, creating an even greater dependence on India. Significantly, as Hussain notes, the Kashmiri "intelligentsia debunked the statist perspectives that connected Kashmir's prosperity with economic aid flowing from India by providing an alternative vision for Kashmir's self-sufficient economic growth."[121] While the tunnel had undoubtedly expanded mobility for Kashmiris in relation to India, Kashmiri geographical imaginaries contested India's *other* territorial restrictions on Kashmir, as well as India's stranglehold over the Kashmir economy.

Finally, the emergence of the nouveau riche with close ties to India led to greater inequality and tension between social classes. Kashmiri novels and literature from this time featured stories of the "moral degradation and urban decadence" rampant in society because of this liberal, wealthy class.[122] And it is here where corruption—another pivotal face of economic planning in the state—became entrenched.

Corruption and the Fraught Realities of Progress

Narratives of corruption centered on how government patronage was leveraged to buy political loyalty. The *Kashmir Affairs* journal published by Balraj Puri bemoaned the nepotism and corruption under Bakshi, particularly in the transport industry, which, according to the report, had "thrown up the largest number of millionaires."[123] This was because Bakshi had centralized the authority to issue permits for the operation of vehicles on various routes, and he "more often than not used it to reward political services."[124] It was not just transport permits that were centralized under the authority of the prime minister; Bakshi also controlled loans, scholarships, and important contracts. The journal declared that Kashmir was the most cooperativized state in India, with nearly 50 percent of families belonging to the cooperative movement, providing them with rural credit. These cooperatives were run by National Conference committees and thus, were highly politicized. It was noted that "the way a permit or loan is granted puts a burden on the conscience of every recipient . . . a sense of guilt due to the way they are patronized."[125]

The journal also questioned the work of the development sector, given that many officials and engineers affiliated with the Public and Works Department utilized lower quality material in order to appropriate a portion of the funds allotted for a given project. In a few cases, officials had "damage[d] roads . . . [and] appropriate[d] a portion of the money spent on repair."[126] Senior officers of the Sindh Valley Hydro Electric Scheme were all suspended for siphoning funds.[127] Although the manifesto had called for protection of Kashmir's forests, deforestation and illegal timber smuggling reached an all-time high.

Accounts of local corruption also appeared in local newspapers, including the *Kashmir Post, Martand, Apna Sansar, Khidmat,* and *Sach*. These papers repeatedly highlighted stories of corrupt government workers, hiring of unqualified candidates, illegal promotions, bribes, and money intended for development schemes going into the pockets of ministers, inspectors, contractors, engineers, and directors. In February 1954, the *Martand* complained that loans intended for artisans and petty traders were "being given to business men who may be able to get loans as a result of their influence both in government circles and National Conference. . . . [They are] depriving deserving people of aid."[128] In another issue, the same paper criticized the government for making promotions, appointments, and transfers based on influence instead of merit, seniority, and experience. It also accused the local municipality of not doing its part to ensure the cleanliness of neighborhoods and not taking stronger action against those who were selling adulterated milk.[129]

Perhaps the strongest criticism was reserved for the officials in the bureaucracy who enjoyed the privileges of working under Bakshi. The *Khidmat*, an otherwise pro-government paper, demanded a review of the private property of all government officials to ascertain whether they were getting money from other means.[130] Others bemoaned that children of government officials and other influential people were selected for loans, training, and educational scholarships, whereas those who had no political influence were left behind.[131] In his memoirs, advocate Hirday Nath Dhar lamented the corruption among the government officials, who had private servants in their homes and spent state funds on furniture, personal travel, and petrol.[132]

These accounts stand in contrast to the reports of progress that the government was circulating. They suggest money was not being spent on income-generating projects but rather on bribing an entire class of government officials. In his study of corruption among bureaucrats in the Indian state of Uttar Pradesh, William Gould highlights how corruption in post-independence India served multiple purposes, enabling local politicians and parties to stake out networks of power and alliances in electoral politics through the use of control over licenses, permits, rationing, and patronage.[133]

Corruption under Bakshi also became a way for the government to create legitimacy in the disputed state and engender new forms of political loyalty.[134] In this context, patronage, interpreted as corruption, was not only tolerated but deployed as a political strategy to the extent of becoming a "policy" pervading both the high levels of government and the everyday local bureaucrats in the civil service, police, and so on. State patronage relied upon the same narratives of "abundance" that underwrote the food subsidization programs. Bakshi was reputed to have said that if a Kashmiri was unable to get rich under his rule, he would never be able to get rich.[135] Here again, we see how the need to obtain political loyalty caused the government to deliberately enact corruption as a modality of control.

Yet, corruption in Kashmir also played a unique role. Discourses on corruption diverted public attention to issues of technical "good governance" and away from the underlying issues of the nature of political sovereignty and India's relationship with Kashmir. Corruption, thus, was an explicit component of economic developmentalism and another means to entrench the Indian occupation. The very fact that the government allowed newspapers to speak of rampant corruption without censure meant that it did not see the topic as a threat to its legitimacy. Perhaps the government intentionally created a space where limited critiques of its governance could be expressed, understanding that when matters of governance were discussed, discourse had already shifted away from deeper questions of political sovereignty. In these public evaluations of Bakshi's government, the expectation that the state should provide good governance was reinforced.

Allegations of corruption were so frequent that eventually the government was forced to respond. In 1955, the government established an anti-corruption tribunal under the chairmanship of Justice M. A. Shahmiri.[136] Its activities, however, were soon suspended, and in 1956, the controversy split the Bakshi cabinet, with G.M. Sadiq leading a breakaway faction called the Democratic National Conference (DNC). In Sadiq's published correspondence with Bakshi from that period, he asserted that the pre-1953 situation that gripped Abdullah's administration was being continued under Bakshi; National Conference workers were authoritarian, and the government's efficiency was "sapped by corruption and malpractice."[137] Bakshi admitted that corruption had not yet been eliminated but said that the administration was "working fine" and indeed had improved. He added that several commissions had been appointed to look into corruption charges and that Sadiq should refrain from discrediting the National Conference, as that would help the opposition.[138] Within less than a year, members of the DNC would once again be absorbed into Bakshi's cabinet. However, the correspondence between the two leaders sheds light on the gravity of the state of corruption. Sadiq would come to power in 1964 and lead the corruption charges against Bakshi and his close associates.

In 1965, a few years after Bakshi stepped down from power, the state of Jammu and Kashmir, now under the chief ministership of G. M. Sadiq, brought a corruption case against him and his associates. The Ayyangar Commission of Enquiry declared, "Between October 1947 to October 1963 . . . [Bakshi] obtained pecuniary and other benefits for himself, for members of his family, for his other relatives and for some other persons in whom he was interested."[139] The investigation revealed that landowners were coerced into selling their land and were not adequately compensated, while others had their land encroached upon. The Bakshi family was also accused of exploiting the Low Income Group Housing Scheme and arranging illegal tiling and forest contracts as well as leases for cars, petrol, and cinemas. Moreover, they used government funds for personal expenses. The case was brought to the Indian Supreme Court—which ironically was given jurisdiction over the state's affairs under Bakshi's rule—and the chief justice found Bakshi to be guilty.

It is not coincidental that this commission took place immediately after Bakshi was unceremoniously asked to step down from power, especially as the Indian government sought to further erode Kashmir's autonomy using the new chief minister (not prime minister), G. M. Sadiq. The Ayyangar Commission of Enquiry was presented as a mechanism of accountability after years of misgovernance and corruption under Bakshi. These internal corrective mechanisms ultimately served the interests of the Indian state and each consecutive client regime by creating a pretense of accountability and redress of political grievances in what was, by default, an illegitimate political setup. Corruption charges against Bakshi also played a different role for the Indian state. By presenting the Kashmir government and its leadership as corrupt, the Indian state was able to deflect from its own responsibility in enabling economies of corruption. It could also claim that Kashmir's corrupt leaders had been unable to rule effectively, delegitimizing greater calls for autonomy even among its own local loyalists and utilizing only those leaders who could effectively seek greater integration with India.

Further, the dependence on India made it so that Kashmir was not able to fulfill its actual economic potential, a process that would result in "de-development."[140] Kashmiris were made to internalize narratives of their idleness and unwillingness to work. Ultimately, India was able to position itself as "singularly capable of providing a means of livelihood to the occupied people."[141] By later positioning Kashmir as a "begging bowl" and decrying the "corruption" of Kashmir's leaders, the Indian government was able to "undermine Kashmiri sovereignty."[142] There would be no introspection into the ways in which India's economic relationship with Kashmir enabled such practices to take root. Bakshi's economic development, reliant on tropes that Kashmir "needed" India, had simply been another mode of control that sustained India's colonial occupation. Thus, during Bakshi's rule, India was able to infiltrate Kashmir by fiscal and not direct military means.

Chapter 5

SHAPING SUBJECTIVITIES
Education, Secularism, and Its Discontents

In the early 1950s, the Department of Education of the Kashmir government received a petition from the town of Sopore. The student chair of the National Students Federation of Sopore, Abdul Samad, made an appeal to establish an intermediate college in the town, describing the central role the town played politically and economically and stating that despite this role, the condition of education in Sopore had been "rendered poor." Students could get educated only until matriculation, he explained, and were forced to go to Srinagar or other cities for higher education. He lamented that "because of this and unprecedented poverty, many of the students are forced to leave their education and their hopes are dashed to the ground."[1] Samad described how the people of Sopore had presented their request to the Dogra government but had been ignored. He declared that "the funeral of the Dogra government has happened and people's rule [*awami raj*] has come and a New Kashmir is born and people who understand the pain and suffering of common people have come to power, we hope that this long-standing demand of people of Sopore, Handwara, and Baramulla will be fulfilled."[2]

Two years into Bakshi's government, the Department of Education had received hundreds of similar petitions from across Jammu and Kashmir.[3] Sent from *mohalla* (neighborhood) committees, public organizations, student groups, villages, and local National Conference party workers, these petitions requested the Department of Education to establish schools and colleges in their areas. One officer in the department declared, "The influx of such applications does not come to an end at all."[4] Unlike Abdul Samad, many of the petitioners were illiterate and signed with their thumbprints.[5] A number of petitions called upon Bakshi's government to keep its promises to build schools or hire new teachers as discussed during his recent tour of their community.[6] Calling Bakshi's rule as *awami raj,* the petitions referred to the progress made under his government and their communities' desire to take part in that development.

It is clear from the petitions that people knew the government had commenced a new education policy; the petitions, thus, provide a sense of how ordinary Kashmiris responded to this program. As the petitions described above illustrate, people expected Bakshi's government, especially in contrast to Dogra rule, to deliver on promises of educational and economic reform. Furthermore, these letters were not limited just to establishing schools or colleges; ordinary citizens wrote letters or petitions of complaint to the government, mobilizing their communities in the pursuit of better educational infrastructure or more teachers, seeking entrance into institutions of higher learning, and obtaining scholarships.

Through state-led advances in education, such as free tuition until the university level, the creation and improvement of primary, secondary, and professional schools, as well as the revision of education philosophy, syllabi, and linguistic policies, the government attempted to shape a secular modern Kashmiri subjectivity. In doing so, the leadership debated the purpose, form, and content of education, and education became central to debates over the identity of Kashmir as it was being produced in this moment. Educational policy drew extensively from the objectives laid out in the Naya Kashmir manifesto. Yet, even though education became a site of collective aspiration, it was also a site of deep contestation, as questions of community representation threatened its implementation on the ground. Debates over education reflected the conflicting aims and complex interests of the Kashmir government as well as the fraught nature of intercommunal relations under secular rule.

To be secular entailed adopting a disposition aware of religious difference while ensuring equal recognition to various religions. However, because the government paid particular attention to the empowerment of Kashmiri Muslims, educational developments, by default, became linked to the cultivation of a modern Kashmiri Muslim subject. As mentioned before, Kashmiri Muslims were the primary demographic the government sought not only to empower but also to bring into line in the new political order. The empowerment of

Kashmiri Muslims entailed the accumulation of power through various economic, political, and social means. This empowerment came at the cost of the group that had previously held the monopoly on education and employment: an elite minority class of Kashmiri Pandits who themselves had already felt discriminated against under the Dogras, who had favored non-Kashmiri Hindus for higher administrative positions. Under the post-Partition governments, their previous stronghold in education was challenged as Muslims began to enroll in schools and colleges in larger numbers and became employed in various educational institutions. In addition, the government's attempts to produce a secular Kashmir alienated a number of Muslim groups and individuals, who argued that these efforts undermined the Muslim identity of the community.

Scholars have critically interrogated the relationship between secularism and the modern state.[7] Hussain Agrama argues, "Secular power works by rendering precarious and even undermining the very categories on which it ostensibly depends and aims to establish."[8] Because the state continuously attempts to draw the line between religion and politics, Agrama maintains that "this ongoing entanglement is a feature of the expanding regulatory capacities of the modern state."[9] Extending this analysis to Kashmir, I argue that despite the attempt to produce a secular, modern identity, educational reconfigurations were already entwined with religious reconfigurations, because religious difference was coded in the policies and administrative practices of the state. As a result, the government's educational policies undermined the aims of the Naya Kashmir manifesto in building a "united people of the state" and produced increased Pandit-Muslim tension, leading the government to become mired in accusations of promoting communalism—favoring one religious community to the detriment of the other.[10] This "ongoing entanglement in the question of religion and politics, for the purpose of identifying and securing fundamental liberal rights and freedoms" expanded the state's regulatory capacity over social life.[11]

More than any other sphere of state-building, education brings our attention to the intersection of the politics of life and local aspirations, and the ways ordinary people made demands on, became a part of, and contested the project of state reform, while also utilizing it for their own ends. Educational reform also shows that while people might not have granted the Bakshi government legitimacy, they accepted and enhanced its authority—enabling the Kashmir government to play a greater role in the regulation of social life.

Kashmiri Muslims and Education under the Dogras (1846–1947)

The Dogras controlled the education of their subjects, a majority of whom were Muslims. However, unlike the princely rulers of Mysore and Baroda, who set up institutions of higher education that served as sites of resistance against colonial rule, the Dogras were far less invested in matters of education.[12] For most of the late nineteenth and early twentieth century, indigenous *madrasas* (for Muslim boys) or *patshalas* (for Pandit boys) imparted basic religious education, Persian, Arabic or Sanskrit, and math to students. The Dogras did not view the promotion of education of the masses as a priority, and specifically for Kashmiris, very little infrastructure was set in place for either Hindus or Muslims.[13]

It was only in 1889, as the British began to exert greater control over the princely state and sent a resident to Kashmir under Pratap Singh, that education became a central component of the drive toward state centralization. Nevertheless, "policies were fraught with ambivalence about mass education in general and Muslim education in particular."[14] This was due in part to Dogra desire to ensure that the state did not have a local elite demanding a role in the bureaucracy, which at the time was primarily composed of non-Kashmiris, including Urdu-speaking Punjabis, as well as a number of Kashmiri Pandits. If the majority community in the state began to get educated, the Dogras assumed they would make demands for employment in the bureaucracy.

At the turn of the century, compelled in part by the colonial state, the Dogras established primary, middle, and higher secondary schools and the Sri Pratap College, the first institution of higher education in the state. The principal beneficiaries of these policies were Kashmiri Pandits, who enjoyed greater access because of their increasing prevalence in the administration. Alongside the efforts of the state and colonial missionaries, private individuals, such as Tyndale Biscoe and Annie Besant, established schools catering to the elite, mostly Kashmiri Pandit and other Hindu families of Srinagar. Muslim socioreligious reform organizations began to prioritize education also, founding schools—including what would later be the Islamia College—for the urban class based in Srinagar.[15] By 1915, all religious and private institutions were under the purview of the state as they were given grants-in-aid. There were no local higher educational and professional schools. Kashmiris had to go either to Aligarh or Lahore for further studies.

Despite these efforts, the educational statistics for Kashmiri Muslims remained dismal compared to the overall number of Muslims and Pandits throughout the state.[16] As more primary schools began to open, the number of Muslim students slowly rose, although in higher education, the number of Muslims remained limited. In 1926, of the 480 students in Sri Pratap College, only 7 were Muslim.[17] Even in 1941, the literacy rates for Muslims were staggering: only 1.6 percent of Kashmiri Muslims could read and write.[18] The statistics for female education were even lower.

Comparing their status with Kashmiri Pandits, in the second decade of the twentieth century, an emerging Muslim leadership composed of upper-class, urban males, which would go on to form the Muslim Conference and later, the National Conference, criticized the Dogras for their discriminatory policies against Kashmiri Muslims. Linking the acquisition of education to better employment opportunities in the administration, as the Dogras had feared, Kashmiri Muslims began to take greater interest in educational affairs, even demanding the involvement of the British colonial state.[19] Interventions like the Sharps Report in 1916 called for the expansion of primary education and scholarships for Muslim students in higher education. The Dogras became defensive, arguing that the responsibility for the education of Kashmiri Muslims belonged to its leadership and that the poor statistics resulted from Muslim apathy toward education, not a lack of opportunities or a policy of discrimination.

To obtain political recognition, groups had to "look like or perform the role of religious communities."[20] Consequently, Muslims began to articulate their demands as a cohesive community, and this focus on "community" became the generative ground for political identity in the colonial era.[21] In response to the events of 1931, the Dogras formed the Glancy Commission, composed of leaders from various religious and regional backgrounds, to look into the grievances of their respective communities. The commission conceded that despite being a majority, Muslims were excluded from the representative institutions of the state.[22] For the improvement of Muslim education, the commission suggested the Department of Education hire more Muslim teachers, employ more religious instructors, or mullahs, to teach Arabic, and provide special scholarships for Muslim students. Most importantly, at the request of the commission, the Department of Education in 1932 created the post of Mohammedan Inspector to manage the educational affairs of Muslim students. The government also selected one Muslim and nine Kashmiri Pandits for scholarships to study abroad. It might be tempting to view these developments as a shift in Dogra attitudes toward Muslim education. However, they were at best conciliatory efforts to quell the unrest, not reflective of a change in Dogra sentiment toward its Muslim subjects. By 1947, a vast majority of Muslims remained illiterate.

While the movement against the Dogras resulted from marginalization in education and employment, it was increasingly seen as divisive along religious (Hindu versus Muslim) lines. The Dogra government created friction between the two communities by casting their interests as divergent and clearly demarcated cultural and religious borders between the two, as well as providing patronage to one over the other. The state used Hinduism to buttress its claims of sovereignty.[23] The Dogras also reified the idea of separate religious communities by providing students with basic instruction in their own religion; they had a policy of Urdu for Muslims and Hindi for Hindus.[24] These policies established a firm ground for tensions to emerge between the two communities.

Kashmiri Pandits and Muslims saw their political interests as widely diverging because of Dogra "patterns of legitimation which allowed the Hindus of Kashmir to exclude Muslims in the contest for the symbolic, political and economic resources of the state."[25] For the elite Pandits, the political leverage resulting from their predominance in the educational and administrative sectors was one that "determined [their] very being."[26] Pandits saw their leverage in state institutions as an intrinsic right. They considered merit as intrinsic to their very being; if Muslims were unable to reach their status, it was on account of their intrinsic lack of merit, and not the structural conditions of the state.

As soon as the first generation of Muslims began demanding special concessions in the late 1920s and 1930s to overcome their educational and representational backwardness, Pandit privileges stood on shaky ground.[27] The Pandit political identity became defined by a shared urgency of restoring their previous stronghold. Any attempts of affirmative action for Muslims became contentious. For example, in 1930, to redress inequalities in employment, a flyer was posted for a job in the Srinagar Municipality welcoming only Muslim applicants. After some Pandits labeled the flyer as "communal"—meaning it explicitly privileged one religious group over another—the flyer was withdrawn.

Kashmiri Muslims who benefitted from educational opportunities under the Dogras recollect this time as one of emerging tensions and polarization along Hindu-Muslim lines. From their writings, we see that before 1947, Muslim students were acutely aware of their second-class status.[28] Not only did Muslim students feel discriminated against in terms of obtaining admission, they also felt acutely disadvantaged in school.[29] They were prevented from organizing to demand better rights, and any attempts to mobilize for better treatment as a community were perceived as a "communal" move.[30]

Director of Education K. G. Saiyidain, a prominent Muslim, who would become the minister of education and the educational advisor to the Government of India, attempted to implement the suggestions made by the Glancy Commission, including improving educational opportunities for Muslims. Saiyidain emerged as a controversial figure among the region's Hindus. They submitted numerous petitions to the maharaja claiming that the department under his leadership discriminated against them. Many called for his resignation. Their complaints revolved primarily around the linguistic policies of the state.

Although Kashmiri was a dominant language, Urdu in the Perso-Arabic script was chosen as the language of the administration and of instruction. This was not unique, as Urdu was the official language of the Punjab as well during colonial rule, despite Punjabi being the dominant language.[31] In Kashmir, there was little debate about the use of Urdu, but debates raged about the script. In 1940, a government order declared that the Devanagari and the Persian scripts should have equal recognition and that textbooks should be printed in both.[32] Teachers were also expected to have knowledge of both scripts. This order was met with resistance from a wide variety of groups within Kashmir, although it was meant to "pacify Hindu opinion, which had become increasingly rancorous . . . against the state's so-called pro-Muslim policies."[33]

In the differentiation of Hindi from Urdu throughout the Northwest Provinces and Oudh, Hindi was seen as being for Hindus and Urdu for Muslims.[34] The proponents of Devanagari were Hindu groups protesting the use of the Perso-Arabic script. In one example, the president of the Jammu Kashmir Hindu Sabha stated that although the government had ordered that the medium of instruction in government schools would be simple Urdu written and taught in both Devanagari and Perso-Arabic scripts, the textbooks were all in Persian and contained Arabic and Persian words. Devanagari textbooks were limited, and Muslim heroes were described in a beautiful language while Hindu heroes were accorded the reverse treatment. He added that the department was carrying out an organized crusade against Hindu culture and Hindu interests.[35] Meanwhile, Abdullah's National Conference complained that the Dogra government and members of the Kashmiri Pandit community were attempting "to foist Hindu culture on Muslims."[36] Newspapers sympathetic to the National Conference saw it as a move to divide Hindus and Muslims within the anti-Dogra movement by imposing two scripts. Separately, the Muslim Conference saw it as "not only an attack on common nationality but also an attack on Islam in Kashmir."[37]

It is important to note that Kashmiris—both Pandit and Muslim—did not raise the issue of the Kashmiri language playing a role in educational and administrative affairs. This was primarily due to the class-based biases of the leadership. If the language of administration or medium of instruction was Kashmiri, it would benefit the masses and the privilege of the elites in both communities would be challenged.[38] The implications for this and other inter-community tensions in the post-Partition period, as we will see, would be significant.

Education in the Naya Kashmir Manifesto

A few years after the contentious 1940 order, when the National Conference met to write the Naya Kashmir manifesto, it prioritized the equality of all citizens of the state in all spheres of life, regardless of their nationality, religion, race, or birth.[39] The manifesto declared that all citizens had a right to education, which would be compulsory and free up until higher education even in the most remote parts of the state.[40] The plan also called for scholarships for poor students in higher education. Education was meant to align with the National Economic Plan, so that it "should not be merely liberal, but also technical," and free vocational education or adult education would also be provided for the workers in factories.[41] The plan called for the creation of district colleges, as well as a network of higher, middle, and primary schools that were liberal as well as technical. The state would also provide research scholarships for training abroad on topics pertaining to the economic plan. Women were given equal rights to men, and the plan called for an increase in women's schools and colleges.

While the languages spoken in the state were Kashmiri, Dogri, Balti, Dardi, Punjabi, Urdu, and Hindi, Urdu was to be the lingua franca of the state, and the primary medium through which education and administrative business would occur. One exception was that the mother tongue of the region was to be the medium of instruction in primary schools.[42] The state was responsible for developing all languages by providing scripts, translations, dictionaries, publishing, and scholarships for study. A "national university" was to focus on the culture of all nationalities in the state. The authors of the manifesto showed a determination to ensure that all regions and communities in the state felt a part of the New Kashmir, a unified state that nonetheless celebrated and developed the diversity of its citizens.

Sheikh Abdullah's government attempted to prioritize the manifesto's educational aims, but it was constrained in a number of ways. During his rule, a number of primary schools opened, as well as the University of Jammu and Kashmir (the first university in the state) in 1948, and the Women's College in 1950.[43] Despite the increase in the education budget as compared to that allocated during Dogra rule, many private and aided schools were shut down. For those that remained, parents had to pay tuition fees, which many could not afford.[44] A number of Muslim teachers and professors also left for (or were exiled to) Pakistan.[45] As with other developmental projects, the department lacked enough funding on its own to finance a number of educational projects. While Abdullah's government was open to taking funds from private bodies, it hesitated to rely on the Government of India.[46] This mirrored Abdullah's insistence on maintaining economic and financial autonomy. In the few newspapers allowed at the time, there were complaints that the tuition fees were high, that the new government was not spending enough on education, and that the quality of education was deteriorating.[47] As we will see, Bakshi's government, just as in matters of economic development, would depart from his predecessor's attitudes against greater Indian investment in education.

Nonetheless, an important development did take place under Abdullah: Kashmiri was made the medium of instruction for primary school children in Kashmiri-speaking areas, although Urdu remained the official language of the state. The Kashmiri Script Committee was set up under the authority of Ghulam Ahmed Ashai (also the first vice chancellor of the new university); its task was to create a modern script that would be rational, more scientific, and easier for the general population to adopt. Members of the committee travelled throughout the region to gain the input of teachers and those well versed in the language. After Abdullah's arrest, however, Ashai was detained and the Kashmiri script project came to a standstill. Nonetheless, the attempt to foreground Kashmiri as the medium of instruction, at least for primary school children, was important; it was linked to the aims of the manifesto, a vision that Bakshi also would depart from.

Once Bakshi came to power, he opened the floodgates to Indian aid; as a result, the Department of Education proposed and implemented a variety of educational projects to assert its vision for education. What was this vision? What steps did the government take to reform education? What was the impact of these policies? It is to these questions we now turn.

A Time to Hope? An Overview of Educational Policy

Bakshi detailed his plans for education during his speech on Radio Kashmir on August 9, 1953, the day after Abdullah's arrest. He promised to improve teacher salaries, abolish fees, provide textbooks, develop the national languages (including Kashmiri, Dogri, and Ladakhi), and provide scholarships, including among Kashmiri Muslims, "Harijans," Sikhs, Ladakhis, and Gujjars and Bakerwals (nomadic groups).[48]

Within weeks, Bakshi's government made education free up to the university level, living up to the ideas of the Naya Kashmir manifesto.[49] The move was groundbreaking. Despite calls to do so in states in India, Kashmir became the only region to institute such a policy.[50] In doing so, Bakshi's government exhibited acute political acumen. The increase in tuition fees under Sheikh Abdullah had resulted in a series of hunger strikes and agitations.[51] The new government wanted to avoid all political complications, and it determined that one of the primary ways to appease Kashmiris in the aftermath of Abdullah's arrest would be to remove fees altogether. According to the government, over 125,000 students were affected by this policy in its first year alone.[52] So many students enrolled that it became difficult for existing institutions to accommodate them, thus spurring a huge drive to construct more schools.

Through the influence of leftists in its administration, Bakshi's government undertook a series of steps making education more accessible to a broad cross-section of Kashmiri society. G. M. Sadiq, appointed the minister of education and health under Bakshi and later chief minister, drafted the educational policy of the government in 1955. Sadiq was an avowed communist, having spent time with leading communists in the subcontinent, including B. P. L. Bedi and his wife, Freda, on educational matters under Abdullah's administration. All three—Sadiq, Bedi, and Freda—were architects of the manifesto, and Sadiq's educational policy plan in 1955 drew heavily from its precursor. Other left-leaning educationists in Kashmir, including the principal of the Women's College, Mehmooda Ahmed, also joined in the implementation of the plan. The high visibility of the communists in educational matters raised eyebrows in anti-communist circles in India. Sumanth S. Bankeshwar of the Society for Defence of Democracy warned of "the indoctrination of the people of Kashmir with communism through the state apparatus," including the distribution of communist literature and political appointees of communist sympathizers throughout the education department.[53]

While charges by critics may have been overstated, the purpose of a progressive educational policy was primarily to meet the economic goals of the state. Before developing the educational policy, the department sought feedback from teachers, students, principals, and chief inspectors. Their reports provided detailed information on the running of schools throughout the state; many wrote of the need to improve school infrastructure and the lack of qualified and engaging teachers.[54] One teacher complained that the current education "system is too bookish and subject matter is far removed from circumstances and phenomena of actual life," a limitation the government sought to overcome.[55]

The policy called for compulsory primary education for all children from age seven to thirteen, after which most were expected to join a technical or trade school. Urdu was to be the primary mode of communication, but most schools also were expected to teach the mother tongue to children. It also detailed ways to improve technical and university education, multipurpose schools, teacher training, youth welfare, and physical education. The budget for education went from nearly 6 percent of the state's total revenue in 1950 to 12 percent by 1956, and the total expenditure on education increased by 500 percent.[56] A large portion of the budget went toward building or improving primary, secondary, and higher secondary schools in both rural and urban areas throughout the state. Emphasis was placed on universal primary education. Mobile schools were also provided for the nomadic Gujjar and Bakerwal groups.[57] The government placed importance not just on urban centers like Srinagar, but throughout the region. The total enrollment of students in 1950 was 107,233. Within a decade, the number had increased to 276,351, an increase of 250 percent; boys' enrollment increased 125 percent and girls' enrollment increased 400 percent. The number of educational institutions also nearly tripled from 1,330 in 1950 to 3,653 by 1960.[58] To keep a wider network of institutions under state patronage, the government gave private and religious institutions grants-in-aid.[59] It also provided a number of scholarships for students of "backward classes"—Muslims were considered backward as were lower castes (a point I turn to later), Ladakhis (who were called "frontier people"), and females. Finally, the government hired thousands of teachers, a majority of whom were Muslim. Many female teachers were hired, and to attract more people to teaching, the government raised their salaries. The total number of teachers employed by the government in 1950 was 4,261; by 1960 the number had more than doubled to 10,330.[60]

Through these initial policies, education became much more accessible to a greater number of people throughout the state, especially Muslims and females. In 1941, only 1.6 percent of Kashmiri Muslims could read and write, but in 1961, close to the end of Bakshi's rule, this increased to 11.03 percent.[61]

Bakshi's government also made critical interventions in higher education by creating professional colleges and increasing access. In 1947, there were 3,029 men and women enrolled in college; by 1960, this number had increased to 8,385.[62] Before Bakshi, there were no engineering or medical colleges in the state. Kashmiris had to go to cities in India or abroad, where they might find limited or no seats for them in medical or engineering schools.[63] Responding to significant pressure from students and their families, Bakshi reached out to Vishnu Sahay, in charge of Kashmir affairs in the Government of India, to establish a medical and engineering college in Srinagar.[64] Sahay wrote to the respective ministries in the Indian government for their opinion, stating, "From the political point of view, the idea is of course attractive as it will help to bring Kashmir and the rest of India together," underscoring once more the political intentions for many of Kashmir's development policies.[65] While the head of the ministry of health, V. K. B. Pillai, agreed that the medical college was a good idea given the "size and geographical situation of the state," he suggested it was the Kashmir government's responsibility to come up with the funds, although the center could provide technical assistance. The head of the ministry of education, Humayan Kabir, was less enthusiastic about the prospect of an engineering college. "There is no case for establishing a separate engineering college in JK," he responded, pointing out that "the state has been assisted liberally by the ministry by finding quite a large number of seats in the existing institutions and that should meet its needs for the present." He added, "You may also kindly impress on the authorities of the state the need to conform to local practice regarding admissions, etc. and not make requests for continual changes, exemptions, and special preference."[66]

Kabir's response—especially the last part—reveals impatience with the demands of the Kashmir government, especially concerning the "special preference" repeatedly invoked. While there is no further correspondence in the available files on this matter, it appears Bakshi managed to overturn Kabir's decision. Both the National Institute of Technology (the engineering college) and the Government Medical College were founded in the second half of his rule. With the development of these professional institutions, thousands of Kashmiris, especially those from Muslim families, enrolled and social mobility became a reality: many began to ascend into the middle and upper classes. Indeed, in contemporary popular discourse, this is one of the most memorable developments of Bakshi's government; he is credited with changing the futures and fortunes of hundreds of families. A vibrant Muslim professional class now replaced the elite class of Muslim and Pandit families that had maintained a financial and social monopoly due to their links to the Dogra state. It is important to note that many who received these scholarships or opportunities were deemed as having "sound and steady political views;" a number of their families were also already involved in or became invested in Bakshi's rule as a result.[67]

Although the government initiated a number of reforms, developments in education were not simply top down. Kashmiri Muslims, clamoring for greater opportunities, also played an agentive role in shaping educational policy. If they ever had misgivings about education under the Dogras, these sentiments were overruled by the proactive approach of the new government. Bakshi's government provided more scope and opportunity for average Kashmiris—and not just an elite group—to advocate for better educational benefits, and people responded enthusiastically. During his Friday *durbar*, tours throughout the state, as well as his visits to Indian states, Bakshi encountered Kashmiris from all walks of life.[68] Many would also write directly to Bakshi urging him to open a school in their village, provide a scholarship or admission for their son or daughter, support an educational journal, approve a text for distribution in schools, or improve the infrastructure of their institutions. Those who sent letters about their situation did not argue their case for admission or a scholarship on grounds of merit. Instead, they provided details of their destitution and their difficult life, including the responsibility of taking care of large or ailing family members. By presenting themselves as "backward," they made emotional appeals to the government, hoping that the government would respond empathetically. These demands were then taken to the Department of Education and inevitably influenced the crafting of state policies.

The agency of ordinary people demonstrated the collective buy-in from Kashmiris for the new project of the Bakshi administration. People saw themselves as deserving of government largesse and also placed their expectations on the government to deliver. Furthermore, despite increased economic and political integration with the Government of India, the Kashmir government exhibited a significant amount of autonomy in its day-to-day decisions at the local level, including formulating education policy and curriculum, the content and medium of instruction, and qualifications for entry into various programs.

Educational Reform: Creating a Modern Kashmiri Subject

Being modern in the context of Kashmir directly contrasted to life under the Dogras, which was seen as a time of backwardness, poverty, superstition, illiteracy, and isolation from the outside world. Modern education involved a desire to cultivate well-rounded students and prepare them for a life of productivity in an increasingly revolutionizing society. The Kashmir government saw investment in education as a significant contribution toward economic growth.[69] Policies and initiatives were thus created to uplift the masses, bringing them into line with middle-class sensibilities of hard work, civic duty, cleanliness, and leisure. In many ways, then, Bakshi's state-building policies were both a class-based program of the Kashmiri elites and upper classes wanting to imbue the middle and lower classes with a particular set of modernizing concerns and attitudes as well as a program in which the latter were active in shaping its implementation on the ground.

The government wanted to ensure that students would be able to be *productive* citizens, ones that could contribute to economic progress. In accordance with the manifesto, emphasis was placed on technical and vocational training to cultivate those with the skills necessary to improve the living standard of the masses. At the primary level, the department created "activity schools," where "children would learn by doing things, things that would be related to their daily life and that would be connected with their immediate surroundings."[70] Craft and play had a prominent place in their education. English was not the primary focus; emphasis was on the mother tongue and Urdu and writing in excellent calligraphy. A standard primary school curriculum consisted of classes in health and hygiene, arithmetic, basic science, civic sense, and basic history and geography of the state and of India. The history of Kashmir was taught through talks and plays about the rudiments of the new social structure, especially the changes brought about by the new government. After their primary schooling, a majority of students went on to trade or technical schools. These "multipurpose" schools at the secondary stage allowed students to learn trades like agriculture, animal husbandry, beekeeping, arts, crafts, sericulture, horticulture, technical skills, and forestry. Learning a particular trade improved a student's chance to obtain employment after completing school. The aim was to produce not just "a skilled craftsmen but an educated citizen also," with a "healthier civic and social sense, an appreciation for culture, ready do their part in bringing about a progressive, modernizing Kashmir."[71]

The government was keen on developing a sense of patriotism for the motherland—which was seen as Kashmir—and pride in the Naya Kashmir program. Attention was paid to the cultivation of a proper civic sense and explaining the different components and capacities of the modern state. History and geography lessons emphasized understanding the five-year plans, land reforms, cooperative societies, modern methods of agriculture, rural reconstruction, scientific inventions, women's empowerment, trade unions, industrialization, the postal system, the health system, and village economies.[72]

With no intermediate schools, qualified students went on to secondary (high) schools, where they prepared for the matriculation exam and potentially for college or university. Secondary education at this point was limited to a select few. The students specialized in streams that depended on the needs of the locality and on the availability of teachers.[73] After matriculation, a majority of students would end their formal education and find employment in trade, commerce, government, and secretarial jobs, while a few went to colleges and universities within Kashmir or outside the state. Many received scholarships so that they could return to Kashmir and teach in the colleges. Others returned as doctors, engineers, lawyers, and bureaucrats.

The government was concerned with the deterioration of discipline and good behavior among the youth. In particular, it wanted to ensure that youth utilized their time in healthy, nonpolitical directions, and it reserved a significant portion of the education budget for "youth welfare."[74] The government organized youth rallies on important occasions—such as India's independence day and Nehru's birthday. As in Nehruvian India, schools and colleges became much more attentive to sports and physical education and the encouragement of art, music, drama, and theater.[75] The Kashmir government took a keen interest in a number of these schemes sponsored by the Government of India. A look at *Lalla Rookh*, the magazine of Amar Singh College, provides a glimpse into the dynamic student life at the time. Many students wrote articles about their experiences with hiking, youth camps, and scouting, activities seen as promoting self-confidence, cooperation, better judgment, and communal harmony.[76]

Bakshi built sports fields, including the still-standing Bakshi Stadium, and students were urged to participate in competitions and tournaments organized by the government. Kashmiri teams also participated in inter-state tournaments in hockey, football, and cricket. In one year alone, over 40,000 rupees were set aside for the organization of sports and physical activities, and the Government of India supported all efforts related to youth welfare.[77] In a letter to the Department of Education, Humayan Kabir of the Government of India's Ministry of Education wrote that "the school of today exists not just for promoting scholarship but for total development of child's personality."[78] To develop a healthier civic and social sense, students were also encouraged to volunteer and participate in social service activities.[79] The arts also received due attention. In 1961, under the auspices of the Tagore Memorial Committee, Bakshi inaugurated Tagore Hall, the first state-of-the-art theater in Kashmir. Performances were held in colleges and schools, and folk dramas were revived. Artists and troupes from India as well as local groups performed for Indian and foreign dignitaries. Kashmiri writers created many of the dramas, which promoted communal harmony, raised awareness of women's and social issues, and propagated principles of the new government (including land reform) and the duties and responsibilities of citizens.

Focus on women's education also defined this period.[80] Not only were female students exhorted to focus on their studies, but they were also involved in a variety of sports and theater. Describing her first day at the Women's College in Srinagar, Shamla Mufti, one of the first women to receive her master's in Kashmir and would later become principal of the Women's College, emphasizes the variety of options available to female students. She recalls, "Some girls had a hockey stick in their hands. . . . Some were talking about badminton matches. . . . Some were in a hurry to go to the library. Some had to go to a drama practice and they were running around for that reason."[81]

The students at the women's college would also go with their professors to nearby villages or downtown Srinagar for various social service projects. Mufti remembers that "they would bathe the kids, clean the houses . . . and let the mothers know how to keep their children away from different sicknesses."[82] These extracurricular activities played an important role in the government's cultivation of a modern subject, one with discipline, service, and a well-rounded personality. All these qualities were to help students play a critical role in state-building activities, influencing their families, relatives, and neighbors.

To cultivate well-rounded individuals, the government also exposed students and teachers to views, people, and institutions outside Kashmir through educational tours and trips. Kashmiri students were sent on tours to cities like Delhi, Amritsar, Agra, and Aligarh through their colleges and through athletic competitions, youth camps, and cultural programs in theater and music.

Arts, sports, and youth welfare were part of nation-building activities in a number of postcolonial contexts, including in India. Yet, in the context of Kashmir's colonial occupation, they were also pivotal to the politics of life and the subsequent politics of depoliticization and containment. Building from understandings of the relationship between sports, culture, and colonialism, the promotion of these activities in Kashmir not only enabled the construction of modern, active, disciplined national subjects but also emotional integration with India. Good-will tours from delegations in India and trips to different cities in India were a way for young Kashmiris to build affective ties with India and Indians. They were intended to show Kashmiris that they were part of a broader project of nation-building and evoke a sense of belonging to the nation. Within Kashmir, the promotion of these activities allowed the Kashmir government to have some level of social control—especially over the youth—that needed to be contained lest they became more politically conscious or, worse, active. The government hoped to not only contain political threats but "actively transform the political positions and dispositions that could produce such threats."[83]

Cultivating "Secularism"

Scholars have argued that secularism in the context of the Indian subcontinent was distinct from its European variant. Rajeev Bhargava argues for a "contextual secularism" in the case of India, which "did not erect a strict wall of separation, but proposes instead a 'principled distance' between religion and state. Moreover, by balancing the claims of individuals and religious communities, it never intended privatization of religion."[84] Yet, there has been limited literature on how the Indian state conceptualized the secular and what the secular actually meant in practice in contrast to the rhetoric around it. In the case of Kashmir, the challenge was not to completely remove religion from the public sphere but to ensure the acceptable modalities through which religious identities could be articulated publicly, while disseminating certain fields of knowledge. What the government did not account for, however, was that religious difference was already coded into its practice and set the terms by which religious claims could inform state policies. For example, Mridu Rai argues that "Jammu and Kashmir's very entry into the [Indian] constituent assembly's deliberations was attended by a religiously informed understanding of its people . . . chiseling Kashmiris into Hindus and Muslims."[85]

The Kashmir government was also interested in cultivating a secular Kashmiri identity, what many have referred to as *kashmiriyat*, or a shared secular syncretic Kashmiri culture. Interestingly, while the Naya Kashmir manifesto called for the encouragement of our "common culture, which includes the culture of all nationalities living in the state," it does not use the term *kashmiriyat*.[86] It appears that the term gained traction only after Sheikh Abdullah returned to power in the 1970s.[87]

The concept of *kashmiriyat* has been discussed by a number of scholars, including the multiple meanings of the term, its origins, and its varying political trajectories.[88] But how did the Kashmir government construct this secular, composite identity, especially since thus far, rights had been granted or denied based on one's religious identity? As we will see, this context placed the desire for the "secular" in tension with actual state policy that was hyper-cognizant of religious enumeration, especially in educational institutions.

In their reports, inspectors from the Department of Education would regularly categorize the number of students and teachers in schools or the scholarships provided for a given year based on their religious affiliation. In one report, the principal of the Amar Singh College proudly informed the government that all Muslims who had applied to the college that year had been accepted, revealing that the same had not been the case for Hindus and Sikhs.[89] This attention to enumeration, as we will see—not unlike the days of the British or the Dogras—led to increased communal polarization. Furthermore, the government's "disavowal of religion in its political calculus and its simultaneous reliance on religious categories to structure and regulate social life" linked the public and the private that the secular state was intended to separate.[90]

Here, I am interested in two primary points. First, the government's construction of a secular Kashmiri subject sought to bring Kashmir in line with the purported secular ideals of the Government of India and away from the two-nation policy upheld by the creation of Pakistan. Yet, the secular ideals of the Government of India were themselves in question at this time.[91] Second, and perhaps more importantly, the emphasis on promoting an *existing* secular identity in fact obscured the state's fears of continued discord between religious communities, a very real possibility given the very structures within the state that enabled perceived or actual religious inequality. In that sense, the government didn't promote a secular identity to reflect reality. It did so to inculcate the attachments and dispositions that would make it a reality.

While there were no overt acts of violence between Muslims and Hindus during the Partition in the Valley, an ethnic cleansing of Muslims had taken place in Jammu under Dogra and right-wing Hindu nationalist auspices. At the same time, tensions arose in the immediate aftermath of the Partition as various Hindu groups contested the Abdullah government's policies, especially land reform, which they saw as an attempt to marginalize them. The government was also concerned about any outwardly Muslim assertions in the public sphere and any rise in the popularity of the Muslim Conference or other pro-Pakistan groups within the state. Indeed, the specter of religious discord was never too far from the minds of Abdullah and Bakshi. This potential discord threatened to undo Kashmir's incorporation into India, which was fundamentally based on the oft-repeated notion that Kashmir, as a Muslim-majority state, had opted for India because its Muslims were "secular" and had rejected the two-nation theory.[92] Anxious about communal tension, the government envisioned educational institutes as one place where they could intervene in order to promote communal harmony. As a result, the political leadership repeatedly encouraged the Department of Education to "ban the scourge of communalism."[93]

The Government of India sent a letter to all state governments to suggest ideas for improving and strengthening communal harmony in educational institutions in the country from both the "general point of view of public peace and security but also from the educational point of view. . . . [The] consequences for misconceptions are far-reaching."[94] In Kashmir, A. A. Kazimi, the non-Kashmiri director of education under Abdullah and partially under Bakshi, collected suggestions to strengthen communal harmony from various stakeholders, including teachers, principals, and school inspectors. They proposed joint celebrations of all festivals by the various communities, suitable songs or talks to promote communal harmony, praise for the virtues of communal harmony in textbooks, intercommunal dinners or celebrations to recognize those who contributed toward the cementing of relations between different communities, common prayers and singing of the national anthem by the whole school before work began, games enabling mutual dependency among members of all communities, the staging of dramas emphasizing communal harmony, the promotion of voluntary social work in diverse communities, studying the language and literature of the other community, and going on hiking trips and excursions where the students lived together in common tents and dined in common areas.[95] One important suggestion, whose avoidance would come to haunt the department, was "non-communal recruitment to the government services and also to promotion to higher education." The suggestions were exhaustive and even included ideas that Hindu students should speak on the anniversaries of Muslim holy prophets and saints, and vice versa.[96] Examples of possible dramas included the life stories of Akbar, Kabir, and other perceived secular figures of Indian history. Moments of communal violence or tensions were to be expunged from the history syllabi, and it was suggested that classrooms be decorated with images of great men and reformers who had done their part in maintaining communal relations.[97]

One of the more intriguing suggestions was to keep teachers busy during the day so they would not have time for talk that exacerbated religious tensions. The occurrence of such talk must have been a concern of the department since on an educational tour in 1958, the new minister of state for health and education, A. G. Trali, urged teachers to "play their role in the democratic movement of the state and not to [involve] themselves into any political group or groupings."[98] The department was also concerned about the types of books, newspapers, and magazines available in the schools and colleges. Any book, paper, or magazine deemed to cause religious friction was banned from educational institutes.[99] An incident arose when a principal of a school ordered for his school library a number of books by Maulana Abu Ala Mawdudi, the founder of the Jamaat-i-Islami, an Islamic political organization that advocated a role for Islam in political life, as well as books by other Islamic scholars. The department admonished him for keeping these books in the library as they held views that were subversive of the ideals of the state; they were removed.[100] Works that mocked Islam, Hinduism, or Sikhism were also banned.

In addition to promoting communal harmony in educational spaces, the department also took a deep interest in rewriting the history syllabi and publishing new textbooks in line with the ideals of the Naya Kashmir manifesto. In detailed directions to the writers of textbooks, the Text Book Committee instructed, "Books are to popularize the ideals of patriotism, tolerance, humanity and encourage a progressive outlook on life in the New Kashmir. Children should be introduced to the cultural heritage of Kashmir in such a manner that they may learn to acquire creative appreciations of this heritage."[101] Under Sheikh Abdullah, there was more emphasis on the history and heritage of Kashmir than of India. The lone exception was to mention the impact of the Indian freedom movement on Kashmir.[102] Writers were encouraged to link history and geography lessons to local events.[103] This slowly changed under Bakshi's government, as more explicit mention was made of historical ties between India and Kashmir.

Kashmiri history was refashioned to make its incorporation into India appear seamless. The writers of the textbooks were urged to focus on the medieval and modern eras of Kashmir, as these eras were seen as best speaking to the secular demands of the contemporary moment.[104] In so doing, the life histories of prominent perceived secular figures such as the famous medieval poets Lal Ded and Nund Rishi and one of the more "inclusive" Muslim rulers, Zain-ul-Abidin, were highlighted.[105] More recent individuals, such as Maqbool Sherwani and Brigadier Usman, both supporters of the National Conference who had been killed in battle against Pathan Muslims in 1947, were also spotlighted to highlight those who upheld the ideals of a secular Kashmir linked to

India. Study of the modern period covered the harsh conditions of Kashmiris under the Dogras and the momentous struggles of the National Conference leadership, which had overcome the scourge of "communalism" (i.e., the Muslim Conference) during the freedom movement in Kashmir. Important figures from different parts of the state appeared in order to create cross-regional unity. Both the medieval and the modern periods provided examples of what was perceived as the "inherent" secular identity of Kashmir and were thus highlighted by the government.

While the construction of the history of Kashmir focused primarily on an agreed upon understanding of a shared secular ethos, the discussion of the historical relationship between Kashmir and India was not always as natural or clear-cut. A few years into the post-Partition period, as the state's political status became firmly entrenched with India, more attention was given to Indian history. Some drafts of the government's syllabi and textbooks were returned to the authors for not including material on Indian history or stories of important Indian nationalist figures such as the Rani of Jhansi, Gandhi, and Nehru. Greater emphasis was placed on Kashmir's historic links with India, especially after Akbar.[106] This was done to trace a natural progression of Kashmir's political future with India. It is important to note that while periodization of Kashmiri history went from periods of Kashmiri rule (whether Buddhist, Hindu, or Muslim) to non-Kashmiri rule, Indian history was demarcated along a religious periodization with distinct periods of Muslim and Hindu rule. Because the government wanted to ensure that this reading of history did not cause any conflict, professors were called in from Delhi to confirm fair representation of the two religious communities in Indian history.[107] Furthermore, the links between the freedom movement in India and the freedom movement in Kashmir were developed, emphasizing their shared anti-feudal, progressive, and secular visions. Nonetheless, in the framing of the relationship, Kashmir was already treated as being separate from India; for example, for school projects students were encouraged to do a project either on India *or* Kashmir. The justification for how the two became intertwined was being constructed *through* these syllabi.

The work of constructing a secular identity for Kashmir was not limited to syllabi and textbooks. The activities of the Archeology, Museums,

Research and Publication Department also worked toward this end. In doing so, the department departed from Dogra policies, which sought to buttress Hindu religious sites and interests.[108] Under Bakshi, the department was now tasked with promoting the ideology of a secular Kashmiri material and literary history. For archeology, the government assembled a list of historic sites important to both Hindus and Muslims, providing funding for their preservation and upkeep.[109] The research and publications department also made sure to collect manuscripts throughout the Valley that dealt with both Hindu and Muslim thought, practice, and philosophy. It collected a number of texts in both Sanskrit and Arabic/Persian and published works on Kashmir's contribution to Persian and Sanskrit literature.[110] By publishing and preserving these manuscripts, especially those that dealt with mysticism and Shaivism, the government was able to position itself as promoting the history and literature of all communities.[111]

Not everyone agreed with the version of history being shaped to give credence to ties with India. In a response note to a prospective textbook, M. A. Beg, who would later form the oppositional Plebiscite Front, critiqued the presentation of Kashmir's history with India, saying it was presented in a manner that made Kashmir seem as if it had always relied on or been a part of India historically. Beg also questioned the popular Hindu myth of Kashmir's founding through an overreliance of the *Rajatarangini* (discussed in chapter 3) and the role of Kashyap Rishi, a Vedic sage of Hinduism. In the Puranas, a Hindu text, Kashyap Rishi is said to have drained the Kashmir Valley to make it inhabitable, after which the term *Kashmir* was derived from his name. Beg stated that this story was a myth but was presented as a fact in the textbooks. He dismissed the notion that non-Kashmiri rulers were liberators and argued that Kashmiri kings were presented in a haphazard manner and, if they were Muslim, almost always discussed in a bad light.[112] Beg was a close associate of Sheikh Abdullah's and thus, served as a potent foil to Bakshi's state-building policies. Painting the government's educational curriculum as anti-Kashmir and anti-Muslim reveals the anxieties about the balance Bakshi's government was attempting to tread, even among those who had previously supported accession to India. Beg's criticism of how the government represented Kashmir's history—and seemed to elide, in particular, its Muslim history—suggests that the curriculum was viewed by some Muslims as narrating an ostensibly secular history that in effect foregrounded Hindu mythologies.

Additional criticism of the government's educational policy came from other Muslim bureaucrats and scholars. Ghulam Hassan Khan, a Kashmiri writer and scholar, argued that the state's educational system was designed to "create a sense of integration, unity, and solidarity" with the "secular and nationalist ideals" of India. . . . "The state's educational system also focused on Indian culture and traditions, refraining from educating Kashmiris about their own history or language."[113] He disagreed with the "government's decision to exclude religious education from the curriculum, arguing that ethical education created a society free from greed, deceit and slander."[114] Although Khan claims that religious education was excluded, that was not the case; indeed, a particular "syncretic" and "apolitical" version of Islam (made tame because of the influence of Hinduism or Indic civilization) was propagated by the state, "reducing Islam to a monolithic form."[115]

Perhaps the most incisive critique came from the Jamaat-i-Islami Kashmir, a sociopolitical organization founded in 1946, which strove to maintain its own identity outside its parent body in India or Pakistan. The Jamaat explicitly critiqued the purported secularism of both the Indian state and the Kashmir state.[116] It organized symposiums in response to the new education policy, including one held in Sopore in 1955. In a three-part article in the paper *Dawat* (published as well in the Jamaat's own paper in Kashmir, *Azan*) linked to the Jamaat-i-Islami in India, the *amir* of the Jamaat, Saaduddin Tarabali, commented on the government's draft educational policy, spearheaded by the left-leaning minister of education, G. M. Sadiq. Tarabali compared Kashmir to South Tyrol, an area annexed by Italy after World War I, whose population was of German descent and spoke German. Italy attempted to provide "such an education and training to this new population, so that when they became adults there would be no differences between them and the imagination of their rulers. . . . They would not recognize their language and ancestors even by mistake. They must be all-over Italian; they had to die for Italy and live for Italy."[117] This, Tarabali suggested, is what India was doing to Kashmir, arguing—in line with the politics of life—that what modern powers could not do with the stick (that is, through use of force), they did through education.

Tarabali's criticism of the government's educational policy was on both technical and ideological grounds. Critiquing the starting age for primary education, he suggested it should be at the age of five and a half years, rather than the government's recommendation of seven years. He argued that at seven years of age, children had already picked up the negative influences of the society around them. He also opposed coeducation, arguing that "cinema, nude pictures, pornographic songs and literature have aroused so much sexual desire that a twelve-year-old is fully aroused by these emotions . . . and schools become centers of mischief in that sense."[118] He pushed back against compulsory education for students, stating that it was known to lead to a high average of absenteeism. Most importantly, however, he declared that theology—which was completely absent—should be compulsory in the education curriculum, especially because religion "helps to create a high level of morality." Developing a society without morality, he argued, was akin to building a house on sand. Strikingly, although Tarabali agreed that physical education and recreation were important, he argued the government's education policy lacked military training and the use of military equipment, which should be an integral component to college education. In addition, he argued that schools should develop a relationship with local hospitals or health centers, and male and female doctors should visit the schools and treat the students for any illnesses. He also urged the government to take public criticism seriously and incorporate it in its policy.

Tarabali argued that the purpose or goal of education was not made clear in the government document and was a source of confusion for the general public. The document claimed that the aim of the new education policy "would be not only to produce skilled craftsmen, but an educated citizen also." However, it did not specify what it meant to be an educated citizen. The textbooks—covering a range of diverse topics—also had no coherent purpose and would lead the students' minds to "wander." His own understanding of the purpose of education relied upon a civilizational gap between the East and the West. He criticized the adoption of Western educational norms and philosophies in the new education policy, arguing that even as the Western world had advanced technologically and obtained a position of leadership, "it had divided the human community and provided the basis for a bloodbath on which man has twice played the Holi of human blood on a large scale," in reference to the two world wars.[119] Western education erected artificial walls "between man and humanity on a national and patriotic basis . . . and those living inside and outside these walls have been taught the process of annihilating each other." Tarabali argued that education itself was the culprit, as only "highly educated people have come forward as leaders to spread this poison. . . . Someone who is illiterate cannot succeed in this." Comparing Western education to a garden, he described how "its poisonous fruit is so sharp and bitter that neither the shade of the trees nor the spring of the garden can withstand this bitterness. . . . The death of the fruit has turned the whole beauty of the garden upside down." He called for new plants to be planted in the garden—a new approach to education—that would not be bitter, but sweet; not deadly, but life-giving. For the leaders of the East to mimic the West would be to jump into a well with one's eyes open.

While Tarabali does not use the term *secularism*, it is evident that it is precisely the form of Western education—steeped in secular values that remove morality and theology from the curriculum—that is to blame for the "bloodbath." For Tarabali, the purpose of education should not be economic or technological advancement but rather, cultivation of a sense of morality and purpose for the citizenry. While the Kashmir government could boast of encouraging a holistic approach to education that incorporated both physical and technical development, Tarabali's ideal educated body went a step further: it was intellectually sound, morally and spiritually disciplined, and physically strong and healthy. By leveraging his critique on civilizational terms, Tarabali went beyond the more expected criticism of the state erasing Muslim identity. Rather, the state's approach to education, based on secular, Western norms, had grave consequences for humanity at large.

The Jamaat implemented its critiques of the educational vision of the government, presenting a competing mode of education that brought together traditional Islamic sciences and modern scientific education. The organization opened a number of private schools throughout the state. Unlike other schools run by Muslim *anjumans* (such as the schools affiliated with the Anjuman Nusrat ul Islam), the schools run by the Jamaat did not receive any grant-in-aids from the state. These schools increased in popularity and reach, especially in major cities and towns outside Srinagar, Yoginder Sikand argues, because they provided middle-class Muslims with an alternative to what they felt was an onslaught by government schools promoting Indian cultural imperialism.[120] While Sikand does not specify what he means by the promotion of "Indian cultural imperialism," it was perhaps the secular nature of the government's curriculum—seen as Indian cultural imperialism—that these families opposed. In addition, many of these schools were also opened in underserved rural areas, which also explains their increased popularity.

Kashmiri, Hindi, or Urdu?

As under the Dogras in the 1930s and 1940s, language was a major and frequent source of tension within the bureaucracy and in schools and colleges, marking continuities between both secular and Hindu modes of governance. The status of Kashmiri, Urdu, and Hindi was hotly contested and became linked to the broader political status of the state. The official language of instruction under the Dogras was Urdu, in both Perso-Arabic and Devanagari scripts, but a number of Hindu organizations felt that the Devanagari script was being sidelined. After the Dogras, Abdullah's government made efforts to promote Kashmiri, even putting together a Kashmiri script committee that was supposed to agree on a common script. Urdu, in both the Perso-Arabic and Devanagari scripts, remained the official language during Bakshi's rule. The status of Kashmiri, however, was unclear, with the government sometimes declaring Kashmiri or another regional language (such as Dogri or Ladakhi) as the medium of instruction in primary schools, and other times Urdu in either script.[121]

The Government of India was particularly interested in the status of Hindi in the various states and sent repeated requests to ask the state governments what was being done for the propagation of Hindi, as it was the national language. Even Karan Singh, in his letters to Nehru, expressed his discomfort with Urdu being the state language of Kashmir, suggesting it was "far from uncontroversial and is open to serious objections" and argued that it was of "great importance that Hindi be given due place in the state at least equal to if not superior than the state language."[122] Initially, Kazimi (director of education) responded that nothing was being done. After repeated requests from the Government of India, in February 1954, Kazimi reported that "Hindustani in both the scripts is the medium of instruction in the primary and middle stages of education. In the high school, no language is compulsory, but Hindi is one of the three languages which can be taken up as an option subject."[123] It is important to note that Kazimi referred to the official language as Hindustani in his correspondence with the Indian authorities and not Urdu, although the latter was the official policy of the government. Perhaps he was attempting to appease the Government of India by situating Hindustani as the middle ground between Hindi and Urdu. The Kashmir government knew that propagating Hindi to the extent desired by the Government of India would have negative repercussions in Kashmir, so it resisted Hindi's broader implementation in the region. Even so, schools received aid to promote Hindi teaching and were also encouraged to purchase subscriptions to Hindi magazines, books, and journals, and a number of the magazines published by the educational institutions had Hindi sections in them. Kazimi argued that Hindi should not be imposed on the people but that people should come to it voluntarily.

The ambiguities in the policies did not pertain just to Hindi, but also to Urdu and Kashmiri. While the official policy rendered it obligatory for teachers to learn both the Devanagari and Perso-Arabic scripts, it remains unclear to what extent this was enforced, or if it was enforced only in those areas where there were significant numbers of students who used both.[124] There was also ambiguity about the use of a script for Kashmiri; in some instances the department mentions the script was complete and waiting for government authorization, and in others that the script was not yet complete.[125] In 1954, however, the committee submitted its report declaring that a majority of the committee members had ruled in favor of the Perso-Arabic script over Devanagari and Roman. The matter, however, was not further developed, nor does it appear to have been implemented.

Because of the country's vast diversity, the Government of India institutionalized a three-language formula in the federal linguistic jurisdiction for each state. The formula— intended to contribute to "ethno-linguistic emancipation"—included Hindi, English, and the regional language of the state.[126] In the case of the Valley, in particular, the regional language was Kashmiri. However, within a few years under Bakshi, Urdu became the primary language of instruction, although efforts to propagate Hindi at the behest of the Government of India continued. Kashmiri was removed from educational institutions, replaced by Urdu even as a medium of instruction for primary schools, a development that went against the Naya Kashmir manifesto. Kashmiri was spoken by nearly 97 percent of the population in the Valley, while Dogri, Pahari, and Ladakhi were spoken in the other regions of the state. Urdu was not the mother tongue of any of the regions of the state, and so the decision to single it out as the language of primary instruction was a surprising one. The government's justification—which remained unsubstantiated—was that "the most widely spoken and understood language in the JK state is Urdu which therefore has naturally been recognized as the regional language for the whole state."[127]

One possible explanation for the decline of Kashmiri under Bakshi is that it was a deliberate attempt by his government to "Indianize" Kashmir in the post-1953 moment; if the masses remained distant from the Kashmiri language, feelings of a distinct Kashmiri sociocultural identity would erode, facilitating better integration with India. This perspective, however, does not provide the entire picture. In the Srinagar State Archives, there are no official directives or correspondence with the Government of India to remove ties to the Kashmiri language—the directives mostly concern the propagation of Hindi. Furthermore, despite Urdu being a regional language, the Government of India was not interested in its promotion, since it had been declared the official language of the state of Pakistan and was increasingly seen as the language of Muslims and Muslim "separatism."

In addition, the Government of India and the Kashmir government attempted to appropriate, not dismiss, Kashmiri for their own purposes. While Kashmiri was demoted in the educational institutions, it was not ignored completely. The Education Department began a Kashmiri research section in the new Research and Publications Department to collect rare Kashmiri manuscripts to preserve Kashmiri heritage. Lalla Rookh, a publishing company affiliated with the government, also began to publish a number of contemporary and historical Kashmiri plays, novels, and collections of short stories.[128] Nonetheless, the government decided not to give Kashmiri official-language status in the three-language policy throughout India. If the issue was not with the Kashmiri language itself, what else led it to be displaced as the medium of instruction? I contend the decision to declare Urdu the primary language of the state was an entirely local one, based on the internal dynamics and agentive role of the Kashmir government.

K. Warikoo makes reference to the variety of ways Urdu was given preference over Kashmiri. For one, Warikoo points out, there were very few Kashmiri language newspapers in circulation. The post-1947 state administration also foiled attempts to promote the Kashmiri language; for example, when the Films Division of the Government of India wanted to dub films in Kashmiri, the government requested that they do it in simple Urdu. It also foiled attempts by Russian publishers to translate Russian classics into Kashmiri. Warikoo argues that the policy against the Kashmiri language reflects the dynamics of "Muslim majoritarianism" in which a religious ethnicity (Muslim-Urdu) has been superimposed over a linguistic ethnicity (Kashmiri) to bring Kashmiri Muslims closer to the concept of the *ummah* (global community of Muslims) and the state of Pakistan. "This task has been carried forward by numerous Islamic political, social and cultural institutions," he states, "all of which have been preaching and promoting Islamic world view" The result, Warikoo argues, is that "a firm ideological base has been prepared to mould the political and cultural views of Kashmiri Muslims on religious lines rather than ethno-linguistic/cultural basis."[129]

Warikoo's argument may ring true for some religious organizations in the Valley, but it does not help us understand why the Kashmiri government promoted Urdu. Further, with its emphasis on "Muslim majoritarianism," it runs the risk of conflating the Kashmir government, composed of Kashmiri Muslims, with Muslim institutions in the state. As we have seen, the government attempted to produce a secular subject in the state's educational institutions; for a bureaucracy and political leadership that arrested people who were pro-Pakistan to cultivate a language policy based on allegiance to Pakistan is unlikely. Indeed, Kashmiri was being displaced from the educational institutions and replaced by Urdu, but Warikoo's account of this being a result of Muslim majoritarianism, as we will see, is inadequate.

Chitrelekha Zutshi, in her discussion of linguistic policies in the state under Bakshi, also argues that Urdu was adopted as the only official language of the state as it was "obviously pandering to increasingly vocal elements in Kashmir that were articulating the Kashmiri identity in Muslim terms."[130] In other words, adopting Urdu was a form of Muslim appeasement. Both Warikoo's and Zutshi's reasoning falls into the trap of equating the promotion of Urdu with Muslim majoritarianism, not taking into account the historical position of Urdu in the state, as well as in the Muslim elite imagination. The removal of Kashmiri from the educational system resulted from various interests: the goals of the Kashmir government, the class-based educational philosophies of people in the Department of Education, and, surprisingly, the demands of some individuals in the broader public. As Ananya Kabir reminds us, it is important not to deny agency and grant Kashmiri speakers "some control over their mother tongue."[131] To do so will reveal some aspects of a "collective psyche."[132]

One of the goals of the post-1947 state was to find coherence among the different regions, including the Valley, Jammu, and Ladakh, and to unify a state identity. In an article entitled "Kashmiri and the Linguistic Predicament of the State," P. N. Pushp argues that "the New Kashmir aspirations were dynamic enough to give the Kashmiri language a chance. The language was made at one stroke a subject of study as well as a medium of instruction. But soon the overcautious bureaucracy . . . viewed the experiment as extremely inconvenient, for, despite its constitutional status, Kashmiri, after all, was a mother tongue likely to inspire other mother tongues of the State also to press for their claims to be accommodated in the school curriculum."[133]

It is a strong possibility, as Pushp suggests, that one of the reasons the bureaucracy found the Kashmiri language inconvenient was that it would inspire the other mother tongues (including Dogri, Ladakhi, and Balti) to press for claims to be better accommodated, since the state was interested in managing discontent of other regions that had erupted in the late Dogra period as well as during Sheikh Abdullah's term, especially with the Praja Parishad in Jammu. Thus, it is possible that Urdu was seen as the language that could unite the various regions of the state.

Yet, this analysis, much like Zutshi's, does not adequately consider the history of the region, the position of Urdu among the Muslim intelligentsia in the subcontinent, and the position of Kashmiri in the eyes of many upwardly mobile Kashmiris. Given years of rule under non-Kashmiris, other languages—Persian, Sanskrit, Urdu, English—were always privileged over Kashmiri.[134] For some Muslim bureaucrats, Kashmiri was, simply put, not seen as a modern language. The Kashmiri Script Writing Committee attempted to modernize the Kashmiri language.[135] The committee met with Kashmiris of various professions to come up with vocabulary dealing with modern subjects, including topics in health, science, and technology. It appears that this effort was more challenging than they had imagined. Thus, the government was at a loss to figure out how to modernize Kashmiri, and it returned its attention to Urdu.[136]

Interestingly, it was not just the Muslim elite or bureaucratic classes that were skeptical about the use of Kashmiri. In the Educational Policy document, Education Minister G. M. Sadiq states, "Many Kashmiris, especially those who belong to towns and who are well-off do not want their children to be taught Kashmiri in schools. They seem to feel that Kashmiri should be taught to children at home, and the schools should teach them Urdu."[137] This perspective was not limited just to urban Kashmiris. Petitions from Kashmiris living in rural areas also asked the Education Department to focus on teaching Urdu in schools as children learned Kashmiri at home. In one example, the parents of students who were taught Kashmiri at the primary level urged the local education officer to teach the students exclusively in Urdu.[138] In their eyes, Kashmiri was the language of the rural, village poor—backward and without the prospect of economic mobility.[139]

When it came to heritage and literature, Kashmiri was promoted through the preservation of old manuscripts and the production of literature in the language, but when it came to the crafting of modern subjects through the education system, it was not deemed appropriate. The promotion of Urdu was linked to the upwardly socially mobile aspirations of the Muslim bureaucracy and the middle and lower classes; it was thus linked to the desire for modernity. Knowing Urdu would provide greater opportunity for Kashmiri Muslims to travel to places like Aligarh, Delhi, or Hyderabad for their studies. Urdu was seen as providing greater status, as well as geographic and intellectual mobility. We must remember that a number of the educationists had obtained their education from Aligarh and were in touch with the developments of the Muslim intelligentsia throughout the subcontinent, including progressive Muslim thought. Kavita Datla discusses the role Urdu played among the Muslim intelligentsia affiliated with Osmania University. She argues that the Muslim educationists did not employ Urdu as a tool to articulate their identitarian claims but as grounds to shape the future of a secular, modernizing national culture with a place for the Muslim past and scholarly traditions.[140] Thus, Urdu was seen as being at the center of a shared secular future (although what that secular future entailed still remained vague).

Datla's argument holds partial resonance for Kashmir, although in the case of Kashmir, the emphasis was more on the class-based aspirations of a group of Kashmiri Muslims instead of the reformulation of Muslim literary and religious traditions. In Kashmir, Urdu had a historical pull—as it was the language of the state under the Dogras—as well as a modern one. Urdu provided the Muslims of Kashmir with an elite language that was also seen as modern. Urdu was initially important for a number of Pandit educationists as well, as many of them were well versed in the language. Indeed, Pandits were the authors of much of the Urdu literature written by Kashmiris.[141]

A look into language syllabi sheds light on how Urdu was viewed vis-à-vis other languages. The Urdu syllabi encouraged teachers to discuss vocabulary and stories relating to the body, dress, food, shelter, animals, transport, objects, occupations, the lives of the great men and women of Kashmir, craft, and agriculture. No reference was made to explicitly Islamic topics, such as stories of the Prophets or any Islamic texts or religious traditions.[142] This was not the case for the Hindi and Punjabi language syllabi. While the Hindi and Punjabi language syllabi dealt with everyday vocabulary relating to the home, school, hygiene, sports, science, and patriotism, they also explicitly made reference to religious stories from the Ramayana, Mahabharata, and the Bhagavad Gita as well as information on the Guru Nanak and other religious figures.[143] The promotion of Urdu was largely articulated in a deliberately nonreligious way. This is unlike Urdu nationalism in Hyderabad, which incorporated Muslim identity to invoke a broader, more universal national identity. Nevertheless, whatever the intentions of the state might have been, a number of Kashmiri Pandits and Hindus in the state (and later scholars) viewed the promotion of Urdu as a "communal" move that favored or appeased Kashmiri Muslims over other groups in the state.

There is a separate but related reason Kashmiri was demoted in educational institutions. The promotion of Kashmiri was seen as a communist conspiracy, as most of the leaders of the Democratic National Conference (who had formed a separate group from Bakshi in the mid-1950s) favored it, including Sadiq and Mir Qasim.[144] Therefore, Kashmiri might also have been a site of contention between the Bakshi group and the communists (who had been deeply involved in the writing of the manifesto) in his administration, underlining another example of how local rivalries impacted policy.

Controversies over Educational Policies

Educational contestations surrounding Pandit-Muslim relations did not pertain just to linguistic policy. They also spilled over into college admissions and employment. From the perspective of some Pandits, their community became marginalized as more and more Muslims began to benefit from the openings provided by the new government. We have already seen that to manage Kashmiri Muslims after accession and the arrest of Sheikh Abdullah, Bakshi's government gave employment and educational seats to Muslims whose families had played a role in providing legitimacy for his rule. After his rule ended, a commission was set up with the support of the Government of India in 1967 to investigate his government's recruitment policies, which were causing tensions between various communities. In its report, the commission declared that "there were instances where recruitment was made without observing the usual formalities. . . . Besides, some appointments were also made from political cadres. . . . [Bakshi] stated that merit could not be the only criterion in these matters . . . [for if it were so,] there would be no place for Muslims . . . and other backward people in the state."[145] Because of the need for Muslim representation in the government and educational institutions, many of these positions were given to Muslims over more "qualified" Pandits. This went against the ideal of representation to protect the interests of the minorities in the state, as articulated in the Naya Kashmir manifesto. In the plan, minorities were given a weightage in the legislative assembly to quell their fears of majoritarianism. Yet, at the same time, the minority-majority logic did not have the same salience in Kashmir, where the Muslims, as a majority, were considered a backward class and thus provided with additional access to benefits often reserved for disempowered minorities.[146] The promise of equality among the various groups was not possible given their starkly different material realities.[147] At the same time—the numerical minorities of the state, including the Kashmiri Pandits, felt that Muslims should not be treated as a backward class.

Two incidents occurred under Bakshi's government that highlight these contestations around educational policies. The first was a government order in 1954 establishing community-based ratios for admissions to colleges. The second was the hiring of teachers within the state. To justify the community-based ratios, Kazimi said, "I feel that the Muslims in Kashmir cannot for some years compete on equal terms with more educationally advanced non-Muslims for admissions in the colleges. It is therefore, very necessary to give them extra facilities."[148] Subsequently, on July 10, 1954, the secretary to government, Ministry of Education, issued an order declaring:

> With a view to affording chance for higher education to all communities, it is hereby ordered that future admissions in the colleges should be regulated as under
>
> | | |
> |---|---|
> | Kashmir: | Hindus (Including Sikhs): 30% |
> | | Muslims: 70% |
> | Jammu: | Hindus (Including Sikhs): 70% |
> | | Muslims: 30%[149] |

Given that Kashmiri Pandits and other non-Muslim students had constituted the vast majority of students in the colleges in Kashmir, this order had significant implications. It had arisen in response to protests and requests by Kashmiri Muslim students that Bakshi's government provide better opportunities for Muslims in higher education. In its efforts to ensure that these protests did not take a political turn, the government projected that a better enrollment of Muslims into the colleges would not only help fulfill its modernizing goals, but also lessen the concerns of the Muslim majority toward Indian rule. Here, we see Kashmiri Muslims utilizing the political dynamics of the state to gain certain material benefits.

In doing so, the government met stiff resistance from the Hindus in Kashmir. Prominent Pandit newspapers, including the *Martand* as well as papers outside Kashmir, criticized this new order vehemently. An article in the *Martand* declared that the "admission into state educational institutions was fixed on a communal basis.... If not revoked, numerous Hindu boys and girls being unable to secure entrance in government colleges would have either to discontinue their studies or go out of the state which would be possible only for a handful of those with some means."[150] The article continued that this order not only went against the "letter and spirit of the Indian constitution but also serves to reveal the true nature of the claims being made by state leaders that they stand for the high principles of secularism and democracy."[151] The government was accused of "dishonest and unscrupulous devices" for achieving their objective and was likely to be challenged in the court of law.

The reaction of the minority press in the state as well as the Indian press led the Department of Education to go on the defensive.[152] The response of the department is quoted here at length. The department acknowledged that:

> not a single voice has been raised in support of this order. The intention of the government is not to ban admission of boys and girls of any particular community but to enable boys belonging to backward classes to get admission in state colleges freely. The government has been spending the major portion of its revenues to impart free education and there it would be absolutely tendentious to suppose that there is any attempt to discourage higher education in case of the more educationally advanced communities. The policies of the government with respect to every sphere of administration are secular and the government is anxious to disallow discrimination against any community or class of people on grounds of religion.... In spite of the order, there have been no instances in which admission has been refused to the non-Muslim boys in Kashmir and Muslim boys in Jammu.[153]

The minority press in the state disputed the latter point, arguing that non-Muslims were unable to secure admission within the limits of the quota reserved for them. They urged the department to issue a clarifying directive stating admission to the colleges would be primarily based on merit, and that backwardness of a particular community would be a secondary consideration.

A number of leading Pandits in the Department of Education, including the education minister, J. N. Bhan, were in support of this government policy. Nonetheless, in contrast to the period under Dogra rule when Muslim students felt marginalized within colleges, criticism now came from certain segments of the Kashmiri Pandit community, who felt that the bureaucracy, now including a significant number of Muslims, was deliberately trying to appease Kashmiri Muslims at Pandit expense.[154] These Pandits viewed the Muslims as taking greater control over the bureaucracy and felt that they were an endangered religious minority; more and more Muslims were entering the state services, being hired as teachers, and being sent outside Kashmir for training and further education.

Evidence of this perception appears in Agha Ashraf Ali's memoirs, where he wrote of the complex relations between Kashmiri Muslims and Pandits during Bakshi's rule. As one of the first Kashmiri Muslims to play a prominent role in the Education Department, he described his close friendships and relationships with a number of Pandit friends and mentors, whom he thanked profusely for their impact on him. At the same time, he described the oppression meted out by the Pandits in government service or among the rural elite against Muslims under the Dogras.[155] He observed that the social position of Pandits declined during Bakshi's government and claimed that the communities at the time saw themselves as two separate nations, as Pandits began to distance themselves from the aspirations of Kashmiri Muslims to become closer to the Indian government.[156] In the educational institutions, he described the Pandit *baradari* (brotherhood) as closely linked, never speaking ill against each other, and rejecting interference in their community's internal affairs. He also acknowledged the fear the community felt once their monopoly on education and employment began to unravel. One of the major incidents that Agha Ashraf raises in his memoir is the reaction of the Pandit community toward the hiring of Kashmiri Muslim teachers. As principal of the Teachers College, Agha Ashraf oversaw a majority of Pandit teachers. As more Muslim teachers were hired into the college, he stated that the Pandit teachers were not happy to receive them.[157] At one point, when he sent two Muslim women for higher training, he described how the Pandits at the school started a corruption case against him, claiming he was acting "communally" and discriminating against Kashmiri Pandits. The issue was raised with Bakshi himself and the complaint was eventually dismissed. By then, Agha Ashraf's reputation had been tarnished. He would go on to claim that those Pandits he had once tried to help were the first to turn against him. He stated that everything he had worked for (secularism, communal harmony) had been destroyed.[158]

For a number of Pandits, especially those within the educational sector, fostering Muslim interests had reached its apogee under Bakshi. According to Professor Mohan Lal Koul, who served in several colleges in the state, after 1947 "all corners in the Valley were rummaged for Muslim graduates, who were put to the Training College, Srinagar for the Diploma in Teaching and . . . directly installed as Headmasters overriding the merit, achievements and claims of the veteran Kashmirian Hindu teachers . . . generating a simmering discontent in the Kashmirian Hindu teachers and Hindu employees in all departments of the government."[159] Koul's reflections are representative of the general sentiments of Kashmiri Pandit educators, many of whom believed they were discriminated against in hiring practices. This is further evidenced by Pandit teachers who went to the state high court with similar charges against the Department of Education. For doing so, Koul accuses Bakshi's men of harassing them. He says that "the goon-brigade reared and raised by Bakshi led an operation against the prominent Hindu teachers . . . putting them to a great humiliation. . . . [The] Prime Minister [has] stooped so low for organising such an operation against the veteran Hindu teachers, who were instrumental in changing the educational scenario of the state."[160] Justice Bahauddin ran the state high court at the time. The primary issue raised at the court was whether the hiring and promotions of new and existing teachers would be based on seniority (which would benefit the Pandits) or educational ability (a phrase that was flexible enough to benefit Muslims). A lengthy debate ensued over the definition of backwardness—whether it entailed social or economic backwardness. Eventually, Pandits concerns were overruled and Muslims were deemed socially backward, signaling once more the paradoxes of minority-majority logics under secular governance, especially in the context of Kashmir.

The issue arose again in the Supreme Court of India in 1968, during G. M. Sadiq's rule in a prominent case entitled *Trikoni Nath vs. the State of Jammu and Kashmir*. The Supreme Court, dissatisfied with the designation of the Muslims as a backward class, declared the current practices of the state unconstitutional.[161] While the Kashmir government upheld the judgment, it devised a plan to continue to allow Muslims to hold their offices as "in-charge" headmasters or educational officers. Agha Ashraf describes how, as a result, he was made to put two headmasters in each school—one based on seniority and one based on educational ability—usually one Pandit and one Muslim in each school. Debates over the hiring practices of the state and discrimination against the Pandits continued, and further cases arose during Sadiq's administration. The issue sparked a number of protests and demonstrations from members of both communities against the policies of the government. Eventually the Kashmir government resorted to detailing the particular castes and occupations among the Muslims, as well as towns in which they resided, that were deemed "backward," instead of marking them all as backward.

Were the Pandits discriminated against in educational policies? The state government's 1967 Commission of Enquiry to investigate recruitment policies also looked into biases for selection into higher education. Interestingly, it found that the number of students belonging to Jammu was much smaller than those from Kashmir, but that "the share of Hindus has been much larger than that of Muslims in all the important courses of study."[162] Furthermore, the commission declared that Hindu students received a much larger share of study loans than Muslims. While the commission had certainly vindicated the practices of the government, at least in regard to discrimination against Kashmiri Pandits, it certainly had a political reason to do so. The commission was motivated in part by a desire to maintain political stability. If it had found the Kashmir government guilty of discrimination against Pandits, it would have caused additional problems for a state that was increasingly struggling to uplift Kashmiri Muslims.

In August 1967, a few years after Bakshi stepped down from power, Parmeshwari Handoo, a Pandit girl, married Ghulam Rasool Kanth, a Kashmiri Muslim, and converted to Islam. Large numbers of Kashmiri Pandits came out on the streets to launch an agitation against the government and the Muslim community, accusing the Muslim boy of forcibly abducting Handoo.[163] The agitation soon spread and took a political turn as Pandits argued that the government, which had decided that Handoo was of age and had willingly married the Muslim boy, was appeasing Kashmiri

Muslims. Kashmiri Muslims led a number of protests in response, which quickly turned into rallies for self-determination.[164] Although the Pandit agitation had been sparked by the immediate incident of the conversion and allegations of forced marriage, the increasing tensions between the two communities gave momentum to the agitation. Indeed, a government commission into the matter noted that the real reason for the agitation was "grave apprehensions amongst the Kashmiri Pandits against an invasion by other communities in their almost exclusive preserve of government activities. They . . . felt aggrieved with measures the government took for the welfare and general interest of the people of the state . . . related . . . to land laws and admission to educational institutions."[165] The report was never published as it "would reopen unpleasant controversies which have communal overtones" and would be against "public interest" in Kashmir—even as the correspondence acknowledged the publication of reports on "communal disturbances" in Indian states.

As a result of the demarcation of differences between Muslims and Pandits, both identified with their respective religious communities, not more closely with the Kashmir government. In this sense, secularism was not about neutrality toward religion, but an active constitution of religious difference and a setting of the terms by which religious claims could be articulated in public and inform state policies. Secular modern governance exacerbated—not alleviated—religious discord. More importantly, the primary driver of these reconfigurations was not religious-political institutions, but the state itself.

Although the Dogra government, which used Hinduism to buttress its claims of legitimacy, and the Bakshi government, which used secularism to advance similar ends, were starkly different, they both exacerbated tensions between Kashmiri Muslims and Pandits. The reason for this lies in the ways in which the modern state recognizes rights based on community identities, which in the case of Kashmir was particularly explosive because of the colonial occupation. Thus, the resulting discord was not an aberration. These consequences are part and parcel of how secular governance operates as well as how colonial occupation functions. While the state on the one hand instigates religious discord, it also subsequently becomes the "neutral" arbiter of religious relations, as evidenced by the court cases that went as far as the Indian Supreme Court. As a result, the logics of colonial occupation and modern secular governance do not simply play into the politics of divide and rule. They also enhance state capacity over all aspects of social life.

Chapter 6

JASHN-E-KASHMIR

Patronage and the Institutionalization of Kashmiri Culture

In 1956, the Kashmir government hosted the first ever Jashn-e-Kashmir, or Festival of Kashmir.[1] The festival, which was intended to bring to light many aspects of Kashmiri culture and "serve as a vehicle of contact between Kashmir and the rest of India," showcased theater, music, poetry, dance, sports, and other events from Kashmir as well as various Indian states.[2] Indian film stars performed *qawwalis* and performances in the newly built Bakshi Stadium, while *kathak* performers regaled audiences in Tagore Hall. Performances were arranged throughout the Kashmir Valley—in Shopian, Kulgam, Pahalgam, Sopore, and Handwara—as well as in Jammu and Leh. *Bhand pather* and *chakri* performances attracted peasants in rural areas.[3] The festival was immensely popular. The Kashmiri pro-freedom leader Syed Ali Shah Geelani, who at the time was affiliated with the Jamaat-i-Islami, remembered a visit to Sopore to meet other party members, but when it was time for prayers at the local mosque, very few people came. "When we inquired about the conspicuous absence of people in the masjid," Geelani recalled, "we were told that people have gone to Jashn-e-Kashmir gala being organized there that day."[4] Not just intended for people in the state, the festival attracted nearly twenty thousand tourists as well as senior leaders from India, including Prime Minister Jawaharlal Nehru.[5] It was the most visible and celebrated embodiment of Bakshi's Kashmir.

In a message to the public at the conclusion of a month-long series of events, Bakshi avowed that the annual festival was a crucial component of his state-building project. "Now that we have earnestly launched schemes for the economic and social regeneration of the people of our state," he declared, "it is necessary that adequate attention should be paid to our cultural heritage so that these traditions are nourished and carried forward."[6] Making reference to the improved standard of living since his government took power, he continued, "Progress would be incomplete if, side by side with these material changes, we ignore our cultural needs. The Festival of Kashmir was started with the purpose of directing public attention towards this aspect of our social life."[7] He noted that the celebration would "provide means of greater contact and fraternization between the people of this place and those living in the rest of India," serving as an important tool of emotional integration.[8] Building on the politics of life, the festival was also intended as a break from "tension and politics" and was "a fitting climax to the conditions of normalcy and stability that followed the change-over in August 1953."[9]

Jashn-e-Kashmir joined a number of cultural developments that were implemented under Bakshi, most importantly culminating in the establishment of the still-standing Jammu and Kashmir Academy for Arts, Culture, and Language (Cultural Academy). These cultural developments were linked to the broader goals of state-building: to establish legitimacy for Bakshi's rule, modernize Kashmiri society, promote socialist development and secular ideals, project normalcy to observers outside Kashmir (which would in turn increase tourism), and foster emotional integration between Kashmir and India. Additionally, the government's interventions in the realm of culture also played a critical role in bureaucratizing Kashmir's emerging cultural intelligentsia, providing them with the resources and platforms to showcase their work.

Culture was a site of activity for a number of global political movements in the first half of the twentieth century, many of which were influenced by communist and socialist ideals. In the era of decolonization, cultural producers were compelled to renegotiate their relationship with the state, while the latter, especially in a number of African and Asian contexts, attempted to absorb, subvert, or suppress the role of the intelligentsia. The Cold War era was replete with cultural propaganda led by both the US (the Congress for Cultural Freedom) and the Soviet Union and managing cultural production was integral to nation and state-building projects.[10]

Not all cultural production in this period was affiliated with the state. In

Kashmir, a number of artists continued to write poetry on religious, mystical, and philosophical themes and utilized literary conventions that preceded the modern era. Nonetheless, I focus primarily on artists who were mobilized to shape the cultural policies of the Kashmir government. Since 1947, the government was active in the promotion of a cultural vanguard, which consisted of writers, poets, and playwrights tasked with the preservation and promotion of Kashmiri culture and heritage, contributing to a distinct sense of Kashmiri cultural nationalism. Both the Kashmir government and the Indian government did not see this Kashmiri cultural nationalism as subversive; rather, it was promoted as being in tandem with—and not a threat to—Indian nationalism. While this process began under Sheikh Abdullah, it expanded under Bakshi, who was able to materialize culture as a component of state-building.

At the same time, however, cultural production should not be seen as just an exercise of a hegemonic state, which political theorist Antonio Gramsci would describe as moral and intellectual processes by which subordinate classes consent to their own domination. While the government utilized culture for its own aims, cultural producers and receivers were agents themselves and found ways to rework, resist, and subvert the narratives of the state, as we find in both India and Pakistan.[11] Bearing this in mind, while we will see how the Bakshi government's interventions in cultural affairs were a deliberate attempt to consolidate government narratives, they were not hegemonic, highlighting how the implementation of the project of cultural reform on the ground was marked by ambivalence, contestation, and dissent. Although the cultural intelligentsia in Kashmir was reliant on government patronage, the bureaucratization of culture under Bakshi produced its own contradictions by eliciting both conformity and resistance.

The Rise of Progressivism in Kashmir

Modern literature in Kashmir emerged during the later half of Dogra rule and was revitalized during Partition. Prior to this period, literature in Kashmir was primarily classical religious and literary texts in Persian and Kashmiri, including *marsiyas, naats, ghazals, masnavis*, and a specific type of Kashmiri poetry called *vaakhs,* popularized by the medieval poet and poetess Shaikh Nur-ud-din (Nund Rishi) and Lal Ded.[12] There was also a vast body of literature in Sanskrit and, to a limited extent, in Arabic. The literary shift to Urdu was reinvigorated in the third and fourth decades of the twentieth century. Two poets who wrote of the suppressed condition of Kashmiris under the Dogras were Ghulam Ahmed Mahjoor (1885–1952) and Abdul Ahad Azad (1903–1948), both of whom attempted to bring the language of poetry to the language of the common man. Both writers wrote in Urdu, although their most revered works are in Kashmiri. Azad was the more revolutionary of the two; he identified as a Marxist and his poetry directly addressed themes of social change and justice.[13]

Leftist thought, which gained popularity among the cultural intelligentsia throughout the subcontinent, also elicited interest in Kashmir. In the 1920s and 1930s, a small number of middle-class Kashmiris went to Punjab for higher education. There, they encountered bustling communist circles that idealized the Russian Revolution.[14] Upon their return to Kashmir, a number of these individuals would play a critical role in the creation of the National Conference and in the drafting of the Naya Kashmir manifesto. In the 1940s and 1950s, Kashmir became a popular site for leading leftist literary figures, including M. D. Taseer, Faiz Ahmed Faiz, Mulk Raj Anand, and K. A. Abbas, many of whom were close friends with Sheikh Abdullah and other members of the National Conference and regularly interacted with the local cultural intelligentsia. Some Kashmiri writers during this period drew their inspiration from the Progressive Writers Association and other prominent leftists and communists in the subcontinent. The Progressive Writers Association was a radical cultural movement created in 1936 in Lucknow and had links to international anti-fascist leftist literary movements. They adhered to the doctrine of socialist realism in their literature and believed that all artistic endeavors had to be for a political purpose in order to reshape society and give expression to people's lives, including the marginalized. While not all members were communists, they were deemed progressive for their anti-imperial and pro-reform views.[15] Kashmiri writers launched their own Progressive Writers Organization, where writers such as Prem Nath Pardesi, Som Nath Zutshi, Ali Mohammad Lone, and Qaisar Qalandhar would meet informally in each other's homes or in the local colleges to recite poetry and read each other's writings.[16] Communist literature was available in the Valley through the Kashmir Book Shop, run by Niranjan Nat Raina, who also ran a communist paper called *Azad*.

Instead of creating their own organization, Kashmiri communists decided to base themselves in "bourgeois nationalism" and strengthen the left -wing faction of the National Conference. This decision was made during a communist study circle in 1942 in Srinagar, where Bakshi was also present.[17] Fazal Elahi Qurban, a well-known communist leader in Lahore who was on a visit to Srinagar, led the meeting. He implored the gathering to adopt Lenin's thesis on the Eastern Question, which appealed to communists in the East to align themselves with anti-imperial movements such as the Indian National Congress, even though they might not be Marxist.[18] On the question of Partition, the Communist Party of India went back and forth in favor of Pakistan, but ultimately decided the idea of Pakistan represented feudalism.[19] As a result, a number of Kashmiri communists, who initially were ambivalent on the question of Pakistan, went along with the party line and became closer to the Indian National Congress.[20] In Kashmir, they joined the struggle against the Dogras, working to abolish landlordism and establish a representative state.

On the cultural front, the authors of the Naya Kashmir manifesto sought to bring together diverse communities in order to celebrate and "encourage our common culture."[21] The manifesto called for a Radio Station in the Kashmiri language, which also would host programs in the other languages of the state (Balti, Dogri, Dardi, Gojri, Hindi, Urdu, and Punjabi). It called for a film and theater association, as well as the encouragement of cultural activities for the youth. The manifesto declared that the ancient monuments of the state should be protected and developed for educational value. Finally, and most importantly, it called for an institute of art and culture.[22] Overall, the cultural plan was meant to promote Kashmiri national unity, secularism, and progressivism.

Under Abdullah's government, the relationship between cultural production and the state shifted. The government mobilized the Cultural Front, consisting of a number of progressively inclined intelligentsia, including women, to combat pro-Pakistan sentiment that had emerged with the remnants of the Muslim Conference and others who were growing disillusioned with the National Conference. The front was to galvanize locals against the incoming Pathan Muslims. Many in the Cultural Front had links to the National

Conference and had been involved in the anti-Dogra agitation. With the collapse of feudalism and the Dogra political order as well as the emergence of what was declared a people's government, the atmosphere was one of triumph and confidence.[23]

Prompted by the cultural intelligentsia's desire to reach out to the Kashmiri-speaking masses, the Kashmiri language was also rejuvenated through the promotion of a particular type of cultural nationalism. The traditional parameters of Kashmiri literature were expanded as writers explored new avenues and styles through poetry, short stories, novels, prose, and theater. Writers affiliated with the Cultural Front composed patriotic songs for the new movement and travelled throughout the region, putting on plays about social change in villages and small towns. Trilokinath Raina, a historian of Kashmiri literature, writes that for the Cultural Front, "art was for life and like social change, it became socialist propaganda."[24] Prominent members of the Marxist Indian Peoples Theater Association (IPTA), including Rajbans Khanna, Shivdan Chohan, Balraj Sahni, and Sheila Bhatia, were deputed to Kashmir to train the local artists.[25] Kashmir became a popular site of activity for a number of Indian leftists, who were attracted to the real possibility of implementing a socialist or communist order under the leadership of the National Conference.[26] The themes of the literature affiliated with the Cultural Front dealt with the promotion of socialism, anti-landlordism, secularism, and communal harmony.[27] One particular play was dedicated to Maqbool Sherwani, a National Conference worker who was killed in 1947 by the Pathan Muslims in the town of Baramulla. Sherwani was memorialized for saving non-Muslims, including Christians in Baramulla, and representing the syncretic cultural ethos of Kashmir. While it is clear that a number of artists had sympathies with leftist ideology, it is difficult to state who was an actual card-carrying member of the Communist Party. Nevertheless, the front was mobilized to meet the political needs of the nascent government.

The Cultural Front was renamed the Cultural Congress and in 1949 began to publish a monthly Kashmiri literary journal, *Kwang Posh*, which ran for nearly twenty-five issues, until it ceased publication in 1956.[28] The journal included short stories and poetry from prominent left-leaning writers of the time, including Dina Nath Nadim, Som Nath Zutshi, Noor Mohammed Roshan,

Rehman Rahi, Amin Kamil, Ghulam Nabi Firaq, Akhtar Mohiuddin, and Aziz Haroon. The themes included land reform, the difficulties of proletarian life, and the emancipation of women, as well as Hindu-Muslim unity. G. M. Sadiq, the minister of education and healthcare and the most prominent leftist in the administration, served as the patron for the journal. Sadiq brought together artists, encouraging them to serve as interpreters of people's struggles and aspirations, as well as demanding social transformation.[29] In a speech to the Cultural Congress in 1950 he declared, "Literature . . . shall expose imperialist, capitalist and feudal designs on the people's freedom and give leadership and direction to their struggle and fight for world peace."[30]

Dina Nath Nadim was one progressive writer who gained prominence at this time, writing clearly as an ideological leftist against war, imperialism, and capitalism. He wrote the first Kashmiri sonnet and opera and experimented with free verse and prose.[31] In the first Kashmiri free verse, "Bi G'avi ni az" (I will not sing today), Nadim freed Kashmiri poetry from its traditional metered poetic forms and sought to create a new ideological role for the writer:

I will not sing today,
I will not sing
of roses and of bulbuls
of irises and hyacinths
I will not sing
Those drunken and ravishing
Dulcet and sleepy-eyed songs.
No more such songs for me![32]

The poem is a patriotic call to arms of sorts; the poet, realizing the futility of poetry that praises nature (of which there was no shortage in Kashmir), is aware that the "wily warmonger with loins girt / lies in ambush for my land."[33] The "warmonger" was Pakistan, and writers were implored to use the power of their pen to mobilize people for the benefit of the Kashmir state against Pakistan's perceived machinations.[34]

While the Cultural Front mobilized most of the progressive poets of the time, not all shared its enthusiasm for the new political order under Abdullah, highlighting the continued ambivalence or opposition from Kashmiri writers to state-led projects of cultural nationalism. Mahjoor, who also served as the chief editor of *Kwang Posh* until 1952, wrote a number of satirical poems against developments in Kashmir. From being the pen behind the National Conference's iconic poem "Arise O Gardner," which encouraged people to overthrow Dogra rule, Mahjoor expressed his disappointment with the new period in his poem *Aazadi* (Freedom):

> In western climes Freedom comes
> With a shower of light and grace,
> But dry, sterile thunder is all
> She has for our own soil.
> Poverty and starvation,
> Repression and lawlessness, -
> It's with these happy blessings
> That she has come to us.[35]

Referring to the "popular" government under Abdullah, Mahjoor speaks of the conditions of "Freedom": poverty, starvation, repression, and lawlessness. "Freedom," he writes, "being of heavenly birth / Can't move from door to door / You'll find her camping in the homes of a chosen few alone." Later in the poem, he writes, "They searched her armpit seven times / To see if she was hiding rice / In a basket covered with her shawl / The peasant's wife brought Freedom home."[36] In these lines, Mahjoor derides the economic policies of Abdullah's government, which forcibly procured rice from farmers, especially in the rural areas. Mahjoor is most remembered for the lines that led to his imprisonment: "Though I would like to sacrifice my life and body for India, yet my heart is in Pakistan," expressing a sentiment that reflected the complex political aspirations of some progressive writers at the time.[37]

The Emergence of a Bureaucratic Cultural Intelligentsia

Although Bakshi had earlier interacted and worked with a number of Kashmiri communists and progressives, he was skeptical of their role within the National Conference and tried to restrict their influence so that they would not get involved in the political opposition.[38] Some were arrested for holding sympathies with Abdullah, while others were mobilized in an effort to limit the progressive forces that could undermine Bakshi's government. The Cultural Congress, which had been set up under Sheikh Abdullah, was disbanded; its members were invited to join the newly created Koshur Markaz, or Cultural Conference.[39] This inevitably led to a split within leftist ranks. Many were accommodated into Bakshi's government, while others grew disillusioned. Peer Giyas-Ud-din, who at the time supported independence of the Kashmiri communists from the National Conference, blames "self-contradiction, . . . ideological differences within [communist ranks], . . . no correct theoretical line, . . . [and] no semblance of independence" for this split.[40]

In his seminal study on Kashmiri literature, Trilokinath Raina describes the years following Sheikh Abdullah's arrest as the "years of disillusion." Following the enthusiasm of the 1940s and the early 1950s, he argues that Kashmiri literature as a whole entered a phase of gloom and frustration, "a decade of despair." Those who remained committed leftists grew distant from the movement, seeing that its leadership was less concerned with the poor and workers and more "concerned with obtaining power."[41] Raina makes reference to Bakshi being one of the primary causes of the end of progressivism in Kashmir. However, he does not address the aims and legacy of Bakshi's cultural project, what it was intended to highlight as well as obscure, and the intricacies of the relationship between the government and the cultural intelligentsia. Indeed, the context on the ground for artists was far more complicated than a betrayal "by those who wore the mask of socialism," as one of the writers of the Cultural Front, Noor Mohammad Roshan, declared.[42]

How was culture a part of Bakshi's state-building project? The government, in an attempt to utilize culture to legitimize its rule, provided patronage for individual artists, published cultural works and magazines, and created cultural institutions that were to define what constituted Kashmiri heritage and culture. Maintaining a monopoly on defining Kashmiri culture, then, was intimately linked to the maintenance of India's colonial occupation, as Kashmiri "culture"—as well as its purveyors—was appropriated by the state.

While some writers may have supported Bakshi on their own, Kashmir's cultural intelligentsia faced significant pressures to join the ranks of his administration. Bakshi provided patronage to individual artists and writers; this included providing funds for their projects, commissions, and employment in the government bureaucracy. Given that most artists were from lower-middle-class backgrounds, financial concerns and the desire to make a steady income were a priority for them, a condition that Bakshi was easily able to exploit. In their correspondence with the Department of Information, many asked for advances for their services to the government. For example, Amin Kamil, who was compiling a text on Habba Khatoon, a sixteenth-century Kashmiri poetess, requested the government provide an advance "so that I may be able to meet the necessary requirements of my family, which are haunting me very much."[43] A few days later, he wrote again, adding, "If any payment due to me from any quarter does not come in time, all my financial arrangements for my family are disturbed and I find myself in a great fix."[44] The department agreed to provide Kamil with a 150-rupee advance.

In another case, Ghulam Nabi Khayal, a Kashmiri poet, writer, and translator, recounted how he had been arrested in 1958 for taking part in protests in favor of Sheikh Abdullah. After spending two years in jail, Bakshi approached him and encouraged him to leave politics since it had a bad effect financially on Khayal's family. In turn, Bakshi offered him a post in the government bureaucracy, gave him five hundred rupees, and told him that his Kashmiri translation of the poetry of Umar Khayyam would be published as a book.[45] Khayal agreed and went on to play an important role in the cultural affairs of the state.

In addition to sponsoring their works and providing them with employment and increased opportunities, Bakshi hired writers for special projects, which included commissioning poems that were performed at Jashn-i-Kashmir and other cultural events. Khayal recalled one incident when "a poet would normally be paid Rs. 20 for a rendition. . . . It was that time that around Sonawari area in north Kashmir there was a devastating flood. Bakshi wanted the poets to write about it, and for their poetry they were paid Rs. 50 each."[46] Bakshi possibly got the idea for generating art during natural disasters from the Indian People's Theater Association, which performed plays about the Bengal Famine and which Bakshi encountered during the days of the Cultural Front. This suggests that Bakshi was drawing upon earlier cultural repertoires. In another instance, poets were commissioned to write poems during an anti-corruption week.[47] Playwrights were also commissioned to produce scripts that could be performed in schools and colleges, promoting government ideology to Kashmir's students.[48] But it was not simply poems and plays about Kashmir that Bakshi commissioned; he also hired poets to write tributes about his benevolent and progressive rule.

These poems were performed at Jashn-i-Kashmir and published in the Department of Information's propaganda journals, including *Kashmir Today* and *Tameer*.[49] The pages of these journals are replete with poems of praise for Bakshi and rely extensively on the politics of life. Narleesh Kumar Shad contributed one such poem, "A Week of Colors" (Haft-i-Rang):

Long live the cause of light
Long live the ambassador of new memory
You are the luster of Kashmir
Love live Khalid-i-Kashmir
Ecstasies in the Valley of Kashmir
House of beauty the Valley of Kashmir
It has your smell of wisdom
That is the flower of the Valley of Kashmir
You changed the destiny of the nation. . . .
I am praying according to "Ghalib" saying
An Architect of Modern Kashmir,
May you live long thousands of years
May each year have fifty thousand days.[50]

In this poem, the writer praises Bakshi, using his nickname "Khalid-i-Kashmir," or the Architect of Modern Kashmir. Bakshi is applauded for changing "the destiny of the nation," from what we imagine to be a period of darkness to one of progress. In another poem, "The Era of Khalid-i-Kashmir," written by Abbas Ali, the writer declares, "Kashmir and Khalid-e-Kashmir are one / people speak your name with every respect." Speaking of the region's new economic prosperity, he continues:

This era has become the era of Khalid-i-Kashmir
The prosperous time is because of you
You made the desert into a garden
Now look how the springs come in a beautiful way.[51]

The mention of the "garden" is especially important given the dire economic situation before Bakshi came to power, and the recurrent trope of the garden in earlier poems (including Mahjoor's).

These poems—which speak of Bakshi's personal characteristics as well as his economic and social policies—were reflective of the government's reliance on writers and poets to promote its narratives of progress. For a group of writers and artists that were oftentimes struggling to meet their financial needs and gain a wider audience, the patronage that Bakshi provided was difficult to reject. Many went on to serve in the lower rungs of government bureaucracy and in 1958 were eventually accommodated in the Cultural Academy. Taking part in the bureaucracy also enabled them to represent Kashmir in international literary functions and meetings. For example, a delegation from Kashmir was invited to attend a Cultural Forum festival in Moscow. Writers such as Akhtar Mohiuddin and Shamim Ahmed Shamim toured to Moscow for the forum.[52] These opportunities allowed Kashmiri writers to travel and gain access to progressive cultural networks outside Kashmir.

Bakshi's ability to utilize the cultural intelligentsia was a point of contention among writers. Some critiqued their new establishment role, despite partaking in it themselves. Nadim, the poet who had played an integral role in Abdullah's Cultural Front, was one of the first whose writings took a turn toward satire and irony. In a biting satirical poem in Kashmiri entitled "Huti Nazran Dolaan Dyaar Matyo," he writes of how bags of money were dangled in front of an artist's eyes. With this imagery, Nadim suggests that Bakshi was bribing the artist to join his fold.[53] He critiques how the artist is now more concerned with financial concerns than the authenticity of his art. In another Kashmiri poem, Nadim satirizes how flattery and sycophancy were becoming a daily routine among the intelligentsia, while "worthwhile attachments were being given short shrift."[54] The creation of a bureaucratic cultural intelligentsia led some to argue that the "left in Kashmir did not cultivate the democratic consciousness of the people to enable them to understand the role of various classes in relation to Kashmir politics. . . . Instead of consolidating itself, its votaries themselves become victims of opportunist power politics."[55] So the inclusion of artists in the government was also seen as an end to the progressive movement.[56]

While a number of analysts criticize the bureaucratization of the cultural intelligentsia under Bakshi, they fail to mention that this type of patronage is precisely how a colonial occupation operates.[57] The politics of life entailed bringing the cultural intelligentsia into the state-building project; such an appropriation enabled complicity, as writers sought coherence amid "incommensurate, conflicting political and ideological commitments," as well as their class aspirations as a result of financial insecurity.[58] The fundamental structures of India's colonial occupation created a situation where writers had to live under its logic and were dependent on the state, "torn between [their] subordination to the state and [their] aspirations for . . . liberation."[59]

Alongside the patronage of artists, Bakshi started a rival journal to *Kwang Posh*, called *Gulrez*, which featured works by those who had joined the Bakshi camp. In approving the journal, the Department of Information noted that it would assist in "disseminating the literature inherited by us from our glorious past and present readers within and without the state with pieces of selected works of the present times."[60] The Department of Information also began the Urdu journal *Tameer*, the Hindi journal *Yojna*, and the English journal *Kashmir Today*, for which it commissioned writers' articles, literature, and poetry. These journals were distributed to individuals and institutions that the government deemed important outside Kashmir, including various embassies, colleges, and government officials, thus providing a broader audience for these works.

With the creation of cultural institutions such as Lalla Rookh Publications, Jashn-e-Kashmir, and the Cultural Academy, and the further development of existing institutions such as Radio Kashmir, the government was able to bring a vast amount of cultural production within its fold. Their creation also led to a shift in the way the cultural history of the region was depicted and a canonization of the authoritative aspects of Kashmiri literature and culture, which was broadly marked as "heritage." These organizations' mandate was to preserve and collect this heritage and also create new works that would embody this vision.

Radio broadcasting played an important role in cultural reform. Radio Kashmir, part of the Broadcasting Corporation of India, was established in 1948 under Sheikh Abdullah's government, to promote the Kashmiri language. It initially served as counter-propaganda to Radio Pakistan and Azad

Kashmir Radio, radio stations in Pakistan and Pakistan-administered Kashmir that Kashmiris listened to follow developments across the border. Under Bakshi, additional programs were created to complement the government's cultural agenda. A number of progressive writers worked for Radio Kashmir, often producing dramas, short stories, and prose on issues of the day as well as propaganda for the government. Many of the programs were in Kashmiri and highlighted the important changes in development and cultural progress. The Kashmiri language was able to expand into a variety of genres, including drama, and was developed further with the use of broadcasting. Radio Kashmir also attempted to bring together Kashmiri musicians trained in classical Sufiana music, who came to the studio to perform live broadcasts.[61] In this way, musicians also came under government patronage. Much like radio stations around the world, Radio Kashmir became a propaganda tool for government policies and actions. Ministers and officials were regularly called upon to detail the activities of their various ministries. An important point about Radio Kashmir is that it prioritized the Kashmiri language—through its programming—as well as Kashmir's syncretic and Perso-Islamic-influenced musical traditions. Unlike in schools, Kashmiri was not completely ignored by the government; it was just seen through the lens of the preservation of culture instead of a means through which the society could modernize. This is perhaps why the promotion of the Kashmiri language was not seen as a threat to either the Kashmir government or the Indian state. Relegated to the sphere of state-led cultural preservation, it was not seen as subversive.

In addition, both Sufiana (Perso-Islamic) music and Hindustani classical music came together through the use of the *santoor,* a hundred-stringed instrument, often made with walnut, that came to the region from Central Asia. By highlighting Kashmir's diverse musical traditions—a confluence of Central and South Asian, Hindu and Muslim—Radio Kashmir attempted to portray Kashmir as a syncretic space with a unique cultural heritage. This important point was also evidenced in the cultural works collected and distributed by Lalla Rookh Publications.

Lalla Rookh Publications

In order to create an umbrella organization for the production and dissemination of social, political, and cultural literature, the Kashmir government established Lalla Rookh Publications in 1955. Lalla Rookh collected, compiled, and produced literature relating to Kashmir and sold and distributed it outside Kashmir.[62] A group of concerned individuals submitted a memorandum to the Kashmir cabinet, detailing the reasons for the creation of Lalla Rookh Publications.[63] The memorandum began by stating, "In addition to the press, the radio, and the cinema, the publication of cheap and readable literature of scientific and literary nature is playing a major part in raising the cultural standards of the masses." However, the memorandum noted that there was too much commercialization in publishing, which "has dampened the spirits of many a talented author." After giving examples of universities and governments around the world that had begun their own publishing companies, the memorandum continued:

> In Kashmir, the necessity for such a concern has long been felt. Our budding and talented scholars, in the absence of a suitable agency to undertake the publication of their works, have languished. . . . Kashmiris have also been deprived of the benefit of studying works of high literary and historical value pertaining to their country since most of them are out of print and therefore very rare and costly.[64]

The memorandum suggested that the Kashmir government start its own publishing agency that would provide Kashmiri writers with an outlet to publish their works. It would also reprint "cheap editions" of important works on Kashmir. Lalla Rookh would be a "private limited company . . . [and] the government should purchase all or most of the shares." It urged the government to establish relationships with booksellers and agents within and outside India. Lastly, it indicated that an independent entity was needed given that anything published by the Department of Information directly would be deemed as propaganda.[65]

The memorandum suggested that Lalla Rookh's purpose would be to "increase the reading culture in Kashmir." Given the rate of illiteracy at the time and the paucity of publishing houses, it is plausible to imagine that writers found it difficult to publish and distribute their works. Thus, the government was able to benefit from this constraint and situate itself as a "savior" for Kashmir's writers. However, it had to do so discreetly, as Lalla Rookh was not intended to serve as "propaganda." Nonetheless, the government was to own all the shares of the company and a minister of information and broadcasting would serve as the chairman, restricting the extent to which Lalla Rookh could be independent. Nevertheless, publishing with Lalla Rookh was attractive for a number of writers, especially because of its links with booksellers outside Kashmir.

A list of Lalla Rookh publications makes it evident that one aim of the organization was to distribute literature from the perspective of the Kashmir government pertaining to Kashmir's political situation as well as a particular projection of Kashmir's cultural and literary history. This list included publications on Kashmir's position in the Security Council, Kashmir's special position in India, and Pakistan's relationship with the United States.[66] The government declared that a book entitled *Kashmir in the Security Council* sold five thousand copies in its first month. These works were primarily in Urdu and English, and some were in Kashmiri.

Alongside these publications, Lalla Rookh also published literature pertaining to Kashmir's cultural heritage. It received an initial 45,000 rupees from the government, and a committee, headed by Pran Nath Jalali and Noor Mohammed Roshan, was created to oversee the organization. Jalali was a leading figure among Kashmiri leftists and Roshan was a writer, and both of them had been active in the state's cultural scene. The committee created a series of panels that were to assemble literature on a variety of topics. Each panel consisted of a number of advisors, who included prominent writers, academics, and poets. Historical works were meant to discuss various periods in Kashmir's history, "bearing close resemblance to our present-day problems [which] will enlighten our people about their past and also deepen their patriotic sentiment."[67] They primarily centered on figures who were deemed "secular"—such as Zain-ul-Abidin, the popular Muslim king in the medieval period, and Kashmir's freedom movement against the Dogras. Publication of cultural works was meant to "make our heritage widely known."[68] The topics of the panels included Kashmir's contribution to Sanskrit literature, Kashmir's contribution to Persian literature, anthology of modern short stories, collected works of Mahjoor, anthology of Kashmiri verse, and Habba Khatoon. While the material was mostly Kashmiri-centric, in an effort to reach out to other regions, Lalla Rookh also published several other works on Dogri art and literature.

Members of the panels were assigned to procure valuable material from the families and heirs of famous Kashmiri writers, including rare historical manuscripts. For example, one panel was tasked with collecting material from the widow of Abdul Ahad Azad, including some of his unpublished poems and personal notebooks.[69] Others were tasked with travelling across Kashmir, especially to rural areas, to collect oral folk tales, proverbs, and songs.[70] Additional panels were set up to commemorate particular cultural figures, including the poetesses Lalleshwari (Lal Ded) and Habba Khatoon. On April 22, 1956, Lalla Rookh celebrated Lalleshwari Day, "paying homage to Kashmir's first and foremost mystic poetess, philosopher, and saint . . . adorned by Kashmiri women as a deity."[71] In directives to the panels, Lalla Rookh Publications requested those who were collecting works of Kashmiri literature to highlight "social realism, romantic narrative, religious narrative, nature depiction, . . . mysticism, devotional verse, elegy."[72]

We have seen how educational policies highlighted purported secular histories and icons of medieval Kashmir. Similarly, Lalla Rookh paid careful attention to Kashmir's contribution to both Sanskrit and Persian literature, underscoring the importance of making a composite, secular national heritage known to people, regardless of the material differences among communities. The Kashmir government attempted to negotiate the contours of multiple civilizations in order to depict Kashmir's unique, composite, and exceptional cultural heritage, leading to a distinct form of cultural nationalism. In addition, through the process of selecting which works would be collected and distributed, the government situated itself as the ultimate arbiter for what would be included in Kashmir's cultural identity. By sending its cultural officers to various parts of the state in search of folk art and manuscripts, the government also became the purveyor of not just the work produced by its artists but also what had been confined to the realm of "folk art." In many ways, then, the government institutionalized what had otherwise been part of oral culture. Given that Lalla Rookh was also publishing political works from the perspective of the government, we should see the collection of these cultural works as being a part of the government's efforts to promote a particular understanding of

Kashmir. What began to be known as Kashmir's "secular culture" was a selective construction and interpretation, borne out of the needs of a particular political moment. Here, the secular is deployed to justify Kashmir's links with India. This might explain why, later on, Kashmiri *cultural* nationalism was a contested terrain for advocates of Kashmiri self-determination, given its appropriation and use by the Kashmir government.

The compilation of the various publications was not without disagreement. Compilers did not have total control over which works would be included; the editors at Lalla Rookh were able to reject some of their suggestions while adding their own. An example is the case of Akhtar Mohiuddin, a Kashmiri short story writer and novelist who was asked to compile an anthology of short stories. Jalali suggested to Mohiuddin that his collection was missing some important authors. Mohiuddin responded that the works of these authors were not "up to the mark."[73] He wrote a follow-up letter asking for his payment for the compilation. Jalali responded at length, writing that the introduction that Mohiuddin prepared was "not an attempt at the serious evaluation of the literary merit of the stories chosen for the anthology." Instead, he argued, Mohiuddin concentrated "on the political motivation of the writers and the political aims of the stories." He continued:

> Our concern does not believe in the fact that the democratic advances made by our people after the autocracy were just an "illusion." We would prefer a literary critic when writing an introduction of a book of this type to give less prominence to an unbalanced and superficial understanding of the political element in art.[74]

Given Jalali's response to Mohiuddin, it is evident that the government used Kashmir's cultural intelligentsia toward a particular end: to highlight the progress that was being made in Kashmir. Mohiuddin's introduction to the anthology, which stated that the advances made after Dogra rule were "just an illusion," was clearly not welcome in the body of work sponsored by the government.

On November 20, 1957, Lalla Rookh Publications was disbanded, and its functions were incorporated back into the Department of Information.[75] The reasons for this are unclear but are potentially related to the creation of the

Democratic National Conference, led by G. M. Sadiq, in 1958.[76] Since a number of those who worked at Lalla Rookh were closely linked to Sadiq, it is possible that the organization was deemed a threat to Bakshi, and it folded. Despite its short existence, however, Lalla Rookh played a critical role in setting the parameters for what constituted Kashmiri culture.

After Lalla Rookh Publications was disbanded, on July 7, 1958, Bakshi's government established the Jammu and Kashmir Academy for Arts, Culture and Languages, or the Cultural Academy.[77] The scope of the Cultural Academy was broader than that of Lalla Rookh Publications, as it also incorporated music, theater, and dance and was especially invested in promoting the regional languages of the Jammu and Kashmir state, including Dogri and Ladakhi. Perhaps responding to tensions among the three regions, the government attempted to ensure that Jammu and Ladakh were represented in the construction of a Kashmiri cultural identity. Jashn-e-Kashmir included cultural performances from Ladakh, Kargil, Poonch, and Jammu. All cultural activities in the region effectively came under the purview of the Cultural Academy, which also developed ties with the Sahitya Akademi in New Delhi. The latter institutionalized a series of awards for Kashmiri writers and poets.

As cultural production increasingly became bureaucratized, a number of traditional art forms suffered and their political relevance was neutralized. One, in particular, was *bhand pather*, a form of satirical theater that was especially popular in rural areas and traced itself to Kashmir's medieval period. *Bhand pather* is a folk form focused on satire and resistance as its main theme. It is performed anywhere and is usually not scripted. Under the Dogras, it was considered a "remover of sorrows" for Muslim peasants who were forced into labor.[78] Travelling *bhands* would utilize *phir kath*, or twisted talk, which would be understandable only to those who were familiar with the local idiom. It was through *phir kath* that Kashmiris were able to decode the serious messages in the comedy, unrecognizable to Mughal, Sikh, and Dogra officers.[79] Nonetheless, as contemporary cultural critic Arshad Mushtaq argues, a number of groups involved in *bhand pather* came under government patronage and were dependent on grants from the Cultural Academy. With this institutionalization of what was an indigenous folk form, Mushtaq states that *bhands* lost their historical independence from the political establishment.[80] Javaid Iqbal

Bhat further suggests that this resulted in a sanitization of the *bhand* form, which had previously contested the bonds of national identity and instead constituted itself in a local logic. Bhat argues that the art form had previously presented a non-idealized version of *kashmiriyat*; although it spoke of ties between religious communities, *bhand* was also attentive to the socioeconomic differences in the state.[81]

This attention to a complex local history was lost when *bhand pather* became institutionalized by the state, which "signified an aggressive appropriation drive to strengthen the larger idea [of a composite, national identity] at the expense of the smaller frames."[82] The loss of a once cherished art is depicted in Salman Rushdie's novel *Shalimar the Clown*. In one scene in the novel, *bhand pather* show is being performed in an auditorium in Srinagar. Inside the auditorium, no one is watching the *bhands*; all are more concerned about slogans that are being chanted outside the auditorium.[83] Having lost its ability to serve as a subversive act against authority—be it Mughal, Afghan, Sikh, Dogra, Indian—the folk form lost its credibility. The story of the *bhand* represents, in many ways, how bureaucratization of a cultural form made it conform to an understanding of a Kashmiri cultural identity that was far removed from its constitutive local logic.

Of and Beyond the State: Literature as a Counter-narrative

While the government had significant influence in cultural affairs, some Kashmiri artists found ways to subvert its narrative, despite being in the government bureaucracy. This suggests that while the government certainly had control over cultural production, it was not hegemonic. I highlight how Kashmiri writers managed to find their own ways of shaping and contributing to literature. The earlier example of Akhtar Mohiuddin's experience with Lalla Rookh suggests that when the government was not interested in promoting literature that contested its aims, artists found refuge in short stories, poetry, and novels, resulting in a particular type of cultural efflorescence in this period that focused on the social issues facing Kashmiri society.[84] Smaller publishing houses, such as Ali Mohammad and Sons, based in downtown Srinagar, independently published these works.

Kashmiri fiction can serve as a counter-discourse and provide a glimpse of history excised from Kashmiri statist and Indian nationalist renderings. It provides a glimpse away from state-directed propaganda and narratives of progress in Kashmir. In the literature from this period, when Jashn-e-Kashmir was being celebrated and Bakshi's rule was posited as the harbinger of progress, a number of writers explored themes of corruption, greed, obsession with money, loss of moral values, and lack of loyalty in their writings, showcasing how these things turned son against father, and neighbor against neighbor.[85] Even as writers explored these themes, however, they did not make any explicit political commentary on Kashmir's political status or future. However, their analysis of the social issues plaguing Kashmiri society can be understood as a critique of Kashmir's political misfortunes, of which Bakshi's state-building project played a part.

Because these writings provided a social, not an explicitly political critique, they were eventually compiled by the Sahitya Akedemi, based in New Delhi, in an attempt to promote literature from various states in the country. In one satirical story by Amin Kamil, "The Cockfight," Shahmal, a woman who is married to Ghulam Khan, wants her husband to buy her an expensive rooster so that she can brag to her neighbor, Jana. It seems Shahmal, who only has two hens, wants the rooster to spite Jana, who has five hens and a rooster. Instead of being the good omen she had hoped, Shahmal is disappointed when she is awakened in the dead of the night by the rooster crowing. She attempts to wake her husband to tell him to kill the rooster, as "it is a creature of ill-omen." However, it is her concern as to how Jana would respond in the morning that worries her most. The next day, she avoids leaving her home and looks with repugnance at the new rooster. She vows to have him killed by her neighbor Samad, who has a reputation for the "as an expert slaughter of fowl." After returning home, she finds her rooster and Jana's rooster, who she had referred to as a "scavenger" rooster, in a cockfight. Seeing her rooster gaining the upper hand, she backtracks on her intention to kill him saying, "A cock of mine may have a thousand vices, he may even crow at the fall of the night; these are of no account in my eyes if he has the proper fighting mettle. This was the type of cock I wanted. Otherwise, is not the market flooded with innumerable stinking, scavenger cocks?" Kamil's short story is considered one of the most widely read in the Kashmiri language. Through a simple tale of two competing housewives and their roosters, the story speaks to jealousy, disappointment, and regret. It is a satirical take on what appears to be increasing greed and competitiveness within Kashmiri society, perhaps an indictment of what the politics of life can result in.

Other writers wrote of how political change in Kashmir only benefitted some, while life was the same for the wretched of the earth.[86] Some also examined the changes wrought by those who had recently acquired wealth through corruption and sycophancy. In Ali Mohammad Lone's short story "The Strange Mohalla," a man who has recently acquired wealth is trying to get an elderly woman who lives in his area out of her house, so that he may take it over.[87] Under the Dogras, there used to be a brothel in the area, and so the neighborhood was one of ill repute. The woman, Farzi Tuj, had lost two of her sons to Kashmir's freedom struggle against the Dogras. Her third son had disappeared during the time of Partition. Because of these tragedies in her life, she "has become mad" and yells obscenities at passersby. The man, Wali Mohammad, "had been a petty shopkeeper, but now he is a big contractor, dealing in lakhs."[88] Speaking of his perceived piety, the writer notes that "the numberless times he rubs his brow on the floor in prayer have left a permanent dark coin-like mark on his forehead, which he wears proudly." Wali Mohammad finds Farzi's presence in his neighborhood intolerable, and he begins to plan a way for her to leave: "To this end he decided to stay here for longer periods and build contacts with the other residents of the neighborhood, greeting them with a smile. . . . He gave a generous donation to the mosque."[89] He hires a broker to buy the house from Farzi, who spitefully rejects the offer. Wali Mohammad then tries to get the support of Sula Gondol, the owner of the local shop where the men of the neighborhood go to smoke and discuss politics. Gondol is however uneasy with Wali Mohammad's anger and tells him to leave Farzi alone. Wali retorts, "Just say the word and I will drag her out by her two feet and throw her out of her house." Gondol becomes angry and bursts, "What gives you the right to say all this, you beggar? Or has all this new-found prosperity gone to your head and made it overflow?"[90] The incident causes all the men and children to come to the shop to see what is happening, and women come out on their balconies and to their windows. Wali Mohammad is forced to walk away. In the end, the author writes:

> Truly it was a strange Mohalla. . . . There is no brothel here now, but a pious *Namazi* [one who prays] is still made fun of, a respectable contractor is humiliated and disgraced just for the sake of a mad old woman. . . . This unfeeling, insensitive Mohalla [neighborhood], at the very mention of whose name people shudder and plug their ears.[91]

"The Strange Mohalla" is not only a critique of the behavior of those with newfound wealth—as a result of the politics of life—but also, through the character of Wali Mohammad, an indictment of their religious hypocrisy. It is no coincidence that Wali is a contractor—an individual who is ostensibly engaged in "development" or "progress." Being a contractor in this period of state-building meant being involved in high-level corruption but still enjoying the benefits of society. In this neighborhood of sexual ill repute, the people—and not the pious contractor—appear to be on the right side of morality with their defense of a woman whose three sons were sacrificed in Kashmir's political struggles. In this story, Lone lodges a critique of the implications of "development" in erasing that sacrifice. The story also speaks to the attempts the contractor makes to lure the people in the neighborhood through money—and the woman's steadfastness against such attempts, perhaps reflecting Kashmir's political dynamics at the time.

While a number of writers offered an indirect social critique of the period, some, like Rehman Rahi, directly took on Bakshi. Perhaps no account of Bakshi's rule was as damning as Rehman's satirical poem in Kashmiri "Maefi Nama" (Apology).[92] Rahi was one of the leading progressive poets of the time. He joined the bureaucracy under Bakshi and took part in Jashn-e-Kashmir and the other cultural projects of the state. However, it appears that his leanings were toward Sadiq and the Democratic National Conference. In the poem, the poet apologizes for having insulted the "gold-laden ruler," referring to Bakshi. Later on, he suggests the ruler was insulted because Rahi had dared to mention the ineffectiveness of a particular policy. Evoking a series of images, the poet satirizes the ruler's dictatorial style ("If someone dares to smell a rose without your due permission, that is mutiny") and his total control over all aspects of life and death:

> If you call a mirage a sea, that will be the reality

If you call blood Zam Zam, who has the guts to say it is not?
If you call stumbling dance, who can question you?
An insane person with whom you are happy, he gets the seal of being a dervish
If you are not ready to tolerate Socrates, you will give him the poison
Who am I to challenge you?

In the next set of lines, Rahi writes of the desires of the people and how they have been quashed:

But then isn't it natural to have a desire
Isn't it natural if in winters, we read the book of the coming Spring
But my lord, if it makes you upset, we will nail the windows
We will tell the breeze that announces the spring that he is suspect
If you give the order, we will burn Gulrez to Ashes
There will be no morning, and after every night, neither will Noashlab seek her prince
We will tell the tulip that Mahjoor was gone out of his mind, that is why he asked for your welfare
Azad was complaining in vain, he was also out of his mind
Why was he raising these issues? It is God who decides who is poor and who is wealthy

The last line, in particular, reflects the poet Azad's socialist ideology and refers to the death of progressive thought under Bakshi. Yet, what is most interesting in these lines is that the people themselves might "nail the windows," perhaps suggesting the widespread compliance that had taken root.

The next set of lines ridicules the institutions in Bakshi's government, referring to their being filled with unqualified individuals, including criminals, as well as the censorship and suppression that led people to curtail their own conscience:

If it was your wish, the cattle thieves will be made judges in your rule
If someone wanted to boast about his intelligence, he was shown his place

The police officers smuggle drugs on your orders
The casinos are thrown open by the mullahs in your order
If you forbid, the newspapers were burnt on roads
Everybody told his conscience that it is absurd to express

In the end, the poet directly takes on the government's lack of legitimacy:

You never had to take the favors of the people
Time was in your favor and made you the king
You sensed the blowing winds, and then you did commerce with the traders
You fulfilled your own desires
Someone's hut was burned, but you added another story to your house

By not having to "take the favors of the people," Rahi suggests that Bakshi never had to seek their approval (through a legitimate transfer of power); instead, he struck a deal with the Government of India and was made king. While a number of Kashmiris suffered losses on account of this deal, Bakshi, according to the poet, benefitted materially.

Two lines, however, lay bare the project of cultural reform—in particular the patronage of the cultural intelligentsia. The poet says, "It is true that I have written poems in praise of you / but it is also a fact that I just want to save my life." These two lines shed light on the fundamental paradox of Bakshi's project of cultural reform. While the cultural intelligentsia did partake in this project, the poet wishes to underscore the pressures that he and others dealt with in a time of great political suppression as well as economic need. These lines signify the immense coercion and contradiction that was involved in maintaining Bakshi's rule, even for those who were seemingly a part of it.

Akhtar Mohiuddin: Storytelling in the Age of Rhetoric

In this last section, I turn to the privately published works of Akhtar Mohiuddin, the short story writer, novelist, and playwright whom we came across earlier regarding his correspondence with Lalla Rookh. Mohiuddin's career spanned the second half of the twentieth century and effectively began under Bakshi's government. He authored a number of collections of short stories, novels, travelogues, and plays. Mohiuddin's first collection of short stories, *Sath Sangar*, was published in 1955, and he was the first Kashmiri to receive the Sahitya Akedemi award in 1958, at the age of thirty. He is also credited with writing the first Kashmiri novel, *Doad wa Dag*, in the early 1950s.

Mohiuddin was born to a middle-class family on April 17, 1928, in Srinagar. He attended Sri Pratap College, and after graduation, he was hired as a clerk in the Abdullah-led Constituent Assembly in 1951. He began his literary career by writing short stories in Urdu and received second place in an international short story contest in 1954 for his story "Pondrich." Soon after, he associated himself with the Cultural Congress and was able to gain a sizeable readership by publishing in the literary journal *Kwang Posh*.[93] Along with a number of other writers, he turned to Kashmiri, feeling that he could express himself better in his native language. Once Lalla Rookh Publications was established, Mohiuddin asked for financial help as he was in dire need. He requested that the publishing house help him sell and distribute his recent book, *Doad wa Dag*.[94] He also presided over a number of panels for Lalla Rookh Publications, including the anthology of short stories mentioned above as well as the creation of a Kashmiri dictionary.[95] After serving in a number of government posts, he was promoted to secretary for the Cultural Academy.

Mohiuddin, like Rahi and Nadim, had to navigate two different roles: government servant and artist. Instead of seeing the two as being in contrast, or of one being in "resistance" to the other, I argue that we need to examine his works as an individual's way of negotiating multiple demands on his or her life. His writings use modernist fictional techniques, including stream-of-consciousness and interior monologue. Mohiuddin moves beyond the Progressives as there are no heroes in his work. To be sure, the self that Mohiuddin depicts is one that is full of contradictions, driven at some points to madness. This self is pushed to its limits by greed, avarice, and loneliness but also, as Mohiuddin makes clear, helplessness. Mohiuddin eventually seeks redemption for his characters, highlighting the fractured nature of society, in which people had to learn how to operate, to function, and as Rahi succinctly wrote, to save their life. As Mohamad Junaid writes, "To tell the story of Akhtar Mohiuddin is to begin to uncover clues to an alternative story of Kashmir itself, and to an ethical ideal for a collective life presently denied its full dignity."[96]

Mohiuddin covers a range of themes in his short stories and novels, which serve as an archive of the everyday—of people's fears, doubts, concerns, strengths, and weaknesses. A common theme of most of his stories, however, is the "desire to expand the interior space of the Kashmiri being, both imagined as a historical figure, dehumanized by subjugation as well as an emergent subject struggling to articulate his or her rights."[97] In the short story "Does Anyone Have the Courage?" he depicts a Kashmiri Pandit mother who is unhappy that a Kashmiri Muslim man is attempting to make conversation with her son on the bus, whereas the man is attempting to make a genuine connection with the boy, hoping that he doesn't appear to him as a "monster."[98] The incident perhaps underscores the suspicion that had emerged among Pandits in light of the developments mentioned in the previous chapter.[99] Yet, as Mohamad Junaid explains, Mohiuddin, although understanding the marginal position of Muslims, "calls on Muslims to remain sensitive to how Pandits might perceive them in the new situation, especially where the old inter-community codes of expected behavior may no longer hold. To him, 'Kashmiriness' means cultivating a certain tenderness towards the other, especially through lending a gentle helping hand to turn that Pandit disposition towards Muslims from fear to disdain to respect and understanding."[100] This understanding is markedly different from the official cultural production of the government that tended to idealize Kashmir's "syncretic" culture; here, Mohiuddin acknowledges the very real tensions and misgivings, as well as histories of inequality and marginalization that exist among Muslims and Pandits, while also creating an ethics of engagement with the internal "other."

In "The Game of the Snowballs," Mohiuddin critiques the hypocrisy of the wealthy class through the story of a man who forced his servant to sit outside in the cold, which led to his death. The same man is later seen grieving at the servant's funeral.[101] In the story "Election," he shows how an election is conducted in Kashmir, through the activities on election day in a particular neighborhood. The rulers already know the results but feel that "some theatrics are essential."[102] And so, hired hands representing the opposition raise green flags (a gesture toward Pakistan), which leads to their homes being stoned. The next day, the party with the red flag (representative of the National Conference) wins, and the same hired hands participate in a victory procession.

In stark contrast to the pages of *Tameer* and *Kashmir Today*, which, as we saw in the first chapter, spoke of the progress being made in the state, these writings make visible the fractures, anxieties, and exploitation that marked the Bakshi and beyond. The short story "Election" highlights the exploitation of democratic norms under the "people's government" and the ways in which elections are manipulated to serve the ruling party. The stories make visible the corruption that comes with newfound wealth as well as the tensions between various communities and various social classes within Kashmiri society. Most importantly, they give expression to the compulsions to compromise that individuals experienced in their day-to-day affairs and that were integral to colonial occupation.

These compulsions are evidenced in Mohiuddin's first novel, *Doad wa Dag*. In the story, Mohiuddin delves into the lives and thought processes of four characters: Fatima and Raja, who are sisters, and Sham Sahib and Abdul Gani. Fatima is the older sister to Raja and is married to Sham Sahib. The sisters are orphaned, and Sham Sahib decides to also take Raja under his care. Fatima is gravely ill, but Sham Sahib, who does not believe in going to hospitals, takes her to the local hakim for help. In the meantime, Sham Sahib's accountant, Abdul Gani, makes a number of advances to Raja, who seems to be attracted to him but is fearful of the consequences of breaching social etiquette. Abdul Gani is depicted as a selfish man; he marries two women, one for her dowry and the other for her looks, but he soon divorces them once he tires of them. Sham Sahib also marries Raja to an older man, who is a widower and has three children; Raja sees him more as a father than a husband and fantasizes about Abdul Gani.

Sham Sahib, who was previously portrayed as a generous, kind man, begins to lose money and is in debt. He takes his anger out on Fatima and beats her. One day, seeing Fatima in such a state, Raja raises her voice and the neighbors intervene. Out of jealousy, it seems that the other men in the neighborhood want to settle scores with Sham Sahib, and they force the husband and wife to get a divorce. Fatima lives with Raja and her husband, who is not happy to have her in the house.

One day, Fatima falls ill and Raja takes her to the hospital. There, she meets Abdul Gani, who takes care of her and makes sure she is well attended. Abdul

Gani tells Raja that he will marry Fatima and take care of her. Raja hastily agrees. After the wedding, she visits her sister, and Abdul Gani persuades her to spend the night. The three sleep in the same room. In the course of the night, Abdul Gani rapes Raja, while Fatima watches, unable to say anything. Raja soon learns that Abdul Gani brings women home and regularly fights with Fatima. She continues to sleep with him, realizing that it encourages him to treat Fatima better. After some time, Fatima dies, and Raja begins to avoid Abdul Gani. He starts to visit her at her home, and her husband becomes suspicious. He divorces her, and after some months, Abdul Gani proposes to her and they get married. She appears happy to marry him but soon realizes his infidelities. One day, Raja realizes she is pregnant, and Abdul Gani is enraged; he does not want to spend money on a child. He hires a midwife to give Raja poison to abort the baby. Raja begins to bleed heavily and is about to die. Abdul Gani, feeling remorse, takes her to the hospital, where she survives. In the end, it appears a change has washed over Abdul Gani, and he transforms, becoming a dutiful husband to Raja.

Doad wa Dag is the story of lower-middle-class Kashmiri society at the cusp of change. What is striking about the narration is that Mohiuddin rejects making any judgments on the morality of the characters. While a few critics have criticized the lack of a moral message in the story, Raina argues that Mohiuddin is not interested in serving as a custodian of moral ethics, setting his works apart from much of the progressive literature in South Asia and perhaps being a defining feature of Kashmiri cultural production at this time.[103] In addition, I suggest that Mohiuddin attempts to give insight to the compulsions that make people act as they do, whether it is Sham Sahib's increasing debt, Raja's desire to save her sister, or even Abdul Gani's obsessive desire to escape poverty. Compulsion seems to drive many of the characters, but Mohiuddin also does not deny them their agency in shaping and justifying how they lead their life. It is a sharp, searing portrayal of society and human relationships—greed, jealousy, desire, selfishness, marital problems, adultery, lust, helplessness—but also of forgiveness and redemption. In one important scene, Abdul Gani is shown as being kind to a dog that had been beaten by a group of rowdy children, portraying a redemptive quality in a man who has otherwise destroyed so many lives. It could be that *Doag wa Dag* serves as a reflection of the broader Kashmiri society, which faced a number of crises in this period of transition. Perhaps Mohiuddin wishes for his readers to sympathize with the decisions his characters take, compromises that he and those around him had to regularly make.

The complex inner worlds that Kashmiris had to navigate are further depicted in the short story "I Can't Tell." The story is set in 1958 in Lal Chowk, the business hub of the city. The narrator is observing a curious scene evolve in the market. Nearly four dozen police officers who are wearing the uniform of the Kashmir Police descend upon the market area. The narrator says that the men are actually from the (Indian) Central Reserve Police but that "the Indian ruler had resorted to this stratagem so that if per chance some news reporter saw them and wrote a report it would be the Kashmiri government which would get a bad name. . . . Centre would remain blameless."[104] In a few minutes, a government strongman, Qadir Chaan, starts to beat a pedestrian. A crowd gathers, and the police charge those who are assembled and shoot tear gas in the air.[105] The next day, the narrator reads the local English and Urdu dailies, which tell the story differently, blaming "anti-national" elements for stirring up trouble. The narrator decides to meet Qadir Chaan. Upon visiting his house, he notes that the family is poor and that Qadir Chaan has a few daughters, one of marriageable age. The narrator familiarizes himself with the family, and Qadir Chaan opens up to him about his life and his many responsibilities. He seeks forgiveness from God for his many sins and feels deep remorse for his actions, but he declares that he has no options. Once the narrator reveals his interest in Qadir Chaan's story, the latter tells his story. He says that after Sheikh Abdullah's arrest, he was poor, and the price of essential items had increased. His mother suddenly died and he was unable to get even a cloth for her shroud due to financial constraints.[106] As a result, he began to feel betrayed by Sheikh Abdullah, whom he saw as being responsible for his financial plight. In a subsequent protest following Abdullah's arrest, a group of people raised slogans in favor of Abdullah. Enraged, Qadir Chaan became angry at their foolishness and started to beat some of the people. One person was killed.[107] He said that Bakshi's brother, Bakshi Rasheed (who was also responsible for developing the Cultural Conference) told him that he could avoid jail as long as he worked for the government. He had to create scenes at various places, so that the police would arrive and "anti-national" elements could be blamed. This would allow the Kashmir government to bolster its security apparatus with funds from India. In turn, Qadir Chaan would receive compensation from the government. Upon hearing this story, the narrator becomes emotional, and declares, "O people intensify your struggle for freedom. . . . Liberate Qadir Chaan from his bondage."[108]

In the story, Mohiuddin sheds light on the dire circumstances that lead individuals to seek government patronage as well as the complex inner moral worlds through which these individuals justify their participation in the system. Perhaps, Mohiuddin sought to give expression to his own helplessness and the helplessness of those around him. A counter-narrative to the politics of life imbues his writings, leaving the narrator/Mohiuddin to ultimately demand liberation from this bondage. Ultimately, we can see Mohiuddin's writings as deeply political, an inward reflection on what a colonial occupation does to a society—the "fragile realm of contestations running through the veins of Kashmir."[109]

In the 1990s, Akhtar Mohiuddin renounced his Padma Shri (the fourth highest civilian award given in India) in the wake of mass killings during the armed movement against Indian rule. He had earlier renounced his Sahitya Akademi award after the hanging of Maqbool Bhat, a Kashmiri pro-freedom leader in the 1980s, which he had campaigned against. In the last two decades of his life, he wrote critical short stories on Kashmir's evolving political solution. His son and son-in-law were both killed in the violence. He dedicated his novel *Jahnamuk Panun Panun Naar* in 1975 to the person "who would fire the first bullet to set things right in Kashmir."[110]

Mohiuddin's story—from having been one of the artists incorporated into the government's cultural intelligentsia to later renouncing national awards for his writings—reflects the complex interplay between conformity and resistance in this chapter, as well as the bureaucratization of culture under a colonial occupation. This is perhaps one of the reasons why Kashmir did not develop a robust, progressive cultural intelligentsia in this period that was critical of the state. Many of Kashmir's progressive intellectuals who provided a moral critique of Kashmiri society were also compromised by the Kashmir government—although Mohiuddin's case was resoundingly more toward resistance than many of his peers. The government needed Kashmir's cultural intelligentsia, and new writers relied on government patronage. Intervening in the realm of culture allowed the government to showcase its capacity not just in terms of publishing particular works but also hosting state-level events that served as symbolic tools to reflect progress in a society that was reeling from political instability. Moreover, it allowed the Kashmiri language to be brought to the masses through new literary forms.

The Kashmir government wanted to ensure that cultural production fit the needs of the political moment. A vast majority of the cultural intelligentsia was incorporated within the purview of the state, tasked with consolidating a Kashmiri culture and heritage that aligned with Indian secular ideals and promoting narratives of progress. At the same time, this incorporation did not mean that these writers were completely subsumed, as evidenced from their contestations within government institutions as well as their writings that were privately published or collected many years later. Many of these appear to be at odds with the narratives of the government in their satirical or critical treatment of developments in Kashmiri society. The bureaucratization of culture, however, led to a decline in the progressive movement and, to a certain extent, leftism in Kashmir. As its former proponents were assimilated into the bureaucracy, there were very few that could maintain the mantle of progressivism.

What does it mean for Kashmir's culture to be defined and shaped in service of a colonial occupation? I conclude that the appropriation of Kashmir's culture by the Kashmir government led cultural production to be deployed in ways that became fundamentally imbricated with government ideology. This is not to say that there is an "inauthentic" versus an "authentic" culture—rather it is important to consider the broader political context in which this cultural consolidation occurred—as well as what was erased in that consolidation. If certain aspects of Kashmiri "culture" were not seen as a threat and given a space by the Indian and Kashmir governments, then it would become harder for later proponents of self-determination to rely on them to craft a heightened sense of cultural nationalism. The implications should not be understated; it crafted a fragmented Kashmiri "self," one for whom the cultural terrain remains deeply contested and suspect.

Chapter 7

THE STATE OF EMERGENCY

State Repression, Political Dissent, and the Struggle for Self-Determination

In his story "The Shadow and the Substance," Kashmiri writer Amin Kamil presents a character named Manohar, the son of Pandit Samsar Chand, who was sent to jail in 1946 for fighting Dogra rule.[1] In the story, Manohar describes himself as a shadow, "the same shadow that accompanies every man. Sometimes it stands in front of him, sometimes behind, now at his right, now to his left." We soon find that Manohar is

> an employee of the Secret Police Service—an informer. You may want to know which Secret Police Service, because there are two such agencies here: the Kashmir Special Staff and the Indian Secret Police. Over here, there are two faces to everything. There is the Indian Reserve Police as well as the state's own Kashmir Police. There is a Central Information Department as well as the state's own Information Department. There are even two flags. . . . Here you will find two parallel governments, two outfits, two secrets, two pairs of hands always held out in their own separate ways, to protect the freedom of individuals. That is why I hasten to explain that I was a shadow from the Indian Secret Police—a nameless being, an informer."[2]

Manohar follows a Muslim man whom he sees in the area of Lal Chowk, near the site of a bomb blast the day before.[3] The man's demeanor makes Manohar suspicious, and he decides to become his shadow, "an orbit within which his body began to move."[4] He follows the man into a restaurant full of officials, lawyers, teachers, poets, and communists, many of whom had also been subject to Manohar's surveillance. The man leaves the restaurant and receives a packet from another man on the street, who urges him to relax and go home. The man replies that people like him are never meant to relax with their families. Manohar becomes suspicious, imagining that the man is responsible for setting off the bomb the previous day. He follows the man to his house, where an elderly woman asks him if he has brought home medicine for his sick wife. The man laments that he has received money from someone but has not gotten the medicine. As the man starts to leave the house again, Manohar begins to feel embarrassed running after the man, but then he hears the elderly woman admonish him, "Why was I telling you that day that you should not take up a job with this Special Staff? But you thought you had hit upon a fortune!"[5] Manohar, understandably, is shocked; the man he has been following was a shadow himself. At the end of the story, he asserts: "This town is full of Shadows."

As Kamil's short story suggests, both the Government of India and the Kashmir government had established their own rigorous systems of surveillance, including informers and multiple intelligence agencies. Manohar's tale highlights how everyone—including government employees—came within the orbit of surveillance to the extent that one "shadow" ends up unintentionally orbiting another "shadow."

A primary reliance on the politics of life did not entail that the state overlooked more sovereign forms of power, including the use of surveillance, violence, and repression, to contain political dissent against its rule. Police and intelligence files from Bakshi's period reveal a sophisticated, organized, widespread, and penetrating security and surveillance grid that criminalized political beliefs and aspirations that did not subscribe to that of the Kashmir and Indian governments. As scholars have argued, policing, surveillance, and emergency laws are colonial techniques of control for monitoring and "managing dangerous populations," especially after the territory has been secured.[6] Emergency laws, as John Reynolds writes, are "deeply implicated in settler-colonialism and related processes of occupation, dispossession, and discrimination."[7] In addition, Ilana Feldman writes that they are at the "heart of the imperial experience," working to shape political and social community and identify the multiplicity of subject positions within a given population.[8]

The raw use of sovereign power under Bakshi generally targeted individuals vocal or active in dissident politics. This was unlike the period after the armed rebellion when it was deployed against the broader collective, perhaps because those at the helm of power during Bakshi's rule still imagined Kashmiris—except for a disgruntled few—were impressionable and amenable to Indian rule as long as they were able to reap its benefits.

Political repression certainly did not begin under Bakshi. The Dogra and Abdullah governments were also politically repressive, and Bakshi drew upon existing repressive strategies, expanding them after Abdullah's arrest. Under the Dogras, the security apparatus had targeted the National Conference leadership; in the waning days of Dogra rule, it also arrested political workers who were pro-Pakistan or opposed the state's accession to India, "long before the tribesmen entered Kashmir."[9] Under Sheikh Abdullah's government, the target of the state's repressive policies were primarily individuals or groups purported to be pro-Pakistan or who rejected the state's accession to India.

Between 1947 and 1953, as head of the Home Department, Bakshi oversaw internal security concerns. Following the end of Abdullah's rule, brutal practices continued and expanded under Bakshi. The government spent a significant part of its budget on police and intelligence. Under Bakshi, Jammu and Kashmir surpassed Indian states in terms of expenditure per citizen on the police.[10]

Politically repressing those who supported Abdullah was integral to the consolidation of Bakshi's rule. At the same time that the Kashmir government was building schools and distributing rice at lower prices, it utilized a series of legal and extralegal measures to arrest or target those who were pro-Abdullah or pro-Pakistan—the two, as we will see, were not wholly commensurate. Nonetheless, under Bakshi, a popular and organized mass movement for self-determination emerged, primarily under the banner of the Plebiscite Front but also under other political and religious formations.

Driven by the belief that any form of political activism calling for a resolution of the Kashmir issue or a plebiscite was a threat to the "security of the state," the Kashmir government developed a series of legal and extralegal practices of surveillance and control. An enduring state of emergency belied what was otherwise being promoted as a democratic order. This indefinite state of emergency was an exercise in colonial control, aimed at suppressing people's political aspirations as well as their agency by marking all dissent as being sponsored by Pakistan. Meanwhile, political dissidents were constrained not only by the repression meted out by the Kashmir government but also the ambiguities inherent in their leadership's demand for self-determination in the context of the UN resolutions and shifting political developments. In addition to a lack of ideological coherence amongst dissidents, one of the primary reasons why the dissident groups were unable to sustain a strong political opposition is that many of the leaders were operating within the same frame of reference and background as those who were officially in power.

Bakshi's Inheritance

On the level of political freedoms, the Naya Kashmir manifesto had been resolutely progressive, guaranteeing freedom of speech, assembly, press, and demonstrations.[11] It also allowed for citizens to join a variety of political and cultural organizations. In providing for equal protection under the law, the plan stated, "No citizen may be arrested or detained except by decision of a Court of Law or by the sanction of the Advocate-General."[12] It also protected the private property and correspondence of its citizens. Perhaps no other aspect of the manifesto was as undermined, however, as the sections that guaranteed political freedoms.

Charles Davenport defines repression as "government regulatory action directed against those who challenge existing power relationships."[13] These regulatory actions vary and include a variety of overt and covert, violent and nonviolent, and state and state-sponsored actions, including harassment of opposition leaders, firing of government employees, restrictions on civil liberties, suspension of habeas corpus, censorship of the press, banning of political parties, and limitations on associations, gatherings, and speech. Other repressive tactics include state-sponsored militias, death squads, torture, disappearances, mass killings, policing and violence against protestors, prevalence of informants and intelligence agencies, and imprisoning and exiling dissidents. Some states also rely on strategies of accommodation involving efforts to negotiate with the opposition, release political prisoners, and co-opt the opposition into the current political system. Bakshi's government relied upon many of these tactics, highlighting the varying types of dissent it sought to subdue.

Although the government faced dissent from different ideological, regional, and religious groups, "political" dissidents in this period—those who were the most criminalized—were primarily those contesting the finality of the state's accession to India and demanding a plebiscite. Aside from the Plebiscite Front and the Political Conference, Muslim religious bodies, such as the Jamaat-i-Islami, were not only pro-Pakistan but also challenged the secular ideals of the Kashmir government. Other groups on the government's radar included individuals or groups in Jammu and Ladakh that wanted greater regional autonomy within the state or further integration with India; leftist or communist groups and trade unions opposed to the unequal distribution of wealth and power under Bakshi; and Sikh and Pandit groups contesting what they perceived as the government's increasing discrimination against their community.

Sheikh Abdullah and his loyalists represented the primary architects of dissent at this time. Although Abdullah later shifted his stance to be more accommodating with the Indian leadership, in the fifties and the early sixties, he was a staunch proponent of Kashmiri self-determination in the face of Government of India and Kashmir government coercion. Even from behind bars, Abdullah inspired the opposition leadership and gained the sympathies of Kashmir's Muslims, as he had in the later decades of Dogra rule. The events surrounding his removal from power had given him a charismatic and moral authority to mobilize the masses on the issue of a plebiscite. Furthermore, Abdullah had supporters in India who were advocating for his release to come to an ultimate agreement with the Kashmir leadership. Because his release would directly challenge Bakshi's hold on power, many of the Bakshi government's repressive measures were specifically leveled toward Abdullah and his supporters.

The first of these repressive practices was the creation of a ragtag group of National Conference workers called the Peace Brigade, a militia dispatched to local neighborhoods, especially those deemed pro-Pakistan. Abdullah's administration had formed the Peace Brigade, and ironically after his arrest, its members went after his supporters. Munshi Ishaq, an emergency officer in the district of Budgam under Abdullah and later one of the founding members of the Plebiscite Front, wrote in his memoirs that the Peace Brigade took the "law and order system in their hands and spread the network of hooliganism and terrorism in villages and cities. . . . The police department also came under them."[14] Ishaq's characterization of the Peace Brigade differs from that of Andrew Whitehead, who, although arguing that the "militia's task was to protect the Kashmiri capital from the Pakistani invaders, and in so doing it buttressed Kashmir's accession to India," posits it solely as defending Kashmir against the Pathan Muslims.[15] Whitehead's account does not address the coercive role the militia played in bolstering the accession and suppressing those opposing it.

When Bakshi came to power, he took control of the Peace Brigades, now with an extensive intelligence network in areas that appeared to have anti-Indian or anti-Bakshi sentiments. Oftentimes in plain clothes and given expansive authority, they would attack or harass those in the opposition, imprisoning and torturing those suspected of dissent, using mainly "their muscles and canes."[16] Their heavy-handed tactics gained them notoriety; they were known to put hot potatoes in the mouths of opponents, place heavy stones on their chests, and brand them with hot irons.[17] They were also accused of molesting women.[18] Ishaq recalled how they would tie pro-Pakistan Kashmiris with grass rope and hold them in their headquarters.[19] The Peace Brigade came to be known in local parlance as *khuftan faqirs*, or late-night beggars, because they would parade around Srinagar city after the last prayer of the day, *khuftan* in Kashmiri.[20] The level of suppression was such that individuals were arrested or beaten if an informant discovered them privately listening to Radio Pakistan or Radio Azad Kashmir.

The Peace Brigade, as well as other police and home guard units, worked in tandem with Ghulam Qadir Ganderbali, the notorious superintendent of police in Srinagar, known for his brutal use of torture and his control over the security apparatus. He oversaw the Kothi Bagh Police Station in the heart of the city, where a number of political prisoners were detained. In addition to the Peace Brigade, the Kashmir police force, as well as the Central Reserve Police Force and the Indian army, were all in operation in Kashmir. Furthermore, a separate government militia made up primarily of Bakshi's followers and National Conference workers, known as the *goggas*, controlled particular neighborhoods, tasked with identifying local individuals who were suspect. In essence, they formed a separate, parallel mode of surveillance for Bakshi.

Given the restrictions on archival research on Kashmir at the National Archives of India, it is difficult to ascertain to what extent and in what way the Government of India was directly involved in managing dissent at this time. What we can gather is that the Indian government had its own intelligence agencies spying on the broader society along with the Kashmir leadership as well as armed police check posts in the region to "tackle large-scale attempt[s] at infiltration, subversion, sabotage, and political conspiracy."[21]

Much of the Indian government's attention was on the border with Pakistan to ward off any attacks, while the Kashmir government focused more on managing dissent internally and producing a "compliant, unthreatening population."[22] Indian officials were primarily concerned with border raids, illicit trade, and people moving across the cease-fire line.[23] They would keep a close eye on those Kashmiris, in particular, who were attempting to come back from Pakistan after Partition and the first India-Pakistan war and settle once more in Kashmir. These individuals—ostensibly refugees now marked as infiltrators—required approval from the local district magistrate granted only when it was ascertained they were not involved in any pro-Pakistan politics and were of "good character."[24] In the police and intelligence files, characterizations of "good character" were not deployed simply for citizenship or resettlement but also for more mundane matters among regular residents such as starting a new newspaper or seeking permits or licenses, signifying the penetrating reach of the surveillance grid into all levels of society and forcing people to retreat from political activity.

The Kashmir government's suppression of local dissent discomforted some in the Indian leadership. The Government of India knew of the activities of the Peace Brigade and other local militias; during a visit to Kashmir, Govind Ballabh Pant, then the Indian home minister, asked Bakshi about the Peace Brigade and whether its activities included breaking up public meetings of Bakshi's opposition gatherings. According to Mir Qasim, a former chief minister and member of Bakshi's cabinet, "Bakshi tried to play it down saying it was a band of a very few and unarmed persons. . . . [In response] Pant said that one goonda can make a thousand men's life miserable."[25] Despite the Government of India's presumed discomfort at the methods used to curb his opponents, Bakshi was given free rein to deal with dissent.[26]

In addition to the numerous surveillance, intelligence, and armed agencies, a series of heavy-handed laws criminalized political dissent. As Duschinski and Bhan argue, if we take into account the role of law in playing a "formative and constitutive role in relation to the social, cultural and political dynamics of occupation," then the series of draconian laws were meant to assert colonial control and "institute a state of emergency and permanent crisis in Kashmir," a dynamic that was fundamental to the logics of occupation.[27] Although international law has yet to legally recognize Kashmir as an occupation—it is critical to understand how "occupation was 'produced in and through' a complex set of legal processes by which a permanent state of emergency [was] established."[28] And while these measures are "always portrayed as being 'temporary' or 'provisional' until the security situation [is] brought [under] control," they in effect create a sense of permanent danger and instability.[29] This, then, creates a situation where state sovereignty is established primarily through the ongoing criminalization of all forms of dissent.

A number of draconian laws, including the Public Security Act, were remnants from the Dogra period.[30] However, the level and extent of suppression during the Bakshi period surpassed that of the Dogras. During the later part of Dogra rule, various political parties, including the National Conference, the Muslim Conference, the Kisan Mazdoor Conference, and the Kashmir Socialist Party, could hold public meetings and annual conferences. Members of these parties even contested in and won elections. There was more restriction on the press under Bakshi than under the Dogras; the latter allowed opposition parties to publish papers whereas the former censored them. Kashmiris living outside the region, even in India, had more freedom to publish papers of varying perspectives than their counterparts in Kashmir.

In 1954, the Supreme Court of India extended its jurisdiction to Kashmir as a means of further integration. That meant that the fundamental rights of citizens guaranteed by India's constitution applied in the region; however, as Sumantra Bose argues, "These civil liberties could be suspended at any time at the discretion of [Kashmiri] authorities in the interest of 'security,' and no judicial reviews of the suspensions would be allowed. In effect, this was carte blanche for the operation of a draconian police state in [Kashmir]."[31] A wide range of laws contributed to the permanent state of emergency. The Public

Security Act curtailed civil liberties and allowed for the confiscation and requisition of any property. The Enemy Agents Ordinance, introduced by Bakshi in 1948, allowed arrest and trial of those suspected of pro-Pakistan leanings, resulting in punishment ranging from imprisonment of ten years to the death penalty.[32] Individuals faced trial in a "designated special court with no right of appeal for persons designated as enemy agents or as persons aiding the enemy."[33] The ordinance applied to those peacefully calling for a plebiscite. Public meetings and processions, unless in support of the ruling party, were forbidden under Article 50 of the Defense of India Rules.[34] The Ingress and Egress Act pushed back to the other side of the cease-fire line any undesirable resident of the state.[35] Various regulations under the Defense of India Rules were also promulgated during the Indochina War of 1962; a number of Kashmiri leaders, including Sheikh Abdullah, were held without trial under these rules.[36] In addition, some government-affiliated individuals lost their jobs for speaking out against the state.[37]

The most commonly applied law was the Preventive Detention Act (1954; PDA), a law separate from the Preventative Detention Act passed by the Indian Parliament in 1952. The PDA allowed the police to detain suspects without a trial for a maximum of five years and was used to arrest thousands of political activists. In correspondence between the Indian government and the Kashmir government (primarily D. P. Dhar, the deputy home minister), there was much discussion over what to disclose to the public as well to those detained. Indian officials in the Ministry of State and the Ministry of Law closely looked over the draft of the Kashmir government's PDA to ensure it could not be challenged in the courts—given that, according to an official in the Ministry of States, the courts were "very jealous of their jurisdiction."[38] Since the Supreme Court had extended its jurisdiction to the Kashmir state, the Indian government appeared concerned that individuals held in preventive detention be provided grounds for their detention as well as legal representation in accordance with the fundamental rights granted in the Indian Constitution. They were concerned that the courts would look into whether "the grounds are clearly stated, the facts supporting the grounds are definite and precise and whether the grounds are properly related to the reason for detention and only to it." Initially, the Kashmir government set up an advisory board to determine whether there was sufficient cause for preventive detention cases. Detention orders could be revoked and then reinstated if "fresh facts have arisen."[39] Yet, realizing that this much oversight could prove to be complicated, the cases sent to the advisory board were restricted to issues of "loyalty of the police, supplies, and foreigners."[40]

For all other cases of preventive detention, there were ambiguities surrounding the purposes of detention—whether they were done in the interest of public safety or peace, maintenance of public order, or security of the state. Security of the state was a more serious crime and entailed protection of the country from foreign aggression (including attempts to overthrow the government, rebellion, or war) while public order involved ordinary breaches of public safety such as protests, riots, or communal incidents but not danger to the state itself. Indian officials encouraged the use of security-of-the-state charges to detain most pro-plebiscite or pro-Pakistan political dissidents, even if their activities did not fall under the purview of the clause. V. Narayanan of the Indian Ministry of States even admitted that "when the grounds for detention . . . are furnished, it is possible that some of them might be viewed as relatable more to the 'maintenance of public order' than the 'security of the state.'"[41] For some of the detainees—including Abdullah—the evidence was in the speeches they delivered, seeking to "inflame communal passions and break up the integrity of the state."[42] Yet, in other cases, there were no specific speeches or actions and thus no definite grounds for detention. Rather, these individuals were said to be "members of a particular group whose object was to do certain things."

Eventually, officials in the Indian government argued that the actual grounds did not have to be disclosed "for reasons connected with the security of the state or the maintenance of public order" if the disclosure went against public interest—a term once more left undefined. The government—and not the court or board—was also supposed to review the case. In effect, the Indian government created a loophole in the law—going against its own constitution—enabling the Kashmir government to detain individuals for years at a time with no judicial oversight—contributing once more to the state of emergency. By not requiring the government to reveal the grounds for detention, the PDA also enabled the criminalization of individuals not only for their political activities but also for their political beliefs.

From the perspective of the Indian and Kashmir governments, the PDA was crucial "in view of the change in situation and circumstances brought about by the American military aid to Pakistan," whereby a "situation may arise in Jammu and Kashmir which would necessitate the entrustment to Government of the maximum measure of authority regarding preventive detention. . . . There might be infiltration, attempts at sabotage, and all manner of activities designed to create a difficult and ugly situation."[43] To justify the draconian laws, the factors causing an "ugly situation" were always depicted as external to the people of the state. There was no acknowledgement of the rights of people to express political dissent or political aspirations. These laws enabled the government to curb dissent but were also an integral part of the organization of state violence and repression. As a result, the state enacted a rule by law—in which the legal form was used to cloak arbitrary power—instead of a rule of law, which, as Rueban Balasubramaniam argues in the case of more contemporary cases of indefinite detention, contrasts with arbitrary power.[44]

As Duschinski and Ghosh argue, "India's occupation of Kashmir is based on a normalized and pervasive logic of punitive containment of Kashmiri dissent and rebellion that produces and is produced by a jurisdiction of suspicion with its origins in colonial power relations."[45] Preventive detention is not extra-constitutional or unconstitutional, nor is it exceptional; rather, it is "written into the logic of occupational constitutionalism."[46]

Parallel to the legal suppression, dissidents also accused government authorities of using extralegal strategies to coerce opposition activists into submission. Munshi Ishaq described how his neighborhood suffered discriminatory treatment because of his political activities. The construction of a road from his house to the main market in the area was stopped.[47] In addition, others accused the government of using strategies of accommodation, which sought to negotiate with or co-opt the opposition. Qari Saifuddin, one of the main leaders of the Jamaat-i-Islami, described how officials in the Central Intelligence Department attempted to bribe him to work on their behalf. "One day a senior CID officer came from Delhi and wanted to meet with me," Saifuddin wrote in his autobiography. "The messenger was my Hindu student. I accepted the meeting with him on my student's request. The officer was trying to convince me with his sweet flattery that I secretly work for him while living in the party, and secretly inform him about the Jamaat-i-Islamis' work . . . so that they will give me valuable compensation as reward. I refused . . . and he became very insistent. After this long discussion, the officer became angry."[48]

The repressiveness of the government's policies toward its dissidents unleashed what Prem Nath Bazaz, a Kashmiri Pandit writer who had once been a member of the National Conference but had grown disillusioned with its increasing authoritarianism, referred to as a "reign of terror" on his visit to Kashmir in the mid-1960s. A state of emergency had become the new normal. These actions, he argued, led to a "complete alienation from India and a yearning for Pakistan. . . . Repression can't keep away Kashmiri Muslims from their pro-Pakistan predilections."[49] He continued that it was only because of persecution that Kashmiri Muslims wanted Pakistan, as the government was unable to win them over.[50] In this perspective, heightened repression solidified anti-India sentiments, resulting in the desire for a different political arrangement—in this case, merger with Pakistan. From the perspective of the Kashmir government, however, it appeared that repression was required to uphold the present political arrangement, given a potential preexisting sentiment for Pakistan, especially among the region's Muslims.

Bazaz's comments regarding Kashmiri Muslims' predilection for Pakistan are important to note. Instead of suggesting that Kashmiri Muslims had a primordial attachment to Pakistan because of shared religious backgrounds, he suggests that this affinity arose "only because of persecution." Paradoxically, according to Bazaz, the government had to use repressive tactics to secure the accession, which assumes that Kashmiris were inclined toward Pakistan to begin with. Yet, for Bazaz, it was these very repressive tactics that undermined the legitimacy of the state, as Kashmiris began to "yearn for Pakistan." I suggest that the yearning was a result of the terms of the plebiscite itself, given that the only two options were to join India or Pakistan. In a way, these terms restricted the range of political possibility in Kashmir. Dissent was more complicated as a result of local rivalries and concerns and did not neatly fit into binaries.

Political Dissent

The Political Conference and the Plebiscite Front were two primary political opposition groups that came to prominence during Bakshi's rule. Since most members of the Muslim Conference, which had opposed accession to India at the time of Partition, had either been arrested or exiled to Pakistan during Abdullah's rule, the members of the Political Conference and the Plebiscite Front were primarily former National Conference supporters who had grown disillusioned with the authoritarian practices of the party or those who were still affiliated with Abdullah and had become wary of what they perceived as the Indian government's increasing interference in Kashmir's affairs and its backtracking on promises of autonomy. These individuals had played a pivotal role in the struggle against Dogra rule, been committed to the Naya Kashmir manifesto, and served in Abdullah's government as ministers, administrators, and educators. They included members like Sofi Mohammed Akbar, who had previously signed arrest warrants in Baramulla against those who were pro-Pakistan.[51] In many ways, they had much more in common with those who were in power in terms of their background in the struggle against the Dogras and their initial commitment to a form of Kashmiri nationalism. Thus, the primary political opposition did not necessarily seek a fundamentally different vision of the state or form of sovereignty but, rather, opposed the authoritarianism of the National Conference and the rise of communalism (or Hindu nationalism), as well as India's backtracking on promises of autonomy.

These factors led them to assert a right to self-determination through a plebiscite. Was the plebiscite slogan a substitute for Pakistan? I argue that what "self-determination" would specifically entail was left vague, although both the parties led people to believe they were presumably in favor of Pakistan. Furthermore, there was ambiguity in how they ascribed a commitment to a secular polity, even as they made appeals to Muslim identity from time to time. The story of the rise and fall of these two organizations sheds light on the difficulty of organizing a coherent opposition in the context of India's colonial occupation but also broader global geopolitical realities.

The Political Conference

In the new political landscape, the Political Conference was one of the first groups that emerged to contest Kashmir's accession to India.[52] Ghulam Mohiuddin Karra, previously associated with the communist wing of the National Conference, founded the group in June 1953, just a few months before Sheikh

Abdullah's arrest. Although Karra was initially more left-leaning, he vacillated toward Pakistan.[53] The Political Conference, although calling for the right to self-determination, described itself as a pro-Pakistan organization and in its meetings was clear that the party stood for accession to Pakistan.[54] A poster of the Political Conference listed the following commitments: withdrawal of forces, immediate and free conduct of plebiscite, long live Pakistan, constitutional struggle, aversion to subversion, and friendship with welfare, fraternity, and world peace.[55] The organization rejected violence and coercion as a method of protest, but its members were asked to be willing to "lie on embers for the protection of the right of self-determination."[56]

My insights into the workings of the Political Conference are based on an oral interview with Pirzada Hafizullah Makhdoomi, a former Political Conference worker and secretary general of the Working Committee, as well as secondary sources. Makhdoomi came from a Sufi *pir* family in the Khanaqah area of the Old City. He entered Amar Singh College in 1952, where he grew interested in politics and served as the college secretary for the National Conference. A curious student, he went to the state's Constituent Assembly, filled at the time with National Conference loyalists, to watch the proceedings. He realized they were "dumb driven cattle," saying, "People would just support the leader (Sheikh Abdullah). There were no elections, no contest."[57] His support for the National Conference subsequently dwindled. His experience suggests it was how the NC operated that led to disillusionment among young students, like Makhdoomi, with the party. Alongside other students at Amar Singh College, he started to hold meetings and demonstrations on the school grounds. Members of the Political Conference became aware of the activities of these students and recruited them into their group. When asked what motivated him to join the Political Conference, he emphasized the right of self-determination. His interpretation of the two-nation theory was that Pakistan was founded to protect the political rights of Muslims, ensuring they had equal rights and representation and were not forever relegated to the status of "minority" in a Hindu majoritarian India. Makhdoomi reiterated it was "not because of Islam." When asked what he meant, Makhdoomi clarified that Pakistan was not meant to be an "Islamic state" (or a theocratic government) but rather, a state for the subcontinent's Muslims to live securely. This sentiment was reiterated by a number of other Kashmiri Muslims from that period, for whom Pakistan—in addition to being a safe haven for the region's Muslims—was a place of economic, filial, and educational ties.[58]

There is some dispute over the origins of the Political Conference. While Makhdoomi claimed that Karra was a sincere activist, Abdullah's autobiography suggests a different account, corroborated by B. N. Mullik, the director of the Intelligence Bureau of India, and Munshi Ishaq. Abdullah said Karra wanted a cabinet position in his administration, but the position was given to G. M. Sadiq. In defiance, Karra left the National Conference to set up the Political Conference. Ishaq also refers to Karra as being opportunistic and wanting to take credit for the movement.[59] After establishing close contacts with Pakistan, Mullik argues that Karra received funding for his political activities in the Valley.[60] Makhdoomi denied this allegation, arguing that Karra had property and didn't need external funding.

Whatever the impetus behind the Political Conference's founding, it appeared to initially gain resonance with large swaths of Kashmiris, especially in Srinagar. Its first main event was a large procession in the Old City, on June 19, 1953, with nearly one hundred thousand people in attendance, according to Makhdoomi. Makhdoomi recalled, "It was held in Nawa Kadal. The leader [Karra] came out and asked the people what they stand for. The people all said Pakistan."[61] As the procession started moving towards Lal Chowk, people began to throw stones at the Indian army vehicles. In his memoirs, Munshi Ishaq remembered that the "city was echoing with the slogan of Pakistan Zindabad (Long live Pakistan). The flags of the National Conference had been torn to shreds."[62] Soon after, the Kashmir cabinet banned the party and placed its leaders in jail.[63] Makhdoomi remembered specifically how Karra had switched from his communist viewpoints toward "becoming more religious," perhaps suggesting that a religious nationalism was soon to gain ground, as leftists or communists began to lose their ideological spark as a result of their affiliation with the National Conference.

The Political Conference's founding members and working committee members consisted of well-known educated Kashmiris, including some Kashmiri Pandits. Pandit Rughonath Vaishnavi, a lawyer, served as vice president of the organization. Like others, he has grown disenchanted with the organization's suppression of dissent and resigned from the party, worried that it wanted to "hold the reins of absolute power to [its] heart's content."[64] In 1952, Vaishnavi's weekly Urdu newspaper, *Jamhoor*, was banned, and he joined forces with Karra to become one of the founding members of the Political Conference. In his unpublished memoirs, he wrote "It was clear that Kashmiris had been 'relegated to the position of slaves' after India gained its independence."[65]

As a Kashmiri Pandit who was a member of a pro-Pakistan organization, Vaishnavi was taunted as "Pakistani *batta*," or Pakistani Kashmiri Pandit.[66] Yet Vaishnavi's support was not for Pakistan, per se, but for the majority of the region's inhabitants, who he believed had the democratic right to determine their future. Vaishnavi eventually resigned from the Political Conference and subsequently wrote a statement in favor of Kashmir's independence as a separate nation-state in a letter to the then president of India, Dr. S. Radakrishnan, on February 25, 1964.[67] Vaishnavi's letter sought to underscore that the people of Kashmir "of whatever religion, creed or community . . . are born of one and the same soil . . . [and] possess a unique sense of belonging to our land of birth."[68] In subsequent letters to other Indian officials, he reasoned that the people of Kashmir have "politically, culturally, and socially held themselves distinct from the rest of the world." An independent Kashmir, he wrote, would be a bridge of peace between India and Pakistan. In response to criticism that it would get overrun by its neighbors, he argued that it would be able to sustain its sovereignty as did the other smaller member states of the United Nations. Being a part of the international community, Vaishnavi stated, would protect Kashmir's territorial integrity.

The reason for his apparent shift toward arguing for an independent state remains unclear. Perhaps, as it was for Makhdoomi, Vaishnavi's initial support for Pakistan was in light of the perception that Pakistan was not an Islamic theocracy but one that would protect the democratic rights of the subcontinent's Muslims. As Pakistan's identity as an Islamic state became more foregrounded with the framing of its constitution, it is possible that Vaishnavi became concerned about what this identity would mean for minorities in the country. His example underscores the evolving ideological shifts among Kashmir's political activists at this time, which were affected by changing political developments and restricted political possibilities that ranged from seeking greater autonomy under the National Conference to seeking a plebiscite that would be in favor of Pakistan, to articulating a vision of independence.

During his time with the organization, Vaishnavi, along with the other leaders of the Political Conference sent letters to the United Nations Security Council and the Government of India. They raised the issue of the lack of civil liberties in the state, rampant police rule, the presence of the armed forces, and political prisoners, as well as the denial of the promised plebiscite.[69] They met with news agencies, both Indian and international. Political Conference leaders kept a close account of political delegations that were coming to India and wrote to various international bodies. Some of these communications, however, were returned to the headquarters of the party without being delivered due to state repression.[70]

In 1960, Makhdoomi travelled to Pakistan to meet its leadership. He recalled becoming angry in a conversation with a Pakistani leader who complained that Kashmiris "were too cowardly to take to the gun." He reminded the official that the struggle for self-determination was a nonviolent one and that India would completely suppress the armed struggle given its sheer advantage. Because of limited sources on the Political Conference, it is difficult to ascertain what the organization believed would occur after a plebiscite. If it declared itself to be for Pakistan, how did it envision Kashmir's relationship with Pakistan? There was a lack of clarity on the goals of the Political Conference, as well as its vision for Kashmir's future—a trait it would share with the Plebiscite Front.

There are a number of reasons for the decline of the Political Conference. Aside from internal dissensions and a weak financial position, it appears the Political Conference's leadership could not compete with the increasing influence of the Plebiscite Front. In the 1950s and 1960s, the front had the support of Sheikh Abdullah, the undisputed leader of the opposition to Bakshi. In an interview with *Kashmir Life*, Makhdoomi asserts that Karra confided in him, "I am defeated. People blindly follow Sheikh. No matter whether he does good or bad to them, but people will support only him."[71] The conference's membership was small in comparison to the front's. In a membership drive in 1964, for example, government intelligence noted that the organization managed to secure only 1,200 members, far less than the Plebiscite Front.[72] The response to the group's appeals appeared to be weak. The leadership also faced a crisis between those willing to dialogue with the Government of India and those who weren't, a process parallel to that of the Plebiscite Front. After the Holy Relic incident, in which a relic of the Prophet Muhammad was stolen from Srinagar's Hazratbal Mosque, leading to weeks of unrest in the region in 1963, Karra became involved in the committee formed to recover the relic, composed of Muslim leaders throughout the Valley, many of whom had been affiliated with the Political Conference and the Plebiscite Front. Subsequently, the organization folded and Karra retreated from politics. Nonetheless, for many years, the role of the Political Conference had been to keep the issue of plebiscite alive, especially in the international arena. Yet, it would be the rise and fall of the Plebiscite Front that would come to define Kashmir's politics in subsequent decades.

The Plebiscite Front

The Plebiscite Front dominated the political scene in Kashmir from its inception in 1955 to its reincorporation into the National Conference after the Sheikh-Indira accord of 1975. Mirza Afzal Beg, once a minister in Sheikh Abdullah's administration, and former legislators from Abdullah's Constituent Assembly founded the Plebiscite Front in August 1955. Many of its leaders were former National Conference officials or workers. Having served time in jail after Abdullah's arrest, Beg was released on parole for health reasons and became the group's first president. On paper, the Plebiscite Front stood for "self-determination through a plebiscite under the UN auspices, withdrawal of the armed forces of both nations from Kashmir, and restoration of civil liberties and free elections."[73] It viewed the state's accession to India as temporary and argued that resolving the Kashmir issue would promote needed amity and goodwill between India and Pakistan.[74] It disputed the right of the Constituent Assembly to decide the future of the state in the absence of representatives from Pakistan-administered Kashmir as well as UN resolutions stating that the Constituent Assembly could not be a substitute for the plebiscite.[75] Sheikh Abdullah was in touch with members of the Plebiscite Front from jail, advising them on their activities, although he was never an official member of the party. Yet, even as the front was clear in its demand for a plebiscite, there was an ideological split among its leadership on the nature of the movement, attitudes toward Pakistan, and level of engagement with the Indian state.

Munshi Ishaq was one of the founding members and a former president of the Plebiscite Front. His son, Munshi Ghulam Hassan, collected Munshi Ishaq's diaries and published them in the form of a memoir entitled *Nida-i-Haq*. In his writings, Ishaq discusses his family background, as well as his involvement with the Plebiscite Front and political developments in Kashmir from the pre-1947 period until the late 1960s. Much of the text addresses the failures of the Kashmir government leadership, whom he believes put their personal concerns over those of the people, as well as the leadership of the Plebiscite Front, whom he accuses of betraying the cause of self-determination.

As one of the few Muslim businessmen, Ishaq played an important financial role for the National Conference's struggle against the Dogras and later served as an emergency officer in Budgam under Sheikh Abdullah's administration. Ishaq writes that he was not in favor of the accession to India and that he had grown increasingly disillusioned with the repressive politics of the National Conference.[76] When he was called by Beg to become a founding member of the Plebiscite Front, he agreed only because Beg claimed that the party's stance was "accession with Pakistan on the cloak of a referendum."[77] Indeed, a number of individuals informed me that Beg and the leadership of the Plebiscite Front let other members and the broader society believe that the front was in favor of merger with Pakistan. Makhdoomi recalled how during their gatherings, they "would raise a green handkerchief and rock salt, both of which was supposed to represent Pakistan" to gain favor with the people.[78] Yet, the leadership never explicitly declared that it was pro-Pakistan, and in its official statements attempted to distance itself from the neighboring country.

After announcing the launch of the Plebiscite Front, Beg and the rest of the leadership began a membership campaign. Thousands of people "readily accepted the Plebiscite Front. . . . Most of the villages, *mohallas*, towns, and cities of the state witnessed a mushroom growth of the Plebiscite Front organization committees."[79] Two months later, the first convention was held in Sopore in September 1955. In November of that year, the government rearrested Beg under the Preventive Detention Act. Other conventions and gatherings were held throughout the state and the organization increased its membership. Many of the front's activities centered on the figure of Abdullah, who had once again retained a larger-than-life hold over the masses. In the front's meetings and rallies, its leaders would encourage people to remain united behind Abdullah, as he would lead them to attain real freedom and social and economic prosperity.[80]

The organization of the Plebiscite Front was highly centralized and hierarchical, with a general council and a central committee at the head of committees at the primary, neighborhood, tehsil, district, and provincial levels. Delegates elected presidents for two-year terms. Each unit had to send a monthly report to the central committee about its activities. Given the highly repressive atmosphere in the state, it is difficult to ascertain how many members the organization had at its peak. However, estimates range from 75,000 to 200,000, not including the masses of people attending the rallies or speeches.[81] In addition, the organization worked with labor unions and student groups, including the Young Men's League and the Student Federation. It regularly raised funds through membership fees, special contributions, grain contributions by peasants, and donations for legal cases and members of families of prisoners. In addition, the front received money from Kashmiris settled in Britain, most from Pakistan-administered Kashmir.

The Plebiscite Front was accused of receiving funds from Pakistan. Both the Government of India and the local Kashmir government charged that Pakistani officials gave money to Begum Abdullah, Sheikh Abdullah's wife, who then gave the funds to the leaders of the organization. When the issue was brought up in court, the members of the front denied the allegation. At the same time, however, it was later alleged that Bakshi himself would provide funds for both the Political Conference and the Plebiscite Front, as well as other groups. The reasons are simple: Bakshi needed to justify the need for a strong security state with unrestricted powers as well as continued Indian support. In correspondence with the Indian leadership, "he used the front and its activities as a justification for many of his acts of omission and commission."[82] Bakshi justified his financing of these groups to Kashmiri journalist Sanaullah Bhat, stating, "The existence of such elements was necessary; otherwise, New Delhi will do anything here it likes."[83] Thus, by portraying instability in the state, Bakshi continued to receive complete support from the Indian government for his activities in Kashmir. Although the front leadership denied this allegation, they conceded that some private individuals might have taken money from the government.[84] While Bakshi was certainly not responsible for the founding and development of these organizations, the possibility that he funded them from time to time suggests that the relationship between dissent and repression was not clear-cut and that at times Bakshi manipulated the "presence" of dissent in order for the Kashmir government to continue to receive funding and support from the Government of India. This highlights how the politics of life also crept into the space of dissent and repression.

The Plebiscite Front used several strategies to promote the plebiscite. The first was propaganda against the Bakshi government. Workers would print posters and circulate pamphlets and news throughout the region. Theater performances would be conducted depicting Abdullah, Beg, and Nehru, where the latter was forced to withdraw troops from Kashmir and hold a plebiscite.[85] The front called for a boycott of elections in 1957 and 1962 in addition to a social boycott of all pro-Indian Kashmiris; people were asked not to cooperate with them in the running of the administration.[86] There were also cases where deceased relatives of pro-Indian political parties were refused burial space.[87] The front regularly held meetings, rallies, and processions; the police or the Peace Brigade broke up many of them. It called for strikes, or *hartaals*, on important occasions, including August 9, the date of Abdullah's arrest.[88] It sought to bring international pressure on India by writing to various delegations and international organizations and sent letters to world forums and regional gatherings of world leaders.[89]

Officially, the front articulated its struggle as a secular, nonviolent, anti-colonial one, often invoking other anti-colonial struggles around the world.[90] Its members noted the irony of India fighting and denouncing imperialism "to free herself from its clutches, playing itself the contemptible game of expansionism immediately after having attained independence."[91] Pushing back against the two-nation theory, the front declared the demand for plebiscite was "not based on religious affinity with this or that country" but a belief in a peaceful and democratic method.[92] The front adopted a number of resolutions reaffirming the organization's faith and desire for communal harmony. It accused British rule of dividing the Hindus and Muslims of the Indian subcontinent.[93] While the organization never used the government-sponsored term *kashmiriyat*, it positioned itself as an organization working for the betterment of all Kashmiris, not just Kashmir's Muslims.[94] In response to government allegations that the Plebiscite Front was communal, it repeatedly declared its commitment to secularism and against communal fanaticism, declaring "We are a secular nation . . . . State can't prosper until it has communal peace. . . . [We] strive for cohesion amongst various communities of [the] population."[95] It called for "true and genuine secularism" to be ingrained in the body politic, although it never detailed what this might entail nor how it might be achieved.[96] Front materials praised Gandhi "as the greatest apostle of truth and nonviolence in the present world." It would go on to declare that Gandhi himself saw how Kashmir had offered a "ray of light" during Partition and protected its minorities despite the "ghastly news of [Muslim] brethren in Jammu at hands of [the] Maharaja and RSS."[97] The front painted Hindu nationalist developments in India and in Jammu as "having disastrous consequences both to the cause of Indian secularism and for the confidence that Kashmiri Muslims had placed on the Indian leadership."[98] The front also repeatedly insisted it was "wedded to the principle of nonviolence and consistent with the high principles of ahimsa and the utility of peace."[99]

Given that many in the leadership of the front had previously been affiliated with the National Conference, the stated commitment to secularism is perhaps not surprising. From these writings, it appears that the rise of communalism in India and its subsequent impact in Jammu with the Praja Parishad was an important reason for many of the front's leaders to question the security of Kashmir's Muslims in India. This, combined with the authoritarianism and repression of the Kashmir government, led to the demand for plebiscite. The leaders of the Plebiscite Front did not contest the ideology behind the Naya Kashmir manifesto—many of them had played a role in shaping it—suggesting that such ideals were not simply the exclusive domain of the state. In one pamphlet that detailed the biographies of Plebiscite Front leaders who were accused in the Kashmir Conspiracy Case, the "secular" credentials of those accused were in full display. They were praised for their role against the "tribal raiders" and their participation in the Peace Brigades, which, as we learned earlier, had played a crucial role in suppressing pro-Pakistan sentiment in Kashmir.[100] They did not distance themselves from or reject their former pivot toward India. They argued instead that their former support for the accession was only because India had made certain promises in favor of an eventual plebiscite.

The front's official commitment to secularism faced criticism among some of its leaders who were pro-Pakistan. It was also in tension with the Front's attempts to spread its platform among the masses in the context of state repression. Since public gatherings were heavily curtailed, leaders of the Plebiscite Front, including Sheikh Abdullah, articulated their policies from a religious platform, including Muslim shrines or mosques in Hazratbal, Khanaqah, Khanyar, and Soura, as well as during festivals and Eid when there were larger congregations.[101] They made reference to the Quran and stories from Islamic history. Munshi Ishaq, in one of his speeches, referred to Imam Hussain's fight for freedom and his martyrdom based on sacrifice, urging the audience to do the same.[102]

It is possible that the front utilized these discourses to appeal to Kashmiri Muslims—not very different from the compulsions of Bakshi's government—especially given the rise of more explicitly religious groups such as the Jamaat-i-Islami. Since the government had gained the monopoly on developmentalist and secular discourses, the front had little maneuverability aside from positioning itself through religious discourses. It had to distinguish itself from the government. In its interactions with the press and communication with international bodies, its leaders relied heavily on secular and liberal tropes of democratic values and the right of self-determination. On the other hand, in their speeches to large congregations in mosques and shrines, they invoked Islamic stories of sacrifice and religious idioms. As a result, the leaders' engagement with ordinary people was mediated by a religious vocabulary, speaking of injustices through an Islamic framework. This is, importantly, how they were able to gain popularity.

Yet, for some in the front, the strategy was not simply instrumentalist but part of a religious nationalism that sought merger with Pakistan. Intelligence reports revealed tension between front members who were more "pro-Abdullah" and those who were "pro-Pakistan." The pro-Abdullah faction included Maulana Syeed Masoodi, who sought to "oust the pro-Pakistan" elements from the party and demanded the release of Sheikh Abdullah, as only he could "devise a just and honorable solution of the Kashmir tangle."[103] In

1960, during Munshi Ishaq's presidency—ostensibly more pro-Pakistan—he advised front workers to "dissolve their differences and hold meetings in mosques, adopt Islamic slogans . . . and try to give a religious-cum social semblance to the party program."[104] The intelligence report indicates that this caused friction among the workers. Other leaders, such as Hakim Habibullah and Sofi Mohammad Akbar, argued that had Kashmiris followed the teachings of Islam, the events of 1947 would not have happened and that the struggle for the right of self-determination was in pursuance of Islamic principles.[105] These divisions between the pro-Abdullah faction (still vague in its overall goal) and the pro-Pakistan faction would increasingly come to the fore in subsequent years. This suggests that "acting politically was not just about acting against or in relation to governing authorities."[106] Indeed, it becomes important to understand the multiplicity of perspectives among the population and the "very significant efforts by people to exercise control over others in their community."[107] During the front's protests however, the Kashmiri masses continued to chant "Sher-i-Kashmir zindabad" (Long live Sheikh Abdullah [Lion of Kashmir]), "Pakistan zindabad" (Long live Pakistan), and "Yeh mulk hamara hai, iska faisla hum karenge" (This nation is ours, we will decide its future).[108] For them, the invocation of all three did not appear contradictory; all three remained internally coherent, giving collective expression to a rejection of India's rule over them.

The Kashmir Conspiracy Case

The year 1958 was an important one for both the Political Conference and the Plebiscite Front. Bakshi's government was facing increasing Indian and international pressure to release Sheikh Abdullah, the only man seen as having the moral authority to settle the Kashmir issue once and for all. Reports in the international media declared that all Abdullah proposed was a "free vote. . . . If that is a crime, then India's claim to Kashmir is obviously an arbitrary seizure of power and falls of its own injustice."[109] Critics claimed that the unlawful arrest of Abdullah had weakened India's position in Kashmir and on the international stage.[110] Mir Qasim wrote in his autobiography that Prime Minister Nehru was eager to make peace with Abdullah. For Bakshi, Qasim recalled, "This was a hard pill."[111] Perhaps Bakshi understood that once

Abdullah was released, his own position in Kashmir would be weakened, as the Government of India would try to make a deal with Abdullah to bring him back to power.

In New Delhi, the Indian Constituent Assembly formed a group to mobilize support in favor of Abdullah's release and against Bakshi. Mridula Sarabhai, Rammanohar Lohia, and Ashok Mehta led these efforts. Sarabhai, a former Congresswoman, had maintained contact with a number of Plebiscite Front leaders, as well as Abdullah, and received criticism in India for her stand, many accusing her of supporting the Plebiscite Front, the Political Conference, and the Muslim Conference.[112]

While a number of Indians viewed Sarabhai in a predominantly negative light for her support of the pro-plebiscite movement, a number of Kashmiri activists at the time, including Anwar Ashai, told me during interviews that she had been sent by Nehru to provide a "soft face" of India. Her purpose, they argued, was to make sure that Nehru still had an open channel of dialogue with Sheikh Abdullah, despite having him arrested. Munshi Ishaq also agreed with this perspective in his memoirs. He stated: "She showed her sympathy with the movement and was interfering in its matters. The mission of this clever woman was to finish Bakshi's government and turn the attention of the freedom movement towards acquisition of authority. . . . In short, Mridula's effort had been for India's interests."[113]

Whether Sarabhai was truly vested in the pro-plebiscite movement or whether she was placed within the leadership of the movement on behalf of the Government of India can be ascertained from later developments. Nonetheless, she played an important role in the state at the time of Abdullah's release in January 1958. In her account *Call for Impartial Inquiry: Pre and Post Hazratbal Incident*, Sarabhai presented the Plebiscite Front's position on Abdullah's release and the tactics of Bakshi's government. She wrote that the purpose of Abdullah's release by the government was not to bring him closer to Nehru to find a permanent solution but "to get India out of embarrassment in the eyes of the world which is caused by Sheikh Sahib's continuous detention and imprisonment."[114] Furthermore, she revealed that "those who are in close touch with the state authorities do not hesitate to say that Sheikh Sahib's release is necessary to re-arrest him and get him punished in the court of law." As soon as Abdullah was released, Sarabhai detailed how the government intended to charge him with a series of crimes so that he would be legally detained and lose whatever position he may still have had in the eyes of Indian officials. She wrote how "notorious goondas were employed to demonstrate against him in order to provoke him and the people of the state. . . . [They would] pose as Sheikites, raise anti-Indian and pro-Pakistan slogans." According to Sarabhai, this would serve as proof of his "antinational and dangerous role" and would be used to excite the Indian press to "get their support to let loose a bloody rule of repression in the interest of security of the state."[115] Sarabhai also accused the Bakshi government of exploding a series of bombs throughout the city "to create an atmosphere of terror," so that the case could be made for Abdullah to be detained for life. In an important revelation, she stated that it was not the Government of India that was furthering tension but rather, the Kashmir government. Nonetheless, she accused the Indian government of turning "a blind eye" to the political developments in the state. Sarabhai's account of the intrigues surrounding Abdullah's release is corroborated by a number of additional sources, including Mir Qasim and B. N. Mullik, the director of the Indian Intelligence Bureau, and it highlights how developments on the ground were as informed by local rivalries (Abdullah-Bakshi) as they were by rivalries between the Indian government and the Kashmir government.[116]

It appeared Bakshi's fears were not unfounded. When Abdullah was released on January 8, there was a surge of popular enthusiasm as people throughout the Valley held processions in his honor. Plebiscite Front workers were told to maintain the peace and bear the atrocities of the government, and to raise only the slogans Sher-i-Kashmir zindabad (Long live the Lion of Kashmir), Free plebiscite, and Hindu Muslim unity zindabad.[117] Notably, pro-Pakistan slogans did not make this list. Abdullah primarily spoke in places of worship—the Hazratbal shrine, Khanaqah-e-Maulla, and the Jamia Masjid. Quoting verses from the Quran and reciting Iqbal's verses, he spoke against the Bakshi administration. At one gathering, he stated, "Those who dishonor you and take away your freedom must eventually fail, provided you persevere in your faith and determination. The decision about Kashmir's future cannot be taken in Karachi or Delhi or Moscow or Washington. Kashmir belongs to the people of Kashmir and they alone can decide its fate."[118] In addition to giving speeches, Abdullah visited the families of those who had been killed in the aftermath of his arrest. In his memoirs, he recalled how "people came out in large numbers. Women formed rows and greeted me singing. . . . It was the women of the same locality who, known for their lively spirit, had become the despair of the Dogra army in the early phase of our movement."[119] In one stroke, Abdullah painted a historical continuity between his quests for self-determination and the struggle against the Dogras in the pre-Partition period.

In his speeches and letters of the time, Abdullah (like some of the other members of the Plebiscite Front) does not explicitly refer to his previous support of Kashmir's accession to India nor to his prior statements that the plebiscite did not need to be held as Kashmir had given its consent to Indian rule. Rather, he foregrounds that the accession was to be temporary, as Nehru himself had pledged to the world community that the people of the state would decide their future affiliations. In one letter, he stated, "Unfortunately, India and Pakistan got bogged down into minor details of plebiscite arrangements." Placing the blame on both India and Pakistan, he argues that "for the last twelve years the gulf between India and Pakistan has widened, and in the process the people of Kashmir have been crushed in every conceivable manner."[120] In creating a historical continuity from the time of the Dogras to Kashmir's movement for self-determination, Abdullah was deliberately vague about the National Conference's earlier support of the accession and was also vague about what "self-determination" would actually entail. This is perhaps because Abdullah was attempting to toe multiple lines: he could not alienate the Government of India by calling for direct accession to Pakistan as that would contravene his stance on a Kashmiri—not Muslim—nationalism, but neither could he alienate the Kashmiri masses by foregoing the cause of plebiscite, which for many of them, may have entailed Pakistan. The question of what "self-determination" meant for the leaders of the Plebiscite Front was thus left undefined.

At the time of his release, local authorities, perhaps not anticipating such a large response from the public, went on the offensive. The Peace Brigade went throughout the state assaulting those who had put up decorations for Abdullah's welcome. Other supporters or members of opposition groups were kept in police custody.[121] On Friday, February 21, however, the situation grew out of control. Abdullah was scheduled to give a speech at the Hazratbal Shrine, and over two hundred thousand people were expected to attend. A "clash" occurred between National Conference workers and workers from the Plebiscite Front and Political Conference, resulting in the death of a National Conference worker, Mohiuddin Banday. Instead of the regular jail officials, the Central Reserve Police Force dealt with the political workers, which Makhdoomi said "was meant to treat us as criminals instead of political dissenters."[122] The government arrested a number of Abdullah's supporters and opposition party members, including Sadr-uddin Mujahid, Sofi Mohammed Akbar, and Pandit Raghunath Vaishnavi. All were detained without warrants. Sarabhai's account gives the names of 255 people arrested from February 21 to March 21. She argues that the Hazratbal Incident was concocted by the state "to create an inflammatory situation to influence international developments."[123] Mir Qasim supports this perspective in his autobiography: "[Hazratbal] was engineered by Bakshi supporters to promote the justification of Sheikh's re-arrest."[124] Such engineered attacks, which are a common feature amid conditions of colonial occupation, became commonplace in subsequent decades. Abdullah wrote a letter to Nehru, complaining of Bakshi's repressive policies. Nehru sent an emissary, Vijaya Lakshmi Pandit, to visit Kashmir and meet with Abdullah. Bakshi became aware of this development, and Abdullah was rearrested under the Preventive Detention Act and sent to Kud Jail in Jammu on April 29.[125]

After Abdullah's second arrest, the government charged members of the Political Conference and Plebiscite Front with conspiracy against the Kashmir state in what became known as the Kashmir Conspiracy Case. The case consisted of the Bomb Case, in which the government accused the groups of planting bombs throughout the city, as well as the Hazratbal Murder Case, which resulted in the death of the National Conference worker. The prosecution claimed to have a list of 300 witnesses and 136 co-conspirators. On May 25, under Sections 121-A and 120-B of the Ranbir Penal Code and Section 32 of the Security Rules, a case was registered against Mirza Afzal Beg and twenty-five others in the court of the special magistrate of Jammu. Official government discourse positioned the events in the state as a law-and-order issue, combined with the specter of a foreign hand. The defendants were accused of joining with Pakistan to overthrow the Kashmir government by violence.[126] The neighboring country was accused of using these individuals in the state to collect military and other intelligence to "carry on pro-Pakistan propaganda and to spread disorder in the state."[127] If convicted, they were liable to face a life sentence or death. A supplementary case was registered for Abdullah, who claimed that Nehru was not in favor of keeping him behind bars but had to concede given the local government's insistence.[128] On the side of the prosecution was a barrister from Calcutta, Mr. Mitra. The lawyers for the defense were Mohammad Latif Qureshi, Mubarak Shah, and Ghulam Mohammad Shah. Mirza Afzal Beg, although accused, also served as legal counsel. Despite repeated requests from Abdullah to Nehru, no lawyer in India came to the aid of the defense. Abdullah argued that the hostile media environment in India toward the case had intimidated potential legal counsel. Eventually, two barristers from London, Mr. Dinglefoot and J. Clerk, served as chief counsel for the defense.

The legal team of the accused collected important documentation, including statements from both sides as well as other important correspondence under the Legal Defense Committee. Although these reports are from the perspective of the accused, they provide important insight into the workings of repression and dissent in the state at the time. For one, the prosecution stipulated that it was Pakistan that sought to inflame communal tensions among the Muslims to work against the government and in favor of Pakistan.[129] It benefitted the Indian state to keep the issue strictly within an India-Pakistan binary, whereby the people of Kashmir who were demanding their political rights could only be seen as agents of Pakistan. The "bogey of Pakistan" was raised to deny Kashmiri agency, a strategic tactic that would gain further currency in subsequent decades. Furthermore, the charge that the Plebiscite Front had instigated communal sentiments in the state allowed the prosecution to paint the front—along with Sheikh Abdullah—as a communal Muslim organization, which would likely deflect any sympathy from external observers.

In turn, the defense for the Plebiscite Front focused primarily on the promises made by the Indian leadership and the United Nations, as well as constitutional and international law, to hold a plebiscite in the state. It sought to contest the government's narrative by stating, "We are neither pro-Pakistan nor anti-India as alleged. We are entirely pro-Kashmir."[130] Arguing against the government's constant invocation of Pakistan, the defense stated that Pakistan was "extraneous to the demand of plebiscite stemming from the people of Kashmir. . . . Why punish people of Kashmir for omissions and commissions of Pakistan?" To the allegation that Pakistan was not removing its troops to fulfill the obligation set out by the UN, the defense asked why that should impinge Kashmir's right to self-determination. It reiterated that the promises of plebiscite were not given by Pakistan but made by India to the people of Kashmir and the international community, even as late as January 1957.[131] The defense's tactics revolved around holding India accountable for its promises, providing a thorough list of times when the Indian leadership had demonstrated its commitment to Kashmiris deciding their own future. Ultimately, the defense attempted to reinstate Kashmiris into their own narrative, arguing that it was not just Pakistan pressing for plebiscite but also the people of Kashmir.[132] The right to self-determination, front leaders argued, was their birthright independent of the UN decision or the support of any country that gave only an international recognition to that right.[133] The prosecution did not directly address any of these points regarding the plebiscite.

Second, the defendants accused the government of attempting to break the determination of the political activists, often through torture. In a number of letters to the magistrate, one of the accused, Ghulam Mohammed Chickan, wrote that the "interrogation center in Srinagar manned by the personnel of the Intelligence Bureau of India has been utilized to subject the accused to process of brain-washing and other third-degree methods in order to extort confessions from them."[134] He requested the protection of the court as he felt his life was endangered since he had disclosed the maltreatment inside the jail.[135] Many of those arrested suffered from serious ailments, especially since most of them were older. Mir Masood Nazir described how the jail authorities "would not allow me to sleep, used to abuse me—somebody scratched my hair, someone slapped me, and some kicked me. These things continued for many days and my condition became so serious that I cannot express it in words."[136] In another letter, an inmate described how he was "tied with chains and was hanged" and "abusive language was used against my religion and prophet" while others were not allowed to sleep for weeks at a time.[137] Nazir was asked to walk barefoot on ice many times and told that if he renounced the demand for plebiscite, the government would employ him. In response to these allegations, the government denied the existence of interrogation centers as described in the torture petitions, stating that "it is absolutely false that any torture is practiced" and that the allegations against the government "are put for use of propaganda utilized by the interested foreign power in making propaganda in the world."[138] Here again, Kashmiris' lived experiences of torture were dismissed as "propaganda" by Pakistan.

In my interview with Makhdoomi, he recalled that the government had told the Central Reserve Police Force officials to keep watch on the workers as they were killers. "So, the lathi charged us, locked us up during the night. We tried to tell them we are all educated, lawyers, professionals, but they tortured us. There were two categories. . . . Category A consisted of higher-level individuals, including ministers and lawyers. Category B was everyone else."[139] Ishaq suggested that this categorization "broke the movement," as the discriminatory standard between the two caused tension among the political activists.[140] Aside from the harsh treatment, Makhdoomi also described the mental stress the workers endured. Many of their families were struggling financially. The Plebiscite Front attempted to collect donations to help them.[141] However, as the pressures inside the jails increased, some workers, lured by Bakshi's promises, made deals with the government. They were allowed to leave the jail and accommodated into various positions. Makhdoomi said that after some months, there were only fifteen or twenty people left, as a vast majority had made a deal with the government.

The Kashmir Conspiracy Case dragged on for years. There was much back-and-forth about the location of the court (the defense wanted the case to be shifted from Jammu to Srinagar), the list of witnesses, the treatment in jail of those who were arrested, and the evidence that was obtained by the prosecution. The accused pleaded innocent to the charges against them, declaring they had not conspired against the Government of India or Kashmir, nor had they any liaison with Pakistan. In response to the charge of conspiracy to overthrow the government, the defense argued that the Plebiscite Front had demonstrated its disregard toward the idea of forming a government and had limited its activity to promoting the right of self-determination.[142] To the charge that it sought to create disaffection against the government, the defense adeptly stated, "It is a commonsense point of view that disaffection against a government can be tried to be caused if and when the public happens to have some affection for it. But on the contrary, if a government has earned enough hatred and notoriety by its own acts and deeds, will necessity arise for sowing disaffection amongst the public against it?"[143] At each turn, the front sought to return to the root issue: the denial of self-determination.

Once the prosecution was finished with their witnesses, the 1962 war between India and China broke out, interrupting the proceedings. Upon the request of the Government of India, which wanted to reconcile with Abdullah, Bakshi was made to withdraw the conspiracy case against the political prisoners. Those who had been accused were eventually released.

Kamraj Plan, Holy Relic Incident, and the End of an Era

After a decade in power, Bakshi Ghulam Mohammed unceremoniously stepped down from power in 1963 under the auspices of the Kamraj Plan. The plan called for the resignation of senior ministers of the Indian National Congress so that they could devote their time to revitalizing the national party after a series of recent electoral losses. Although Bakshi was not a member of the Congress, he offered his resignation alongside other state ministers. To his and many Kashmiris' surprise, Nehru accepted his resignation. It appeared that the Government of India was becoming increasingly wary of Bakshi's leadership—as it had been of Abdullah's—and used the pretext of the Kamraj Plan to remove him from office. The reasons were not made explicitly clear. However, it appears that the level of corruption and political repression under Bakshi was of serious concern to the Indian leadership.[144] In addition, the Government of India was pushing to give Kashmir the same status as Indian states by converting the title of Prime Minister to Chief Minister and removing Kashmir's "special status" within the Indian union, an abrogation of Article 370. Bakshi was staunchly opposed to both moves, and so the utility of Khalid-i-Kashmir was no more.

After Bakshi stepped down from power, he selected his successor, Khwaja Shamsuddin, as the next head of state. The Holy Relic Incident occurred a few months into Shamsuddin's term in office and took the government and Indian leadership by surprise. In December 1963, a sacred relic of the Prophet Muhammad was stolen. For days, despite the cold and snow, there were mass protests throughout the state, with hundreds of thousands of people in the streets, demanding a return of the relic. Schools, offices, and businesses remained closed. Although the Kashmir and Indian governments took steps to recover the relic, anger did not abate. The protests soon turned against the local political establishment, and Bakshi and his family were accused of stealing the relic so that the resulting political outcry would force the Government of India to reappoint Bakshi as head of state. Property owned by the family was damaged and set on fire. The Indian media wrote about the "harrowing tales of continuous repression which Kashmiris suffered."[145] The relic was recovered less than a month later under mysterious circumstances.[146] Shamsuddin, however, lasted only one hundred days in power, after which G. M. Sadiq, seen as more compliant with the Government of India, replaced him. During the agitation, groups within the state had gained traction, increasingly turning their attention to Kashmir's unresolved political status and demanding a plebiscite in the state. As anti-state activity grew, Department of Home files reveal that hundreds of workers of the Plebiscite Front and other groups were detained from 1964 to 1966. Their families repeatedly wrote to the government authorities requesting a release on humanitarian grounds due to health concerns or financial duress. Many of the detainees were made to write bonds to get released, declaring that they would not get involved in political activities.[147]

In the aftermath of the Holy Relic Incident, Sadiq's government realized it needed a different tactic to manage dissent in the state. In consultation with the Government of India, Sadiq decided to pursue a policy of political "liberalization." Previously banned political groups and newspapers of oppositional perspectives were allowed to operate more freely. As a result, new political parties and student groups emerged, and the number of newspapers with diverse perspectives increased. Student groups such as Student and Youth League were far more critical and radical than the leaders of the Plebiscite Front, taking direct inspiration from the Algerian struggle against the French. They also critiqued the Indian state's attempts to distract Kashmiri students from their struggle for freedom through cultural imperialism, by imposing the Indian national anthem in educational institutions.[148] The decade following Bakshi's rule subsequently paved the way for large-scale student and pro-plebiscite politics, underscoring the tenuous nature of his state-building project. Students—both boys and girls—took to the streets, demanding a plebiscite be held in the state.[149] Some were vocally pro-Pakistan. Given the attempts the Bakshi government had made to ensure that the educational institutions stay free of political activities and instead cultivate pro-Indian sentiments, these protests took the government by surprise. New parties such as the Awami Action Committee, a group of Muslim leaders and organizations formed during the Holy Relic Incident, and the Jamaat-i-Islami became more engaged in pro-plebiscite politics.[150] As explicitly socioreligious parties, they created a larger space for a religiously inflected discourse in the movement for self-determination.

Bakshi was arrested under the Defense of India Rules for stirring up agitation against Sadiq's government. He was released for health reasons and in 1967, was elected to the Indian Lok Sabha, where he remained a member until 1971 and tried to play a bigger role in Indian politics. He died in July 1972, as one account narrates, "lonely and unpopular."[151] Unlike other political dynasties in Kashmir, Bakshi commanded that no one from his family should join politics, a wish they have fulfilled until today.[152] Just three years after his death, the trajectory of Kashmir's politics would dramatically shift once more.

Compromise and Betrayal

For over a decade, the Plebiscite Front's most important tactic had been the boycott of general elections, especially given that participation in the elections was offered to the international community as proof that Kashmiris were content under Indian rule and that democracy was in practice. The leaders also asserted the elections were rigged in Bakshi's favor. In 1957, the legislators had all run unopposed, since before the nomination papers were filed, there had been much repression.[153] In 1962, however, the front faced a crisis. Many had been released from jail and there was a split in its leadership regarding the elections. A number of leaders were interested in running for election and gaining power through that route, while others were against it. Some ran during the 1962 elections and were expelled from the party.[154] The front prepared for subsequent elections in 1967 and 1972, but the government declared the organization unlawful before the elections. Mir Qasim wrote that the popularity of the front was such that had its leaders run for elections, they would have certainly won, given that Bakshi's rule had been "brutal."[155]

Because of their changing stance on the elections, some members split from the front and called themselves the Ishaq group, led by Munshi Ishaq. In his memoirs, Ishaq recalled that during a press conference, he argued that elections could not serve as a substitute for a plebiscite and that those within the Plebiscite Front who had participated in elections did not represent the front as a whole. In response, the party leaders of the Plebiscite Front declared Ishaq "dishonest and treacherous." However, word of the deviation quickly spread and "students and youngsters protested in Srinagar and in other areas of the Valley, in which tear gas, stones and baton-charge was used on them. For getting these protests under control, the government implemented arrests on a large scale."[156]

In his writings, Ishaq accused a few members of the executive committee of the Plebiscite Front as well as the Political Conference of being under the influence of the Indian and Kashmir governments. He said most were concerned with obtaining power and did not hesitate to look after their own interests before that of the movement. The government repeatedly approached and pressured the leaders to compromise, but Ishaq stated that a movement that had "shaken the foundations of India" would have been able to give the people their freedom if the "leadership had sincerity instead of lust of power."[157]

Consequently, it appeared that Sheikh Abdullah and Beg were preparing to work within the Indian constitution and reconcile with the Indian leadership, now headed by Nehru's daughter, Indira Gandhi. This culminated in the Sheikh-Indira Accord of 1975 and led to the perception that the leadership of the Plebiscite Front was "pursuing a struggle for [obtaining] power all the time" instead of being genuine about the cause of plebiscite.[158] Sheikh Abdullah and Beg converted the front into the National Conference once again, and the issue of the plebiscite was rendered obsolete, as all discussions on Kashmir's future were to occur within the framework of the Indian constitution. Both men took the reins of power.

To the detractors of the accord, it seemed that the primary leaders of the front had used the organization as a negotiating tool with the Government of India, in an attempt to secure power for themselves or perhaps negotiate greater autonomy for Kashmir. This is perhaps why they had been deliberately vague about what "self-determination" entailed and what would occur after a plebiscite, as well as their relationship with Pakistan. This begs the question of why the front deliberately allowed people—including its own members—to believe that their struggle for self-determination was ultimately for Pakistan. Perhaps the leadership believed that it would be the only way to galvanize ordinary Kashmiris who, as Bazaz had declared, were "yearning for Pakistan." Critics argued that the front used the "idea" of Pakistan to make political inroads within Kashmiri society.

Alternatively, Gockhami argues that the front's leaders became disillusioned with Pakistan's infiltration across the border in 1965 during Operation Gibraltar—which led to another India-Pakistan war and the Treaty of Tashkent—and only further solidified the status quo.[159] The leaders became further disillusioned during the 1971 war, when East Pakistan became the newly independent state of Bangladesh. Plebiscite Front leaders saw both events as indicative of the failures of the Pakistan state, as well as its inability to serve as a safe haven for the region's Muslims, and they became more amenable to negotiating with India. For those who remained committed to the idea of the plebiscite (and Pakistan), the shift in stance was devastating. Ishaq bemoaned the fact that despite the "priceless sacrifices of people, the end of the freedom movement came in the form of political slavery, and the worst economic conditions."[160]

Political dissent in this time primarily revolved around the politics of plebiscite. But what exactly did it mean to demand a plebiscite? What exactly did groups like the Plebiscite Front and the Political Conference want?

The demand was either deliberately or inadvertently ambiguous. For some, a plebiscite was simply a substitute for a merger with Pakistan. Since India already controlled Jammu and Kashmir, demanding a UN-mandated plebiscite would have entailed seeking the other of the two options: Pakistan. Those who sought this merger did so for a variety of reasons: religious nationalism and wanting to be a part of a Muslim state and/or a fear of what would happen to Muslims in India, especially with the rise of Hindu nationalism. In this case,

Pakistan represented a safe haven for the region's Muslims. For others, the demand for a plebiscite was a rejection of state repression and maladministration and India's turning back on promises made to the people and the international community. For many, the demand for plebiscite was also a placeholder for whatever Sheikh Abdullah, the most popular leader at the time, decided. This is why a group like the Political Conference, even though it was explicitly pro-Pakistan, did not gain as much traction. Abdullah represented a popular form of Kashmiri nationalism that could not be fully accommodated into the India-Pakistan binary, and yet, it had very little maneuverability given the restricted nature of the plebiscite options. It was, therefore, easily co-opted. Given the ambiguities around Abdullah's own political commitments, ranging from independence to strategizing around greater autonomy, it is difficult to parse what self-determination would have entailed for the people or what would have occurred after a plebiscite.

In many ways, the tangle between the Muslim Conference and the National Conference on questions of nationalism, secularism, and sovereignty was reproduced in the Plebiscite Front. The lack of ideological coherence was costly. It remained difficult to sustain a strong political opposition since many of the leaders operated within the same frame of reference and background as those who were officially in power. Dissent, therefore, was by no means revolutionary. This would come later, as global developments in the 1970s and 1980s transformed how Kashmiris resisted Indian rule. Nonetheless, while state repression effectively neutralized the primary political parties operating in this period, the two parties played an important role in mobilizing an entire generation of Kashmiris that became politically invested in the right to self-determination.

CONCLUSION

In a graveyard in Naseem Bagh, near Srinagar's Hazratbal shrine, Jammu and Kashmir police guard the grave and mausoleum of Sheikh Abdullah. Despite his championing and going to jail for the cause of Kashmiri self-determination, in the 1990s, when an armed popular uprising against Indian rule erupted, police were stationed around the clock at Abdullah's grave. Young Kashmiri rebels threatened to desecrate the grave, viewing him as a "sellout" after his 1975 accord with the Government of India.

Some miles away in a discreet graveyard in the Shah-i-Hamdan shrine in downtown Srinagar lies another grave, that of Bakshi Ghulam Mohammad, perhaps considered a greater "sellout" in popular memory. Yet, even during the tumultuous nineties, when anti-India sentiments were high, Bakshi's grave remained unguarded. Today, when asked, most Kashmiris do not even know where it is located. His legacy remains a contested one. Even a political activist of the Political Conference, a group that opposed his rule, declared, "For his own political gain, he sold Kashmir to India. But he also did a lot for . . . Kashmiri Muslims. He built schools, gave them jobs, built infrastructure."[1] This simple sentiment allows us to see the importance and relevance of Bakshi's decade of rule in its time and today.

Strategies such as the politics of life build, maintain, and sustain colonial occupations. They enable political subjectivities that are paradoxical in their demands and aspirations, forcing individuals to reconcile their desire for political freedom with their desire to lead "normal," economically stable lives.[2] Through the Bakshi government's patronage of individuals and institutions, Kashmiris were provided with the prospect for social mobility, resulting in an emergent Muslim middle and professional class that was deeply reliant on the local state for educational and economic opportunities. Yet, with such a restricted range of political possibility, people inevitably found themselves navigating their everyday lives "on the spectrum defined by resistance and collaboration and marked by a bit of both."[3] This was, fundamentally, the legacy of Bakshi's decade in power.

Just as colonial occupation changes the subjectivities of those it governs, it is itself not static either. It continuously shifts its modes of control, at times exercising brute power, while at other times utilizing strategies of emotional integration, normalization, and empowerment. Sometimes, all of these exist simultaneously, making and remaking the relationship between the colonial state and occupied society and between different communities within an occupied society. This is precisely why it becomes critical to preserve the *difference* between modes of power and governmentality that operate for citizens (in this case, of India) as well as occupied subjects (of Kashmir). My book has shown the many ways in which this takes place in the realms of development, education, and culture. In contexts where the colonizing state is nominally democratic, colonial occupations become particularly complex to identify, especially when they utilize the politics of life. This is also what makes a colonial occupation "complicated"; these are precisely the strategies that prolong a sense of its intractability and inevitability.

In the period before the armed popular uprising of the late 1980s, India attempted to nationalize and integrate the people of Jammu and Kashmir utilizing a series of client regimes, including Bakshi's. After the end of Bakshi's rule, many state policies that were intended to manage the population continued. These processes—such as the commodification of culture, deployment of tourism (especially for the Amarnath Yatra) and cinema, propaganda and the control of media narratives, criminalization of dissent, patronage toward a comprador class, and economic development, among others—served as important bureaucratic and institutional sites to entrench the colonial occupation. Yet, despite undertaking an extensive project of economic, educational, and cultural development, the Kashmir government, supported by the Indian government, was unable to win over the hearts and minds of Kashmiri Muslims. The sentiment of a majority of Kashmiri Muslims, even those who were participating in the bureaucratic state, remained not only at odds with the goal of Kashmir's greater integration and assimilation into the Indian union, but also in favor of self-determination.

The contradictions of the politics of life and increased repression came to the fore in the late 1980s with a popular mass uprising and armed resistance against Indian rule. While elements of the politics of life continued, India deployed a brutal regime of military occupation and counterinsurgency that engaged in massacres, human rights violations, and war crimes. The indirect rule of the client regimes was done away with, as India imposed central rule either through the governor or the president of the Indian union. Hundreds of thousands of Indian soldiers and paramilitary forces descended into Kashmir and became a permanent fixture in the landscape, alongside their bunkers, concertina wires, armed vehicles, and expanding cantonments. Laws such as the Armed Forces Special Powers Act gave Indian forces complete impunity. Kashmiris became subject to a series of massacres, enforced disappearances, extrajudicial killings, rapes, torture, and crackdowns. The politics of life turned to the politics of bare life. Every aspect of life in Kashmir was militarized as necropolitical power emerged as the primary mechanism of control over a population demanding *azadi*, or freedom. Even in this phase, the millions of Kashmiris demanding freedom were presented as instigators from Pakistan, and the indigenous nature of the armed rebellion was dismissed as Pakistan-sponsored, once more denying the people of Kashmir their agency. Furthermore, in the period after 9/11, India appropriated the war on terror to further represent the movement for freedom and self-determination as terrorism. While the politics of life was meant to show Kashmiris the benefits of acceding to India, eliminating their distinct history and identity through assimilation, the military occupation was meant to quash their desire for freedom and make them realize that the cost of resistance was simply too high and that they were better off yielding to India's rule over them. While India suppressed the armed movement, its brutal modes of control during the three decades after the armed rebellion failed too, as Kashmiris continued to express their resistance to Indian rule through all forms of anti-colonial resistance and mass popular uprisings.

Building a Settler-Colony

If the attempt in the first two phases of India's colonial occupation over Kashmir was to incorporate the people into the nation-state—either through the assimilationist politics of life or the more violent military occupation—the attempt in the third phase is to eject them altogether. India's Hindu nationalist groups have long viewed Kashmir's Muslim-majority demographic as its primary problem and have consistently called for the complete integration of Jammu and Kashmir into India. On August 5, 2019, the Hindu nationalist government of Narendra Modi, upholding its campaign promises to the Indian public, abrogated Article 370, split Jammu and Kashmir from the region of Ladakh, and made both into union territories, directly under the control of the Indian government. The Indian government, with deliberate irony, called this the heralding of yet another "Naya Kashmir." Subsequently, it passed a series of laws that opened up land and residency rights (previously protected by Article 35A of the Indian constitution and granted to "permanent residents" of the state) to Indian citizens. These changes, which strengthen and foreground India's settler-colonial modalities of control in Kashmir, seek to demographically alter the Muslim majority into a minority by bringing an influx of Indian (Hindu) citizens and businesses to settle in Kashmir. In this phase, settler-colonization emerges as direct elimination.

Demographic engineering will result in an ethnic cleansing of Kashmir's Muslim-majority population. There is no pretense anymore of Kashmiri Muslims belonging to India, nor even of India as a secular state. There are other changes that mark this phase, too. Kashmir's client regimes or local intermediaries for Indian colonial rule—like those propped up during Bakshi's period—have been marginalized. Most senior ministers and bureaucrats are now Indian, and government employment for Kashmiri Muslims remains threatened. Instead of indirect colonial rule, India has embarked on direct settler-colonial rule, which erases the amount of negotiation Kashmiris at large can now have with the state.

Nonetheless, there are continuities in terms of the modes of control throughout the three phases from 1947 until the present, showing the overlapping nature of forms of colonialism, settler-colonialism, and occupation. India continues to depict a state of "normalcy" in Kashmir, not just for the international community but also for the Indian public. This is done through strict control over media and information, as well as an entirely machinery dedicated to propaganda. While refusing to allow entry to foreign journalists or human rights groups, in 2019, months after the abrogation, a delegation of far-right European Union MPs were invited to tour Kashmir—reminiscent of the visit of the leaders of the Soviet Union during Bakshi's era. Kashmiri participation in elections—which are often an attempt to address issues of governance—is depicted as acceptance of Indian rule. More recently, electoral redistricting marginalizes the Muslim vote in favor of Hindus, making elections an integral part of the settler-colonial project. Earlier practices of censorship have escalated as Kashmiri journalists, activists, human rights defenders, and academics are targeted by draconian laws and anti-terrorism legislation, as well as detention or suspension, creating a general atmosphere of fear and self-censorship and making it difficult for developments on the ground to get reported. Kashmiris are prevented from gathering, protesting, and mobilizing.

Meanwhile, tourism and cinema have remained critical vehicles to both depict Kashmir as a beautiful haven for the unquenchable Indian gaze as well as amplifying Hindu nationalist claims over Kashmir, especially through the extensive promotion of the Amarnath Yatra. Kashmir remains a popular site for Indian cinema, often strategically oriented as the borderland from which to resist the enemy (Pakistan) or a space of pain and eventual redemption in the Indian national narrative. While current exigencies of the Indian nationalist narrative mean that a different Kashmiri subject (a terrorist, a victim-turned-perpetrator, or the good patriotic Kashmiri) is often presented than that of the films of the 1950s and 1960s, the otherization of the Kashmiri and claims over territory, as well as other colonial tropes that abound in such films, remain.

Remnants of the politics of life appear through the Indian army's strategic use of Sadhbhavna, or Operation Goodwill, to depict itself as the savior of Kashmiris by engaging in development activities and opening up schools, camps, and activities for Kashmiri youth, including "educational and national integration" tours. On the economic front, government jobs are the largest source of employment for Kashmiris, though this may change as the settler colonial process privileges Indians over Kashmiris. India still seeks to create a dependency on its economy—however, dependency is created in a different manner and meant to economically stifle Kashmiris so that they will refrain from civil disobedience. A politics of scarcity—further exacerbated by months and months of *hartals*, or strikes, during moments of severe political unrest—has overshadowed Bakshi's providence of abundance. Furthermore, the abrogation will enable an intensified form of resource extraction for Indian and international capital investment as well as further ecological degradation.

Education remains a site for the creation of subjectivities. Kashmiri schools, colleges, and universities remain under heavy surveillance, and no student activism is allowed. Teachers are suspended or arrested if they express any sympathies with the pro-freedom movement. As settler-colonization accelerates, attempts are made to enforce Hindi in educational institutions, as well as an even more Hindu-nationalist-inspired understanding of Kashmir's history and subsequent "belonging" to India. Schools are increasingly required to host flag-raising ceremonies or sing the Indian anthem (with threats of arrest if they do not comply), and students are forced to participate in other spectacles of national integration. Culturally, the state continues to coopt and promote Kashmiri artists, often featuring them as examples of Kashmiri youth that have excelled under India and can serve as role models for otherwise wayward youth. Festivals and cultural events, often directly under the auspices of the Indian army, continue to be organized in order to promote the narrative of normalization as well as emotional integration.

As India's modes of control have evolved, so too has Kashmiri resistance to its rule, ranging from a new wave of armed rebels, political mobilizations, and civil disobedience to everyday forms of defiance and endurance. Most of the pro-freedom leaders—especially after August 2019—have been detained under draconian laws, and preventive detention remains a primary mechanism through which India exerts its sovereign control over political mobilizations. Furthermore, all evidence of India's massive human rights violations are portrayed as "propaganda" by the neighboring country (Pakistan) or justified as targeting "terrorists." There remains very little space for Kashmiris to express themselves and to resist the changing developments around them without being deemed as a threat to national sovereignty and subsequently charged under anti-terror legislation and arrested or killed. The India state's divide-and-rule policies have also exacerbated tensions among Kashmir's diverse communities.

A "Democratic" Colonial Occupation

Examining Indian state-formation from the perspective of Kashmir sheds light on India's "descent" into an authoritarian, undemocratic, Hindu-majoritarian state. In recent years, political developments under Modi's Hindu nationalist government have led to fears of genocide against Indian Muslims, as well as an increasing realization of their second-class citizenship. State-backed pogroms, violence, and the transformation of the educational, cultural, and legal machinery have enabled that process.

In scholarship and advocacy efforts against Hindu nationalism, there is a tendency to reinforce the idea that India was once secular, pluralistic, and democratic but has now been transformed into an "ethnonationalist state" that commits human rights violations.[4] There is no question that the rise of Hindu nationalism has exacerbated India's challenges and that things have gotten categorically worse. Yet, with this increasing nostalgia for an earlier version of India as a result of rampant Hindu nationalism in India today, the inherent violence of that secular, liberal order (as well as its entanglements with Hindu majoritarianism) is expunged. This nostalgia completely erases how colonialism and domination were at the root of Indian state-formation, not just in Kashmir, but in other places as well. More importantly, Kashmir and the other regions at the "margins" or "frontiers" of the national narrative were not an exception, but remain integral to India's state-formation as a (settler) colonial power. To put it simply: India's foundational moment cannot be viewed as separate from its colonial occupation of Kashmir. Treating Kashmir as an exception (especially when Kashmir was employed to symbolize the Indian "nation"), while lauding India's otherwise "secular" or "democratic" character is akin to denying settler-colonization in the context of US state-formation. In some ways, we can see Kashmir and other zones of colonial occupation as a test case for the Indian state to practice various forms of power: disciplinary, sovereign, biopolitical, and necropolitical. These strategies would be utilized in the "mainland," too, especially against populations that are deemed a threat—Muslims, Dalits, and tribal communities—and more recently, anyone who does not align with the Hindu nationalist project. Therefore, instead of looking for inspiration in a rather uninspiring past, would it not be better to envision more imaginative and liberatory futures?

One of the striking features of colonial occupation is that it exists across multiple political formations—authoritarian, fascist, democratic, socialist, capitalist, and secular. In the context of India, it exists in a country that is nominally democratic and secular. This helps us consider the co-constitutive relationship between the nation-state and colonial occupations. What may be different across these state-forms are the modalities of control that are utilized—such as the politics of life—as well as how these colonial occupations are legitimized by the nation-state and dealt with by the international community. Ultimately, however, the case of Kashmir forces us to rethink our categories of colonialism and (post-) colonialism, secularism, and democracy, as well as our strategies for solidarity and liberation.

NOTES

Introduction

1. The term *state of Jammu and Kashmir* refers to the territory that came under Indian control after the first India-Pakistan war of 1948. It includes the regions of Jammu, the Kashmir Valley, and Ladakh. When referring to the entire state, I use the terms *Jammu and Kashmir* and *Kashmir* alternatively. I will use the term *Kashmir Valley* when referring specifically to one of the regions within the state. The princely state of Jammu and Kashmir, however, incorporates the regions that were under the rule of the Dogras during the British colonial period and also includes the regions that eventually came under Pakistan's control, including Azad Kashmir and the Northern Areas (today's Gilgit-Baltistan). My use of the term *Kashmiri* signifies a political, not ethnic, category of those who are state subjects of the entire princely state of Jammu and Kashmir, unless I use the term *Kashmiri Muslim* or *Kashmiri Pandits* to specify ethnic, Kashmiri-speaking Muslims or Pandits (Kashmiri Hindus) in the Kashmir Valley.

2. Gopal, *Selected Works of Jawaharlal Nehru*, vol. 19, 381–82.

3. Sinha, *Colonial Masculinity*.

4. Von Bogdandy et al., "State-Building"; Whaites, "States in Development."

5. Von Bogdandy et al.

6. For example, Bose, *Kashmir: Roots of Conflict, Paths to Peace*; Behera, *Demystifying Kashmir*; Ganguly, *The Crisis in Kashmir*; Chowdhary, *Jammu and Kashmir*; Varshney, "India, Pakistan, and Kashmir"; Tremblay, "Nation, Identity and the Intervening Role of the State"; Verma, *Jammu and Kashmir at the Political Crossroads*. These texts, to a greater or lesser extent, seek to explain the underlying reasons for the armed uprising of the late 1980s and offer correctives on how India can "reclaim" Kashmir.

7. Duschinski et al., *Resisting Occupation in Kashmir*, 13–14. In their introduction, the editors describe spaces of political liminality as spaces of "in-betweenness," defined by legal provisionality as an administered territory.

8. Rai, *Hindu Rulers, Muslim Subjects*, 4.

9. Snedden, *The Untold Story of the People of Azad Kashmir*; Ali, *Delusional States*.

10. Noorani, *Article 370*, 1.

11. Bhan, *Counterinsurgency, Democracy, and the Politics of Identity in India*, 6.
12. Bhan, 8.
13. Bhan, 10.
14. Duschinski and Bhan, "Introduction: Law Containing Violence."
15. In 1944, the National Conference, the leftist anti-monarchical political party led by Sheikh Abdullah published the Naya Kashmir manifesto, a plan for better educational and economic rights, as well as a responsible government in the state. The next chapter will discuss how Bakshi drew from this manifesto in his state-building policies.
16. Trouillot, *Silencing the Past*, 9
17. Trouillot, 9.
18. The term *politics of life* comes from Neve Gordon's conceptualization of Israel's attempts to "secure the existence and livelihood" of its Palestinian inhabitants. See Gordon, *Israel's Occupation*, 2.
19. Here, I am drawing from literature of Michel Foucault's use of governmentality and disciplinary and biopower modes of control, which are what enables the "politics of life." Foucault defines *governmentality* as "the ensemble formed by institutions, procedures, analyses and reflections, the calculations and tactics that allow the exercise of this very specific albeit complex form of power." Governmentality targets the national body politic. *Biopower* is a type of governmentality that increases the organization of the population in order to increase productivity; it is reliant on "a form of power concerned with the fostering of life rather than the command over death" (the latter using necropolitics, a concept developed by Achille Mbembe). *Disciplinary power* "constitutes individuals and objects as authors of knowledge and power, but it does so with a specific goal in mind—the creation of docile workers and obedient citizens." See Barclay, *Outcasts of Empire*, 21–33. However, as Emily Yeh argues, "The rise of biopower does not replace sovereign and disciplinary modes of power. Rather, all three modes are applied in different combinations at different times, and reinforce rather than contradict each other." See Yeh, *Taming Tibet*, 13.
20. Trisal, "In Kashmir, Nehru's Golden Chains."
21. Kashmir scholars have discussed the role that development plays in obscuring colonialism. Nitasha Kaul has referred to the notion of coloniality as development as "econonationalism," where "supposed liberatory ideas are rhetorically deployed to mask a dehumanizing subjugation." See Kaul, "Coloniality and/as Development in Kashmir"; Zia, "The Haunting Specter."
22. *Pandits* is the term used for Kashmiri Hindus, who are upper-caste Brahmins that follow a regionally specific form of Shaivism (known as Kashmiri Shaivism). As a religious minority, Pandits remained under 5 percent of the total population

of the Valley during Dogra rule and declined after 1947. Historically, they served as an administrative, bureaucratic class under the various rulers and were better educated and more privileged in obtaining employment than Kashmiri Muslims. After 1947, many Kashmiri Pandit bureaucrats were closely aligned with India's national project in Kashmir.

23. Abdullah, *The Blazing Chinar*, 420.

24. In this book, references to "Indian states" do not include the state of Jammu and Kashmir, but rather those states that effectively became a part of the Indian Union and were not an "international dispute."

25. A number of Kashmiri Pandits also opposed Kashmir's accession to India, including Prem Nath Bazaz and Pandit Raghunath Vaishnavi. On the whole, however, Kashmir Pandits overwhelmingly supported the accession.

26. For a detailed examination of the different trajectories of Ladakh and Jammu, see Chowdhary, *Jammu and Kashmir*.

27. Intelligence reports by the Indian government in the waning months of Sheikh Abdullah's rule also suggest this. Ministry of States, Kashmir Section, Government of India, "Intelligence Reports Re: Muslim Affairs in JK State," file no. F.8 (6)K/53, National Archives of India.

28. Bhan, *Counterinsurgency, Democracy, and the Politics of Identity in India*, 9.

29. Misri, "Disabling Kashmir," 76–77.

30. Osuri, "Imperialism, Colonialism and Sovereignty."

31. Shohat, "Notes on the "Post-Colonial," 102.

32. Duschinski and Bhan, "Third World Imperialism and Kashmir's Sovereignty Trap," 323; Joseph Massad, "The 'Post-colonial' Colony"; Junaid, "Tehreek History Writers of Kashmir," 264; Anand, "China and India."

33. McDonald, *Placing Empire*, xiv.

34. Osuri, "Imperialism, Colonialism, and Sovereignty," 3–5.

35. Bhan, Duschinski, and Misri, *Routledge Handbook of Critical Kashmir Studies*, 319.

36. Osuri, "The Forms and Practices of Indian Settler/Colonial Sovereignty in Kashmir."

37. By "modes" or "mechanisms" of control, I draw from Neve Gordon, who argues that these do not include just the "coercive mechanisms used to prohibit, exclude, and repress people, but rather the entire array of institutions, legal devices, bureaucratic apparatuses, social practices, and physical edifices that operate both on the individual and the population in order to produce new modes of behavior, habits, interests, tastes, and aspirations." See Gordon, *Israel's Occupation*, 3.

38. Osuri, "The Forms and Practices of Indian Settler/Colonial Sovereignty in Kashmir," 342.

39. Mbembe, "Necropolitics," 27.

40. Ghosh, "Solidarity-Givers of India and Destiny of the Kashmiri Tehreek."

41. Junaid, "Death and Life under Occupation," 166.

42. Baruah, *In the Name of the Nation*, 32.

43. Falk, "Afterword," 222; Duschinski and Bhan, "Introduction: Law Containing Violence."

44. Junaid, "Death and Life under Occupation," 172.

45. Duschinski et al., *Resisting Occupation in Kashmir*, 2; Duschinski and Bhan, "Introduction: Law Containing Violence," 6–7; Zia, *Resisting Disappearance*, 54.

46. Hussain, *The Jurisprudence of Emergency*.

47. Duschinski and Ghosh, "Constituting the Occupation," 1.

48. Duschinski and Ghosh, 1.

49. Bhan and Duschinski, "Occupations in Context."

50. Bhan, Duschinski, and Misri, "Critical Kashmir Studies," 7.

51. Bhan, Duschinski, and Misri, 7.

52. Rowe and Tuck, "Settler Colonialism and Cultural Studies"; Bhandar and Ziadah, "Acts and Omissions."

53. Mushtaq and Amin, "'We Will Memorise Our Home,'" 3012.

54. Mushtaq and Amin, 3017.

55. Rashid, "Theatrics of a 'Violent State,'" 224.

56. Mushtaq and Amin, "We Will Memorise Our Home," 3017; Bhan, Duschinski, and Misri, "Critical Kashmir Studies," 10.

57. Mushtaq and Amin, 3023; Nabi and Ye, "Of Militarisation, Counter-Insurgency and Land Grabs in Kashmir," 62.

58. Wolfe, "Settler Colonialism and the Elimination of the Native," 387.

59. Wolfe, 390

60. Hallaq, *Restating Orientalism*, 214.

61. Hallaq, 215.

62. Wolfe, "Settler Colonialism and the Elimination of the Native," 388.

63. Kauanui, "'A Structure, Not an Event'"; Barakat, "Writing/Righting Palestine Studies."

64. Bhan, Duschinski, and Misri, "Critical Kashmir Studies," 10.

65. Wolfe, "Settler Colonialism and the Elimination of the Native," 401.

66. Junaid, "Death and Life under Occupation," 161.

67. Mbembe, "Necropolitics."

68. Bhan, *Counterinsurgency, Democracy, and the Politics of Identity in India*; Bhan, "Infrastructures of Occupation."

69. Simpson, *Mohawk Interruptus*.

70. Haley Duschinski, personal correspondence with author, May 31, 2022.

71. For other studies on state-building and legitimization in occupied or politically liminal spaces, see Feldman, *Governing Gaza*; Yeh, *Taming Tibet*; Gordon, *Israel's Occupation.*

72. Mamdani, *Neither Settler nor Native.*

73. Namakkal, *Unsettling Utopia*, 8.

74. Prashad, *The Darker Nations*, xvii.

75. Haley Duschinski, personal correspondence with author, May 31, 2022.

76. Prashad, *The Darker Nations*, 12

77. Baruah, *In the Name of the Nation*, x.

78. Baruah, ix–7; Purushotham, *From Raj to Republic*, 2; Anderson, *The Indian Ideology.*

79. A notable exception is Bérénice Guyot-Réchard's work on the India-China border in the Himalayas. She describes the "intimate entanglement between the imperial and the national [that] has shaped China's and India's expansion in particular ways," as well as the ways in which India's "long freedom struggle and professed unity-in-diversity ideal coexist with imperial strategies towards Kashmir or Nagaland." See Guyot-Réchard, *Shadow States*, 3.

80. Baruah, *In the Name of the Nation*, 43.

81. Chakrabarty et al., *From the Colonial to the Postcolonial*, 7.

82. Chakrabarty et al., 7.

83. Mongia, *Indian Migration and Empire*, 5.

84. Kanjwal, "The Violence on Kashmir."

85. Dar, "Dear Prof. Chatterjee."

86. Zia, "Sanctioned Ignorance and the Crisis of Solidarity for Kashmir," 355.

87. Junaid, "Tehreek History Writers of Kashmir," 254.

88. Junaid, 255.

89. Junaid, 255.

90. Zutshi, *Kashmir: History, Politics, Representation*, 5.

91. For an example of this framing, see Chatterjee, "Kashmir is the Test Bed." About the term *internal colonialism*, Goldie Osuri argues that it is based on an understanding of uneven development and still assumes the unity of the nation-state or that the borders of the nation-state are a given even if it is "colonizing those within." Osuri, "Imperialism, Colonialism, and Sovereignty," 5. For further critiques of this conceptualization, see Junaid, "Tehreek History Writers of Kashmir," 263.

92. Varshney, "India, Pakistan, and Kashmir."

93. Chowdhary, "Kashmir in the Indian Project of Nationalism," 154.

94. Junaid, "Tehreek History Writers of Kashmir," 263.

95. Needham and Rajan, *The Crisis of Secularism in India.*

96. Bhargava, "The Distinctiveness of Indian Secularism."

97. Khalidi "Hinduising India: Secularism in Practice"; Zamindar, *The Long Partition and the Making of Modern South Asia*; Sherman, *Muslim Belonging in Secular India*; Gyanendra Pandey, "Can a Muslim Be an Indian?"; Umar, "Constructing the 'Citizen Enemy'"; Anderson, *The Indian Ideology*, 140–51.

98. Ganguly, "The Crisis of Indian Secularism."

99. Mahmood, *Religious Difference in a Secular Age*, 2.

100. *Selected Works of Jawaharlal Nehru*, vol. 17, 76–78.

101. Junaid, "Tehreek History Writers of Kashmir," 259.

102. Bhan, Duschinski, and Misri, "Critical Kashmir Studies," 10.

103. Bhan, Duschinski, and Misri, "Critical Kashmir Studies."

104. Bhan, Duschinski, and Misri, "Critical Kashmir Studies"

105. Bhan, Duschinski, and Misri, "Critical Kashmir Studies," 260.

106. Sherman, Gould, and Ansari, *From Subjects to Citizens*; Siegel, *Hungry Nation*; Menon, *Planning Democracy*; De, *The People's Constitution*; Sherman, *Muslim Belonging in Secular India*; Ansari, *Life after Partition*; Haines, *Building the Empire, Building the Nation*; Prakash, Menon, and Laffan, *The Postcolonial Moment in South and Southeast Asia*; Toor, *The State of Islam*; Daechsel, *Islamabad and the Politics of International Development in Pakistan.*

107. An important corrective to this body of work is the recently published monograph *What Happened to Governance in Kashmir* by Aijaz Ashraf Wani. Wani examines the policies and strategies adopted by the Indian state and the local Kashmiri governments to grapple with the multiple problems of state-building and argues that in an actively contested state like Kashmir, democracy and governance are always guided and controlled.

108. Feldman, *Governing Gaza*, 17. In an essay in *Himalaya*, I explore this tension of Kashmiri Muslims who joined the bureaucracy in the aftermath of Partition and how it did not necessitate their acceptance of Indian rule. Kanjwal, "Reflections on the Post-Partition Period."

109. Giving Sheikh Abdullah the credit for implementing the policy of free education is a recurring theme in a number of works. See Akhter, *Kashmir Women Empowerment and National Conference*, 142; and Wani, "Political Assertion of Kashmiri Identity," 138.

110. Bose, *Kashmir: Roots of Conflict, Paths to Peace*, 68.

111. Chowdhary, *Jammu and Kashmir*, 80; Behera, *State, Identity, and Violence*, 107–8.

112. Behera, *State, Identity, and Violence*, 114. Bose, *Roots of Conflict, Paths to Peace*, 72; Chowdhary, *Jammu and Kashmir*, 34. Sumit Ganguly describes Bakshi's government as showing "scant regard for tolerating honest dissent, [squelching] civil liberties, and [engaging] in widespread electoral malpractice." See Ganguly, *The Crisis in Kashmir*, 43.

113. Bose, *Roots of Conflict, Paths to Peace*, 68.

Chapter 1

1. Kak, *Khalid-I-Kashmir*, iv.

2. While it is commonly understood that Bakshi was only an "8th pass," there are some reports that he completed the ninth grade. See Kak, *Khalid-i-Kashmir*.

3. Junaid, "Youth Activists In Kashmir." Sheikh Abdullah's autobiography is an important social history of Kashmir during the Dogra period. It details how Kashmiri Muslims felt and were treated under the Dogras as well as their attempts at political mobilization. See Abdullah, *The Blazing Chinar*, 1–69.

4. Rai, *Hindu Rulers, Muslim Subjects*, 150–56.

5. Malik, *Kashmir: Ethnic Conflict and International Dispute*, 26.

6. Malik, 25.

7. *Begar* involved any form of work that the state forced its subjects to do, including projects such as building roads. Workers received little to no payment. See Malik,, 26.

8. Junaid, "Youth Activists in Kashmir," 369; and Hussain, *Kashmir in the Aftermath of Partition*, 28.

9. Rai, *Hindu Rulers, Muslim Subjects*, 206.

10. Malik, *Kashmir: Ethnic Conflict and International Dispute*, 10.

11. Junaid, "Youth Activists in Kashmir," 9–10.

12. Robinson, *Body of Victim, Body of Warrior*, 34–35.

13. Robinson, 35.

14. Thorp, *Cashmere Misgovernment*.

15. Rai, *Hindu Rulers, Muslim Subjects*, 294

16. Para, *The Making of Modern Kashmir*, 19.

17. Hasrat Ghadda, interview with author, Srinagar, August 27, 2014.

18. Tak, "Bakshi Number," 100.

19. Hasrat Ghadda, interview with author, Srinagar, August 27, 2014.

20. Hussain, *Kashmir in the Aftermath of Partition*, 34.

21. Malik, *Kashmir: Ethnic Conflict and International Dispute*, 31. A months-long strike at the Government Silk Factory in Srinagar against low wages and mistreatment resulted in Dogra soldiers killing ten workers.

22. Chandra, "The National Question in Kashmir," 36.

23. Malik, *Kashmir: Ethnic Conflict and International Dispute*, 33

24. For an overview of Sheikh Abdullah's life and impact on Kashmir, see Para, *The Making of Modern Kashmir*.

25. Malik, *Kashmir: Ethnic Conflict and International Dispute*, 34.

26. Malik, 35.

27. Malik, 35. See Hussain, *Kashmir in the Aftermath of Partition*, 38–39.

28. Rai, *Hindu Rulers, Muslim Subjects.*

29. Hussain, *Kashmir in the Aftermath of Partition*, 36; Malik, *Kashmir: Ethnic Conflict and International Dispute*, 45; Zutshi, *Languages of Belonging*, 130.

30. Malik, 38–53.

31. Groups like the All India Muslim Kashmir Committee, which included the poet and philosopher Muhammad Iqbal, as well as leaders of the Ahmedi Muslim committee and the Ahrars based in Punjab, had taken a great interest in what was happening to Kashmir's Muslim population under the Dogras. They would agitate outside the state, hold conferences, and publish material on the topic. See Malik 39–44.

32. Iffat Malik suggests three potential reasons for Abdullah's conversion of the Muslim Conference into the National Conference: enmity with Mirwaiz Yusuf, the genuine conversion to nationalist politics, and the desire to participate on the all-India political stage, which could happen only if the movement was expanded to include all communities in the state. See Malik, *Kashmir: Ethnic Conflict and International Dispute*, 48–49. For the role of Prem Nath Bazaz in the conversion of the Muslim Conference into the National Conference, see Zutshi, *Languages of Belonging*, 279.

33. For a deeper discussion on the reasons why Sheikh Abdullah and others decided a secular nationalist organization would better suit their goals, as well as the challenges in carrying this out, see Rai, *Hindu Rulers, Muslim Subjects*, 274–80.

34. Ganai, "Dogra Raj and the Struggle for Freedom," 177.

35. Zutshi, *Languages of Belonging*, 262.

36. Bazaz, *The History of Struggle for Freedom in Kashmir*, 168.

37. For a more detailed analysis of the manifesto, see Kaul, "On Naya Kashmir."

38. Robinson, *Body of Victim, Body of Warrior*, 40.

39. *New Kashmir*, 10.

40. *New Kashmir*, 5.

41. *New Kashmir*, 7.

42. Bose, *Kashmir: Roots of Conflict, Paths to Peace*, 25.

43. *New Kashmir*, 19–20.

44. *New Kashmir*, 22.

45. Zutshi, *Languages of Belonging*, 275–89. Jinnah's May–June 1944 visit to Kashmir also played a role in the revival of the Muslim Conference. See Zutshi, 287–88.

46. Zutshi, 275.

47. Hussain, *Sheikh Abdullah*, 146.

48. Schofield, *Kashmir in Crossfire*, 110.

49. When referring specifically to the manifesto, I use the term "Naya Kashmir

manifesto." When referring broadly to the progressive project of state-building/reform, I use the term "Naya Kashmir."

50. Malik, *Kashmir: Ethnic Conflict and International Dispute*, 57. Zutshi also details how Abdullah and the National Conference attempted to appease Kashmiri Muslims at this time, creating a religious trust to look over religious spaces of worship and installing a printing press on the grounds of a mosque in Srinagar. For more on Abdullah's decreasing popularity, see Zutshi, *Languages of Belonging*, 265–67.

51. Robinson, *Body of Victim, Body of Warrior*, 40.

52. Bakshi Ghulam Mohammad, *Why Hunger Strike: Truth vs. Kashmir Government*, pamphlet, Department of Information, Srinagar State Archives, n.d.

53. Zutshi, *Languages of Belonging*, 308–10; Para, *The Making of Modern Kashmir*, 140.

54. Iffat Malik states that while Mirwaiz Yusuf Shah was in favor of joining Pakistan, some of the Jammu-based leaders of the Muslim Conference preferred independence. Malik, *Kashmir: Ethnic Conflict and International Dispute*, 60.

55. Chowdhary, viii. Chitrelekha Zutshi has argued that Sheikh Abdullah's decision to accede to India was as a result of political pragmatism instead of "unequivocal acceptance of India." See Zutshi, *Languages of Belonging*, 308. For more on the period around accession see, Para, *The Making of Modern Kashmir*, 122–52.

56. Zutshi, *Languages of Belonging*, 305.

57. Para writes of a letter from Bakshi Ghulam Mohammad to Munshi Ishaq, in which Bakshi reveals that he was in touch with the Indian National Congress and that Nehru hoped that Lord Mountbatten, viceroy to the subcontinent, would secure Kashmir in India's favor. Nehru also wrote a letter to Mountbatten suggesting that the only appropriate choice for Kashmir would be to accede to India. See Para, *The Making of Modern Kashmir*, 130–31.

58. Para, 129.

59. Malik, *Kashmir: Ethnic Conflict and International Dispute*, 62–63.

60. Zutshi, *Languages of Belonging*, 305.

61. Junaid, "Youth Activists in Kashmir," 77.

62. Robinson, *Body of Victim, Body of Warrior*, 41.

63. Naqvi, "The Killing Fields of Jammu"; Snedden, *The Untold Story of the People of Azad Kashmir*, 37–63; Robinson, *Body of Victim, Body of Warrior*, 48–52.

64. Chatta, "Terrible Fate: Ethnic Cleansing of Jammu Muslims in 1947."

65. Junaid, "Youth Activists in Kashmir," 77–79.

66. Robinson, *Body of Victim, Body of Warrior*, 42.

67. Para, *The Making of Modern Kashmir*, 145.

68. Para, *The Making of Modern Kashmir*, 145.

69. Whitehead, "The People's Militia," 153.

70. Whitehead, 153–54.

71. Junaid, "Youth Activists in Kashmir," 13–14.

72. Lamb, *Birth of a Tragedy: Kashmir 1947*, 130–32.

73. Malik, *Kashmir: Ethnic Conflict and International Dispute*, 67–69.

74. Robinson, *Body of Victim, Body of Warrior*, 43.

75. Robinson, 49.

76. Robinson, 51.

77. Duschinski et al., *Resisting Occupation in Kashmir*, 7.

78. Rashid, "Theatrics of a 'Violent State,'" 216.

79. Junaid, "Youth Activists in Kashmir," 162.

80. Rashid, "Theatrics of a 'Violent State,'" 222.

81. Rashid, 225; Junaid, "Youth Activists in Kashmir," 15.

82. Rashid, "Theatrics of a 'Violent State,'" 217–18.

83. Malik, *Kashmir: Ethnic Conflict and International Dispute*, 67.

84. Copland, "The Abdullah Factor," 224.

85. Junaid, "Youth Activists in Kashmir," 15.

86. For more on Junagadh and Hyderabad, see Snedden, *Understanding Kashmir and Kashmiris*, 149–52.

87. Malik, *Kashmir: Ethnic Conflict and International Dispute*, 86.

88. Purushotham, *From Raj to Republic*, 77–126.

89. Robinson, *Body of Victim, Body of Warrior*, 43.

90. After accession, the National Conference decided that Karan Singh would be given the role of "sadar-i-riyasat," a symbolic head of the state. His role was primarily to keep India's leadership abreast of developments in the state.

91. For more on political and social developments inside Azad Kashmir and its relationship to the Pakistan state, see Snedden, *The Untold Story of the People of Azad Kashmir*; Robinson, *Body of Victim, Body of Warrior*.

92. Qasim, *My Life and Times*, 43–48. Shahla Hussain details the authoritarian actions and economic mismanagement of Sheikh Abdullah's government, as well as how he sought to suppress aspirations for alternate political futures. See Hussain, *Kashmir in the Aftermath of Partition*, 79–90.

93. Whitehead, *The People's Militia*.

94. Malik, *Kashmir: Ethnic Conflict and International Dispute*, 95

95. Duschinski and Ghosh, "Constituting the Occupation."

96. Duschinski and Ghosh; Malik, *Kashmir: Ethnic Conflict and International Dispute*, 95. Emphasis added.

97. Malik, 96.

98. Malik, 96.

99. Duschinski and Ghosh, "Constituting the Occupation."

100. Noorani, *Article 370*, 7–14.

101. Hussain, *Kashmir in the Aftermath of Partition*, 100.

102. Snedden, "Would a Plebiscite Have Resolved the Kashmir Dispute?," 76.

103. As Christopher Snedden argues, "The ruling party in J&K . . . used a variety of electoral malpractices to ensure favourable election outcomes. These have included at various times, singly or in combination: rejecting nominations; creating intimidatory pre-election environments; controlling the press; enrolling 'ghost' voters; distributing ballot papers in advance; improper use of government machinery during elections; absenting scrutineers; exiling rivals; and kidnapping or detaining candidates." See Snedden, 80.

104. Zia, *Resisting Disappearance*, 54.

105. Qasim, *My Life and Times*, 46.

106. Qasim, 44.

107. Schofield, *Kashmir in Crossfire*, 171. Hussain, *Kashmir in the Aftermath of Partition*, 104–11.

108. Para, *The Making of Modern Kashmir*, 182–85; Hussain, 103.

109. Malik, *Kashmir: Ethnic Conflict and International Dispute*, 98.

110. Behera, *State, Identity and Violence*, 85.

111. For more on the Praja Prashad, see Hussain, *Kashmir in the Aftermath of Partition*, 111–14.

112. Alam, *Jammu and Kashmir 1949–1964*, 50–53.

113. Para, *The Making of Modern Kashmir*, 186.

114. Alam, *Jammu and Kashmir 1949-1964*, 52-53.

115. Zutshi, *Languages of Belonging*, 314.

116. Ministry of States, Kashmir Section, Government of India, "Intelligence Reports Re: Muslim Affairs in JK State," 1953, file no. F.8 (6)-K/53, National Archives of India.

117. Ministry of States, "Intelligence Reports re Muslim Affairs in JK State."

118. Ministry of States, "Intelligence Reports re Muslim Affairs in JK State."

119. Ministry of States, "Intelligence Reports re Muslim Affairs in JK State."

120. Abdullah, *The Blazing Chinar*, 349.

121. Behera, *State, Identity and Violence*, 61. One example that Abdullah highlights is that Sardar Patel wanted the University of Kashmir to join with the University of East Punjab, which Abdullah protested. See Abdullah, *The Blazing Chinar*, 353–58.

122. Para, *The Making of Modern Kashmir*, 178–81.

123. Puri, *Kashmir Towards Insurgency*, 46.

124. For varying accounts of Sheikh Abdullah's arrest, see Korbel, *Danger in Kashmir*; Singh, *Heir Apparent: An Autobiography*; Abdullah, *The Blazing Chinar*; Hussain, *Kashmir in the Aftermath of Partition*,115–20; Para, *The Making of Modern Kashmir*, 188.

125. Malik, *Kashmir: Ethnic Conflict and International Dispute*, 105, The reasons that led to Abdullah's dismissal are also detailed in the correspondence between Nehru and Karan Singh during the Praja Parishad agitation.

126. Korbel estimates that between thirty and eight hundred were killed, while Kashmiri journalist Sanaullah Bhat, in *Kashmir in Flames*, says that nearly fifteen hundred people were killed. Korbel, *Danger in Kashmir*, 242–44. See also Bhat, *Kashmir, 1947–1977 Tak*, 72.

127. Qasim, *My Life and Times*, 68.

128. Qasim, *My Life and Times*, 70.

129. Khan, "Evolution of My Identity," 14.

130. Mir Nazir Ahmed, interview with author, Srinagar, December 15, 2013; Nazir Bakshi, interview with author, Srinagar, November 18, 2013; Pirzada Hafizullah Makhdoomi, interview with author, Srinagar, November 17, 2013.

131. Nazir Bakshi, interview with author, November 18, 2013.

132. Pirzada Hafizullah Makhdoomi, interview with author, November 17, 2013.

133. Abdullah, *The Blazing Chinar*, 373.

134. Mullik also states that Bakshi was more pragmatic and realized that Kashmir's welfare depended on its unity with India and apprehended that Kashmir would be swamped by the tribal invasions and would lose its identity if it acceded to Pakistan. See Mullik, *My Years with Nehru*, 14.

135. Nazir Bakshi, interview with author, Srinagar, November 18, 2013.

136. Bakshi, interview with author.

137. Bakshi, interview with author.

138. Hassan Shah, interview with author, Srinagar, June 13, 2014.

139. Gash, *Bakshi Ghulam Mohammad.*

140. Hassan Shah, interview with author, Srinagar, June 13, 2014.

141. Pirzada Hafizullah Makhdoomi, interview with author, Srinagar, November 17, 2013.

142. Tak, "Bakshi Number," 39.

143. Feldman, *Governing Gaza*, 16.

144. Feldman, 20.

145. Kak, *Khalid-i-Kashmir*, 138.

146. Tak, "Bakshi Number," 41.

147. Tak, 14.

148. Hassan, *History Revisited.*

149. Government of Jammu and Kashmir, *Jammu and Kashmir, 1953–1954, A Review of the Achievements of Bakshi Government.*

150. Tillin, "Asymmetric Federalism," 546.

151. Bazaz, *The Shape of Things in Kashmir*, 15.

152. Noorani, *The Kashmir Question*, 73.

153. Noorani, 73.

154. Kanjwal, "Reflections on the Post-Partition Period."

155. Kanjwal.

156. Kanjwal.

157. Kanjwal.

Chapter 2

1. Department of Information, "Transport Facilities and Issue of Press Cards to Press Correspondents," in Accession Register no. 282 of 1954–55, Srinagar State Archives.

2. Rosenthal, quoted in *Kashmir through Many Eyes*, Lalla Rookh Publications, Department of Information and Broadcasting, Accession No: 56206, Nehru Memorial Museum and Library, 3.

3. Rosenthal, *Kashmir through Many Eyes*, 3.

4. Special correspondent, *Economist London*, November 22, 1956, in *Kashmir: An Open Book*, 6.

5. Zinkin, quoted in *Kashmir through Many Eyes*, 8.

6. Zinkin, *Kashmir through Many Eyes*, 8.

7. Special representative, *Sunday Times London*, July 26, 1955, in *Kashmir: An Open Book*, 5.

8. Grimes, "Kashmir's Ruler Hears the Poor," *New York Times*, September 15, 1960.

9. Comments from *Morgon-tidningen* (a Swedish government party paper), n.d., in "Kashmir Newspaper Clippings," Indian Council of World Affairs (Sapru House), New Delhi.

10. "India, Pakistan, Kashmir," *New York Times*, August 14, 1953.

11. "India, Pakistan, Kashmir."

12. James Burke, "Indian troops rounding up pro-Abdullah demonstrators," *Life* Picture Collection, August 1953, http://images.google.com/hosted/life/81d45508d56580ed.html.

13. James Burke, "Pro-Abdullah demonstrators running from police after takeover by Bakshi Ghulam Mohamed," *Life* Picture Collection, August 1953, http://images.google.com/hosted/life/5b337255182d7858.html.

14. "A Big New Challenge for UN," editorial, *Life*, February 11, 1957, 38.

15. Ghosh, "Crisis Constitutionalism, Permanent Emergency."

16. Department of Information, "Magazine 'Kashmir' Produced by Ministry of Information and Broadcasting," in Accession Register no. 206 of 1951, Srinagar State Archives.

17. Department of Information, "Visit of Press Correspondents to the State," in Accession Register no. 215 of 1948, Srinagar State Archives. Emphasis added.

18. Department of Information, "Proposed Publication of *Kashmir Today*," in Accession Register no. 228 of 1950, Srinagar State Archives.

19. Department of Information, "Correspondence between JM Zutshi and PM Bamzai, Officer at Information and Broadcasting," December 10, 1951, Srinagar State Archives,.

20. Department of Information, "Publication of Advertisements in *Kashmir Today*, *Tameer*, and *Yojna*," in Accession Register no. 43 of 1966, Srinagar State Archives.

21. Department of Information, "*Tameer*, *Yojna*, and *Kashmir Today*," in Accession Register no. 18 of 1952, Srinagar State Archives.

22. Department of Information, "Revising the Mailing List for Distribution of the Publicity Literature and Press Releases issued by the Information Department," in Accession Register no. 39 of 1955, Srinagar State Archives.

23. Department of Information, "Supply of 200 Community Receivers by Government of India," in basta 11, Year 1954–1960, Radio, Srinagar State Archives.

24. Department of Education, "Setting Up of Information Centers at Various Places in JK State," November 22, 1961, in Accession Register no. 324 of 1961, Srinagar State Archives.

25. Department of Education, "Setting Up of Information Centers."

26. Department of Information, "Grant of Permission for Starting Newspapers 1955–1959," in Accession Register no. 166–173 of 1953, Srinagar State Archives.

27. Department of Information, "Grant of Permission for Starting Newspapers."

28. Department of Information, "List of Newspapers Considered Suitable from a Commercial Viewpoint to Receive Government of India Ads," 1958, Srinagar State Archives.

29. Department of Information, "Accreditation of Press Correspondents for the Year 1955," in Accession Register no. 46 of 1955 (file no. 1376/c-117/55), Srinagar State Archives.

30. Department of Information, "List of Newspapers."

31. Department of Information, "Jai Sudesh Sansar 26-9-1955," in Accession Register no. 162 of 1954–1955, Srinagar State Archives.

32. Department of Information, "Action Against the *Sach* Jammu under the Press and Publication Act 1989," in Accession Register no. 71 of 1958, Srinagar State Archives.

33. Department of Information, "Banning Publication of Local Newspaper or Other Actions against Them," in Accession Register no. 331–345 of 1958, Srinagar State Archives.

34. Department of Information, "Mr. Sahni, Srinagar Correspondent for *London Times*," in "Correspondence between RC Raina and J. N. Zutshi," Srinagar State Archives.

35. Trumbull, "Abdullah Ousted as Kashmir Chief, " *New York Times*, August 9, 1953.

36. "Kashmir after August 9, 1953," *Amrita Bazar Patrika*, May 2, 1955, 8.

37. Deshbandhu, *61, Constitution House*.

38. Department of Information, Letter from On Dhar to J. N. Zutshi, May 25, 1956, file 2601, Srinagar State Archives.

39. "Economic Policies of the Bakshi Government," in "Kashmir Newspaper Clippings," Indian Council of World Affairs (Sapru House), New Delhi.

40. "Economic Policies of the Bakshi Government."

41. Department of Information, "Permission Sought by the Local and Foreign Correspondents," in Accession Register no. 155 of 1954–1955, Srinagar State Archives.

42. Department of Information, "Permission Sought by the Local and Foreign Correspondents."

43. Department of Information, "Permission Sought by the Local and Foreign Correspondents."

44. Department of Information, "Permission Sought by the Local and Foreign Correspondents."

45. Department of Information, "Visit of Press Correspondents to the State," in Accession Register no. 215 of 1948, Srinagar State Archives.

46. Department of Information, "Transport Facilities and Issue of Press Cards to Press Correspondents," in Accession Register no. 282 of 1954–55, Srinagar State Archives.

47. Department of Information, "Transport Facilities and Issue of Press Cards."

48. Department of Information, "Permission Sought by the Local and Foreign Correspondents," in Accession Register no. 155 of 1954–1955, Srinagar State Archives.

49. Department of Information, "Issue of Articles for Special Supplements of Different Papers in and outside the State," in Accession Register no. 299 of 1958, Srinagar State Archives.

50. Department of Information, "Advertisement File," in Accession Register no. 72 of 1955, Srinagar State Archives.

51. Department of Information, "Advertisement File."

52. Raghavan, "Kashmir on the March."

53. Political Correspondent, *Amrita Bazar Patrika,* March 1955, in *Kashmir through Many Eyes*, 1.

54. Kalhan, "Report on Kashmir," *Hindustan Times*, 14.

55. Kalhan, 14.

56. Raghavan, "Kashmir on the March."

57. Political correspondent, *Amrita Bazar Patrika*, 8.

58. Kanjwal, "The Violence on Kashmir."

59. These talks began before the coup and commenced formally on August 17, 1953, for a three-day period.

60. Singh, quoted in Alam, *Jammu and Kashmir 1949–1964*, 147.

61. Singh, quoted in Alam, 147–48.

62. In a letter to Sheikh Abdullah on January 12, 1949, Nehru assured him that this "business of plebiscite is still far away and there is a possibility of the plebiscite not taking place at all." Gopal, *Selected Works of Jawaharlal Nehru*, vol. 9, series 2, 198. Elsewhere, Nehru stated, "Towards the end of 1948, it became clear to me then that we would never get the conditions which were necessary for a plebiscite so I ruled out the plebiscite for all practical purposes." Gopal, vol. 19, 322–30.

63. Ankit, *The Kashmir Conflict*, 26–27.

64. Ahmad, "The Politics of the Major Powers," 118–19.

65. Kumar, *Anglo-American Plot against Kashmir*, 6.

66. Vent and Monier, "Kashmir and the Kashmir Impasse."

67. Ankit, *The Kashmir Conflict*, 2.

68. Ankit, *The Kashmir Conflict,* 62, 104–8; Bazaz, "Politics in Kashmir." See Abney, "Behind the Kashmir Coup," 19; Vent and Monier, "Kashmir and the Kashmir Impasse."

69. "A Big New Challenge for UN," editorial, *Life*, February 11, 1957, 38.

70. "Kashmir after August 9, 1953," *Amrita Bazar Patrika*, 1955, 7.

71. There has been much intrigue surrounding the role of Adlai Stevenson, a US presidential candidate who traveled to Kashmir and met with Sheikh Abdullah. Stevenson was accused of presenting the "independent Kashmir" dream to Abdullah.

72. Ankit, *The Kashmir Conflict*, 57–60.

73. "Partition to Tashkent," *Kashmir Life*, December 21, 2016, excerpted from Mahapatra, "Russia and the Kashmir Issue since 1991," http://www.kashmirlife.net/partition-to-tashkent-127104/.

74. Ankit, *The Kashmir Conflict,* 108.

75. Ankit, *The Kashmir Conflict,* 112.

76. "Periodical Political Reports from Missions—Indian Delegation to UN New

York," Ministry of External Affairs, Kashmir Branch, file no. M/52/1329/107 1952, National Archives of India.

77. Ahmad, "The Politics of the Major Powers," 134–35.

78. These military agreements were to create an alliance against the rising tide of communism. For more on the impact of the US-Pakistan military alliance, see Afroz, "The Cold War and United States Military Aid to Pakistan."

79. S. K. "The Kashmir Dispute after Ten Years."

80. Alavi, "Pakistan-US Military Alliance."

81. Ahmad, "The Politics of the Major Powers," 215.

82. "India Asks Withdrawal," *New York Times*, March 21, 1954, 45.

83. For more on the role of the Soviet Union and the effects of the US-Pakistan military alliance, see Ahmad, "The Politics of the Major Powers," 145–68, 201–47. On the role of the United States, see Colway-Sympson, "The Kashmir Dispute in World Politics."

84. Rosenthal, "Survey of Kashmir Shows Region Firmly Welded to Indian Rule, 3.

85. Department of Information, "Visit of Foreign Correspondents and Journalists to the JK State," Accession Register no. 114 of 1956, Srinagar State Archives.

86. Sherman, *Muslim Belonging in Secular India.*

87. "Policies Not Affected," *New York Times*, February 23, 1954, 11.

88. "Pakistan Backed on Kashmir Issue," *New York Times,* December 27, 1954.

89. Mekkawi, "Egypt and India."

90. "Kashmir Gets Egyptian Offer," *New York Times*, February 17, 1950.

91. Mekkawi, "Egypt and India," 59–70.

92. Government of Jammu and Kashmir, Press Notes, July 20, 1955, Government Press Library.

93. Government of Jammu and Kashmir, Press Notes, November 19, 1955, Government Press Library.

94. "In Kashmir Bid," *New York Times*, April 11, 1954, 27.

95. "Kashmir Newspaper Clippings," Indian Council of World Affairs (Sapru House), New Delhi.

96. "Kashmir Newspaper Clippings."

97. Government of Jammu and Kashmir, Press Notes, November 1, 1955, Government Press Library.

98. Government of Jammu and Kashmir, Press Notes, October 1, 1955, Government Press Library.

99. Government of Jammu and Kashmir, Press Notes, February 13, 1958, Government Press Library.

100. Government of Jammu and Kashmir, Press Notes, July 16, 1963, Government Press Library.

101. Government of Jammu and Kashmir, Press Notes, July 16, 1963, Government Press Library.

102. *Kashmir Today* 1, no. 2 (1956): 5.

103. Mekkawi, "Egypt and India," 80.

104. Government of Jammu and Kashmir, *Inside Pakistan-Held Kashmir*, 2.

105. Government of Jammu and Kashmir, *Inside Pakistan-Held Kashmir*, 4.

106. Government of Jammu and Kashmir, *Inside Pakistan-Held Kashmir*, 14.

107. Government of Jammu and Kashmir, Press Notes, February 13, 1955, Government Press Library.

108. "Arabs Asked to Aid Pakistan," *New York Times*, April 25, 1957, 12.

109. Nehru had earlier visited the Soviet Union, where he had been warmly received. During that visit, the Soviet Union and India agreed not to join in any action or coalition directed against the other.

110. "Soviet Leaders Are Cheered in Kashmir," *New York Times*, December 10, 1955, 4.

111. Government of Jammu and Kashmir, *Soviet Leaders in Kashmir*.

112. Abdul Khaliq, interview with author, Maryland, September 15, 2020.

113. Abdul Khaliq, interview with author .

114. I am indebted here to Lisa Wedeen's work on Syria and the power of spectacle and state propaganda in not only producing political power but also inviting transgressions. See Wedeen, *Ambiguities of Domination*, 6.

115. Wedeen, 6.

116. "Partition to Tashkent," excerpted from Mahapatra, "Russia and the Kashmir Issue since 1991."

117. Government of Jammu and Kashmir, *Soviet Leaders in Kashmir*.

118. Ahmad, "The Politics of the Major Powers," 126.

119. Alam, *Jammu and Kashmir 1949–1964*.

120. "The Russians in Kashmir," *New York Times*, December 11, 1955, 212.

121. Ahmad, "The Politics of the Major Powers," 243; James, "Moscow Vetoes Kashmir Inquiry," *New York Times*, February 21, 1957, 1.

122. Ankit, *The Kashmir Conflict*, 187, 236.

123. Earl Clement Attlee, *Evening Star*, November 20, 1956, in *Kashmir, as Others See It* (Srinagar: Lalla Rookh Publications, Department of Information and Broadcasting), Nehru Memorial Museum and Library.

Chapter 3

1. Department of Information, "Grant of Permission for Shooting of Films in the JK State," in Accession Register no. 624 of 1969, Srinagar State Archives.

2. This practice began as early as 1947, as nationalist films like *Kashmir Hamara Hai* showcased how the first Kashmir war between India and Pakistan served as an

ideological battle in which Kashmir became the "prize" and a sign of India's "vindication" over the two-nation theory. Here, Kashmir's centrality to articulations of Indian nationhood need to be understood. The events of Kashmir in 1947 were situated as the "final act in the struggle for Indian independence," while erasing the conditions in which it became a part of India. See Gaur, "Kashmir on Screen," 62–64, 81.

3. "Grant of Permission for Shooting of Films in the JK State."

4. Meenu Gaur examines two early films that were made in Kashmir, although they were outside the genre of "holiday films." One was *Barsaat* (1949). Here, the "landscape of Kashmir becomes the outward manifestation of the desired interior wholeness of the romantic subject in Hindi cinema." See Gaur, "Kashmir on Screen," 171.

5. Both Gaur and Ananya Jahanara Kabir have also argued that the developments in color film "had a direct impact on the growing popularity of Kashmir as a filming location." Eastmancolor, in particular, was a "heightening filter for this new simultaneity of two different kinds of pleasures"—the Kashmir Valley and more contemporary youthful excitements. See Gaur, "Kashmir on Screen," 190; Kabir, *Territory of Desire*, 38.

6. "Grant of Permission for Shooting of Films in the JK State."

7. Department of Information, "Screening of Travel Films in India," 1955, in basta no. 15 of 1953–1969, Srinagar State Archives. The Films Division films were usually screened before every film shown across India and were an important forum for nation-building, development, and integration for the nascent state. See Despande, "Indian Cinema and the Bourgeois Nation-State"; Deprez, "The Films Division of India."

8. Kabir, *Territory of Desire*, 38.

9. Barclay, "Peddling Postcards and Selling Empire," 85.

10. McDonald, *Placing Empire*, xv.

11. McDonald, xv .

12. McDonald, xv .

13. McDonald, xv .

14. Pedersen, "Peace through Tourism"; Chauhan and Khanna, "Tourism: A Tool for Crafting Peace Process"; Chari, Chandran, and Akhtar, "Tourism and Peace Building in Jammu and Kashmir."

15. Skwiot, *The Purposes of Paradise*, 2.

16. Department of Information, "How About a Holiday in Kashmir?" *India Weekly*, n.d., Newspaper Clippings, Srinagar State Archives.

17. Kabir, *Territory of Desire.*

18. Omkar Nath Kaul, "Kashmir Welcomes You," and P. N. Madan, "Kashmir and Its Tourist Industry," *Kashmir Today* 3 (July–August 1959), Government of Jammu and Kashmir, Department of Information, Srinagar State Archives.

19. "Message from Minister for Health and Tourism," *Kashmir Today* 3 (July-August 1959), Government of Jammu and Kashmir, Department of Information, Srinagar State Archives.

20. Similarly, Anirudh Despande also argues that postcolonial Indian cinema largely represented India as a normatively Hindu, upper-caste, patriarchal space. See Despande, "Indian Cinema and the Bourgeois Nation-State."

21. Gaur, "Kashmir on Screen," 44.

22. Ahmad, "Orientalist Imaginaries," 167–68.

23. Kabir, *Territory of Desire,* 15.

24. Ahmad, "Orientalist Imaginaries," 173.

25. Ahmad, 176.

26. Kabir, *Territory of Desire*, 4, 14.

27. Kabir, 17.

28. Kabir, 66.

29. Ahmad, "Orientalist Imaginaries," 180.

30. Ahmad, 180.

31. "Procedure for Issuing Kashmir Entry Permits," in Ministry of States, Kashmir Section, Government of India, "Tourist Traffic in Kashmir," file no. 10(3)-K/54, 1954, p. 43, National Archives of India.

32. Ministry of States, Kashmir Section, Government of India, "Decision That Travelers to the Jammu and Kashmir State from the Rest of India, and Vice Versa, Should Obtain Permits from the Defense Ministry and the Jammu and Kashmir Governments Respectively," file no. 4(1)-K/48, 1948, 4, National Archives of India.

33. Ministry of States, Kashmir Section, Government of India, "Kashmir Entry Permits," file no. F.10 (24)-K/53, 1953, National Archives of India.

34. Ministry of States, "Decision That Travelers to the Jammu and Kashmir State," 12.

35. "Procedure for Issuing Kashmir Entry Permits," 17.

36. "The Tourists Paradise," *Kashmir Today* 3 (July-August 1959), Government of Jammu and Kashmir, Department of Information, Srinagar State Archives.

37. Ministry of States, Kashmir Section, Government of India, "Tourist Traffic in Kashmir," file no. 10(3)-K/54, 1954, pp. 14–15, National Archives of India.

38. Ministry of States, "Tourist Traffic in Kashmir," 22.

39. Ministry of States, "Tourist Traffic in Kashmir," 22.

40. Department of Information, "Notes from Ministry of Tourist Planning Meeting, Feb. 2, 1950," in "Correspondence re: Tourist Publicity," Accession Register no. 218 of 1946, Srinagar State Archives.

41. Department of Information, "Notes from Ministry of Tourist Planning Meeting."

42. Itoo, "Tourism Industry of Kashmir."

43. Department of Information, "Kashmir to Spend Rs. 1,57,00,000 for New Tourist Resorts," *Mirror*, September 1, 1962, Srinagar State Archives.

44. Kabir, *Territory of Desire*, 10–12.

45. *Guide to Kashmir*, 18.

46. *Guide to Kashmir*, 18.

47. *Kashmir Calling: A Tourist's Guide*, 15.

48. *Kashmir Calling: A Tourist's Guide*, 16.

49. Kabir, "Nipped in the Bud?," 90.

50. Department of Information, Government of Jammu and Kashmir, "Tourist Notes," *Kashmir Today* 3 (July-August 1959), Srinagar State Archives.

51. "How About a Holiday in Kashmir?" *India Weekly*.

52. Department of Information, "Tourist Notes," *Kashmir Today*.

53. Kabir, *Territory of Desire*, 38.

54. Department of Information, Government of Jammu and Kashmir, Tourism advertisements, Srinagar State Archives.

55. The Films Division of India also made short documentaries on the seasons—*Spring in Kashmir* and *Magic of the Mountain*, which covered the summer and early fall.

56. McGowan, "Mothers and Godmothers of Crafts."

57. *Kashmir Calling: A Tourist's Guide*, 8.

58. *Guide to Kashmir*, 10–16.

59. *Guide to Kashmir*, 15.

60. Sarup, *Travel Guide to Kashmir*, 88.

61. Kabir, *Territory of Desire*, 114.

62. Kabir, 114.

63. Kabir, 114.

64. Kabir, 118.

65. Ministry of Information and Broadcasting, *Kashmir*, 10.

66. Ministry of Information and Broadcasting, *Kashmir*, 10.

67. "Kashmir Newspaper Clippings," Indian Council of World Affairs (Sapru House), New Delhi.

68. *Guide to Kashmir*, 7.

69. Indeed, Nehru himself spoke of Kashmir as an inheritor of Indo-Aryan traditions, "making Kashmir central to articulations of Indian belonging and origins." See Gaur, "Kashmir on Screen," 178.

70. Bhan, "'In Search of the Aryan Seed,'" 77.

71. Bhan, 79.

72. Bhan, 78.

73. Department of Information, "Draft Proposal," letter from M. N. Malhotra, General Manager, Movie Makers, to Department of Information, November 22, 1954, Srinagar State Archives.

74. Department of Information, "Draft Proposal."

75. Barclay, "Peddling Postcards and Selling Empire," 86.

76. Kabir, *Territory of Desire*, 40.

77. Kabir, 41.

78. Gaur, "Kashmir on Screen," 313.

79. Kabir, *Territory of Desire*, 91.

80. Despande, "Indian Cinema and the Bourgeois Nation-State," 101.

81. Ahmad, "Orientalist Imaginaries," 173–74.

82. Ahmad, 178.

83. Nehru, quoted in Ministry of Information and Broadcasting, *Kashmir*, 4.

84. Bhan, "Infrastructures of Occupation," 81.

85. *Guide to Kashmir*, 2.

86. Gaur, "Kashmir on Screen," 173–74.

87. Department of Information, "Letter from Miss Mahmooda Ahmad Ali, Government College for Women, Srinagar, to Mr. Ghulam Mohi-ud-din," file no. S-A8-18/CS-55, June 12, 1955, Srinagar State Archives.

88. Department of Information, "Letter from Miss Mehmooda Ahmed Ali."

89. Department of Information, "Draft Proposal," letter from M. N. Malhotra.

90. Ministry of Information and Broadcasting, *Kashmir*, revised, May 1962.

91. McDonald, *Placing Empire*, 48.

92. *Magic of the Mountain*, Films Division of India.

93. *Kashmir Calling: A Tourist's Guide*, 9.

94. Ministry of Information and Broadcasting, *Kashmir*, 9.

95. Sarup, *Travel Guide to Kashmir*.

96. Kabir, *Territory of Desire*, 14.

97. *Magic of the Mountain*, Films Division of India.

98. Ministry of Information and Broadcasting, *Kashmir*, 7.

99. Department of Information, Tourism advertisements, Srinagar State Archives.

100. Kabir, *Territory of Desire*, 39.

101. Gaur, "Kashmir on Screen," 3.

102. Gaur, 108.

103. Ministry of Information and Broadcasting, *Kashmir*.

104. Sarup, *Travel Guide to Kashmir*, 18

105. Kumari, *Kashmir Greets You*, 3.

106. Bashir, *Kashmir: Exposing the Myth*, xvi.

107. Kabir, *Territory of Desire*, 85.
108. Kabir, 102.
109. Gaur, "Kashmir on Screen," 32.
110. *Kashmir Calling: A Tourist's Guide*, 7.
111. Kabir, *Territory of Desire*, 100.
112. Koul, *Srinagar and Its Environs*, 2–3.
113. *Kashmir Calling: A Tourist's Guide*, 9.
114. Ministry of Information and Broadcasting, *Kashmir*, 8.
115. *Guide to Kashmir*, 23
116. *Beautiful Kashmir: Visitors Best Guide*, 43.
117. Kabir, *Territory of Desire*, 91. Gaur mentions that "the mythology of the mountains in Kashmir is such that they are identified with the male gods, in particular Shiva. Further, the Lake is believed to be Goddess Uma or Parvati, the wife of Shiva reborn as Kashmir." See Gaur, "Kashmir on Screen," 172.
118. Koul, *Srinagar and its Environs*, 29.
119. Sarup, *Travel Guide to Kashmir*, 19.
120. *Kashmir Calling: A Tourist's Guide*, 7.
121. Bashir, *Kashmir: Exposing the Myth*, 39–51.
122. "Draft Proposal," letter from M. N. Malhotra.
123. Kabir, *Territory of Desire*, 81, 90.
124. Kabir, 169.
125. Gaur, "Kashmir on Screen," 314.
126. *Guide to Kashmir*, 12.
127. Kumari, *Kashmir Greets You*, 3.
128. Singh, *Pilgrimage to Shree Amarnath Kashmir*.
129. Visitors Bureau, *Notes for Visitors to Kashmir*.
130. For more on the history of the Amarnath pilgrimage as well as how it has changed since 1990, see Jammu and Kashmir Coalition of Civil Society, *Amarnath Yatra*.
131. Sarup, *Travel Guide to Kashmir*, 116.
132. *Hindu Mountain Pilgrimage aka Himalayan Pilgrimage* (1955).
133. Singh, *Pilgrimage to Shree Amarnath Kashmir*, 24.
134. *Himalayan Pilgrimage* (1960).
135. Gaur argues that "the journey to Kashmir is marked by a search for origins, and Kashmir signifies all that is incorruptible and eternal, and therefore a repository of essential values. The sacred Kashmiri mountains are a symbol of purity and origins in this film, and also a place for healing, and an escape from the horrors of the self." See Gaur, "Kashmir on Screen," 180–81.
136. Government of Jammu and Kashmir, Press Notes, October 14, 1963, Government Press Library.

137. Ahmad, *Management of Tourism in Jammu and Kashmir*, 45.

138. Ministry of State for Tourism, Department of Information, "List of tourists," 1964, 1–12, Srinagar State Archives.

139. Gaur, "Kashmir on Screen," 216.

Chapter 4

1. Directorate of Information and Broadcasting, *Crisis in Kashmir Explained.*

2. Directorate of Information and Broadcasting, *Crisis in Kashmir Explained*, 8.

3. Directorate of Information and Broadcasting, *Crisis in Kashmir Explained*, 9.

4. Directorate of Information and Broadcasting, *Unanimous Vote of Confidence in Bakshi Government*, 30.

5. Directorate of Information and Broadcasting, *Crisis in Kashmir Explained*, 8.

6. Directorate of Information and Broadcasting, *Crisis in Kashmir Explained*, 4.

7. Directorate of Information and Broadcasting, *Crisis in Kashmir Explained*, 4.

8. Directorate of Information and Broadcasting, *Crisis in Kashmir Explained*, 8.

9. Directorate of Information and Broadcasting, *Unanimous Vote of Confidence in Bakshi Government*, 16.

10. Directorate of Information and Broadcasting, *Crisis in Kashmir Explained*, 12.

11. Ferguson, *The Anti-Politics Machine*, xv.

12. See Ganguly, *The Crisis in Kashmir*; Behera, *State, Identity, and Violence*; Prakash, "The Political Economy of Kashmir since 1947," 1.

13. Prakash.

14. Prakash, 2058.

15. Ganguly, *The Crisis in Kashmir*.

16. Prakash, "The Political Economy of Kashmir since 1947."

17. Bhan, "Morality and Martyrdom," 192.

18. Thomas Blom Hansen argues that this understanding of the role of the state was embraced by nationalist political elites in the postcolonial world from across the political spectrum, who were anxious to transform their states into normal nation-states. See Hansen and Stepputat, "Introduction," *States of Imagination*,10–13.

19. *Kashmir* (Bombay: All India State's People's Conference, January 1939), accession no. 954.6 G9, Nehru Memorial Museum and Library.

20. *New Kashmir*, 23.

21. *New Kashmir*, 24.

22. *New Kashmir*, 26.

23. *New Kashmir*, 26.

24. *New Kashmir*, 30.

25. *New Kashmir*, 33.

26. *New Kashmir*, 34.

27. Aziz, "Economic History of Modern Kashmir," 5.

28. The condition of the Kashmiri peasants in the late nineteenth century has been detailed in Walter Lawrence's *The Valley of Kashmir*.

29. Jagirs were land grants given by the Dogras to political loyalists. *Muafis* were grants of charity to individuals or institutions, while *mukararis* were cash grants given to individuals, saintly people, or institutions. See Aziz, "Economic History of Modern Kashmir," 56–61.

30. Aslam, "Land Reforms in Jammu and Kashmir."

31. Aslam, 59.

32. Despite the weaknesses of the land reforms, Javeed ul Aziz observes that they did have an important impact on those peasants who benefited from social, cultural, and health advancements. Those families who were empowered by these reforms would also view Sheikh Abdullah as a "messiah" and provide an everlasting support base to him. See Aziz, "Economic History of Modern Kashmir," 89.

33. Thorner, "Kashmir Land Reforms"; Aslam, "Land Reforms in Jammu and Kashmir."

34. Thorner, 999.

35. Thorner, 1002.

36. Aziz, "Economic History of Modern Kashmir," 69.

37. Ministry of Home Affairs, Kashmir Section, "Scheme of Financial Integration with the Center for Jammu and Kashmir," file S. 59 156 EB Part (a), National Archives of India.

38. Ministry of Home Affairs, "Scheme of Financial Integration."

39. The Indian constitution of 1950 distinguished between four types of states. Jammu and Kashmir was considered a "part B state," along with Hyderabad, Madhya Bharat, Mysore, Patiala and East Punjab States Union, Rajasthan, Saurashtra, and Travancore-Chochin. These states were former princely states or unions of princely states, governed by a *rajpramukh*, appointed by the president of India.

40. Ministry of Home Affairs, Kashmir Section, "Scheme of Financial Integration with the Center for Jammu and Kashmir," file no. R20-K/53, 1953, National Archives of India.

41. Ministry of Home Affairs, "Scheme of Financial Integration," 3.

42. Ministry of States, Kashmir Section, "DIB Reports Regarding General Conditions in Jammu and Kashmir. File No 8-K/53, National Archives of India.

43. Malik, *Kashmir: Ethnic Conflict and International Dispute*, 107.

44. Ministry of Home Affairs, Kashmir Section, "Scheme of Financial Integration."

45. Ministry of Home Affairs, Kashmir Section, "Scheme of Financial Integration."

46. *Kashmir in India*, 2.

47. Aziz, "Economic History of Modern Kashmir," 12.

48. Prakash mentions that this changed in the 1970s, when the center set its aid policy at 30 percent grants and 70 percent loans. The reason for this shift is not given. Prakash, "Political Economy of Kashmir since 1947," 2053.

49. Puri, "Central Aid to Kashmir."

50. Puri.

51. Puri.

52. Hussain, *Kashmir in the Aftermath of Partition,* 139. At the start of Bakshi's rule, the Indian government loaned 182.25 lakh rupees to the J&K government. By 1960, this had increased to 718.50 lakhs.

53. As Shahla Hussain details, this would change after 1970, when Kashmir became a "special category" and received a majority of loans over grants. This "prevented economic growth and increased the state's debt burden" as the "state government was forced to divert its resources to debt service, rather than to productive investments and industrial growth." See Hussain, 173.

54. Hussain, 138.

55. Government of Jammu and Kashmir, "Reply to Critics," 2.

56. Government of Jammu and Kashmir, "Aid from India," 3.

57. Government of Jammu and Kashmir, "Aid from India," 3–4.

58. Government of Jammu and Kashmir, "Text of Speech Broadcast by Bakshi Ghulam Mohammad."

59. Government of Jammu and Kashmir, Press Notes, October 15, 1953, Government Press Library.

60. Government of Jammu and Kashmir, "Kashmir at a Glance."

61. Government of Jammu and Kashmir, *The Constitution of Jammu and Kashmir*, 5.

62. Government of Jammu and Kashmir, *Jammu and Kashmir, 1953–1954, A Review of the Achievements of Bakshi Government.*

63. "Kashmir after August 9, 1953," 14, 1955.

64. Aziz, "Economic History of Modern Kashmir."

65. Raghavan, "Kashmir on the March."

66. Government of Jammu and Kashmir, "Aid from India," 5.

67. "Kashmir after August 9, 1953."

68. Zutshi, *Languages of Belonging*, 105–13.

69. Government of Jammu and Kashmir, Press Notes, February 26, 1954.

70. Ministry of Food and Agriculture, Government of India, "Allocation of Rice to Jammu and Kashmir State during 1956-57," file no. 54 (13)/56-BPII, 1956, National Archives of India.

71. Ministry of Food and Agriculture, "Allocation of Rice to Jammu and Kashmir State."

72. Ministry of Food and Agriculture, Government of India, "Jammu and Kashmir: Supply of Rice during the Food Year 1957–1958," file no. 54 (6) 57-BP, vol. 1, National Archives of India.

73. Siegel, "'Self-Help Which Ennobles a Nation,'" 977.

74. Sherman, "From 'Grow More Food' to 'Miss a Meal,'" 1.

75. Government of Jammu and Kashmir, "Reply to Critics," 2.

76. Siegel, "'Self-Help Which Ennobles a Nation,'" 1016.

77. Chowdhary, *Politics of Identity and Separatism*. "To wean the support of people away from Sheikh Abdullah, the Centre and the state therefore adopted the policy of, to use the words of Habibullah, 'literally buying the Kashmiris back,'" 80–81. Bakshi, therefore, started an era of subsidized economy of the state.

78. Chowdhary.

79. Aziz, "Economic History of Modern Kashmir," 131.

80. Kalhan, "Report on Kashmir."

81. Aziz, "Economic History of Modern Kashmir," 139.

82. Government of Jammu and Kashmir, *Sonawari: Field of Gold.*

83. Aziz, "Economic History of Modern Kashmir," 65.

84. Aziz, 117.

85. Aziz, 218.

86. Main Official Resolution, moved at the 22nd Plenary Session of the All Jammu and Kashmir National Conference at Baramulla.

87. Aziz, "Economic History of Modern Kashmir," 159.

88. Kak, *Khalid-i-Kashmir,* 97.

89. Government of Jammu and Kashmir, *Address to the Joint Session of the Jammu and Kashmir Legislature by Sadar-i-i-Riyasat*, February 9, 1959.

90. Hussain, *Kashmir in the Aftermath of Partition,* 171.

91. Government of Jammu and Kashmir, "Some Basic Statistics," 22–52.

92. Government of Jammu and Kashmir, Press Notes, December 24, 1953.

93. Kak, *Khalid-I-Kashmir*, 102.

94. "Bakshi Birthday Number."

95. Government of Jammu and Kashmir, "Some Basic Statistics."

96. Mathrani, "The Conquest of Banihal."

97. Mathrani.

98. Aziz, "Economic History of Modern Kashmir," 46.

99. Ministry of Home, Kashmir Section, "Financial Assistance by the Government of India on the Execution of the Banihal Tunnel Project," file no. F.21.(2)-K/54, National Archives of India.

100. In April 2017, Prime Minister Modi celebrated the Banihal Tunnel by fore-

grounding the "power of stones." He chastised youth who used stones as weapons against the Indian military, while praising those who used them to build roads and tunnels instead. See Bhan, "Infrastructures of Occupation," 71–72.

101. Bhan, 83.

102. Gash, *Bakshi Ghulam Mohammed*, 29.

103. A. M. Rosenthal, "Kashmir Awaits New Power Unit, To Be Inaugurated during 1955," *New York Times*, July 30, 1955.

104. Kak, *Khalid-i-Kashmir*, 104.

105. Haines, "'Concrete Progress,'" 195.

106. Kalhan, "Report on Kashmir," 9.

107. Daechsel, "Sovereignty, Governmentality and Development in Ayub's Pakistan," 154.

108. Bhan, "Infrastructures of Occupation," 72.

109. Bhan, 74.

110. Hussain, *Kashmir in the Aftermath of Partition,* 141.

111. Hussain. 141.

112. Puri, *Kashmir Affairs*.

113. Government of Jammu and Kashmir, "Some Basic Statistics."

114. Puri, *Kashmir Affairs*.

115. Puri.

116. Puri.

117. Puri.

118. More information on the falling income of the industries can be found in Puri, "The Budget of Kashmir."

119. Puri, *Kashmir Affairs*.

120. Hussain, *Kashmir in the Aftermath of Partition,* 145.

121. Hussain, 146.

122. Hussain, 150.

123. Puri, *Kashmir Affairs*.

124. Puri, *Kashmir Affairs*.

125. Puri.

126. Puri.

127. Government of Jammu and Kashmir, Press Notes, September 6, 1954, Government Press Library.

128. *Martand*, 2-3-1954, Local Press News Round-Ups, Government Press Library, Srinagar.

129. *Martand*, 2-14-1954.

130. *Khidmat*, 22-6-1954, Local Press News Round-Ups, Government Press Library, Srinagar.

131. *Sach* 16-7-1954, Local Press News Round-Ups, Government Press Library, Srinagar.

132. Dhar, *Memoirs at the Bar*, 39.

133. Gould, *Bureaucracy, Community and Influence in India*, 173.

134. Gould, 1.

135. Mir Nazir Ahmed, interview with author, Srinagar, December 15, 2013; Haksar, *The Many Faces of Kashmiri Nationalism*, 37.

136. Government of Jammu and Kashmir, Press Notes, January 1, 1955, Government Press Library,.

137. Government of Jammu and Kashmir, "Bakshi-Sadiq Correspondence, June–July 1957."

138. Government of Jammu and Kashmir, "Bakshi-Sadiq Correspondence, June–July 1957."

139. Department of Home, *Jammu and Kashmir Government Gazette*, January 30, 1965, Jammu and Kashmir State Archives.

140. The concept of de-development has been used in the context of the Gaza Strip, where socioeconomic dependence was created with Israel in order to suppress any attempt by Gazan residents to become economically autonomous. See Roy, *The Gaza Strip*.

141. Junaid, "Death and Life under Occupation," 176.

142. Bhan, "Morality and Martyrdom," 198–99.

Chapter 5

1. Department of Education, "Opening of a College at Sopore," file 1414, 16/Schools/1949, Srinagar State Archives.

2. Department of Education, "Opening of a College."

3. While the Department of Education received petitions for the opening up of educational institutions during Sheikh's rule, the numbers were significantly greater under Bakshi.

4. Department of Education, "Opening of Schools," file 1410 Nil/1955, Srinagar State Archives.

5. Department of Education, "Demands from Public for Opening of Schools, via Telegrams, Letters," file 1334 247-B/55/1955, Srinagar State Archives.

6. Department of Education, "Opening of Schools."

7. Asad, *Formations of the Secular*; Mahmood, *Religious Difference in a Secular Age*; Agrama, *Questioning Secularism*.

8. Agrama, 26.

9. Agrama, 29.

10. *New Kashmir*, 39.

11. Agrama, *Questioning Secularism*, 29.

12. Manu Bhagavan has shown how these rulers were critically involved in promoting institutions that emphasized an indigenous modernity. See Bhagavan, *Sovereign Spheres*.

13. Malik, *Kashmir: Ethnic Conflict and International Dispute*, 24–27.

14. Zutshi, *Languages of Belonging*, 173.

15. See Dar, "Role of Socio-Religious Reform Movements among Muslims in Kashmir"; Sikand, "The Emergence and Development of the Jama'at-i-Islam"; Zutshi, "Religion, State, and Community."

16. Zutshi, *Languages of Belonging*, 182. In 1910, only 15 Muslim males had completed higher education as compared to 453 Hindu males (per thousand of population) in the Jhelum Valley. By 1921, the number for Muslims had increased to only 19, and for Hindus, 508. These numbers were much less than for Muslims in other princely states or in British India. Although literacy rates for Muslims were lower there than for Hindus, the difference was not as striking as in Kashmir and also not applicable everywhere because in some provinces, the rates were comparable, if not higher.

17. Rasool and Chopra, *Education in Jammu and Kashmir*.

18. Sikand "The Emergence and Development of Jama'at-i-Islam," 732.

19. The Kashmiri Muslim elites presented a memorandum to viceroy Lord Reading on his visit to Kashmir in 1924. They demanded government jobs and better educational facilities for Muslims, in addition to rights for peasants, the abolition of forced labor, and the restoration of all mosques currently under the control of the Dogras to the Muslim community. For more on the 1924 memorandum, see Rai, *Hindu Rulers, Muslim Subjects*, 255.

20. Rao, "Ambedkar and the Politics of Minority," 130 .

21. Rao, "Ambedkar and the Politics of Minority."

22. Rai, *Hindu Rulers, Muslim Subjects*, 275.

23. Rai explores this in particular through Dogra patronage of Hindu religious sites over Muslim sites. Rai, 183–223.

24. Zutshi, *Languages of Belonging,* 193–94.

25. Rai, *Hindu Rulers, Muslim Subjects,* 14.

26. Rai, 245.

27. Rai, 244–49.

28. Ali, *Kuch to Likhye*, 29.

29. Agha Ashraf Ali details incidents of discrimination against Muslim students in his memoir, including one when almost all the Hindu students participated in a walkout when he was selected by a professor to serve as the secretary of the Historical Society in his college. See Ali, 27.

30. Ali also notes an incident when the principal of the college informed him to end a "Muslim block" of students he had organized to demand better rights.

31. Mir, *The Social Space of Language*.

32. Zutshi, *Languages of Belonging*, 268.

33. Zutshi, 273.

34. See King, *One Language, Two Scripts*.

35. Department of Education, "Resolutions Passed by the Different Sabhas, Anjumans and Societies," file 1250, C/8/17/1944, Srinagar State Archives.

36. Zutshi, *Languages of Belonging*, 269. Both Zutshi and Hussain have also argued that Abdullah was cognizant of how his position on the script controversy would impact his support from Muslims at a time when that support was already diminishing. Non-Muslims saw his response as indication that the National Conference would not respect their cultural rights. See Hussain, *Kashmir in the Aftermath of Partition*, 53.

37. Zutshi, *Languages of Belonging*, 270.

38. Zutshi, 194–95.

39. *New Kashmir*, 13.

40. *New Kashmir*, 39.

41. *New Kashmir*, 38.

42. *New Kashmir*, 21.

43. The university initially was only an examining body. Under Bakshi, it would go on to have its own departments and programs.

44. In a response to a critique of closing private and aided schools in the newspaper *Desh Sewak*, the undersecretary to the minister of education stated that this action's sole objective was to put education on "national lines" and purge educational institutions of "communalism and other sectarian ideologies which are stressed in denominational institutions." See Department of Education, "Closed Schools That Were Private and Aided," file 237, Edu-10.15/NIL, Srinagar State Archives.

45. Department of Education, "Personal File of Nazir ul Islam," file 36, Edu-A-15/6.1.36, Srinagar State Archives.

46. Department of Education, file 75, Edu/106/D/5, Srinagar State Archives; and Department of Education, "ISS Organization Relief to the Universities," File 95, Edu 82-50, Srinagar State Archives. In files from Abdullah's period, the department would largely ignore correspondence pertaining to education from the Government of India, which often frustrated Indian officials, who would have to send repeated reminders. See Department of Education, "Proceeding of the 15th Meet of the Central Advisory Board of Education," file 155, Edu-179/UG/12-8-49, Srinagar State Archives.

47. Department of Education, "Criticism of Papers," file 1684 50/Edu/1952, Srinagar State Archives.

48. Directorate of Information and Broadcasting, *Crisis in Kashmir Explained,* 10–11. *Harijan* was the term used by Gandhi for Dalits at the time.

49. Government of Jammu and Kashmir, *Jammu and Kashmir, 1953–1954, A Review of the Achievements of Bakshi Government.*

50. Taylor Sherman explains that the provision for free education, which had been a directive in the Indian constitution, appeared only in the Third Plan for the Government of India and was eventually dropped because of scarce resources after the Indochina War of 1962. See Sherman, "Education in Early Postcolonial India."

51. Department of Education, "Enhancement of Tuition Fees of Science Students," file 1651, Edu-726-US/1948, Srinagar State Archives.

52. Government of Jammu and Kashmir, *Jammu and Kashmir, 1953–1954, A Review of the Achievements of Bakshi Government.*

53. Sumanth S. Bankeshwar, *Conspiracy in Kashmir*, Society for the Defence of Democracy (Bangalore: Ananth Printing Works, 1955), 18, Accession no. 954.6042/J5, Nehru Memorial Library.

54. Department of Education, "Tour of Chief Inspectors," file 1096, 108-E/53, Srinagar State Archives.

55. Department of Education, "Improvements in Education Department," file 1692, PS-19/33/1953, Srinagar State Archives.

56. Seru, *History and Growth of Education in Jammu and Kashmir*, 176.

57. Department of Education, "Allotment of Schools for Gujjars and Bakarwals," file 1007, 53-B/53/1954, Srinagar State Archives.

58. Seru, *History and Growth of Education in Jammu and Kashmir*, 150.

59. These institutions were run by various Muslim *anjumans* or Hindu societies. For Muslims, they combined the study of Arabic and the Quran with math and sciences.

60. Rasool and Chopra, *Education in Jammu and Kashmir*, 591.

61. Sikand, "The Emergence and Development of Jama'at-i-Islam," 732–33.

62. Government of Jammu and Kashmir, *Expansion of Education.*

63. Ministry of States, Kashmir Section, "Medical Training-Reservation of Seats for Kashmir Nominees," file no. 2(17)-K/53, National Archives of India.

64. Ministry of States, Kashmir Section, "Suggestion of Shri Bakshi Sahib to Start an Engineering College Somewhere in Jammu and Kashmir," file no. F.2. (18)-K/54, National Archives of India.

65. Ministry of States, "Suggestion of Shri Bakshi Sahib."

66. Ministry of States, "Suggestion of Shri Bakshi Sahib."

67. Department of Education, "Grants of Scholarships for the Study of Foreign Languages Abroad," file 1001, Edu-278/C/54/1954, Srinagar State Archives.

68. Hassan Shah, interview with author, Srinagar, June 12, 2014.

69. Dale, "Learning to Be . . . What?," 408.

70. Sadiq, *Our Educational Policy.*

71. Sadiq, 12–13.

72. Department of Education, "Admin Reports of Amar Singh and Other Colleges," file 1828, Nil/1953, Srinagar State Archives.

73. Sadiq, *Our Educational Policy*, 14.

74. Department of Education, "Youth Welfare," file 359, Edu-490/C/54/26-3-55, Srinagar State Archives.

75. Department of Education, "Organization of Sports and Physical Activities," file 1538, 441-B/58/1959, Srinagar State Archives.

76. *Lala Rookh* (Amar Singh College magazine, Srinagar), November 1954.

77. Department of Education, "Organization of Sports and Physical Activities."

78. Department of Education, "Organization of Extra Curricular Activities in Schools," file 319, Edu-586-55/10.11.55, Srinagar State Archives.

79. *Lala Rookh,* November 1954.

80. For more on state-sponsored feminism under Naya Kashmir, see Kanjwal, "The New Kashmiri Woman."

81. Mufti, *Chilman se Chaman,* 119.

82. Mufti, 196.

83. Feldman, *Governing Gaza*, 211.

84. Bhargava, "The Distinctiveness of Indian Secularism."

85. Rai, "The Indian Constituent Assembly and the Making of Hindus and Muslims in Jammu and Kashmir," 205–6.

86. *New Kashmir*, 40.

87. I wish to thank Toru Tak for this observation.

88. For more on the debates over *kashmiriyat* see Rai, *Hindu Rulers, Muslim Subjects*; Madan, "Kashmir, Kashmiris, Kashmiriyat"; Puri, "Kashmiriyat: The Vitality of Kashmiri Identity"; Bamzai. *Bonfire of Kashmiriyat*; Hangloo, "Kashmiriyat: The Voice of the Past Misconstrued"; Tak, "The Term Kashmiriyat"; Zutshi, *Languages of Belonging*; Khan, *Parchment of Kashmir*; and Khan, *Islam, Women, and Violence in Kashmir: Between India and Pakistan.*

89. Department of Education, "Acceptance at Amar Singh College in 1955," Srinagar State Archives.

90. Mahmood, *Religious Difference in a Secular Age*, 25.

91. Zamindar, *The Long Partition and the Making of Modern South Asia.*

92. As Rai details, in 1953, Nehru proclaimed: "Kashmir is symbolic as it illustrates that we are a secular State, that Kashmir, with a large majority of Muslims, has nevertheless, of its own free will, wished to be associated with India." See Rai, "The Indian Constituent Assembly," 213.

93. Department of Education, "Communal Harmony in Educational Institu-

tions: Steps to Be Taken to Promote It," file 102, Edu-336/50.1.5.50, Srinagar State Archives.

94. Department of Education, "Communal Harmony in Educational Institutions: Steps to Be Taken to Promote It."

95. Department of Education, file 995, H-20-8-54, Srinagar State Archives.

96. Department of Education, "Communal Harmony in Educational Institutions: Suggestions from Various People," file 1961, 129-ExA/1954, Srinagar State Archives.

97. Department of Education, "Communal Harmony in Educational Institutions: Suggestions from Various People."

98. Department of Education, "Communal Harmony in Educational Institutions: Suggestions from Various People."

99. Department of Education, "Communal Harmony in Educational Institutions: Suggestions from Various People."

100. Department of Education, "Communal Harmony in Educational Institutions: Suggestions from Various People."

101. Department of Education, "Textbook Advisory Board, Arabic and Muslim Religious Instructions and General Correspondence Thereon," file 771, 77/1949, Srinagar State Archives.

102. Department of Education, "Textbook Advisory Board."

103. Department of Education, "Textbook Advisory Board."

104. Department of Education, "Textbook Advisory Board."

105. In his book, Khalid Bashir details the ways in which the life and histories of other Muslim rulers, including Sultan Sikander, have been deliberately misinterpreted. This is similar to what has happened with the Mughal emperor Aurangzeb. In contrast, Sultan Zain-ul-Abideen is a figure akin to the Mughal emperor Akbar, re-historicized as being the ideal secular Muslim by proponents of *kashmiriyat*. See Bashir, *Kashmir: Exposing the Myth behind the Narrative*.

106. Department of Education, "Improvement and Changes of Textbooks," file 1017, 200/T/1953, Srinagar State Archives.

107. Department of Education, "Improvement and Changes of Textbooks."

108. Rai, *Hindu Rulers, Muslim Subjects*, 192–224.

109. Department of Education, "Research and Publication Department Correspondence," file 72, Edu-524-D/30.6.51, Srinagar State Archives.

110. Department of Education, "Research and Publication Department Correspondence."

111. Department of Education, "Compilation of a Publication for 3 Years Period of Present Popular Government Ending October 1950," file 91, A/836/50, Srinagar State Archives.

112. Department of Education, "Compilation of a Publication for 3 Years Period."

113. Hussain, *Kashmir in the Aftermath of Partition*, 152.

114. Hussain, 152–53.

115. Majid, "Confronting the Indian State."

116. Majid.

117. Saaduddin Tarabali, "Hakumat Kashmir Ki Taleemi Palicy Ka Jaiza," and "Hamari Taleemi Palicy," *Azaan*, June and October 1955. I would like to thank Abdul Haseeb Mir for providing me with these two articles.

118. Tarabali, "Hakumat Kashmir."

119. Tarabali, "Hamari Taleemi Palicy."

120. Sikand, "The Emergence and Development of Jama'at-i-Islam," 733–34.

121. Department of Education, file 1463, 685-A/51/1958, Srinagar State Archives.

122. Alam, *Jammu and Kashmir 1949-1964*, 152.

123. Department of Education, "Propagation of Development of Hindi in the States," file no. 192, 442-C-54/27.1.54, Srinagar State Archives.

124. Department of Education, "Orders Making Obligatory for Teachers to Learn Both Hindi and Urdu Scripts." file 1172, 958-C/55/1955, Srinagar State Archives.

125. Department of Education, "Scheme of Printing of Text Books by Well Acquainted Technical Hands," file 1257, 404/T/1956, Srinagar State Archives; Department of Education, "Charts Showing Scripts of Languages Shown in the 8th Scheduled to the Constitution Language Commission in Bombay," file 918, Edu-B-836-55/1955, Srinagar State Archives.

126. Mabry, "Speaking to the Nation," in *Nationalism, Language and Muslim Exceptionalism*, 150.

127. Department of Education, ""Propagation of Development of Hindi in the States," file 192, 442-C-54, Srinagar States Archives.

128. Department of Education, "Development of Original Language," file 1261, 410/5/1956, Srinagar State Archives. Ananya Kabir also argues that Kashmiri remained popular orally, in ways that escape the prevalent "colonialist binaries between the written and oral domains." See Kabir, "Koshur Today," 182.

129. Warikoo, "Language and Politics in Jammu and Kashmir."

130. Zutshi, *Languages of Belonging*, 319.

131. Kabir, "Koshur Today," 187–88.

132. Kabir, 187–88.

133. Pushp, "Kashmiri and the Linguistic Predicament of the State."

134. Kabir, "Koshur Today," 187–88.

135. Department of Education, "Report of the Kashmiri Script Writing Committee," file 1642, Edu-5/1952, Srinagar State Archives.

136. For an article on the status of Kashmiri as a majority-minority language, Makhan Tickoo interviewed a number of educationists and individuals and asked them about their perceptions of the Kashmiri language. He found that many of them have a poor opinion of the language, and even question if it is a language, given it does not have "grammar rules" and that it borrows heavily from the vocabulary of other languages. See Tickoo, "When is a Language Worth Teaching?"

137. Sadiq, *Our Educational Policy*, 9.

138. Department of Education, "Scheme of Printing of Text Books by Well Acquainted Technical Hands," file 1257, 404/T/1956, Srinagar State Archives.

139. For a more contemporary study of a "private conflict between different linguistic loyalties and loves" in Kashmir and the estrangement of Kashmiris from their native language, see Ananya Kabir, "A Language of One's Own?," 144. Kabir argues that English and Urdu compete with Kashmiri in terms of "affect and prestige" and are "symptomatic of deeper levels of psychic splintering."

140. Datla, *The Language of Secular Islam.*

141. For more on the emergence of Urdu in Kashmir, see Bhat, "Emergence of the Urdu Discourses in Kashmir."

142. Department of Education, "Language Syllabi," Srinagar State Archives.

143. Department of Education, "Language Syllabi."

144. Thank you to Abir Bazaz for pointing me toward this plausible explanation.

145. Government of Jammu and Kashmir. *Report of the Jammu and Kashmir Commission of Inquiry*, 74.

146. In a number of reports for scholarships, "Harijans" in Jammu, Muslims in Kashmir, and Buddhists in Ladakh were deemed "backward."

147. In direct contrast to what was happening in Kashmir, Taylor Sherman notes that in the case of Hyderabad, Muslims were increasingly being erased from government positions. See Sherman, *Muslim Belonging in Secular India.*

148. Department of Education, "College Admissions," 1954, file 1006, Edu 249-D/54/1954, Srinagar State Archives.

149. Department of Education, "College Admissions."

150. Department of Education, "College Admissions."

151. Department of Education, "College Admissions."

152. There is also some reference made in the files held at the Srinagar State Archives about discussions with the Ministry of Home of the Government of India on the admissions issue. However, because access to some Indian government files on Kashmir is restricted, it is difficult to ascertain what the position of the Government of India was on this issue.

153. Department of Education, "College Admissions."

154. The land reforms under Sheikh Abdullah's government also raised substan-

tial criticism from the Hindu community, because a majority of the landlords who lost land were Hindu and the tillers who gained the land were Muslim. See Rai, *Hindu Rulers, Muslim Subjects*, 283.

155. Ali, *Kuch to Likhye,* 108.

156. Ali, 112.

157. Ali, 117.

158. Ali, 125.

159. Koul, *Kashmir Past and Present.*

160. Koul.

161. Supreme Court of India, Triloki Nath and Anr vs State of Jammu and Kashmir and Ors (April 1968).

162. Government of Jammu and Kashmir, "Commission of Inquiry," 72.

163. Bazaz, *Ahead of His Times, Prem Nath Bazaz.*

164. In the mid-1960s, after Bakshi stepped down from power and the Holy Relic incident that occurred soon after, schools in Kashmir erupted in protest against Indian rule, undermining the government's attempts to secure them as a depoliticized space. See Kanth, "Women in Resistance," 43; Pandit, "Schools of Resistance."

165. *Report of the Commission of Inquiry on Communal Disturbances*, file IS-212-A/67, Srinagar State Archives.

Chapter 6

1. Government of Jammu and Kashmir, "Publication on the Occasion of the Kashmir Festival," 2–3, Srinagar State Archives.

2. Government of Jammu and Kashmir, "Publication on the Occasion of the Kashmir Festival,"3.

3. *Bhand pather* is a form of folk theater, which traces its roots to the pre-Mughal period in Kashmir. The *bhands* were troupes of performers that travelled from village to village. Their performances focused on social issues, usually with a satirical bent. *Chakri* is a form of folk music that uses musical instruments like the harmonium, the rubab, the sarangi, and the nout. See Bhat, "Loss of a Syncretic Theatrical Form."

4. Maqbool, "A Cultural Psy-Op."

5. "Srinagar Diary," *Kashmir Today* 1, no. 1 (September 1956): 1.

6. Government of Jammu and Kashmir, "Message by G. M. Bakshi," Srinagar State Archives.

7. Government of Jammu and Kashmir, "Message by G. M. Bakshi."

8. Government of Jammu and Kashmir, "Message by G. M. Bakshi."

9. "Srinagar Diary," 1.

10. For more on Cold War cultural politics, see Saunders, *The Cultural Cold War*; Scott-Smith, *The Politics of Apolitical Culture.*

11.See Toor, *The State of Islam*, 89; Sutoris, *Visions of Development.*

12. Raina, *A History of Kashmiri Literature*, 36–65.

13. G. R. Malik, "A Brief Survey of Kashmiri Literature."

14. Whitehead, "The People's Militia."

15. For a background on the Progressive Writers Association in the subcontinent, see Toor, *The State of Islam*, 52; Ahmed, *Literature and Politics in the Age of Nationalism*; Jalil, *Liking Progress, Loving Change.*

16. Raina, *A History of Kashmiri Literature*, 111.

17. Giyas-Ud-din, *Jammu and Kashmir State and Society*, 55.

18. This position was in contrast to M. N. Roy's more radical stance. Roy was the founder of the Communist Party of India and believed that Indian communists should denounce the Indian National Congress and Gandhi as bourgeois.

19. As Kamran Asdar Ali details, this official CPI line evolved from essential agreement in the 1930s with the idea that India was one nation to a policy of national self-determination for each national and cultural group within India in the early 1940s and then to the one-nation idea in 1946. While the Partition plan was officially approved and a separate Communist Party of Pakistan created, the formal party line was to see Pakistan a result of feudal interests. See Ali, *Surkh Salam.*

20. Haksar, *The Many Faces of Kashmiri Nationalism*, 17.

21. *New Kashmir*, 40.

22. *New Kashmir*, 40.

23. Raina, *A History of Kashmiri Literature*, 111.

24. Raina, 112.

25. The Indian People's Theater Association began in Bangalore in 1941. The association wrote and performed radical political theater, especially in rural areas, about Japanese aggression, anti-fascism, the Bengal famine, landlordism, and the exploitation of workers. See Waltz, "The Indian People's Theatre Association."

26. K. A. Abbas made the film, *Kashmir Toofan Mei* (Storm over Kashmir) in 1949, while Balraj Sahni would make Kashmir the subject of a number of his later films.

27. Kachru, "Dina Nath Nadim."

28. Prior to *Kwang Posh*, there was a Kashmiri language newspaper, *Gaash*, run by Ibn-i-Mahjoor (the son of Mahjoor) in 1940, although it had limited circulation. A number of college magazines, including SP College's magazine *Pratap* and *Lala Rookh* of Amar Singh College, also published fiction and prose in Kashmiri.

29. Raina, *A History of Kashmiri Literature*, 113. Some, like Parimoo, have argued that Sadiq and other prominent leftists began the Cultural Front because they did not enjoy much public support. See Parimoo, *Kashmiriyat at Crossroads*, 217.

30. Raina, *A History of Kashmiri Literature*, 113.

31. Raina, 117.

32. Raina, 117.

33. Kachru, "Dina Nath Nadim."

34. Nadim's Kashmiri short story "Jawabi Card" was also a tribute to the Kashmiri men and women who fought for the National Conference during 1947.

35. Razdan, "*Aazaadee* by Mahjoor."

36. Razdan.

37. Zutshi, *Languages of Belonging*, 2.

38. Giyas-Ud-din, *Jammu and Kashmir State and Society*, 62.

39. Bakshi Rashid, Bakshi Ghulam Mohammed's brother, founded the Cultural Conference. Hasrat Ghadda, interview with author, Srinagar, August 27, 2014.

40. Giyas-Ud-din, *Jammu and Kashmir State and Society*, 66.

41. Hasrat Ghadda, interview with author, August 27, 2014. Ghadda had been a member of the Cultural Congress and later went on to serve in the Cultural Academy. In my interview, he said that the progressive movement in Kashmir lost its fervor as many of its stalwarts were accommodated into the state bureaucracy.

42. Raina, *A History of Kashmiri Literature*, 134.

43. Department of Information, "Advance to Mr. Amin Kamil against Rawa Rupi and Habba Khatoon: 150 Rupees Given," year 1955, basta 101-139, file 106, Srinagar State Archives.

44. Department of Information, "Advance to Mr. Amin Kamil."

45. Tak, "Bakshi Number," 35.

46. Maqbool, "A Cultural Psy-Op." In an issue of *Indian Literature*, J. L. Kaul writes that there were also plays that were written and performed depicting people's struggles against the floods. One was entitled *Kun Kath*. See Kaul, "Kashmiri Literature."

47. Department of Information, "Payment of Royalty for the Contributions to Department Journals—*Kashmir Today*, *Tameer*, and *Yojna*," year 1956, basta 854-856, file 854, Srinagar State Archives.

48. Department of Information, "Milchar—Staged on 27th Jan 1958—At Nedous Hall," year 1958, basta 299-304, file 304, Srinagar State Archives.

49. These journals would issue a "Bakshi number," containing a series of hagiographic articles and poems about Bakshi.

50. Shad, "A Week of Colors," *Tameer* 5, no. 25 (July 1960): 15. I would like to thank Urwa Sahar for assistance in the translation.

51. Ali, "The Era of Khalid-i-Kashmir" *Tameer* 5, no. 25 (July 1960): 127.

52. Department of Information, "Supply of Information to the State Dept's Agencies and Newspapers Outside the State," year 1958, basta 299-304, file 302, Srinagar State Archives.

53. Raina, *A History of Kashmiri Literature*, 136.

54. Raina, 136.

55. Giyas-Ud-din, *Jammu and Kashmir State and Society*, xviii.

56. While a vast number of communists and leftists affiliated themselves with the Kashmiri state, not all did so. Nandita Haksar tells the story of Sampat Prakash, a Kashmiri Pandit trade union leader, who struggled with his communist ideology as well as his Kashmiri nationalism. He grew disillusioned with the Soviet Union for supporting India's stand and was disturbed by the arrest of Sheikh Abdullah. See Haksar, *The Many Faces of Kashmiri Nationalism*, 35.

57. For more on the political subjectivities of Kashmiri bureaucrats, including reasons why they joined the state bureaucracy, see Kanjwal, "Reflections on the Post-Partition Period."

58. Kanjwal, 41.

59. Duschinski et al., *Resisting Occupation in Kashmir*, 14–15.

60. Department of Information, "Approval Gulrez," file 1825, B-8/1952, Srinagar State Archives.

61. Sufiana music was based on Persian spiritual poetry and used instruments like the santoor, sitar, tabla, and saz.

62. Department of Information, Private Secretariat, Government of Jammu and Kashmir, "Government Order No. 1.D.51 of 1957," November 27, 1957, Srinagar State Archives.

63. Department of Information, "Establishment of a Publishing Agency as Government Concern—Lalla Rookh Publications," July 24, 1953, memorandum for submission to the Cabinet, NO. I7B/3068/53, Srinagar State Archives.

64. Department of Information, "Establishment of a Publishing Agency."

65. Department of Information, "Establishment of a Publishing Agency."

66. Department of Information, "Statement Showing the Position of Lalla Rookh Publications," Srinagar State Archives.

67. Department of Information, "Plan of Publication," Srinagar State Archives.

68. Department of Information, "Plan of Publication."

69. Department of Information, "Correspondence with Ibn-i-Mahjoor—Lalla Rookh Publications," year 1955, basta 101-139, file 101- 67/56, Srinagar State Archives; Department of Information, "Compilation of Anthology of Kashmiri Prose," year 1955, basta 101-139, file 118, Srinagar State Archives.

70. Department of Information, "Correspondence with Ibn-i-Mahjoor."

71. Department of Information, "Panel for the Anthology of Kashmiri Verse," year 1955, basta 101-139, file 117, Srinagar State Archives.

72. Department of Information, "Panel for the Anthology of Kashmiri Verse."

73. Department of Information, "Letter to Mr. Jalali," year 1955, basta 101-139, Srinagar State Archives.

74. Department of Information, "Letter to Mr. Jalali."

75. Department of Information, "Winding Up of Lalla Rookh Publications," year 1958, basta 69-80, file 72, Srinagar State Archives.

76. G. M. Sadiq, D. P. Dhar, and Mir Qasim, who were all members of Bakshi's administration, broke off and created a political opposition under the Democratic National Conference, which was opposed to the high-handedness and corruption occurring in the state. Members of the cultural intelligentsia, especially those with communist sympathies that were loyal to G. M. Sadiq, joined the DNC. However, in 1960, Bakshi managed to bring the DNC within his fold. See Puri, "Jammu and Kashmir," 231.

77. Department of Information, Government of Jammu and Kashmir, "July 9, 1958" Press Notes, 1958, Srinagar State Archives.

78. Bhat, *Loss of a Syncretic Theatrical Form*, 41.

79. Bhat, 41.

80. Mushtaq, "1990 Was a Wakeup Call for Kashmir Theater."

81. Bhat, *Loss of a Syncretic Theatrical Form*, 52.

82. Bhat, 52.

83. Rushdie, *Shalimar the Clown*.

84. Some of these writers are Mirza Ghulam Arif Beg, Amin Kamil, Ali Mohammed Lone, Bansi Nirdosh, Rehman Rahi, Mohammed Hajini, Ghulam Nabi Gowhar, Dina Nath Nadim, and Sofi Ghulam Mohammad.

85. See Amin Kamil, "The Cockfight," in *Contemporary Kashmiri Short Stories*, 15–25. Also see Bansi Nirdosh, "To Slavery Born," in *The Stranger Beside Me*, 63–71; Sofi Ghulam Mohammad, "The Paper Tigers," in *Kath: Stories from Kashmir*, 124–32. All three stories revolve around the increasing greed and desire for material things and how poorly people were willing to treat each other for more money.

86. In the poem "Rubaaiyat," Mirza Ghulam Arif Beg writes: "Strange was the division made by God / of the gains of political revolution / bullets to the people / to the leaders wealth; these got pain and sickness / those affluence and wine." See Beg, "Rubaaiyat," in *Mahjoor and After*, ed. Trilokinath Raina, 49; Taj Begum Renzu, "The Beggars at the Durgah," in Mattoo, *Kath*, 132–39.

87. See Ali Mohammad Lone, "The Strange Mohalla," in Mattoo, *Kath*, 72–84.

88. Lone, 77.

89. Lone, 78.

90. Lone, 82.

91. Lone, 83.

92. Rehman Rahi, "Maefi Nama," in *Siyah Roodi Jaryan Manz*, 20–24. I would like

to thank Raashid Maqbool for helping me with the translation of this Kashmiri poem.

93. "Akhtar Mohiuddin and Ali Mohammad Lone."

94. Department of Information, "*Doad wa Dag*: Correspondence between Akhtar Mohiuddin and Department of Information," Srinagar State Archives.

95. For a more thorough analysis of Mohiuddin and his work, including his critique of Indian nationalist and Brahmanical narratives of Kashmir's "origin story," see Junaid, "To Be Kashmiri in the Present."

96. Junaid, 155.

97. Junaid, 155.

98. Junaid, 172.

99. Mohiuddin, "Does Anyone Have the Courage?" in Mattoo, *Kath,* 68–72.

100. Junaid, "To Be Kashmiri in the Present," 173.

101. "The Game of the Snowballs," in Mohiuddin, *Looking into the Heart of Life*, 124.

102. Mohiuddin, "Election," in *Short Stories of Akhtar Mohiuddin*, 74.

103. Raina, *History of Kashmiri Literature*, 209.

104. Mohiuddin, 30.

105. Mohiuddin, 35.

106. Mohiuddin, 59.

107. Mohiuddin, 60.

108. Mohiuddin, 73.

109. Junaid, "To Be Kashmiri in the Present," 172.

110. Handoo, "The Prophesy."

Chapter 7

1. Amin Kamil was a poet, short story writer, and novelist from South Kashmir.

2. Kamil, "The Shadow and the Substance," in *Kath: Stories from Kashmir*, 37–43.

3. Kamil, 38.

4. Kamil, 38.

5. Kamil, 42.

6. Berda, "Managing Dangerous Populations."

7. Reynolds, *Empire, Emergency, and International Law*, 11.

8. Feldman, *Police Encounters*, 8.

9. Prem Nath Bazaz, *Truth about Kashmir*, 2.

10. Bayley, *The Police and Political Development in India*, 67–69.

11. *New Kashmir*, 13.

12. *New Kashmir*, 13.

13. Davenport, "The Weight of the Past."

14. Ishaq, *Nida-i-Haq*, 192.

15. Whitehead, "The People's Militia," 155–58.

16. Handoo, "Ikhwanis of the Yore?"

17. Qasim, *My Life and Times*, 82.

18. Haksar, *The Many Faces of Kashmiri Nationalism*, 38.

19. Ishaq, *Nida-i-Haq*, 192.

20. Handoo, "Ikhwanis of the Yore?"

21. Mullik, *My Years with Nehru: Kashmir*, 56.

22. Feldman, *Police Encounters*, 16.

23. Department of Home Affairs, "Minutes of Civil Military Intelligence Liaison, Committee Meeting from 20th Feb 1954," file 150, IS-32-A/54, Srinagar State Archives.

24. Department of Home Affairs, "Repatriation from Pakistan," file IS-125/49, Srinagar State Archives.

25. Qasim, *My Life and Times*, 77.

26. Bose, *Kashmir: Roots of Conflict, Paths to Peace*, 72.

27. Duschinski and Bhan, "Introduction: Law Containing Violence," 1.

28. Duschinski and Bhan, 1.

29. Duschinski and Bhan, 1.

30. Duschinski and Ghosh detail the use of the J&K Public Security Act during the National Conference–led Quit Kashmir movement against the Dogras in 1946. It "was the first in a series of legislations allowing for preventive detention and other far-reaching restrictions on public political activity on grounds of public order. It provided for indefinite preventive detention, proscription of newspapers and bans on strikes, public gatherings . . . in the interest of the security of the State, public order, and general public." See Duschinski and Ghosh, "Constituting the Occupation," 6.

31. Bose, *Kashmir: Roots of Conflict, Paths to Peace*, 69.

32. Bazaz, *The Shape of Things in Kashmir*, 13.

33. Duschinski and Ghosh, "Constituting the Occupation," 16.

34. Duschinski and Ghosh, 16. See also Abdullah, *The Blazing Chinar*, 462.

35. *The Kashmir Conspiracy Case*, Report 7: Mohiuddin Shawl (Srinagar, Legal Defense Committee, 1964), 58.

36. Lockwood, "Sheikh Abdullah and the Politics of Kashmir," 384. Lockwood argues that the enforcement of the Defense of India Rules as a result of the Indo-chinese War caused a huge debate in the Indian Parliament surrounding the state of emergency. Critics of the law complained that it would undermine India's repu-

tation as a free and democratic country, while those who were in favor of continuing the emergency regulations and Abdullah's detention (which included Hindu nationalist parties) argued that they were needed to ensure the country's sovereignty. After the rules expired in January 1968, the Indian Parliament passed the Unlawful Activities Prevention Act on December 20, 1967. Lockwood suggests that the act was partly passed in order to pacify those who supported the state of emergency. Lockwood explains, "This bill has given the authorities sweeping powers to imprison anyone found guilty of questioning India's sovereignty over territory to which it has established official claim" (385). This meant that Kashmiri opposition leaders who contested the accession could be held under this law.

37. Qari Saifuddin and Saad Uddin, two leaders of the Jamaat-i-Islami, were asked to leave their teaching positions because of their criticism of the state in their speeches. They resigned from the government school and focused on developing more Jamaat schools. See Saifuddin, *Vadi-i-Purkhar*, 51.

38. Ministry of States, "Preventative Detention," Kashmir file no. 11 (6) K, National Archives of India.

39. Ministry of States, "Preventative Detention."

40. Ministry of States, "Preventative Detention."

41. Ministry of States, "Preventative Detention."

42. Ministry of States, "Preventative Detention."

43. Ministry of States, "Preventative Detention."

44. Balasubramaniam, "Indefinite Detention," 119.

45. Dushchinski and Ghosh, "Constituting the Occupation," 2.

46. Duschinski and Ghosh, 8-10.

47. Ishaq, *Nida-i-Haq*, 266.

48. Saifuddin, *Vadi-i-Purkhar*, 28.

49. Bazaz, *A Last Chance for India in Kashmir*, 3. Bazaz, a Kashmiri Pandit, was a former National Conference leader who worked with Sheikh Abdullah and was seen as one of the primary influences on Abdullah for converting the Muslim Conference to the National Conference. After seeing the increasing repression of the NC leadership and its close alliance with the Indian National Congress, he left the party and began the Kisan Mazdoor Conference, which was a pro-plebiscite party, with leanings toward Pakistan. Under the NC leadership, he was exiled to Delhi for his political activities, and a number of party members were arrested. Abdul Salam Yatu, who was the president of the party, was exiled to Pakistan. From Delhi, Bazaz published a series of pamphlets on the political intrigues in the state, all the while calling for a plebiscite. In 1964, he visited Kashmir and wrote *A Last Chance* about the Bakshi period.

50. Bazaz, 10.

51. Anwar Ashai, interview with author, Srinagar, February 21, 2014.

52. Under Abdullah's government, those contesting the accession were the Muslim Conference, the Kisan Mazdoor Conference, and the Socialist Party. A majority of the Muslim Conference leaders had been exiled to Pakistan, many of them leading the Azad Kashmir government, while Prem Nath Bazaz of the Kisan Mazdoor Conference was exiled to Delhi. See Sathu, *Beyond the Iron Curtain in Kashmir*.

53. Bazaz, *Rise of Communism in Kashmir*, 7.

54. Lockwood, "Sheikh Abdullah and the Politics of Kashmir," 387; Department of Home, DIG CID Daily Diaries from August 8, 1961," file IS-32(G)/59, Srinagar State Archives.

55. Gockhami, *Kashmir: Politics and Plebiscite,* 112.

56. Gockhami, 113.

57. Pirzada Hafizullah Makhdoomi, interview with author, Srinagar, November 17, 2013.

58. For more on Kashmiri Muslim's views of Pakistan at this time, see Kanjwal, "Reflections on the Post-Partition Period."

59. Ishaq, *Nida-i-Haq,* 248.

60. Abdullah, *The Blazing Chinar*, 324. Some analysts claim that Bakshi Ghulam Muhammed himself instigated Karra to begin the Political Conference, so that Abdullah could be undermined in the eyes of New Delhi and Bakshi would be able to gain more power in Kashmir. See Gockhami, *Kashmir: Politics and Plebiscite*, 35.

61. Pirzada Hafizullah Makhdoomi, interview with author, November 17, 2013.

62. Ishaq, *Nida-i-Haq,* 248.

63. Ali and Limaye, "Report on Kashmir," 10.

64. Bhan, "How Rughonath Vaishnavi's Life."

65. Bhan, 6.

66. Bhan, 9.

67. The contents of this letter to the president were narrated by Vaishnavi in a submission addressed to the 1965 People's Convention, organized by the Plebiscite Front to bring together a diverse set of stakeholders and come to an understanding of the resolution of the Kashmir issue. See All Jammu and Kashmir Plebiscite Front, *The People's Voice in J&K State*.

68. All Jammu and Kashmir Plebiscite Front.

69. Gockhami, *Kashmir: Politics and Plebiscite*, 118.

70. Gockhami, 116.

71. Bhat, "A Different Politician."

72. Department of Home, "CID Diaries," file IS-45-D/64, Srinagar State Archives.

73. Bose, *Kashmir: Roots of Conflict, Paths to Peace*, 73.

74. Gockhami, *Kashmir: Politics and Plebiscite*, 59.

75. Bhat, "The Plebiscite Front," 171.

76. Ishaq, *Nida-i-Haq,* 261.

77. Ishaq, 267.

78. Pirzada Hafizullah Makhdoomi, interview with author, November 17, 2013.

79. Bhat, "The Plebiscite Front."

80. Department of Home Affairs, "Fortnightly Report of District Magistrate for the Period Ending 15th July 1962," file 13-134-A/62, Srinagar State Archives.

81. Bhat, "The Plebiscite Front," 175.

82. Munshi Ghulam Hassan, interview with author, February 26, 2014, Srinagar; Bhat, "The Plebiscite Front," 177.

83. Bhat, *Kashmir in Flames.*

84. Bhat, "The Plebiscite Front," 177.

85. Department of Home, "DIG CID Daily Diaries from August 8, 1961," file IS-32(G)/59, Srinagar State Archives.

86. Department of Home, "Fortnightly Reports Ending 15th June 1962," file IS-7-A/62, Srinagar State Archives.

87. Singh, *Heir Apparent: An Autobiography.*

88. Department of Home, "Office of District Magistrate Anantnag, Fortnightly Confidential Diary of Anantnag District Ending 31 Dec. 1961," file IS-4-A/62, Srinagar State Archives.

89. Bhat, "The Plebiscite Front," 179. Bhat notes that the front did not attempt to gain the favor of communist or communist-allied countries given the USSR's shift toward India in this period.

90. Department of Home, "Fortnightly Reports Ending 15th June 1962," file IS-7-A/62, Srinagar State Archives.

91. Ghulam Mohiuddin Shah, Ex. Sec. JK Plebiscite Front, "Aching Kashmir Demands," written statement U/S 342 Cr. P.C. Report no. 2, Serial 10, All Jammu and Kashmir Legal Defense Committee (Shaheedgunj, Srinagar, 1961).

92. Shah, "Aching Kashmir Demands."

93. Bhat, "The Plebiscite Front," 191.

94. The Kashmir Conspiracy Case, Report 7: GM Shah (Srinagar, Legal Defense Committee, 1964), 15.

95. Shah, "Aching Kashmir Demands," 15.

96. The Kashmir Conspiracy Case, Report 7, Series 9: Mohiuddin Shawl (Srinagar: Legal Defense Committee, n.d.), 14

97. Shah, "Aching Kashmir Demands, 15; Abdul Ahad Lone (publicity secretary, Jammu and Kashmir Plebiscite Front), "Kashmir Problem: True Side of Picture," rejoinder of Plebiscite Front president to Nehru's observations on Kashmir made during his Srinagar speech on July 19, 1961 (Srinagar: Legal Defense Committee). I

would like to thank Shabir Mujahid for allowing me access to some of the archival sources on the Plebiscite Front.

98. The Kashmir Conspiracy Case, Report 1: Kh Mubarak Shah (Delhi: Raj Art Press, Deputy Ganj, n.d.), 82, Accession no. 954.6042 J9, Nehru Memorial Library.

99. The Kashmir Conspiracy Case, Report 7, Series 3: Khwaja Ali Shah's written statement (Srinagar: Legal Defense Committee, n.d.), 14

100. "Who Is Who in Kashmir Conspiracy Case?," Report no. vii (Srinagar: Legal Defense Committee, n.d.).

101. Gockhami, *Kashmir: Politics and Plebiscite,* 70.

102. Gockhami, 187.

103. Department of Home, "DIG CID Daily Diaries from August 8, 1961," file IS-32(G)/59, Srinagar State Archives.

104. Department of Home, "Annual Administration Report of the Call Dept for the Year 1959–1960," file 15-226-A/60, Srinagar State Archives.

105. Department of Home, "Fortnightly Reports of D. Magistrates Pertaining to Fortnight Ending 15.8.1962," file IS.169 A/62, Srinagar State Archives.

106. Feldman, *Police Encounters,* 18

107. Feldman, 18.

108. Department of Home, "Fortnightly Reports of D. Magistrates Pertaining to Fortnight Ending 15.8.1962."

109. "Kashmir's 'Lion' on Trial," *New York Times*, October 26, 1958.

110. Lockwood, "Sheikh Abdullah and the Politics of Kashmir," 384.

111. Qasim, *My Life and Times,* 72.

112. Deshbandhu, *61 Constitution House.*

113. Ishaq, *Nida-i-Haq*, 270.

114. Sarabhai, *Call for Impartial Inquiry*, 13.

115. Sarabhai, 14.

116. In *My Years with Nehru: Kashmir,* B. N. Mullik writes, "When Sheikh Sahib was released, we knew he would engage in activities that would provide us with further evidence against him. That is why we were in no hurry to file a suit against him."

117. Sarabhai, *Call for Impartial Enquiry*, 31.

118. Abdullah, *The Blazing Chinar*, 456–57.

119. Abdullah, 457.

120. Abdullah, 457.

121. Sarabhai, *Call for Impartial Enquiry*, 34.

122. Pirzada Hafizullah Makhdoomi, interview with author, November 17, 2013.

123. Sarabhai, *Call for Impartial Inquiry.*

124. Qasim, *My Life and Times,* 87.

125. Abdullah, *The Blazing Chinar*, 463–64.

126. Mullik, *My Years with Nehru: Kashmir*, 51. For the official charge, see *Kashmir Conspiracy Case,* Report 1 (Delhi: Raj Art Press Deputy Ganj n.d.).

127. *Kashmir Conspiracy Case*, Report 1 (Delhi: Raj Art Press Deputy Ganj, n.d.), iii.

128. Abdullah, *The Blazing Chinar,* 466.

129. *Kashmir Conspiracy Case,* Report 1, 10.

130. Shah, "Aching Kashmir Demands."

131. Lone, "Kashmir Problem: True Side of Picture"; M. A. Beg, "Kashmir Case for Plebiscite," Report No. IX (ii), Topic No. 1 (Srinagar: Legal Defense Committee, n.d.). Beg quotes V. P. Menon saying in the UN that India will not dishonor international obligations in 1957.

132. Lone, 4.

133. Lone, 15.

134. *Kashmir Conspiracy Case*, Report 1, 10.

135. *Kashmir Conspiracy Case*, Report 1, 10.

136. *Kashmir Conspiracy Case*, Report 1, 14.

137. *Kashmir Conspiracy Case*, Report 1, 22.

138. *Kashmir Conspiracy Case*, Report 3 (Srinagar: Legal Defense Committee, 1964).

139. Pirzada Hafizullah Makhdoomi, interview with author, November 17, 2013.

140. Ishaq, *Nida-i-Haq,* 272.

141. Bhat, "The Plebiscite Front."

142. Shah, "Aching Kashmir Demands" 13.

143. Shah, 13.

144. Widmalm, *Kashmir in Comparative Perspective*, 40.

145. Bazaz, *The Shape of Things in Kashmir.*

146. See Gauhar, *Hazratbal.*

147. Department of Home, "Bahudin S/o Ghulam Mohmad R/o Mira Masjid Sgr." file CK/DIR/65-139, Srinagar State Archives.

148. Department of Home, "CID Diaries," file IS-45-D/64, Srinagar State Archives.

149. Mohammed, *Srinagar: My City, My Dreamland,* 15.

150. The Jamaat-i-Islami's primary role under Bakshi had been to establish a number of schools. It did not directly intervene in the political realm. Only in the late sixties under Sadiq's liberalization policies did it begin to consider a greater political role. See Gockhami, *Kashmir: Politics and Plebiscite*, 152–54.

151. Tak, "Bakshi Number."

152. Asma, "Lost Prime Minister."

153. *Kashmir Conspiracy Case,* Report 7, 67.

154. *Kashmir Conspiracy Case,* Report 7, 101.

155. Qasim, *My Life and Times.*
156. Ishaq, *Nida-i-Haq*, 19.
157. Ishaq, *Nida-i-Haq*, 307.
158. Ishaq, 99; Gockhami, *Kashmir: Politics and Plebiscite,* 250–51.
159. Gockhami, *Kashmir: Politics and Plebiscite*, 240–41.
160. Ishaq, 362.

Conclusion

1. Pirzada Hafizullah Makhdoomi, interview with author, Srinagar, November 17, 2013.
2. Kanjwal, "Reflections on the Post-Partition Period," 56.
3. Fazili, "Police Subjectivity in Occupied Kashmir."
4. Chakravarti et al., "Hindutva's Threat to Academic Freedom."

BIBLIOGRAPHY

Archives and Libraries

Amar Singh College Library, Srinagar, Kashmir
- *Lala Rookh Magazine*

Government Press Library, Srinagar, Kashmir
- Local Press News Round-Ups
- Press Notes

Indian Council of World Affairs (Sapru House), New Delhi, India
- "Kashmir Newspaper Clippings"

Iqbal Library, Kashmir University, Srinagar, Kashmir

Jammu and Kashmir State Archives, Srinagar, Kashmir
- Department of Education
- Department of Information and Broadcasting
- Home Department

National Archives of India, New Delhi, India
- Ministry of External Affairs, Kashmir Branch
- Ministry of Food and Agriculture
- Ministry of Home Affairs, Kashmir Section
- Ministry of States, Kashmir Section

Nehru Memorial Museum and Library, New Delhi, India

Press Information Bureau Library, Srinagar, Kashmir
- *Kashmir Today*
- *Tameer*

Research and Publications Department, Srinagar, Kashmir

Recorded Interviews

Ahmed, Mir Nazir. Srinagar, December 15, 2013.

Ashai, Anwar. Srinagar, February 21, 2014.

Ashai, Asmat. Ellicott City, Maryland, December 2, 2014.

Bakshi, Nazir. Srinagar, November 18, 2013.

Chishti, M. A. Srinagar, February 27, 2014.

Fazili, Ehsan, Srinagar, August 18, 2014.

Fazili, Mushtaq. Srinagar, August 24, 2014.
Ghadda, Hasrat. Srinagar, August 27, 2014.
Hassan, Munshi Ghulam. Srinagar, February 26, 2014.
Khaliq, Abdul. Maryland, September 15, 2020.
Makhdoomi, Pirzada Hafizullah. Srinagar, November 17, 2013.
Mattoo, Neerja. Srinagar, May 24, 2014.
Mir, Abdul Sattar. Srinagar, August 29, 2014.
Mohammed, Zahid Ghulam. Srinagar, November 14, 2013.
Pandit, Nighat Shafi. Srinagar, May 5, 2014.
Shah, Hassan. Srinagar, June 12, 2014.
Shah, Dr. Naseer Shah. Srinagar, June 25, 2014.

Newspaper Articles, Journals, Online Sources

Amrita Bazar Patrika
Azaan
Hindustan Times
Indian Express
Life Magazine
New York Times

"Arabs Asked to Aid Pakistan." *New York Times*, April 25, 1957, 12.

"Arjun Dev Majboor—A Conversation." *Kashmir Sentinel*, n.d. Kashmiri Pandit Network. Accessed August 16, 2016. http://www.ikashmir.net/majboor/conversation.html.

Asma, Syed. "Lost Prime Minister." *Kashmir Life*, July 21, 2014. http://www.kashmirlife.net/lost-prime-minister-issue20-vol06-62396/.

Bhat, Saima. "A Different Politician." *Kashmir Life*, April 12, 2020. https://kashmirlife.net/a-different-politician-229228/.

Grimes, Paul. "Kashmir's Ruler Hears the Poor: Prime Minister Receives Petitioners on Friday in the Capital." *New York Times*, September 15, 1960.

Handoo, Bilal. "Ikhwanis of the Yore?" *Kashmir Life*, July 21, 2014. http://www.kashmirlife.net/ikhwanis-of-the-yore-issue20-vol06-62400/.

———. "The Prophesy." *Kashmir Life*, July 6, 2015. http://www.kashmirlife.net/the-prophecy-issue-16-vol-07-81750/.

"India Asks Withdrawal: U.S. Observers in Kashmir Draw Protest at U.N." *New York Times*, March 21, 1954, 45.

"India, Pakistan, Kashmir," editorial. *New York Times*, August 14, 1953.

"In Kashmir Bid: Offers to Mediate Between India and Pakistan." *New York Times*, April 11, 1954, 27.

James, Michael. "Moscow Vetoes Kashmir Inquiry: Bars Any Move by Security

Council to Use U.N. Troops to Promote Plebiscite Previous Motions Cited." *New York Times*, February 21, 1957, 1.

Kachru, Braj B. "Dina Nath Nadim." *Naad*, n.d. Kashmiri Pandit Network. Accessed August 16, 2016. http://www.ikashmir.net/nadim/article2.html.

Kalhan, D. N. "Report on Kashmir." *Hindustan Times*. Reprint, Srinagar: Lalla Rookh, 1955.

Kashmir after August 9, 1953. Series of articles in *Amrit Bazar Patrika*. Reprinted by Department of Information, Jammu and Kashmir. New Delhi: Caxton Press Private, 1955.

"Kashmir Gets Egyptian Offer." *New York Times*, February 17, 1950.

Mathrani, H. P. "The Conquest of Banihal." *Hindustan Standard* (Calcutta), December 2, 1956.

Mushtaq, Arshad, "1990 Was a Wakeup Call for Kashmir Theater," interview by Moazum Mohammad. *Kashpost* (blog), July 8, 2015. http://kashpost.blogspot.qa/2015/07/1990-was-wakeup-call-for-kashmir-theatre.html.

Naqvi, Saeed. "The Killing Fields of Jammu: How Muslims Became a Minority in the Region." *Scroll.in*, July 10, 2016. https://scroll.in/article/811468/the-killing-fields-of-jammu-when-it-was-muslims-who-were-eliminated.

"Pakistan Backed on Kashmir Issue: Moslem Leaders in 14 Lands Endorse Karachi Demand for Early Settlement." *New York Times*, December 27, 1954.

"Policies Not Affected: Turkish-Pakistani Tie Will Not Alter Views on Mid-East." *New York Times*, February 23, 1954, 11.

Puri, Balraj, ed. *Kashmir Affairs* 3, no. 9 (January–February), 1961.

Raghavan, G. N. S. *Kashmir on the March*. Series of articles in *Indian Express*, October 1956. Reprinted by Department of Information, Jammu and Kashmir. New Delhi: Caxton Press, November 1956.

Razdan, Vinayak. "*Aazaadee* by Mahjoor: The Freedom Song of Kashmir." Translated by Trilokinath Raina. SearchKashmir. July 23, 2008. http://www.searchkashmir.org/2008/07/aazaadee-by-mahjoor-freedom-song-of.html.

Rosenthal, A. M. "Survey of Kashmir Shows Region Firmly Welded to Indian Rule: Time, Money, Hard Work and Power Are Main Factors in New Delhi's Favor—Talk of a Plebiscite Considered Academic." *New York Times*, July 28, 1955, 3.

"The Russians in Kashmir." *New York Times*, December 11, 1955, 212.

Tarabali, Saaduddin. "Hakumat Kashmir Ki Taleemi Palicy Ka Jaiza," *Azaan*, June 1955.

———. "Hamari Taleemi Palicy," *Azaan*, October 1955.

"Soviet Leaders Are Cheered in Kashmir; Bulganin Asks a Renewal of Ancient Ties." *New York Times*, December 10, 1955, 4.

Trumbull, Robert. "Abdullah Ousted as Kashmir Chief. " *New York Times*, August 9, 1953.

Dissertations and Theses

Ahmad, Bashir. "The Politics of the Major Powers towards the Kashmir Dispute: 1947–1965." Ph.D. diss., University of Nebraska, 1972.

Aziz, Javeed ul. "Economic History of Modern Kashmir: With Special Reference to Agriculture (1947–1989)." Ph.D. diss., University of Kashmir, 2015.

Colway-Sympson, Patricia. "The Kashmir Dispute in World Politics," Ph.D. diss., St. John's University, 1968.

Ganai, Muhammad Yousuf. "Dogra Raj and the Struggle for Freedom in Kashmir 1932–1947." Ph.D. diss., University of Kashmir, 2015.

Gaur, Meenu. "Kashmir on Screen: Region, Religion and Secularism in Hindi Cinema." Ph.D. diss., School of Oriental and African Studies, University of London, 2010.

Junaid, Mohamad. "Youth Activists in Kashmir: State Violence, Tehreek, and the Formation of Political Subjectivity." Ph.D. diss., Graduate Center, City University of New York, 2017. https://academicworks.cuny.edu/gc_etds/2123/.

Mahapatra, Debidatta Aurobinda. "Russia and the Kashmir Issue since 1991: Perception, Attitude and Policy." Ph.D. diss., Jawaharlal Nehru University, 2004.

Mekkawi, Zaki Awad El Sayed. "Egypt and India, a Study of Political and Cultural Relations, 1947–1964." Ph.D. diss., Jawaharlal Nehru University, 2008.

Published Government Records

Directorate of Information and Broadcasting. *Crisis in Kashmir Explained*. Srinagar: Lalla Rookh Publications, 1953.

———. *Unanimous Vote of Confidence in Bakshi Government—An Account of the Proceedings of the State Legislature on the Motion of Confidence in Bakshi Government Adopted on October 5, 1953*. Srinagar: Lalla Rookh Publications, 1953.

Government of Jammu and Kashmir. *Address to the Joint Session of the Jammu and Kashmir Legislature by Sadar-i-i-Riyasat, February 9, 1959*. Jammu: Government Press, 1959.

———. "Aid from India, Text of the Speech of Bakshi Ghulam Mohammed, Prime Minister, JK in the State Assembly on March 17, 1955." *Kashmir Today Series*, 2. Srinagar: Jammu and Kashmir Ministry of Information, 1955.

———.*Bakshi-Sadiq Correspondence, June–July 1957*. Srinagar: Lalla Rookh Publications, 1957.

———. *The Constitution of Jammu and Kashmir*. Jammu: Ranbir Government Press, 1956.

———. *Expansion of Education*. Srinagar: Lalla Rookh Publications, 1961.

———, Kashmir Bureau of Information. *Inside Pakistan-Held Kashmir*. New Delhi: Eastern Printing Press.

———. *Jammu and Kashmir, 1953–1954, a Review of the Achievements of Bakshi Government*. Srinagar, Jammu and Kashmir Directorate of Information and Broadcasting, 1954.

———. *Kashmir at a Glance*. Accession no. 5619. Nehru Memorial Museum and Library.

———. *Message by G. M. Bakshi*, October 8, 1956.

———. *Publication on the Occasion of the Kashmir Festival*. Government of Jammu and Kashmir, 1955. Accession no. 105, in Years: 1955, 101–39. Srinagar State Archives.

———. "Reply to Critics." *Kashmir Today Series*, 1. Srinagar: Jammu and Kashmir Ministry of Information.

———. *Report of the Jammu and Kashmir Commission of Inquiry*, December 1968.

———. *Some Basic Statistics*. Jammu: Ranbir Government Press, 1964.

———. *Sonawari: Field of Gold*. Department of Information, August 1964. Srinagar State Archives.

———. *Soviet Leaders in Kashmir*. Srinagar: Lalla Rookh Publications, 1955.

———. *Text of Speech Broadcast by Bakshi Ghulam Mohammad from Radio Kashmir Srinagar on July 26, 1957*. Jammu: Ranbir Government Press, 1957.

Guide to Kashmir. New Delhi: Publications Division, Tourist Traffic Branch, Ministry of Transport, April 1954.

Kashmir: An Open Book. Srinagar: Lalla Rookh Publications, n.d.

Kashmir in India. Delhi: Caxton Press, n.d.

Kashmir through Many Eyes. Srinagar: Lalla Rookh Publications, Department of Information and Broadcasting, n.d. Accession no. 56206, Nehru Memorial Museum and Library.

Main Official Resolution, moved at the 22nd Plenary Session of the All Jammu and Kashmir National Conference at Baramulla. Directorate of Information Library, Government of Jammu and Kashmir, Srinagar, Kashmir.

Ministry of Information and Broadcasting. *Kashmir Calling: A Tourist's Guide*. Publications Division, Government of India, July 1951.

Ministry of Information and Broadcasting, Publications Division, Government of India. *Kashmir*. Bombay: New Jack Printing Works, 1956.

New Kashmir. New Delhi: Kashmir Bureau of Information, n.d.

Sadiq, G. M. *Our Educational Policy: Government of Jammu and Kashmir*. Jammu: Ranbir Press, 1955.

Supreme Court of India. Triloki Nath and Anr vs. State of Jammu and Kashmir and Ors, on 23 April 1968. http://indiankanoon.org/doc/1006376/.

Tak, M. Ashraf, ed. "Bakshi Number." *Sheeraza.* Srinagar: Jammu and Kashmir Academy of Art, Languages and Culture, n.d.

Visitors Bureau, His Highness Government, Jammu and Kashmir. *Notes for Visitors to Kashmir*. Srinagar: Brooks Artistic Press, 1946.

Wreford, Captain R. G. *Census of India, 1941,* vol. 22, *Jammu and Kashmir,* parts 1 and 2. Jammu: Ranbir Government Press, 1943.

Published Primary Sources

Abdullah, Mohammad Sheikh. *The Blazing Chinar: An Autobiography.* Translated from the Urdu by Mohammad Amin. Srinagar: Gulshan Publishers, 2013.

Alam, Jawaid. *Jammu and Kashmir 1949–1964: Select Correspondence between Jawaharlal Nehru and Karan Singh.* New Delhi: Penguin Books, 2006.

Ali, Agha Ashraf. *Kuch to Likhye, Loag Kehte Hain.* Srinagar: Shalimar Art Press, 2010.

Ali, Sadiq, and Madhu Limaye. *Report on Kashmir*. Bombay: Praja Socialist Publication, February 1954.

All Jammu and Kashmir Plebiscite Front. *The People's Voice in J&K State: Proceedings of the Special Convention Held in July 1965, Shahi Masjid, Mujahid Manzil.* In private archives of Shabir Mujahid.

"Bakshi Birthday Number." *Lala Rookh: A Magazine of the Amar Singh College* 24, no. 1 (July 21, 1963).

Bankeshwar, Sumanth S. *Conspiracy in Kashmir,* Society for the Defence of Democracy. Bangalore: Ananth Printing Works, 1955.

Beautiful Kashmir: Visitors Best Guide. Srinagar: Rinemisray Publishers. Research and Publication Department Library, Srinagar, n.d.

Bhan, Mona. *How Rughonath Vaishnavi's Life and Biography Can Provide Important Glimpses into the Political Culture of Kashmir from the 1930s until the 1990s*. Self-published pamphlet, 2016.

Bharati, Hriday Kaul, ed. *Contemporary Kashmiri Short Stories*. New Delhi: Sahitya Akademi, 2005.

Dhar, Hirdey Nath. *Memoirs at the Bar.* Jammu: Sher-i-State Printers, 1968.

Gash, Sofi G. A. *Bakshi Ghulam Mohammad: A Memorial Volume.* Srinagar: College Printing Press, 1982.

Himalayan Pilgrimage (*1960*). British Pathé. https://www.youtube.com/watch?v=pEnL7vUvgss.

Hindu Mountain Pilgrimage aka Himalayan Pilgrimage (*1955*). British Pathé. https://www.youtube.com/watch?v=uMcPAzFYD8M.

Ishaq, Munshi Mohammad. *Nida-i-Haq*. Edited by Munshi Ghulam Hasan. Published diaries and memoir of Munshi Mohammad Ishaq, Srinagar: KBF Printers, 2014.

Kak, O. N. *Khalid-i-Kashmir Bakshi Ghulam Mohammad: Through My Eyes*. Accession no: 12033. Srinagar, Jammu and Kashmir: Research and Publications Department, n.d.

Koul, Samsar Chand. *Srinagar and Its Environs*. Mysore: Wesley Press, 1952.

Kumari, Vijay. *Kashmir Greets You: Guide to Lalla Rookh*. Srinagar: Chronicle Publishing House, 1973.

Mahajan, Dina Nath, and Mohammad Ayub Khan. *Kashmir: An Integral Part of India*. Published by S. Kulbir Singh, Secretary, Provincial National Conference, Jammu. New Delhi: Caxton Press, n.d.

Mattoo, Neerja, ed. *Kath: Stories from Kashmir*. New Delhi: Sahitya Akademi, 2011.

———. *The Stranger beside Me: Short Stories from Kashmir*. Srinagar: Gulshan Books, 1994.

Mohiuddin, Akhtar. *Doad wa Dag*. Srinagar: Ali Mohammad and Sons, n.d.

———. *Looking into the Heart of Life: English Translations of Some Kashmiri Short Stories of Akhtar Mohiuddin*. Translated by Azhar Hilal. Srinagar: Alhayat Printographers, 2010.

———. *Short Stories of Akhtar Mohiuddin*. Translated by Syed Taffazull Hussain. Self-published, 2015.

Mufti, Shamla. *Chilman se Chaman*. (Autobiography in Urdu of Shamla Mufti, former principal of Government Women's College, Maulana Azad Road.) Srinagar: Meezan Publishers, 1994.

Mullik, B. N. *My Years with Nehru: Kashmir*. Delhi: Allied Publishers, 1971.

Qasim, Syed Mir. *My Life and Times*. Bombay: Allied Publishers, 1992.

Saifuddin, Qari. *Vadi-i-Purkhar*. Srinagar: Markazi Maktaba Jama'at-i-Islami Jammu and Kashmir, 1980.

Sarabhai, Mridula. *Call for Impartial Inquiry: Pre and Post Hazratbal Incident*. New Delhi, 1958.

Sarup, G. R. *Travel Guide to Kashmir*. New Delhi: Asia Press, 1955.

Singh, Karan. *Heir Apparent: An Autobiography*. Vol. 1. New York: Oxford University Press, 1982.

———. *Pilgrimage to Shree Amarnath Kashmir*. April 13, 1954. Research and Publication Department Library, Srinagar.

Secondary Sources (Books, Book Chapters, Articles)

Abney, Arthur. "Behind the Kashmir Coup." *New Leader* 36, no. 39 (September 28, 1953).

Afroz, Sultana. "The Cold War and United States Military Aid to Pakistan 1947–1960: A Reassessment." *South Asia: Journal of South Asian Studies* 17, no. 1 (June 1994): 57–72.

Agrama, Hussein Ali. *Questioning Secularism: Islam, Sovereignty, and the Rule of Law in Modern Egypt.* Chicago: University of Chicago Press, 2012.

Ahmad, Aijaz. "The Progressive Movement in Its International Setting." *Social Scientist* 39, no. 11–12 (2011).

Ahmad, Mirza Nazir. *Management of Tourism in Jammu and Kashmir*. New Delhi: Dilpreet Publishing House, 2010.

Ahmad, Rafiq. "Orientalist Imaginaries of Travels in Kashmir: Western Representations of the Place and People." *Journal of Tourism and Cultural Change* 9, no. 3 (2011).

Ahmed, Talat. *Literature and Politics in the Age of Nationalism: The Progressive Episode in South Asia 1932–1956.* London: Routledge, 2009.

"Akhtar Mohiuddin and Ali Mohammad Lone." *Indian Literature* (journal published by Sahitya Akademi) 2, no. 2 (April–September 1959): 89–92.

Akhter, Shahzada. *Kashmir Women Empowerment and National Conference*. Srinagar: Jay Kay Books, 2011.

Alavi, Hamza. "The State in Postcolonial Societies: Pakistan and Bangladesh." *New Left Review*, no. 74 (July–August 1972).

———. "Pakistan-US Military Alliance." *Economic and Political Weekly* 33, no. 25 (June 20–26, 1998): 1551–57.

Ali, Ahmed. "The Progressive Writers Movement in Its Historical Perspective." *Journal of South Asian Literature* 8, no. 1–4 (1977–78).

Ali, Kamran Asdar. *Surkh Salam: Communist Politics and Class Activism in Pakistan 1947–1972*. Oxford: Oxford University Press, 2015.

Ali, Nosheen. *Delusional States: Feeling Rule and Development in Pakistan's Northern Frontier.* Cambridge: Cambridge University Press, 2019.

Anand, Dibyesh. "China and India: Postcolonial Informal Empires in the Emerging Global Order." *Rethinking Marxism* 24, no. 1 (2012): 68–86.

Anderson, Perry. *The Indian Ideology*. London: Verso Books, 2013.

Ankit, Rakesh. *The Kashmir Conflict: From Empire to Cold War, 1945–1966.* London: Routledge, 2016.

Ansari, Sarah. *Life after Partition: Migration, Community and Strife in Sindh, 1947–1962.* Oxford: Oxford University Press, 2015.

Asad, Talal. *Formations of the Secular: Christianity, Islam, Modernity*. Stanford, CA: Stanford University Press, 2003.

Aslam, Mohamed. "Land Reforms in Jammu and Kashmir." *Social Scientist* 6, no. 4 (November 1977): 59–64.

Balasubramaniam, Rueban. "Indefinite Detention: Rule by Law or Rule of Law." In *Emergency and the Limits of Legality*, edited by Victor Ramraj. Cambridge: Cambridge University Press, 2008.

Bamzai, Sandeep. *Bonfire of Kashmiriyat: Deconstructing the Accession*. New Delhi: Rupa & Company, 2006.

Barakat, Rana. "Writing/Righting Palestine Studies: Settler Colonialism, Indigenous Sovereignty and Resisting the Ghost(s) of History." *Settler Colonial Studies* 8, no. 3 (2018): 349–63.

Barclay, Paul. *Outcasts of Empire: Japan's Rule on Taiwan's "Savage Border," 1874–1945*. Oakland: University of California Press, 2018.

———. "Peddling Postcards and Selling Empire: Image-Making in Taiwan under Japanese Colonial Rule." *Japanese Studies* 30, no. 1 (2010).

Baruah, Sanjib. *In the Name of the Nation: India and Its Northeast*. Redwood City, CA: Stanford University Press, 2020.

Bashir, Khalid. *Kashmir: Exposing the Myth Behind the Narrative*. Delhi: SAGE Publications, 2017.

Bayley, David. *The Police and Political Development in India*. Princeton, NJ: Princeton University Press, 2015.

Bazaz, Nagin. *Ahead of His Times, Prem Nath Bazaz: His Life and Work*. New Delhi: Sterling Publishers, 1983.

Bazaz, Prem Nath. *Does India Defend Freedom or Fascism in Kashmir?* New Delhi: Kashmir Democratic Union, June 1952.

———. *The History of Struggle for Freedom in Kashmir*. Srinagar: Gulshan Publishers, 1945.

———. *A Last Chance for India in Kashmir*. New Delhi: Pamposh Publications, n.d.

———. "Politics in Kashmir." *New Leader* 41, no. 14 (April 7, 1958).

———. *Rise of Communism in Kashmir*. New Delhi: Kashmir Democratic Union, August 1952.

———. *The Shape of Things in Kashmir*. New Delhi: Pamposh Publications, 1965.

———. *Truth about Kashmir*. New Delhi: Kashmir Democratic Union, October 1950.

Behera, Navnita Chadha. *State, Identity, and Violence: Jammu, Kashmir, and Ladakh*. Delhi: Manohar Publishers, 2000.

———. *Demystifying Kashmir*. Washington, DC: Brookings Institution, 2006.

Berda, Yael. "Managing Dangerous Populations: Colonial Legacies of Security and Surveillance." *Sociological Forum* 28, no. 3 (September 2013): 627–30.

Bhagavan, Manu. *Sovereign Spheres: Princes, Education and Empire in Colonial India*. New York: Oxford University Press, 2003.

Bhan, Mona. *Counterinsurgency, Democracy and the Politics of Identity in India: From Warfare to Welfare?* New York: Routledge, 2013.

———. "Infrastructures of Occupation: Mobility, Immobility and the Politics of Integration in Kashmir." In *Kashmir and the Future of South Asia*, edited by Ayesha Jalal and Sugata Bose. New York: Routledge, 2020.

———. "'In Search of the Aryan Seed': Race, Religion and Sexuality in Indian-Occupied Kashmir." In *Resisting Occupation in Kashmir*, edited by Haley Duschinski, Mona Bhan, Ather Zia, and Cynthia Mahmood. Philadelphia: University of Pennsylvania Press, 2018.

———. "Morality and Martyrdom: Dams, Dharma, and the Cultural Politics of Work in Indian Occupied Kashmir." *Biography* 37, no. 1 (Winter 2014): 191–224.

Bhan, Mona, and Haley Duschinski. "Occupations in Context: The Cultural Logics of Occupation, Settler Violence, and Resistance." *Critique of Anthropology* 30, no. 2 (2020): 1–13.

Bhan, Mona, Haley Duschinski, and Deepti Misri. "Critical Kashmir Studies: Settler Occupations and the Persistence of Resistance." In *Routledge Handbook of Critical Kashmir Studies*, edited by Mona Bhan, Haley Duschinski, and Deepti Misri. New York: Routledge, 2022.

———, eds. *Routledge Handbook of Critical Kashmir Studies*. New York: Routledge, 2022.

Bhandar, Brenna, and Rafeef Ziadah. "Acts and Omissions: Framing Settler Colonialism in Palestine Studies." *Jadaliyya.com* (ezine), January 14, 2016. https://www.jadaliyya.com/Details/32857.

Bhargava, Rajeev. "The Distinctiveness of Indian Secularism." In *The Future of Secularism*, edited by T. N. Srinivasan, 20–53. New York: Oxford University Press, 2007.

Bhat, Javaid Iqbal. "Loss of a Syncretic Theatrical Form." *Folklore: Electronic Journal of Folklore*, no. 34 (2006): 41–42.

Bhat, M. Ashraf. "Emergence of the Urdu Discourses in Kashmir." *Language in India* 11, no. 9 (September 2011) 156–68.

Bhat, Roop Krishen. "The Plebiscite Front: Its Organisation, Strategy and Role in Kashmir's Politics." *Political Science Review* 10, no. 3–4 (1971).

Bhat, Sanaullah. *Kashmir in Flames: An Untold Story of Kashmir's Political Affairs*. Srinagar: Ali Mohammad and Sons, 1981.

———. *Kashmir, 1947–1977 Tak*. Srinagar: Ali Mohammad and Sons, 1980.

Bose, Sumantra. *Kashmir: Roots of Conflict, Paths to Peace*. Cambridge: Harvard University Press, 2003.

Chakrabarty, Dipesh, Rochona Majumdar, and Andrew Sartori, eds. *From the Colo-*

nial to the Postcolonial: India and Pakistan in Transition. New York: Oxford University Press, 2007.

Chakravarti, Ananya, Purnima Dhavan, Manan Ahmed, Supriya Gandhi, Dheepa Sundaram, Audrey Truschke, and Simran Jeet Singh. "Hindutva's Threat to Academic Freedom." Opinion. Religion News Service, July 7, 2021. https://religionnews.com/2021/07/07/hindutvas-threat-to-academic-freedom/.

Chandra, Prakash. "The National Question in Kashmir." *Socialist Scientist* 13, no. 6 (1985): 35–56.

Chari, P. R., D. Suba Chandran, and Shaheen Akhtar. *Tourism and Peace Building in Jammu and Kashmir*. Washington, DC: United States Institute of Peace, 2011.

Chatta, Illays. "Terrible Fate: 'Ethnic Cleansing' of Jammu Muslims in 1947." *Journal of Pakistan Vision* 10, no. 1 (2009): 117–40.

Chatterjee, Partha. "Kashmir Is the Test Bed for a New Model of Internal Colonialism." *The Wire*, August 28, 2019.

Chauhan, Vinay, and Suvidha Khanna. "Tourism: A Tool for Crafting Peace Process in Kashmir, J&K, India." *Tourismos: an International Multidisciplinary Journal of Tourism* 4, no. 2 (August 2009): 69–89.

Chowdhary, Rekha. *Identity Politics in Jammu and Kashmir*. New Delhi: Vitasta, 2010.

———. *Jammu and Kashmir: Politics of Identity and Separatism*. New York: Routledge, 2016.

———. "Kashmir in the Indian Project of Nationalism." In *The Parchment of Kashmir*, edited by N. A. Khan. New York: Palgrave Macmillan, 2012.

Copland, Ian. "The Abdullah Factor: Kashmiri Muslims and the Crisis of 1947." In *The Political Inheritance of Pakistan*. London: Palgrave Macmillan, 1991.

———. "Islam and Political Mobilization in Kashmir, 1931–34." *Pacific Affairs* 54, no. 2 (Summer 1981): 228–59.

Daechsel, Markus. *Islamabad and the Politics of International Development in Pakistan*. Cambridge: Cambridge University Press, 2017.

———. *The Politics of Self-Expression: The Urdu Middleclass Milieu in Mid-20th Century India and Pakistan*. New York: Routledge, 2006.

———. "Sovereignty, Governmentality and Development in Ayub's Pakistan: The Case of Korangi Township." *Modern Asian Studies* 45, no. 1 (2011).

Dale, Roger. "Learning to Be . . . What? Shaping Education in Developing Societies: Introduction to the Sociology of Education." In *Introduction to the Sociology of Developing Societies*, edited by Hamza Alavi. London: Palgrave, 1982.

Dar, Huma. "Dear Prof. Chatterjee, When Will You Engage with the 'Discomfort' of Indian Occupied Kashmir?" *Pulse* (blog), September 10, 2015. https://pulse-media.org/2015/09/10/dear-prof-chatterjee-when-will-you-engage-with-the-discomfort-of-indian-occupied-kashmir/.

Dar, Showkat Ahmad. "Role of Socio-Religious Reform Movements among Muslims in Kashmir." *International Journal of Innovative Research and Development* 2, no. 5 (2013).

Datla, Kavita. *The Language of Secular Islam: Urdu Nationalism and Colonial India.* Honolulu: University of Hawaii Press, 2013.

Davenport, Charles. "The Weight of the Past: Exploring Lagged Determinants of Political Repression." *Political Research Quarterly* 49, no. 2 (1996): 377–403.

De, Rohit. *The People's Constitution: Everyday Life of Law in the Indian Republic.* Princeton, NJ: Princeton University Press. 2018.

Deprez, Camille. "The Films Division of India—1948–1964—The Early Days and the Influence of the British Documentary Film Tradition." *Film History* 25, no. 3 (2013): 149–73.

Despande, Anirudh. "Indian Cinema and the Bourgeois Nation-State." *Economic and Political Weekly* 42, no. 50 (December 15–21, 2007): 95–101.

Deshbandhu. *61 Constitution House.* Srinagar: Brocas Printing Press, 1954. (Available at Nehru Memorial Museum and Library, New Delhi.)

Duschinski, Haley, and Mona Bhan, "Introduction: Law Containing Violence: Critical Ethnographies of Occupation and Resistance." *Journal of Legal Pluralism and Unofficial Law* 49, no. 3 (2017): 253-67.

———. "Third World Imperialism and Kashmir's Sovereignty Trap." In *Routledge Handbook of Critical Kashmir Studies*, edited by Mona Bhan, Haley Duschinski, and Deepti Misri. New York: Routledge, 2022.

Duschinski, Haley, Mona Bhan, Ather Zia, and Cynthia Mahmood, eds. *Resisting Occupation in Kashmir.* Philadelphia: University of Pennsylvania Press, 2018.

Duschinski, Haley, and Shrimoyee Nandini Ghosh. "Constituting the Occupation: Preventive Detention and Permanent Emergency in Kashmir." *Journal of Legal Pluralism and Unofficial Law* 49, no. 3 (2017): 314–37.

Falk, Richard. "Afterword: Refining the Optic of Occupation." In *Everyday Occupations: Experiencing Militarism in South Asia and the Middle East*, edited by Kamala Visweswaran. Philadelphia: University of Pennsylvania Press, 2013.

Fazili, Gowhar. "Police Subjectivity in Occupied Kashmir: Reflections on an Account of a Police Officer." In *Resisting Occupation in Kashmir*, edited by Haley Duschinski, Mona Bhan, Ather Zia, and Cynthia Mahmood, 184–210. Philadelphia: University of Pennsylvania Press, 2018.

Feldman, Ilana. *Governing Gaza: Bureaucracy, Authority, and the Work of Rule (1917–1967).* Durham, NC: Duke University Press, 2008.

———. *Police Encounters: Security and Surveillance in Gaza under Egyptian Rule*. Stanford, CA: Stanford University Press, 2015.

Ferguson, James. *The Anti-Politics Machine: Development, Depoliticization, and Bureaucratic Power in Lesotho*. Minneapolis: University of Minnesota Press, 1994.

Ganguly, Sumit. *The Crisis in Kashmir: Portents of War, Hopes of Peace*. Cambridge: Cambridge University Press, 1997.

———. "The Crisis of Indian Secularism." *Journal of Democracy* 14, no. 4 (2003): 11–25.

Gauhar, G. N. *Hazratbal: The Central Stage of Kashmiri Politics*. New Delhi: Virgo Publications, 1998.

Ghosh, Pothik. "Solidarity-Givers of India and Destiny of the Kashmiri Tehreek." *Radical Notes*, May 10, 2017. https://radicalnotes.org/2017/05/10/solidarity-givers-of-india-and-destiny-of-the-kashmiri-tehreek/.

Ghosh, Shrimoyee Nandini. "Crisis Constitutionalism, Permanent Emergency and the Amnesias of International Law in Jammu and Kashmir." *Third World Approaches to International Law Review*, May 28, 2020.

Giyas-Ud-din, Peer. *Jammu and Kashmir State and Society: Communist Movement in Kashmir*. Jammu: Jay Kay Book House, 1999.

Gockhami, Abdul Jabbar. *Kashmir: Politics and Plebiscite, 1955–1975*. Srinagar: Gulshan Books, 2011.

Gopal, Sarvepalli, ed. *Selected Works of Jawaharlal Nehru, December 1948–February 1949*, ser. 2, vol. 9. nehruselectedworks.com.

--------. *Selected Works of Jawaharlal Nehru, November 1951–March 1952*, ser. 2, vol. 17. nehruselectedworks.com.

———. *Selected Works of Jawaharlal Nehru, July–October 1952*, ser. 2, vol. 19. nehruselectedworks.com.

Gordon, Neve. *Israel's Occupation*. Berkeley: University of California Press, 2008.

Gould, William. *Bureaucracy, Community and Influence in India: Society and the State 1930s–1960s*. London: Routledge, 2011.

Guyot-Réchard, Bérénice. *Shadow States: India, China and the Himalayas, 1910–1962*. Cambridge: Cambridge University Press, 2016.

Haines, Daniel. *Building the Empire, Building the Nation: Development, Legitimacy and Hydro-Politics in Sind, 1919–1969*. Oxford: Oxford University Press, 2013.

———. "'Concrete Progress': Irrigation, Development and Modernity in Mid-Twentieth Century Sind." In *From Subjects to Citizens: Society and the Everyday State in India and Pakistan, 1947–1970*, edited by Taylor Sherman, William Gould, and Sarah Ansari. New York: Cambridge University Press, 2014.

Haksar, Nandita. *The Many Faces of Kashmiri Nationalism*. New Delhi: Speaking Tiger Books, 2015.

Hallaq, Wael, *Restating Orientalism: A Critique of Modern Knowledge*. New York: Columbia University Press, 2018.

Hangloo, Rattan Lal. "Kashmiriyat: The Voice of the Past Misconstrued." In *The Parchment of Kashmir: History, Society and Polity*, edited by Naya Ali Khan. New York: Palgrave Macmillan, 2012.

Hansen, Thomas Blom, and Finn Stepputat, eds. *State of Imagination: Ethnographic Explorations of the Postcolonial State*. Durham, NC: Duke University Press, 2001.

Hassan, Khalid Wasim. "History Revisited: Narratives on Political and Constitutional Changes in Kashmir (1947–1990)." Working Paper 233. Bangalore: Institute for Social and Economic Change, 2009.

Hussain, Nasser. *The Jurisprudence of Emergency: Colonialism and the Rule of Law*. Ann Arbor: University of Michigan Press, 2003.

Hussain, Shahla. *Kashmir in the Aftermath of Partition*. Cambridge: Cambridge University Press, 2021.

Hussain, Syed Taffazull. *Sheikh Abdullah—A Biography: The Crucial Period 1905–1935*. Bloomington, IN: Wordclay, 2008.

Itoo, Mushtaq Ahmad. "Tourism Industry of Kashmir, 1947–1989." *International Journal of Management and Sustainability* 2, no. 4 (2013): 63–71.

Jalil, Rakhshanda. *Liking Progress, Loving Change: A Literary History of the Progressive Writers' Movement in Urdu*. Oxford: Oxford University Press, 2014.

Jammu and Kashmir Coalition of Civil Society. *Amarnath Yatra: A Militarized Pilgrimage*, May 5, 2017. Report. https://jkccs.wordpress.com/2017/05/05/amarnath-yatra-a-militarized-pilgrimage/.

Junaid, Mohamad. "Death and Life under Occupation: Space, Violence, and Memory in Kashmir." In *Everyday Occupations, Experiencing Militarism in South Asia and the Middle East*, edited by Kamala Visweswaran. Philadelphia: University of Pennsylvania Press, 2013.

———. "Tehreek History Writers of Kashmir: Reconstructing Memory at the Margins of Postcolonial Empire." In *Routledge Handbook of Critical Kashmir Studies*, edited by Mona Bhan, Haley Duschinski, and Deepti Misri. New York: Routledge, 2022.

———. "To Be Kashmiri in the Present: Politics, Ethics, and History in the Work of Akhtar Mohiuddin." In *A Desolation Called Peace: Voices from Kashmir*, edited by Ather Zia and Javaid Iqbal Bhat. New Delhi: Harper Collins, 2019.

K., S. "The Kashmir Dispute after Ten Years." *The World Today* 14. no. 2 (February 1958): 61–70.

Kabir, Ananya Jahanara. "Koshur Today: Death, Survival or Revival." Paper presented at Innovations and Reproductions in Cultures and Societies, Vienna, December 9–11, 2005.

———. "A Language of One's Own? Linguistic Underrepresentation in the Kashmir Valley." In *The Shock of the Other: Situating Alterities*, edited by Silke Horstkotte and Esther Peeren. Amsterdam: Rodopi, 2007.

———. "Nipped in the Bud? Pleasure and Politics in the 1960s 'Kashmir Films,'" *South Asian Popular Culture* 3, no. 2 (2005): 83–100.

———. *Territory of Desire: Representing the Valley of Kashmir.* Minneapolis: University of Minnesota Press, 2009.

Kanjwal, Hafsa. "The New Kashmiri Woman: State-Led Feminism in 'Naya Kashmir.'" *Economic and Political Weekly* 53, no. 47 (2018).

———. "Reflections on the Post-Partition Period: Life Narratives of Kashmiri Muslims in Contemporary Kashmir." *Himalaya: The Journal of the Association of Nepal and Himalayan Studies* 38, no. 2 (2018): 48–53.

———. "The Violence on Kashmir Is Epistemological as It Is Physical." *Jadaliyya*, December 11, 2009. https://www.jadaliyya.com/Details/40341.

Kanth, Fatimah. "Women in Resistance." *Economic and Political Weekly* 53, no. 47 (2018).

Kauanui, J. Kehaulani. "'A Structure, Not an Event': Settler Colonialism and Enduring Indigeneity." *Lateral* 5, no. 1 (2016).

Kaul, J. L. "Kashmiri Literature." *Indian Literature* 1, no. 1 (October 1957): 93–96.

Kaul, Nitasha. "Coloniality and/as Development in Kashmir: Econonationalism." *Feminist Review* 128, no. 1 (2021).

Kaul, Suvir. "On Naya Kashmir." In *Routledge Handbook of Critical Kashmir Studies*, edited by Mona Bhan, Haley Duschinski, and Deepti Misri. New York: Routledge, 2022.

Khalidi, Omar. "Hinduizing India: Secularism in Practice." *Third World Quarterly* 29, no. 8 (2009).

Khan, Mohammad Ishaq. "Evolution of My Identity vis-à-vis Islam and Kashmir." In *The Parchment of Kashmir: History, Society, Polity*, edited by Nyla Ali Khan, 13–36. New York: Palgrave MacMillan, 2012.

Khan, Nyla Ali. *Islam, Women, and Violence in Kashmir: Between India and Pakistan.* New York: Palgrave Macmillan, 2010.

———, ed. *The Parchment of Kashmir: History, Society, Polity*. New York: Palgrave Macmillan, 2012.

King, Christopher R. *One Language, Two Scripts: The Hindi Movement in Nineteenth-Century North India.* Bombay: Oxford University Press, 1994.

Korbel, Josef. *Danger in Kashmir*. Princeton, NJ: Princeton University Press, 1966.

Koul, Mohan Lal. *Kashmir Past and Present: Unravelling the Mystique*. New Delhi: Sehyog Prakashan, 1994. https://archive.org/details/kashmir-past-and-present-unravelling-the-mystique-mohan-lal-kaul/mode/2up.

Kumar, Vijay. *Anglo-American Plot against Kashmir*. Bombay: People's Publishing House, 1954.

Lamb, Alastair. *Birth of a Tragedy: Kashmir 1947*. Oxford: Oxford University Press, 1994.

———. *Crisis in Kashmir 1947–1966*. London: Routledge, 1966.

———. *Kashmir: A Disputed Legacy 1846–1990*. Hertford: Roxford Books, 1991.

Lawrence, Walter. *The Valley of Kashmir*. London: H. Frowde, 1895. https://archive.org/details/valleyofkashmiroolawruoft/mode/2up.

Lockwood, David E. "Sheikh Abdullah and the Politics of Kashmir." *Asian Survey* 9, no. 5, (May 1969).

Mabry, Tristen James. *Nationalism, Language and Muslim Exceptionalism*. Philadelphia: University of Pennsylvania Press, 2015.

Madan, T. N. "Kashmir, Kashmiris, Kashmiriyat: An Introductory Essay." In *The Valley of Kashmir: The Making and Unmaking of a Composite Culture*, edited by Aparna Rao. Delhi: Manohar, 2008.

Mahmood, Saba. *Religious Difference in a Secular Age: A Minority Report*. Princeton, NJ: Princeton University Press, 2016.

Majid, Iymon. "Confronting the Indian State: Islamism, Secularism and the Kashmiri Muslim Question." *International Journal of Asian Studies* 19, no. 1 (January 2020): 1–14. https://doi.org/10.1017/S1479591420000479.

Malik, G. R. "A Brief Survey of Kashmiri Literature." *Muse India*, no. 6 (2006). http://www.museindia.com/viewarticle.asp?myr=2006&issid=6&id=225.

Malik, Iffat. *Kashmir: Ethnic Conflict and International Dispute*. New York: Oxford University Press, 2002.

Mamdani, Mahmood. *Neither Settler nor Native: The Making and Unmaking of Permanent Minorities*. Cambridge, MA: Harvard University Press, 2020.

Maqbool, Raashid. "A Cultural Psy-Op." *Kashmir Life* 21 (July 2014).

Massad, Joseph. "The 'Post-colonial' Colony: Time, Space, and Bodies in Palestine/Israel" In *The Persistence of the Palestinian Question: Essays on Zionism and the Palestinians*. New York: Routledge, 2006.

Mbembe, Achille. "Necropolitics." *Public Culture* 15, no. 1 (2003).

McDonald, Kate. *Placing Empire: Travel and the Social Imagination in Imperial Japan*. Oakland: University of California Press, 2017.

McGowan, Abigail. "Mothers and Godmothers of Crafts: Female Leadership and the Imagination of India as a Crafts Nation (1947–1967)." *South Asia: Journal of South Asian Studies* 44, no. 2 (2021).

Menon, Nikhil. *Planning Democracy: Modern India's Quest for Development*. Cambridge: Cambridge University Press, 2022.

Mir, Farina. *The Social Space of Language: Vernacular Culture in British Colonial Punjab*. Berkeley: University of California Press, 2010.

Misri, Deepti. "Disabling Kashmir." In *Routledge Handbook of Critical Kashmir Studies*, edited by Mona Bhan, Haley Duschinski, and Deepti Misri. New York: Routledge, 2022.

Mohammed, Zahid Ghulam. *Srinagar: My City, My Dreamland*. Srinagar: Gulshan Publishers, 2011.

Mongia, Radhika. *Indian Migration and Empire: A Colonial Genealogy of the Modern State*. Durham, NC: Duke University Press, 2018.

Mushtaq, Samreen, and Mudasir Amin. "'We Will Memorise Our Home': Exploring Settler Colonialism as an Interpretive Framework for Kashmir." *Third World Quarterly* 42, no. 12 (2021).

Nabi, P. G., and J. Ye. "Of Militarisation, Counter-Insurgency and Land Grabs in Kashmir." *Economic and Political Weekly* 50, no. 46–47 (2015).

Namakkal, Jessica. *Unsettling Utopia: The Making and Unmaking of French India*. New York: Columbia University Press, 2021.

Needham, Anuradha Dingwaney, and Rajeswari Sunder Rajan, eds. *The Crisis of Secularism in India*. Durham, NC: Duke University Press, 2007.

Noorani, A. G. *Article 370: A Constitutional History of Jammu and Kashmir*. New Delhi: Oxford University Press, 2011.

———. *The Kashmir Question*. Bombay: Manaktalas, 1964.

———. "The Legacy of 1953." *Frontline Magazine*, August 29, 2008.

Osuri, Goldie. "The Forms and Practices of Indian Settler/Colonial Sovereignty in Kashmir." In *Routledge Handbook of Critical Kashmir Studies*, edited by Mona Bhan, Haley Duschinski, and Deepti Misri. New York: Routledge, 2022.

———. "Imperialism, Colonialism, and Sovereignty in the (Post)Colony: India and Kashmir." *Third World Quarterly* 38, no. 11 (2011): 2428–43.

Pandey, Gyanendra. "Can a Muslim Be an Indian?" *Comparative Studies in Society and History* 41, no. 4 (1999): 608–29.

Pandit, Huzaifa. "Schools of Resistance—A Brief History of Student Activism in Kashmir." *Postcolonial Studies* 22, no. 1 (2019): 95–116.

Para, Altaf Hussain. *The Making of Modern Kashmir: Sheikh Abdullah and the Politics of the State*. New York: Routledge, 2019.

Parimoo, P. *Kashmiriyat at Crossroads: The Search for a Destiny; Based on the Diaries of Late Pt. Dina Nath Parimoo*. Published by P. Parimoo, 2010. https://archive.org/details/CYwP_kashmir-at-crossroads-the-search-for-a-destiny-p-parimoo/mode/2up.

Pedersen, S. Bechmann. "Peace through Tourism: A Brief History of a Popular Catchphrase." In *Cultural Borders and European Integration*, no. 31, edited by M.

Andrén 29–37. Göteborg: Centrum för Europaforskning vid Göteborgs universitet, 2017.

Prakash, Gyan, Michael Laffan, and Nikhil Menon, eds. *The Postcolonial Moment in South and Southeast Asia.* London: Bloomsbury, 2019.

Prakash, Siddhartha. "The Political Economy of Kashmir since 1947." *Economic and Political Weekly* 35, no. 24 (June 10, 2000).

Prashad, Vijay. *The Darker Nations: A People's History of the Third World.* New York: New Press, 2008.

Puri, Balraj. "The Budget of Kashmir: What the Center Means to the State." *Economic Weekly*, April 15, 1959.

———. "Central Aid to Kashmir: Effect of Finance Commission's Recommendation." *Economic Weekly*, May 19, 1962.

———. *Kashmir Insurgency and After.* New Delhi: Orient Blackswan, 2013.

———. "Kashmiriyat: The Vitality of Kashmiri Identity." *Contemporary South Asia* 4, no.1 (1995).

———. *Kashmir towards Insurgency*. Delhi: Orient Longman, 1993.

———. *Jammu: A Clue to Kashmir Tangle.* New Delhi: Photo Flash Press, 1966.

———. "Jammu and Kashmir." In *State Politics in India*, edited by Myron Wiener. Princeton, NJ: Princeton University Press, 1968.

Purushotham, Sunil. *From Raj to Republic: Sovereignty, Violence, and Democracy in India.* Redwood City, CA: Stanford University Press, 2021.

Pushp, P. N. "Kashmiri and the Linguistic Predicament of the State." In *Jammu, Kashmir and Ladakh: Linguistic Predicament*, edited by P. N. Pushp and K. Warikoo. Delhi: Har-Anand Publications, 1996.

Rahi, Rehman. *Siyah Roodi Jaryan Manz* [Under the dark downpours]: *A Collection of Kashmiri Poems.* Srinagar: Delhi: JK Offset Printers, 1958.

Rai, Mridu. *Hindu Rulers, Muslim Subjects: Islam, Rights and the History of Kashmir.* Princeton, NJ: Princeton University Press, 2004.

———. "The Indian Constituent Assembly and the Making of Hindus and Muslims in Jammu and Kashmir." *Asian Affairs* 49, no. 2, 205–21.

Raina, Trilokinath, ed. *A History of Kashmiri Literature.* New Delhi: Sahitya Akademi, 2002.

———. *Mahjoor and After: Modern Kashmiri Poetry.* New Delhi: Sahitya Akademi, 2005.

Rao, Anupama. "Ambedkar and the Politics of Minority: A Reading." In *From the Colonial to the Postcolonial: India and Pakistan in Transition*, edited by Dipesh Chakrabarty, Rochona Majumdar, and Andrew Sartori, 137–58. New York: Oxford University Press, 2007.

Rashid, Iffat. "Theatrics of a 'Violent State' or 'State of Violence,': Mapping Histories and Memories of Partition in Jammu and Kashmir." *South Asia: Journal of South Asian Studies* 43, no. 2 (2020).

Rasool, G., and Chopra, Minakshi. *Education in Jammu and Kashmir: Issues and Documents*. Jammu: Jay Kay Book House, 1986.

Reynolds, John. *Empire, Emergency, and International Law.* Cambridge: Cambridge University Press, 2017.

Robinson, Cabeiri deBergh. *Body of Victim, Body of Warrior: Refugee Families and the Making of Kashmiri Jihadists*. Berkeley: University of California Press, 2013.

Rowe, Aimee Carrillo, and Eve Tuck. "Settler Colonialism and Cultural Studies: Ongoing Settlement, Cultural Production, and Resistance." *Cultural Studies <-> Critical Methodologies* 17, no. 1 (2017): 3–13.

Roy, Sara. *The Gaza Strip: The Political Economy of De-Development*. Washington, DC: Institute for Palestine Studies, September 1, 1995.

Roy, Srirupa. *Beyond Belief: India and the Politics of Postcolonial Nationalism.* Durham, NC: Duke University Press, 2007.

Rushdie, Salman. *Shalimar the Clown*. London: Random House, 2006.

Sathu, Jagan Nath. *Beyond the Iron Curtain in Kashmir*. New Delhi: Kashmir Democratic Union, January 1952.

Saunders, Frances Stonor. *The Cultural Cold War: The CIA and the World of Arts and Letters.* New York: New Press, 1999.

Schofield, Victoria. *Kashmir in Crossfire.* London: I. B. Tauris, 1996.

Scott-Smith, Giles. *The Politics of Apolitical Culture: The Congress for Cultural Freedom and the Political Economy of American Hegemony 1945–1955*. London: Routledge, 2002.

Seru, S. L. *History and Growth of Education in Jammu and Kashmir 1872–1973*. Srinagar: Ali Mohammed and Sons, 1977.

Sherman, Taylor. "Education in Early Postcolonial India: Expansion, Experimentation and Planned Self-Help." *History of Education* 47, no. 4 (2018).

———. "From 'Grow More Food' to 'Miss a Meal': Hunger, Development and the Limits of Postcolonial Nationalism in India, 1947–1957." *South Asia: Journal of South Asian Studies* 36, no. 4 (2013).

———. "Migration, Citizenship, and Belonging in Hyderabad 1946–1956." In *From Subjects to Citizens: Society and the Everyday State in India and Pakistan, 1947–1970*, edited by Taylor Sherman, William Gould, and Sarah Ansari, 90–118. New York: Cambridge University Press, 2014.

———. *Muslim Belonging in Secular India: Negotiating Citizenship in Postcolonial Hyderabad.* Cambridge: Cambridge University Press, 2015.

Sherman, Taylor, William Gould and Sarah Ansari, eds. *From Subjects to Citizens:*

Society and the Everyday State in India and Pakistan, 1947–1970. New York: Cambridge University Press, 2014.

Shohat, Ella. "Notes on the 'Post-Colonial.'" *Social Text*, no. 31/32, Third World and Post-Colonial Issues, 1992.

Siegel, Benjamin. *Hungry Nation: Food, Famine and the Making of Modern India.* Cambridge: Cambridge University Press, 2018.

———. "'Self-Help Which Ennobles a Nation:' Development, Citizenship, and the Obligation of Eating in India's Austerity Years." *Modern Asian Studies* 50, no. 3 (May 2016): 975–1018.

Sikand, Yoginder. "The Emergence and Development of the Jama'at-i-Islami of Jammu and Kashmir (1940s–1990)." *Modern Asian Studies* 36, no. 3 (2002): 705–51.

Simpson, Audra. *Mohawk Interruptus: Political Life across the Borders of Settler States*. Durham, NC: Duke University Press, 2014.

Sinha, Mrinalini. *Colonial Masculinity: The 'Manly Englishman' and the 'Effeminate Bengali' in the Late Nineteenth Century*. Manchester: Manchester University Press, 1995.

Skwiot, Christine. *The Purposes of Paradise: US Tourism and Empire in Cuba and Hawai'i.* Philadelphia: University of Pennsylvania Press, 2012.

Snedden, Christopher. *Understanding Kashmir and Kashmiris.* London: Hurst Publishers, 2015.

———. *The Untold Story of the People of Azad Kashmir.* New York: Columbia University Press, 2012.

———. "Would a Plebiscite Have Resolved the Kashmir Dispute?" *South Asia: Journal of South Asian Studies* 28, no. 1 (2005).

Sriprakash, Arathi, Peter Sutoris, and Kevin Myers. "The Science of Childhood and the Pedagogy of the State: Postcolonial Development in India." *Journal of Historical Sociology* 32, no. (2019): 345–59. https://onlinelibrary.wiley.com/doi/10.1111/johs.12246.

Sutoris, Peter. *Visions of Development: Films Division of India and the Imagination of Progress, 1948–75.* London: Hurst Publishers, 2015.

Tak, Toru. "The Term Kashmiriyat." *Economic & Political Weekly* 48, no. 16 (2013).

Thorner, Daniel. "Kashmir Land Reforms: Some Personal Impressions." *Economic and Political Weekly*, September 12, 1953, no. 37 (1953), 999–1002.

———. *The Shape of Modern India.* New Delhi: Allied Publishers, 1980.

Thorp, Robert. *Cashmere Misgovernment.* Calcutta: Wyman Bros, 1868.

Tickoo, Makhan. "When Is a Language Worth Teaching? Native Languages and English in India." *Language, Culture and Curriculum* 6 (1993): 225–39.

Tillin, Louise. "Asymmetric Federalism." In *The Oxford Handbook of the Indian Con-*

stitution, edited by Sujit Choudhary, Madhav Khosla, and Pratap B. Mehta. Oxford: Oxford University Press, 2019 (45–67).

Toor, Saadia. *The State of Islam: Culture and Cold War Politics in Pakistan.* London: Pluto Press, 2011.

Tremblay, Reeta Chowdhari. "Nation, Identity and the Intervening Role of the State: A Study of the Secessionist Movement in Kashmir." *Pacific Affairs* 69, no. 4 (Winter 1996–97): 471–97. https://www.jstor.org/stable/2761183.

Trisal, Nishita. "In Kashmir, Nehru's Golden Chains That He Hoped Would Bind the State to India Have Lost Their Lustre." *Scroll.in,* November 30, 2015. https://scroll.in/article/772211/in-kashmir-nehrus-golden-chains-that-he-hoped-would-bind-the-state-to-india-have-lost-their-lustre.

Trouillot, Michel-Rolph. *Silencing the Past: Power and the Production of History.* Boston: Beacon Press, 1995.

Umar, Sanober. "Constructing the 'Citizen Enemy'—The Impact of the Enemy Property Act of 1968 on India's Muslims." *Journal of Muslim Minority Affairs* 39, no. 4 (2019): 457–77.

Varshney, Ashutosh. "India, Pakistan, and Kashmir: Antinomies of Nationalism." *Asian Survey* 31, no. 11 (1991): 997–1019.

Vent, Herbert, and Captain Robert B. Monier. "Kashmir and the Kashmir Impasse." *The Social Studies* 49, no.2 (February 1, 1958).

Verma, Pratap Singh. *Jammu and Kashmir at the Political Crossroads.* New Delhi: Vikas Publishing, 1994.

Visweswaran, Kamala. *Everyday Occupations: Experiencing Militarism in South Asia and the Middle East.* Philadelphia: University of Pennsylvania Press, 2013.

von Bogdandy, A., S. Häussler, F. Hanschmann, and R. Utz. "State-Building, Nation-Building, and Constitutional Politics in Post-Conflict Situations: Conceptual Clarifications and an Appraisal of Different Approaches." *Max Planck Yearbook of United Nations Law Online* 9, no. 1 (2005): 579–613. https://doi.org/10.1163/187574105X00138.

Waltz, Michael. "The Indian People's Theatre Association: Its Development and Influences." *Journal of South Asian Literature* 13, no. 1–4 (Fall-Winter-Spring-Summer 1977–1978): 31–37.

Wani, Aijaz Ashraf. *What Happened to Governance in Kashmir?* Oxford: Oxford University Press, 2018.

Wani, Gull Mohamad. "Political Assertion of Kashmiri Identity." In *The Parchment of Kashmir: History, Society and Policy*, edited by Nyla Ali Khan. New York: Palgrave Macmillan, 2012.

Warikoo, K. "Language and Politics in Jammu and Kashmir: Issues and Perspectives." In *Jammu, Kashmir and Ladakh: Linguistic Predicament*, edited by P. N. Pushp and K. Warikoo. Delhi: Har-Anand Publications, 1996.

Wedeen, Lisa. *Ambiguities of Domination: Politics, Rhetoric and Symbols in Contemporary Syria*. Chicago: University of Chicago Press, 1999.

Whaites, Alan. "States in Development: Understanding State-Building." London: Department of International Development, 2009.

Whitehead, Andrew. "The People's Militia: Communists and Kashmiri Nationalism in the 1940s." *Twentieth Century Communism: A Journal of International History* 2 (2010): 141–68.

Widmalm, Sten. *Kashmir in Comparative Perspective: Democracy and Violent Separatism in India*. London: Routledge, 2014.

Wolfe, Patrick. "Settler Colonialism and the Elimination of the Native." *Journal of Genocide Research* 8, no. 4 (2006).

Yeh, Emily. *Taming Tibet: Landscape Transformation and the Gift of Chinese Development*. Ithaca, NY: Cornell University Press, 2013.

Zamindar, Vazira. *The Long Partition and the Making of Modern South Asia: Refugees, Boundaries, Histories*. New York: Columbia University Press, 2007.

Zia, Ather. "The Haunting Specter of Hindu Ethnonationalist-Neocolonial Development in the Indian Occupied Kashmir." *Development* 63 (2020).

———. *Resisting Disappearance: Military Occupation and Women's Activism in Kashmir*. Seattle: University of Washington Press, 2019.

———. "Sanctioned Ignorance and the Crisis of Solidarity for Kashmir." In *Routledge Handbook of Critical Kashmir Studies*, edited by Mona Bhan, Haley Duschinski, and Deepti Misri. New York: Routledge, 2022.

Zutshi, Chiterekha, ed. *Kashmir: History, Politics, Representation*. Cambridge: Cambridge University Press, 2018.

———. *Languages of Belonging: Islam, Regional Identity and the Making of Kashmir*. New York: Oxford University Press, 2004.

———. "Religion, State, and Community: Contested Identities in the Kashmir Valley, c. 1880–1920." *South Asia: Journal of South Asian Studies* 23, no. 1 (2000): 109–28.

INDEX

ALSO PUBLISHED IN THE SOUTH ASIA IN MOTION SERIES

Boats in a Storm: Law, Migration, and Decolonization in South and Southeast Asia, 1942–1962
Kalyani Ramnath (2023)

Life Beyond Waste: Work and Infrastructure in Urban Pakistan
Waqas H. Butt (2023)

Dust on the Throne: The Search for Buddhism in Modern India
Douglas Ober (2023)

Mother Cow, Mother India: A Multispecies Politics of Dairy in India
Yamini Narayanan (2023)

The Vulgarity of Caste: Dalits, Sexuality, and Humanity in Modern India
Shailaja Paik (2022)

Delhi Reborn: Partition and Nation Building in India's Capital
Rotem Geva (2022)

The Right to Be Counted: The Urban Poor and the Politics of Resettlement in Delhi
Sanjeev Routray (2022)

Protestant Textuality and the Tamil Modern: Political Oratory and the Social Imaginary in South Asia
Bernard Bate, Edited by E. Annamalai, Francis Cody, Malarvizhi Jayanth, and Constantine V. Nakassis (2021)

Special Treatment: Student Doctors at the All India Institute of Medical Sciences
Anna Ruddock (2021)

From Raj to Republic: Sovereignty, Violence, and Democracy in India
Sunil Purushotham (2021)

The Greater India Experiment: Hindutva Becoming and the Northeast Arkotong
Longkumer (2020)

Nobody's People: Hierarchy as Hope in a Society of Thieves
Anastasia Piliavsky (2020)

Brand New Nation: Capitalist Dreams and Nationalist Designs in Twenty-First-Century India
Ravinder Kaur (2020)

Partisan Aesthetics: Modern Art and India's Long Decolonization
Sanjukta Sunderason (2020)

Dying to Serve: the Pakistan Army
Maria Rashid (2020)

In the Name of the Nation: India and Its Northeast
Sanjib Baruah (2020)

Faithful Fighters: Identity and Power in the British Indian Army
Kate Imy (2019)

Paradoxes of the Popular: Crowd Politics in Bangladesh
Nusrat Sabina Chowdhury (2019)

The Ethics of Staying: Social Movements and Land Rights Politics in Pakistan Mubbashir
A. Rizvi (2019)

Mafia Raj: The Rule of Bosses in South Asia
Lucia Michelutti, Ashraf Hoque, Nicolas Martin, David Picherit, Paul Rollier, Arild Ruud and Clarinda Still (2018)

Elusive Lives: Gender, Autobiography, and the Self in Muslim South Asia
Siobhan Lambert-Hurley (2018)

Financializing Poverty: Labor and Risk in Indian Microfinance
Sohini Kar (2018)